Study Skills For D...

Feedback Form

If you subject area does not already use one, ask your subject tutors if they will fill this one in for you for each piece of written work you submit.

Name	Good	Satisfactory	Needs Improvement	Suggestions
Answers question?				
Refers to appropriate sources?				
Use of sources				
Balance between sources and own ideas				
Argument				
Analysis				
Reasoned conclusion				
Use of charts, diagrams etc.				
General layout, contents, page numbers etc.				
Punctuation, paragraphing				

Being Aware

In the academic system, being right or wrong isn't really the point. The point is to be aware. If you've attempted to do something and it hasn't quite worked, that doesn't matter if you honestly evaluate:

- **What you did:** Your research questions, research and methods.
- **What happened:** Did you get the answers you expected? What problems did you come up against; how did you solve them?
- **Why you think it happened:** Could you have prepared better or foreseen problems?
- **What you should have done:** Were you too ambitious? Did you miscalculate the time you needed? Should you have used a different method?
- **What you now know and could use to make improvements next time:** For instance, only about one third of questionnaires get returned – unless you put everyone in a room and go through them with the respondents and answer any questions, though most will not give up more than 20 minutes or so for this.

Four Communication Principles

Remember, in academic communication you should always be:

- **Honest:** Only say things you can provide evidence for and always say where you got them from. Hearsay and personal experience, while interesting, don't constitute academic evidence.
- **Relevant:** Make sure that what you say is relevant to the topic under discussion and keep to the point.
- **Clear:** Make everything clear to the reader or listener to help him follow the proceedings. Assume he's an intelligent non-expert in your subject. Provide headings and a framework – a 'how to read' or 'how to listen' so that he can follow the stages in your argument.
- **Real:** Explain what needs to be explained. That means give definitions or explanations of ideas or processes that may not be known to the non-expert intelligent reader. However, don't explain that which is common knowledge.

For Dummies: Bestselling Book Series for Beginners

Study Skills For Dummies®

Cheat Sheet

Key Critical Thinking Skills

- **Reflecting on what you're told.** Take time out to consider your reaction to information. Do you agree with it, are you surprised or excited by it, or do you think it links to other information you have? If you disagree or disbelieve it, why? What would it take to convince you?

- **Observing how information is presented.** Is it in a paragraph, a table, an illustration, a graph, map or chart? Can you think of ways to improve the way information you have read about is presented?

- **Comparing new information with previous knowledge.** Does the new information extend or confirm your previous knowledge, by adding more instances, or contradict it because the results are different?

- **Considering the status or reputation, skills and abilities of the people who give you information.** Always ask what the possible bias of any information source might be: What's in it for them?

- **Distinguishing between fact, hypothesis and opinion.** Facts are what there is evidence for. Hypotheses are theories or ideas which need to be tested by academic enquiry. Opinion is personal. Based on impressions, experience and perhaps limited research, you can't demonstrate opinion objectively.

- **Identifying the conclusion of an argument.** Conclusions are what you are left with (or meant to be) after a discussion or argument. Conclusions, like the truth, are not always simple.

- **Identifying the stages in an argument.** The stages in an argument show the links between the information given and the conclusion.

- **Evaluating the quality of the evidence presented.** How good is the evidence? Where and who did it come from? How was it acquired? Always ask who gains and who loses.

- **Being aware of what hasn't been discussed and wondering why not.** Sometimes data is missing from a data set. Always ask what the data is not telling you, as well as what it is.

- **Analysing and evaluating the argument.** Evaluating data means giving it a value – not quite marks out of ten but sufficient to answer these questions: Is the argument or conclusion good? Does it explain all the circumstances or only some? Does it have flaws, or leave awkward examples out? How could I make it better?

- **Making inferences, decisions and judgements.** Making an inference is when you draw a conclusion from what is suggested but not explicitly stated. Decisions usually involve choices, and come after you have evaluated the different possibilities. Judgements, similarly, come after evaluations and usually state a preference for one thing over another after you have investigated both.

- **Weighing up the evidence and presenting your own argument.** Weighing up the evidence includes evaluating and judging it, and it could be that none of the theories or arguments given seem to work in all cases, so you may have an argument of your own to present.

For Dummies: Bestselling Book Series for Beginners

Study Skills FOR DUMMIES®

by Doreen du Boulay

WILEY

A John Wiley and Sons, Ltd, Publication

Study Skills For Dummies®

Published by
John Wiley & Sons, Ltd
The Atrium
Southern Gate
Chichester
West Sussex
PO19 8SQ
England

E-mail (for orders and customer service enquires): cs-books@wiley.co.uk

Visit our Home Page on www.wiley.com

Copyright © 2009 John Wiley & Sons, Ltd, Chichester, West Sussex, England

Published by John Wiley & Sons, Ltd, Chichester, West Sussex

For general information on our other products and services, please contact our Customer Care Department within the U.S. at 877-762-2974, outside the U.S. at 317-572-3993, or fax 317-572-4002.

For technical support, please visit www.wiley.com/techsupport.

Wiley also publishes its books in a variety of electronic formats. Some content that appears in print may not be available in electronic books.

British Library Cataloguing in Publication Data: A catalogue record for this book is available from the British Library

ISBN: 978-0-470-74047-7

Printed and bound in Great Britain by TJ International Ltd, Padstow, Cornwall

10 9 8 7 6 5 4 3 2 1

WILEY

About the Author

Doreen du Boulay taught undergraduate and postgraduate subject courses in Education and Applied Linguistics, study skills and skills for specific subjects at the universities of Aberdeen, Warwick and Sussex for longer than she cares to remember – over twenty years. She taught students from a range of backgrounds and with many different needs, and wrote the Sussex University study skills web pages.

She was an assessor of pre-university courses for overseas students in British universities for BALEAP (British Association of Lecturers in English for Academic Purposes) for ten years, a consultant with the British Council for training courses in Algeria, Poland and Zambia and for Banque Indo-Suez training courses in English for employees. She was seconded by the University of Aberdeen to work in local oil and gas companies with their overseas employees.

Having begun her career as an organisation and methods analyst, she turned to secondary school teaching, first in Zambia, then in Shropshire and Scotland, before becoming a university teacher. She has always benefited from having several feet, centipede-like, in several camps – as a subject tutor, skills tutor and course assessor, and working in industry – and has always tried to pass on insights from this mixture of experience. She took early retirement due to vision problems and now works freelance.

Dedication

To Zoe, Jan and Huw, my children: always an inspiration.

Acknowledgements

I would like to thank all the colleagues and students over many years who taught me so much, especially Godfrey Yeung, Scherto Gill and Earl Kehoe, who allowed me to refer to their work.

I would also like to thank editors Simon Bell and Wejdan Ismail for their support and suggestions in producing this book during a difficult time in my life.

Publisher's Acknowledgments

We're proud of this book; please send us your comments through our Dummies online registration form located at www.dummies.com/register/.

Some of the people who helped bring this book to market include the following:

Acquisitions, Editorial, and Media Development

Development Editor: Simon Bell

Content Editor: Jo Theedom

Commissioning Editor: Wejdan Ismail

Publishing Assistant: Jennifer Prytherch

Copy Editor: Anne O'Rorke

Technical Editor: Eileen Lafferty

Executive Editor: Sam Spickernell

Executive Project Editor: Daniel Mersey

Cover Photos: © Somos/Veer

Cartoons: Ed McLachlan

Composition Services

Project Coordinator: Lynsey Stanford

Layout and Graphics: Christin Swinford

Proofreader: Laura Albert

Indexer: Claudia Bourbeau

Contents at a Glance

Introduction 1

Part I: Study Skills Basics 7
Chapter 1: Planning for Success 9
Chapter 2: Tutors and Student Support 27
Chapter 3: Becoming a Critical Thinker 41
Chapter 4: Embracing ICT Skills 53

Part II: Becoming an Active Learner 65
Chapter 5: Learning Actively in Lectures, Seminars and Tutorials 67
Chapter 6: Grappling with Group Work: Workshops, Seminars
    and Presentations 83
Chapter 7: Taking Notes During Lectures 99
Chapter 8: Making Use of Feedback 113

Part III: Gathering Your Evidence 125
Chapter 9: Research Methods and Tools....................................127
Chapter 10: Finding Answers: Reading and Research 149
Chapter 11: Taking Notes for Your Purposes: Not the Book's 167
Chapter 12: Using the Internet as a Research Tool 183
Chapter 13: Tackling the Building Blocks: Numbers and Figures...........199

Part IV: Getting It Down on Paper.......................... 219
Chapter 14: Pulling Your Ideas Together in Writing 221
Chapter 15: Grasping Writing Process Basics 237
Chapter 16: Looking at Form, Function and Style........................255

Part V: Final Reckoning: Surviving
(And Enjoying) Exams.................................... 271
Chapter 17: Mastering Memory Strategies 273
Chapter 18: Preparing for Your Exams 287
Chapter 19: Coping with the Countdown to Your Exams 305

Part VI: The Part of Tens 323

Chapter 20: Ten Time-saving Techniques 325
Chapter 21: Ten Ways to Have Fun While Studying 333
Chapter 22: Ten Essay Writing Tips 341

Index 349

Table of Contents

Introduction 1
   About This Book 1
   Conventions Used in This Book 2
   What You're Not to Read 2
   Foolish Assumptions 2
   How This Book Is Organised 3
      Part I: Study Skills Basics 3
      Part II: Becoming an Active Learner 3
      Part III: Gathering Your Evidence 3
      Part IV: Getting It Down on Paper 4
      Part V: Final Reckoning: Surviving (And Enjoying) Exams 4
      Part VI: The Part of Tens 4
   Icons Used in This Book 5
   Where to Go From Here 5

Part 1: Study Skills Basics 7

Chapter 1: Planning for Success 9
   Getting to Grips with Student Life Basics 10
      Finding your way around 11
      Checking out who's who 12
      Other important locations 13
   Behaviour and Etiquette 14
      Departmental culture 16
      Sorting out problems 16
   Organising Your Study 18
      Putting together your timetable 18
      Group study 20
      Keeping a Learning Diary 21
   Give Me a Break! Using Your Downtime 24
      Taking daily breaks 24
      Working out weekly breaks 25

Chapter 2: Tutors and Student Support 27
   Working Out Your Welfare 28
      Getting Set for Student Life 28
      Using the Student Union 29
      Finding help, support or counselling 29

Living on campus 30
Getting Help with Health Issues 32
Facing financial matters 32
Coming to Terms with Tutors 33
Personal tutors 33
Examining Study Support 36
Behaviour and Responsibilities 38
Knowing your responsibilities 38
Preventing plagiarism 38

Chapter 3: Becoming a Critical Thinker 41

What Is Critical Thinking? 41
Scoping out the skills of critical thinking 42
Making an academic argument 44
Analysing Claims and Evidence 47
Necessary and sufficient conditions 48
Evaluating the evidence 49
Having an academic opinion 50
Developing your academic voice 51

Chapter 4: Embracing ICT Skills 53

Understanding the Technology You Need 53
Handling the hardware 53
Surveying the software 55
Connecting to the Internet 57
Working out WiFi 58
Browser beware: Restricted access material 59
Sampling Systems Learning and Support 60
Assessing ICT Pitfalls 62

Part II: Becoming an Active Learner 65

Chapter 5: Learning Actively in Lectures, Seminars and Tutorials. . .67

Preparing for a Lecture 68
Looking at Lectures 69
Sizing Up Seminars 72
Sorting out types of seminar 72
Preparing to participate in seminars 74
Knowing who does what in seminars 75
Perusing personality types in seminars 76
Testing Out Tutorials 79
Personal tutorials 80
Subject or project tutorials 80

Chapter 6: Grappling with Group Work: Workshops, Seminars and Presentations 83

   The Benefits of Group Work...84
   Working Out Workshops 85
      Using workshops for self-study.................................87
      Using workshops for preparation..............................87
      Getting the workshop organised................................88
   Giving Presentations in Seminars.......................................90
      Kinds of seminar 90
      Engaging your audience..91
      Managing the seminar 92

Chapter 7: Taking Notes During Lectures 99

   Matching Your Expectations Against Reality.........................100
   Preparing the Ground for Great Notes..................................100
      Identifying different types of lectures 101
      Taking your place 101
      Handling handouts..101
   Weighing Up Ways of Note-taking 102
      Making notes on paper..103
      Making notes on a laptop...104
   Organising Your Thoughts 105
      When and what to note..106
   After the Lecture: Adapting and Reflecting on Your Notes....109
      Building a bibliography..109
      Following up on lecture notes.....................................111

Chapter 8: Making Use of Feedback............................113

   Finding Out About the Formal Feedback System 113
      Knowing what you get feedback on.............................114
      Understanding the marking system and
         minimum requirements..115
      Bouncing back from a low grade 116
   Getting Early Feedback on Coursework 116
      After the Event – What Tutors Say and What They Mean 117
      Putting yourself in your tutor's shoes 123
      Understanding how tutors think.................................123
      Making feedback a two-way process...........................124

Part III: Gathering Your Evidence 125

Chapter 9: Research Methods and Tools 127
Developing Hypotheses 127
Devising a Theoretical Framework.. 129
   Choosing a theoretical framework 129
   Relating framework to hypothesis.................................... 130
Choosing Your Research Method.. 131
   Qualitative research 132
   Quantitative research.. 132
   Longitudinal studies 133
Delving into Data Sources and Access 134
Reviewing Your Research Tools.. 135
   Developing research questions.. 136
   Constructing case studies 138
   Querying with questionnaires 139
   Outlining observation... 140
   Evaluating experiments.. 141
   Approaching action research 143
   Investigating interviews 144
   Assessing storytelling 145
Avoiding Pitfalls.. 146

Chapter 10: Finding Answers: Reading and Research 149
Reviewing Reading Lists 150
   Identifying what you really need to read 150
   Balancing your reading 151
Reading as Research – Finding Answers to the Right Questions 152
   Creating research questions 152
   Refining your reading and researching techniques.................. 153
Homing In On How Texts Are Organised.................................... 156
   Section organisation, function and usefulness 156
   Paragraph structure 158
Exploring Other Media Resources.. 159
   Using audio-visual resources 159
   Sharing Resources and Reading Groups.............................. 163

Chapter 11: Taking Notes for Your Purposes: Not the Book's 167
Knowing What You Need from Your Note-Taking 167
Getting Credit for Reading.. 168
   Choosing the right sources 169
   Understanding your purpose in reading and note-taking.......... 169
Developing Your Note-Taking Skills.. 170
   Tabulating notes from several sources................................ 172
   Summary skills 175

Comparing and contrasting.................................176
Analysis...178
Critiquing and text analysis.............................180
Citation/quotation and note cards....................182

Chapter 12: Using the Internet as a Research Tool **183**
Online Dos and Don'ts......................................183
Browser beware: inappropriate web pages...........184
Accommodating balance and bias......................184
Avoiding Internet plagiarism............................185
The Internet as a Life-Saver..............................187
Sourcing books..187
Online research tools......................................188
Approaching E-Learning...................................195

Chapter 13: Tackling the Building Blocks: Numbers and Figures **199**
Dealing with Numbers......................................200
Statistics and statistical significance 200
Percentages 201
Fractions, formulae and decimals.....................202
Mean, median and mode.................................204
Standard deviation...206
Illustrating Your Data......................................208
Pie charts...209
Bar charts 210
Histograms...211
Bell curves 212
Flow charts...213
Technical diagrams 214
Graphs...215
Tables..216

Part IV: Getting It Down on Paper *219*

Chapter 14: Pulling Your Ideas Together in Writing **221**
Understanding the Anatomy of Academic Writing................221
Paying attention to parts and functions 223
Exploring alternative methods..........................223
Using Models..224
Where to find models.....................................225
Knowing what to be wary of.............................225
Surveying Set Titles..226
Using what you know......................................227
Mind maps and initial ideas.............................228
Guideline 'wh' questions..................................230

Creating Working Titles 230
Considering Your Orientation 232
Making Outline Plans 232
        Discussing your ideas with friends 233
        Seeking agreement from tutors 234

Chapter 15: Grasping Writing Process Basics 237

Organising Your Writing 237
Organising Your Information 238
Presenting Your Information 241
        Using tables 242
        Using graphs and charts 244
        Using diagrams and other visual representations 245
Reviewing Your Writing Order 247
        Looking at overall logic 252
        Getting draft feedback 253

Chapter 16: Looking at Form, Function and Style 255

Balancing Formality and Personal Voice 255
Using Citations, References, Footnotes and Quotations 257
        Placing footnotes 259
        Using longer quotations 260
Watching Your Back – Making Claims and Hedging 261
Observing Other Language Features 263
        Gender awareness 263
        Use of pronouns 264
        Avoiding passive forms 265
        Cutting out contractions 266
        Addressing the dreaded apostrophe 267
        Other punctuation 268
        Acting on Acronyms 269

Part V: Final Reckoning: Surviving (And Enjoying) Exams 271

Chapter 17: Mastering Memory Strategies 273

Key Information and Memory Strategies 273
Remembering Key Points and Sequences 275
        Mastering Mnemonics 275
        Assessing audio stimuli 275
        Learning with loci 276
        Other ways to remember key facts 278
Making Memory and Logical Links 279
        Developing a historical perspective 279
        Making memory maps 280

Revising from Notes 281
Making Memories 283
Collating and Recycling Information 284
Reflecting on Beliefs and Feelings 286

Chapter 18: Preparing for Your Exams 287

Examination Requirements and Conditions 288
    Assessing the importance of your exams 288
    Touching on timetabling 288
    Sorting out your individual needs 289
    Allowing for illness and anxiety 289
Perusing Past Papers 290
Reading Up on Rubrics 290
    Essay-type questions 293
    Multiple-choice questions 297
Strategies to identify common topics 299
Testing Yourself 300
Timetabling the Pre-Exam Period 301

Chapter 19: Coping with the Countdown to Your Exams 305

A Time and Place for Everything 306
    Making time for revision – and life's necessities 306
    Keeping a healthy mind in a healthy body 308
    The economics of time, self-bribery and treats 309
Getting Down to It: Sitting Your Exams 311
    Last minute exam behaviour checks 311
    Exam Day Preparation 313
    Approaching Oral Exams 315
After the Exams 318
    Understanding the marking process 318
    Querying an exam mark 320

Part VI: The Part of Tens 323

Chapter 20: Ten Time-saving Techniques 325

Asking Direct Questions 325
Planning to Do Things at the Best Time 326
Prioritising Your Workload 327
Nobody's Perfect – Thank Goodness! 328
Avoiding Procrastination 328
Learning to Say 'No' 329
Having A Quiet Place and Time 330
Building In Some Flexibility 330

Using Big Blocks of Time for Big Tasks.....................................331
Big Projects Need Big Plans 331
Revisiting Reading Lists..332

Chapter 21: Ten Ways to Have Fun While Studying...............333

Being the Best Host 334
Throwing Perfect Parties..334
Joining Up 335
Getting Out in the Local Community 335
Supporting Sweet Charity 336
Working as a Student Helper..337
Reporting for Duty..337
Discovering DJing 338
Diving into Student Politics 339
Being a Mentor or Coach 339

Chapter 22: Ten Essay Writing Tips 341

Getting Feedback You Can Use...341
Defining Your Terms 343
Finding Your Voice..343
Avoiding Style Giveaways...344
Sorting Out Your Verb Grammar 345
Using Gerunds..345
Exchanging Essays 346
Allowing Reflection Time and Self-criticism..........................347
Assessing Your Satisfaction Levels 347
Overcoming Blocks 348

Index *349*

Introduction

Welcome to *Study Skills For Dummies*! So, what are study skills, and why do you need them? Read on. While your subject of study is concerned with *what* you learn, study skills are to do with *how* you learn. Study skills help you use the content of your course as efficiently as possible, so that you get the most out of the efforts you put into your work. They provide you with a basic toolkit of resources to select from and apply to any situation, and each new situation gives you more practice and more confidence in yourself. The skills you practise at college or university will also stand you in good stead in the world of work afterwards. They can help you, for instance, present yourself well at interview, network effectively or challenge with confidence the small print in contracts or other documents.

For most people, going to college or university is their first experience of independence and it can be daunting as well as exciting. For this reason, in this book I take a broad view of study skills so as to include wellbeing as a basic requirement for fruitful studies. The people you meet and interact with, as well as being a joy in themselves – or a problem to solve – contribute to your learning process and skills development. Good students are lively, chatty and well-rounded people who learn from each other as well as their tutors.

About This Book

Study Skills For Dummies aims to help every student get the most from themselves and their studies. Not by burning the midnight oil in a garret and forsaking everything and everyone else – far from it. This book explains some of the reasoning behind how things work in the academic world, the duties and responsibilities of students and their tutors and how and where to seek out answers when something is not clear to you. Knowledge is power and helps to put you in charge of your learning.

The book offers practical strategies to help you use your time effectively and avoid stress, with suggestions for particular tasks like understanding essay titles and taking notes. Regular preparation, followed by discussion or self-reflection on what you've learned or how your views have changed in the light of these experiences, are the bedrock of your learning experience. This process of revisiting what you've learned strengthens not only your memory for information – a great help later on, when the exams come round – but also your own ideas and views. It also helps you construct your arguments in favour of your views: this process is central to your academic development.

In other words, wherever possible, this book shows you how to kill at least two birds with one stone, but you can dip into any chapter and find practical suggestions for solving the problems or tackling the tasks at hand.

Conventions Used in This Book

To help you navigate through this book, I've set up a few conventions:

- *Italic* is used for emphasis and to highlight new words or terms that are defined.

- **Boldfaced** text is used to indicate the action part of numbered steps.

- Website addresses appear in `monofont`, so that they stand out on the page.

- Sidebars (the grey boxes you come across from time to time) are extra background information that you can take or leave.

What You're Not to Read

Because this book is about putting you in charge so that you can easily find what you need, I've also made it easy for you to identify 'skippable' material. This stuff, although interesting and related to the topic at hand, isn't essential for you to know:

- **Text in sidebars:** The sidebars are fun, and you'll learn from reading them, but they aren't essential reading. They share anecdotes, examples or background information only, although I hope they are helpful.

- **The stuff on the copyright page:** Save your time. You should only read what you need to and there's nothing here of any interest, even if you're doing a publishing degree.

Foolish Assumptions

In writing this book, I've assumed that one of the following is true about you.

- You are in your last year of school considering embarking on a course of study at college or university.

- You have already started a course at college or university.

- You are returning to education after a break to take a higher degree and need some revision.

✔ You are taking a Foundation course instead of 'A' levels.

✔ You want the best value from your investment (both financial and physical) in education at university, and you want to know how to get it.

How This Book Is Organised

Study Skills For Dummies is divided into six parts, with each part broken into several chapters. Each chapter is, in turn, broken up into several sections. Each part brings together related material. The table of contents gives you more details of each chapter.

Part I: Study Skills Basics

This part introduces you to the nitty-gritty of being at university telling you about the overall set-up, academic requirements, how things work and how you can develop the basic tools you need to be a successful student. Here's where you find out about critical thinking, and those essential ICT skills you have to have in modern college education.

Part II: Becoming an Active Learner

One thing you need to get straight from the start is that a college or university education is not something that just happens to you. It's something you do. Active learning is about asking questions of the information you are taught, and using your critical skills to transform simple facts into understanding. This part covers the various sorts of learning experience you are going to become accustomed to, from intimate seminar groups to lectures in which you might be one of a hundred or more participants. It also stresses the two-way nature of education, accustoming you to the idea of seeking and giving feedback.

Part III: Gathering Your Evidence

This part deals in detail with an area which might be relatively new to you: independent research. At college or university you are in control of your own learning. Part III takes you through all you need to know about acquiring the raw material for knowledge and understanding. I tell you how to find the information you need, where to find it, and how to go about incorporating it into your own work.

Part IV: Getting It Down on Paper

Being able to express your views concisely in writing is a key skill for any student, almost regardless of which course they are on. The chapters in this section show you how to structure your written work effectively and how to use the sort of language appropriate to academic communication. They also stress the key principles of academic communication: honesty, clarity, relevance, and reality. Whether you're writing lab reports or a dissertation, this part shows you how to get your thoughts down in the most efficient way you can. Writing is about showing what you know and using that as a basis to find out new things – about yourself as well as your subject. Just as poems and whodunits have an expected form, so does academic writing. This part helps you to base your ideas in academic 'fact' and be creative.

Part V: Final Reckoning: Surviving (And Enjoying) Exams

Even if you're studying a subject where a large component of your final grade is made up of coursework, the chances are that you'll have to sit exams at some point. This part deals with understanding exam questions, tips for remembering detailed information and advice on making the exams period as enjoyable as it possibly can be. If you prepare properly for your exams, there's really nothing to worry about, and this section shows you how to develop the confidence to sail through with flying colours.

Part VI: The Part of Tens

It's a _For Dummies_ book, so there must be a Part of Tens. The chapters in this section offer chunks of sound advice to enhance your experience of student life. I talk about how to maximise the time you have available, how to work _and_ have a good time at university, and finish up with ten great ideas for making your essays stand out from the crowd.

Icons Used in This Book

The icons used in this book help you to find different kinds of information that may be useful to you.

This icon highlights practical advice to make study skills work for you. Tips are the inside info you need to make the most of your study time.

This icon is a friendly reminder of important points to take note of. Carry these away with you, and you won't go far wrong.

You'll find this icon beside real-life instances of the particular topic I'm discussing, to help you get a grip on the issues.

The ideas and information you'll find next to this icon tend to be a bit more technical or mathematical than the rest of the book. I'm not saying the info isn't interesting, but don't get bogged down in it. You can still get the big picture, so feel free to skip this stuff.

This icon marks things to avoid of be wary of. If you see this icon, steer clear of whatever it is I'm warning you against.

Where to Go From Here

For Dummies books are organised so that you can dip in practically anywhere. You don't have to start at Page 1 and keep going until the index. In fact that isn't a great idea at all.

Having said that, it might be an idea to start with Part I, which really does cover the basics of student life. After that, the world – or at least the book – is your oyster. Use the Contents Pages and the Index to find the stuff you really need and want to know about. And enjoy!

Part I
Study Skills
Basics

In this part . . .

So now you're a student. What do you do now? This part gets you up to speed on the essentials of student life. In it I cover the people and places you need to know, the ways in which you need to organise yourself and both your responsibilities as a student and those of others towards you.

I also talk about the very basic skills you need to acquire to be a successful and engaged student. Not just the techie stuff, although I cover that, but the crucial skills of critical and analytical thinking which underpin your time as a student – and set you up for life.

Chapter 1

Planning for Success

· ·

In This Chapter

▶ How course elements fit together – who's who and what's what

▶ Reviewing rules and behaviour

▶ What's in store and taking control

▶ Balancing work and leisure

· ·

A very exciting phase in your life is about to start – new teachers, new classmates, new things to study about your chosen subject. If you're away from home for the first time, you need to work out new strategies to get yourself up on time without the person or pet that used to perform that function. You'll discover, sadly, that the washing fairy who used to transform piles of discarded clothes into sweet-smelling, smoothly ironed wearable articles is a myth – or didn't accompany you to your new address. You'll learn a lot about yourself. You might turn out to be a highly talented omelette maker, write the best essay on fluoridisation and freedom in your study group or score a hat trick at hockey, a sport you never played at school.

Some things you can do nothing about, like not growing another six inches if it's not in your genes. However, there are plenty of things you can improve by developing strategies and planning, and the good thing about planning is that it doesn't take very long. You can do it in small doses, and it can make a big difference. In addition, planning will save time so that you can have more fun, and some planning will itself be fun and certainly a lot more interesting than watching paint dry. Knowing how to do things – having good study skills – is just as important as knowing what's what!

Getting to Grips with Student Life Basics

When you arrive at your college, you will normally be given a student information pack which will include:

- General information about student life at your particular university or college, such as:

  - A campus map

  - Significant term dates

  - Information about the library

  - Details of shopping and banking facilities

  - An introduction to the sports centre

  - All you need to know about the health centre

  - Information on campus safety and security

  - A guide to the Students Union

  - General academic rules and regulations relating to exams, handing in work late, and plagiarism

- Specific information about your course, including:

  - The names of tutors, (note your year tutor in particular)

  - The academic school office that deals with you subject area

  - Contact numbers and emails for help and support

  - The term or year programme of topics for each course of study

  - The recommended reading, probably on a weekly basis

  - The methods of on-going assessment

  - The dates of examinations

A lot of the information is useful to consult as the need arises, so keep it safe. In study terms, your timetable for the term is your road map showing how much of your time is structured by the formal elements of your couse. The weekly elements consist of timetabled classes, ranging from wholly taught lecture courses and seminars (which probably include contributions from class members) to workshops and laboratory work, which may take the form of supervised group or individual work. Each class will be allocated a particular room and tutor. If you are lucky, your weekly timetable may be set out for you by your subject office. If not, the school office will give you the code numbers for the classes you have to attend so that you can find the time, place and tutor from the overall room allocations timetable, normally available in the reception area of most campus buildings or with the porters.

Finding your way around

The academic department in which you study may be part of a *school* or a *faculty,* depending on which is the preferred term in your university. The school (faculty) or department office will supply you with a blank timetable so that you can fill in your classes and don't need to carry all the room bookings information round with you.

You also need the campus map (ask the school (faculty) or department office for one if you aren't given one). This should at least give you the building names or numbers, if not the room numbers. Room numbers are usually allocated like for hotel rooms – 102 means first floor room 2, and 210 second floor room, though this may vary. Lecture theatres usually have a name or code to indicate what they are and seminar rooms may just have a building code or name and number. See Chapters 5 and 6 for more on lectures and seminars.

Take your timetable and campus map and spend an hour or so finding all the rooms you will use or visit using the checklist which follows this paragraph as a guide. The teaching rooms can be in different buildings and some distance from your subject home base area, so note the loos and cafes in passing. There is normally a ten minute gap between classes, so knowing where you have to get to when you have one class immediately after another will tell you if there is only time for a loo break, not a coffee break.

- Lecture theatres
- Seminar rooms
- Tutors' offices (get the room numbers from the school office)
- School office and secretaries or admin. staff offices
- Common rooms and cafes near the teaching rooms
- Locker space near teaching rooms
- Toilets near the teaching rooms
- Laboratories, including computer labs or *clusters* (groups) of computers available for students to use in open plan areas and the Language lab
- Main library, departmental library and places for self-study (check opening hours)
- Students Union offices
- Student Health Centre
- Sports centre and gymnasium
- Shower facilities

- ✔ Lock-ups for bikes
- ✔ University Book shop
- ✔ Student Union and other shops – grocery, launderette, stationery
- ✔ Student bars and Refectory

Checking out who's who

When you have found each tutor's office, check the important information pinned to the door: the time of their office hour and the name of the person who provides their secretarial or administrative support, each with their internal phone numbers and email addresses. This is important information to get in contact or leave a message at short notice, if you are ill or get held up. The teaching staff will be out of their rooms teaching for much of the time, so messages are best left with or at least copied to their secretary, probably working in the school office or nearby. Tutor's office hours are a guaranteed time when tutors will be in their offices and available to students. Find out more about what tutors do in Chapter 2.

Although appointments may not be necessary, it's worth either suggesting a time to call within the office hours (by email or internal phone) in case the tutor is expecting other students. That way, you don't have to wait around. If you can't do that, get there a bit early to be first in line. Your time is just a valuable as your tutor's and an extra half hour in the library might be more useful than waiting outside a door.

Take a book to read just in case you have to wait.

When you have found the teaching rooms, your various subject tutors' offices, their office hours, phone numbers and email addresses, the phone numbers and email addresses of those who deal with their administration, where their offices are located (they might be some distance away from the tutor's) make yourself a 'Who's Who to keep with your class timetable as shown in Figure 1-1. The information on Tutors' doors tends to be the most up to date. Check again at the beginning of the next term in case office hours have changed.

You will note that two tutors who teach you can have office hours at the same time and you may have a lecture at the time of an office hour. However, students are not expected to contact tutors on a regular basis and office hours are arranged for when a tutor is not teaching. If you have a bigger or on-going problem, you should probably contact your year or personal tutor, if you have one. It may also be possible to arrange a different meeting time with a tutor.

Name	Position	Room No.	Phone	Email	Office hours
Janet. K.	Tutor, ECS.3	D15	896677	Janet.K@ any.ac.uk	Wed. 3.00 – 4.00
Prof. Wilks	Tutor, ECS.5	D27	896223 (sec) 896224	Wilks@ any.ac.uk	Wed. 3.00 – 4.00
Mrs P. Jones	Admin Janet K.	School Office D10	896666	p.jones@ any.ac.uk	Leaves 5.00pm
Emma P.	Socs 2 lecture & seminar	A35	896555	Emma.p@ any.ac.uk	Wed. 10 – 11.00
Dave B.	Tutor, Socs 1. Lecture+ seminar	A32	896523	Dave.n@ any.ac.uk	Mon. 12.00 – 1.00
Miss J. Wiles	Admin Emma P. & Dave B	A26	896529	j.wiles@ any.ac.uk	Leaves 4.00pm
John.R	Year tutor	A30	896532	J.rowe@ any.ac.uk	Thurs. 2.00 – 3.00
Jessie K.	personal tutor	A36	896539	jessie@ any.ac.uk	Mon. 2.00 – 3.00
Mrs T. King	Admin. Jessie & John	A40	896547	t.king@ any.ac.uk	Not in Friday

Figure 1-1:
A Typical
Who's Who

Other important locations

You probably went on a campus visit, either when you visited to find out if
the college was for you or not, or perhaps during *Freshers' week* – the first
week of the first term of the university year. If you haven't been on a tour
of the library already, sign up for one at the reception desk. You will be
shown where the books and journals in your subject area are located, how
to reserve books, use the *interlibrary loan system*, (a system which allows
you to borrow books from other university libraries if your university library
doesn't have a copy available) and how to find out whether books you want
are held by the library, on loan or available, and what library information you
can access on line. In short, all the practical information you need to start
borrowing. Check the library opening times.

Find out the location of the open access computers on campus. Some might
be set up with special facilities or programmes for drawing technical diagrams or learning languages and will normally have a resident technician to

help with any hitches. Check when the technician is available. The computer laboratory will normally be open outside their working hours. Check Chapter 4 for more detail on ICT skills.

The Student Union bar will normally be the cheapest place to buy alcohol. Bars with names which include 'Senior' or are in research unit buildings are often aimed at staff or older students and will be more expensive. The same is true of cafes – the Union café will be cheaper. However, prices on campus are generally relatively low and slightly more expensive cafes often provide a range of daily newspapers to peruse while you sip your coffee. Campus newspapers – official and student – should also be available. (You can often buy at least one 'quality' newspaper like the *Guardian, Times. Independent, Telegraph, Financial Times* very cheaply on campus for as little as 10p.)

The Student Health Centre will have doctors on campus and may also provide dentists and opticians as well as a counselling service. There is often also a dispensary or chemist shop. It's a good idea to register with the health professionals on campus if you can, as they will have a good idea of your overall health profile. In addition, you may find there is a sick bay for on campus nursing if you are too ill to look after yourself where you can get plenty of TLC, and there will be First Aiders in all buildings. At the entrance to each building there is normally a notice telling you where the First Aid post in the building is and the name of the First Aider, usually next to the Fire regulations.

Behaviour and Etiquette

The rules of academic engagement between students and tutors normally mean that *professors* (the highest level of university teacher, with an international reputation) or *deans* (the heads of the faculties or schools have their phones more or less permanently switched through to their secretaries, who usually have an office adjacent to that of the academic in question. You might be lucky and get through to them directly if they teach you and you have a query related to your course, but you normally have to go through their secretaries. This is very positive for you, as a secretary is much more likely to get you any general information that you need. If you want something from the horse's mouth, you'll probably have to make an appointment. This might take a while if the professor you want to speak to is about to leave on a trip to the swamps of central Africa. Senior staff are generally a bit more distant than tutors, lecturers, senior tutors (the next level up from tutor/ lecturer) or readers (the level below professor) because of the range of tasks they carry out within a tight schedule.

Testing out academic titles

Men in suits or smartly dressed women in high heels are usually part of the administration or bureaucracy in a university or college. They are also more likely to be referred to by their title – Mr, Mrs, Dr – than many of the academic staff, by both students and other staff members. Exceptions are perhaps professors or deans, whose secretaries tend to use their titles when talking to them, at least in the presence of others.

By contrast, it is sometimes difficult to tell the difference between students and younger members of staff. Possibly the holes in staff jeans are a little smaller and in not quite such revealing places! You may have been used to calling your teachers by their first names at school and so won't be surprised if that is the case at college.

When in doubt wait to see how other people refer to your tutors and the administration staff to their faces – which can be quite different to how they refer to them when they're not there. The best thing to do is ask what he or she would like to be called. They may offer you the same courtesy.

If you phone a tutor/lecturer, senior tutor or even a reader who teaches you they are quite likely to answer their phone. It is normally switched through to their secretaries only when they are teaching or not in the university. A tutor may answer the phone even if they are taking a tutorial in their room. If they do answer, you should ask if they're busy. They will probably ask you to ring back later at a fairly precise time if they are teaching (because their time is quite tightly allocated) or offer to ring you. You can always check their timetable with their secretary so that you don't disturb them when they're teaching. Secretaries (sometimes called administration staff) always know timetables, although certain maverick tutors will go walkabout at other times without telling their secretaries where they've gone. Most administrative staff can provide the information you need, so its always worth asking them first. The Vice Chancellor, the administrative head of the university, usually welcomes new students at the start of term (there may even be drinks and nibbles). Some have an 'open door' policy and keep an office hour for students or have general receptions with students once or twice a year so that you can speak to them. They also take a keen interest in the feedback from students – in most cases, you fill in a questionnaire at the end of each course of study with your impressions and suggestions. Check out Chapter 2 for more on tutors and what they do.

Departmental culture

Every department within an institution has its own culture. In some, you will find students, tutors, even professors, and administrative staff sitting together and chatting informally in the department cafe. Tutors may thus be very approachable, especially if they are creatures of habit and tend to be in the same place at the same time on a regular basis. Other places may be more formal – or the offices of the various department members may not be close together, so they can't so easily be found outside their offices or teaching time. In this case, the more formal structure through the administrative staff will help you get hold of who you need.

Generally speaking, the administrative staff keep all the records, rules and regulations and are at the forefront of organising the marks, timetables and other data for your course. They will also probably have copies of any handouts or lecture notes you missed, as well as copies of previous exams. They may even have sample copies of old exam answers. See Chapters 17 to 19 for more on how to survive – even enjoy – exams.

If you need any help with any of the day to day running of the course, course papers and so forth, then the school office for your subject area should be your first port of call. Make friends with all the people in the school office and make sure you know who the ones on your list are, in particular the secretaries to your tutors. These people are likely to be able to find out most of things you need to know and can save you (as is their job) from bothering a tutor about something the tutor can't help you with anyway. This saves you time. Departmental staff can usually suggest the best person to ask if they don't know the answer themselves. They are generally the calm in the middle of the storm, keeping the ship on course.

Administrative staff tend to go home quite early or may work staggered hours. They may not work every day, so be careful to note their work times on your 'Who's Who' list so that you know when as well as where to find them.

Sorting out problems

Once you have sorted out your weekly timetable – rooms, times and tutors with their associated administrative help and know where to find people – there may be a problems concerning the formal requirements of your course. Again, try the school office or administrative staff first as it is likely to be a problem they've come across before. If they don't have a solution, they will know who to ask. If it's a strictly academic (rather than organisational) question, then you might try the year tutor. The sort of issue you might encounter includes:

✔ **Timetable problems.** If you are studying two or more subjects, then you may have a timetable clash. Various possible solutions exist.

- One of the courses may be repeated at another time or in another term, so you may be able to switch to that one.

- If you only have to miss part, not the whole of a class, you may be able to catch up the part you miss with the help of your subject tutor.

- You may be able to substitute another course for one of the clashes, one that is equivalent in value for your degree. (Some institutions, especially those with visiting overseas students, assign credits to comply with European, American, or International systems. Some courses may be worth six credits, others ten. These can be added to the students' credits when they get back home. The credit system shows the minimum number of courses a student needs to take and pass. They will still get marks for each course according to degree level standards – first, upper/lower second, third, pass.)

- If your subject tutor needs to see you or give you a tutorial, your tutorial takes precedence. It will be a one-off clash and may be the only time your tutor is free.

- If a seminar clashes with a lecture, then the seminar normally takes precedence. In many cases, lectures are repeated with different groups, so you may be able to join another. Sometimes lectures are taped and can be viewed later. Always make sure the lecturer or tutor of the class you may have to miss and their secretary are aware of your problem. There may be another solution.

✔ **Course requirements and assignments.** Just as you might have to prioritise the classes you attend, you might sometimes have to prioritise your study time and leave some things out when you're in a tight corner. To make the best judgements, you need good information.

- Find out whether there are exams every term or once or twice a year and whether you have to pass them all to pass the course for the year. Some may count towards your degree – others not – you need to know which. See Chapters 17 for more on exams.

- Find out how many essays you have to write and their due dates – whether you can expect to write one a week or one a fortnight – for example, and how they are assessed.(See Chapter 8 for more on feedback and assessment) Do all the marks count or perhaps the best three out of five, for example? Do you have to do longer, *essays* once a term, perhaps twice as long as other essays and do they count for more thanweekly or fortnightly essays? Is a term essay, say, worth twice the marks of a weekly essay? What is the overall base level mark you need to get to pass the course for the term or year?

- Depending on the course you're doing, you may have to carry out laboratory work, group or individual projects or experiments. It's important to know how they are assessed in relation to other work. Again, if a project is worth twice the marks of a weekly essay and you are pressed for time, you might put more effort into the project. Some assignments might not be assessed, but you need to complete them as a first step to another assignment which is assessed.

- In general, some forms of work are likely to be obligatory or certainly more important than others in terms of marks, so find out which is which. Some work may not be graded, for example, first essays, as the idea is to give you feedback and hints, but no penalties. This gives you a chance to experiment a bit and try out ideas, so this type of assignment has a different kind of value for you.

- Find out what the penalties are for failing to hand in work, failing a course or term assessment, and whether you can resit exams or rewrite essays with low marks. On some courses every essay counts, but on some it's the best of three, for example.

If you have the information you need, you can avoid difficulties. If, for example, you already have the essay grade average you need for one course with one essay in hand, but your essay grades are low for another course, better put your effort into the essay for the second course. It's always better to get things right in the first place rather than carryi the burden of extra work on to the next term, but there are usually ways to put things right, so never give up!

Organising Your Study

You should now have a good idea of the formal requirements and obligations and the framework for the term – the classes to attend, assignments to complete and exams to pass – and some idea of the routes you will take to get to and from classes, the library and a hot coffee. Even if you haven't yet met your tutors, you know where they hang out, at least some of the time. You probably will have met some classmates during Freshers Week and people studying other subjects who might live in the same place. You are gradually building up a picture and an understanding of the various relationships that will develop.

Putting together your timetable

You have your timetable and assignment due dates. You can now build in your preparation and other studies. The timetable in Figure 1-2 is simplified.

Timetable	Monday	Tuesday	Wednesday	Thursday	Friday
9–11	Lecture LT2		***Hand in assignment		***Hand in assignment
11–1.00		Lecture LT4	Seminar S4		Workshop group project
2.00–4.00	Seminar S2			Lecture LT3	
4.00–6.00				Seminar S3	
6.00–9.00		Project			

Figure 1-2: A typical timetable

Seminars and lectures may have only one hour slots and although teaching can go on till 9.00 p.m., this doesn't happen very often. You may have only eight hours of formal teaching per week – or a lot more. In this plan, there are two assignment preparation or hand-in days per week. Each lecture has a follow-up seminar (with the same number) on the same topic and there is some project/workshoptime.

The timetable in Figure 1-2 has three topics to prepare reading for each week, one for each lecture/seminar pair. The two exercises are based on the lecture/seminars of the previous week. Maths, Economics, and Technical students as well Arts students who need to handle large amounts of information will almost certainly have regular exercises to practise using the formulae and methods introduced to them each week. (See Chapter 12 for more on handling numbers and figures.) Other exercises may be translations for language students, short experiments or other tasks which give practice in some of the methods or principles discussed in class. The workshop and projects relate to the third topic of the previous week, which is not assessed through an assignment, but through a report at the end of term. Any term examination is likely to include at least one topic from each week, though there will be a choice. Your reading list for each topic will tell you the main or core reading.

You will probably find that one or two texts cover several topics over a number of weeks. See if you can borrow them from the departmental library, reserve them from the main library or buy them second-hand from the Student Union or other bookshop, especially if they are recommended to buy in the reading list. Buying a copy will probably save you time and possibly your sanity, and you won't have to go through the hunting down process again before exams, as there will almost certainly be exam questions based upon highly recommended texts. You can always resell it later and get some of your money back.

This means you can prepare for lectures and essays and exams – to a certain extent – at the same time and as you go along. However, the immediate planning is about how to use the space in your time-table for each week and where to study. You could prepare by reading for Lecture 2 on Friday afternoon and then prepare the related questions for Seminar 2 – you could ask for examples or explanations for things you haven't understood – after Lecture 2 on Monday morning. You have a two hour break between the lecture and seminar on Monday, and, taking out time for lunch, you can probably do a good hour's study before the seminar. You need to think where you would like to study, like the library, and whether on your own or with classmates, probably those attending the same seminar with you might be the most useful.

Learning is mainly a co-operative process at college or university, rather than competitive. Your main competitor is yourself, to improve and learn as you go along. However, being co-operative doesn't mean you won't have arguments! It means sharing your thoughts and rationally defending them, and listening to those of others. Putting things into words is in itself a learning process. Take a look at Chapter 3 for more on developing an academic argument, and Chapters 14 to 16 for how to express yourself in writing.

It may seem a bit early, but the subject or school office may well have copies of recent exams that you can look at or get a copy of. You may be able to view them on line. This is important, especially if you have exams each term. You should be able to detect a thread between the exam questions and lecture/seminar topics to bear in mind and keep on the back-boiler. If you can't detect a thread or an exam question seems to relate to a minor topic, this is a question you can bring up in the relevant seminar. Check out Chapter 18 for more on effective revision.

Group study

Your seminar groups – there may be a different group of people in each seminar – are perhaps the best group for doing co-operative work. For example, you could set up a group to share texts, including reserving, borrowing or buying them, or even share reading and discussing them. You may have time to have a short follow-up meeting about the seminar you've just attended. This is where common rooms are useful, as you need a big enough space for several people to chat in. It is not easy to find unused teaching rooms during the day time, though you might find it easier later in the afternoon. In any case, you are liable to be evicted. See Chapters 5 and 6 for more on seminars and group study.

If you make yourself into an 'official' regular study group, you may find the Student Union can help you find a room or your tutor can persuade room bookings to tell her which rooms are free at a certain time and to inform her if they get booked up later, so you can use them for the time being. What you don't want is to traipse round looking for a room as people will drop by the wayside and lose impetus. Get a place to meet sorted out.

You need to decide on group priorities. For example, text sharing for exams could be a timetabled priority so each member of the group knows who has (or should have) read each text and members can contact each other to discuss them before the exam if they wish or have time.

Although one person may take the main lead and present the main points from reading texts each week, everyone needs to do some reading. Text/reading study group meetings work best after the lecture and before the seminar, to give everyone more to comment on in the seminar. The commitments of the other students may be the best way to decide on study group membership – groups of up to nine or ten are fine, as this means each student takes the lead for one week each terms. The seminar group could be sub-divided if it is larger than this.

With luck, most people will have read some of the main background texts that you were sent to read over the summer and so have basic understanding of the lecture and seminar topics. This background reading can serve as a baseline for the discussion of further reading and is an excellent starting-off point to broach the subject of sharing reading texts and reading and reporting groups by asking: 'What did you think of . . . ? Did it make sense to you, did you agree with what it said about . . . ?'

Discussions of reading will probably lead to other useful discoveries by group members, suc as online journals or archives with articles written by recommended authors. Some of these may be more up to date than the books on your list. As the saying goes, 'It pays to talk' and you learn from each other.

Keeping a Learning Diary

You should have a class timetable, with hand-in dates, a preparation reading programme with links to exam questions, and possibly a reading group timetable. Make the most out of your plans and preparation by keeping a *learning diary*. This could be a conventional desk-type diary or a simple note-book. Although lap tops are very convenient, they can't be used quite everywhere and jottings are easier to add to paper – especially in the middle of the night. A page or double-page spread for each day is best, with the smaller weekly timetable (see Figure 1-2) available to refer to at the beginning.

The weekly timetable shows the balance of classes, heavy and light days, days when you have to get up early and days when it will be tempting to sleep in. If possible, leave most of the week-end free for non-study matters, though you might want to swap a Saturday afternoon of study for some study-free hours during the week. Wednesday afternoons usually have no classes to allow time for participation in sport, but you don't have to do sports on Wednesdays, as long as you have a balance of activities. Such a balance is easier to achieve on a weekly basis, which is why the timetable is useful to have to hand within your Learning Diary.

The learning diary can work as both a daily organiser and a planner to remind you what you have to do, where you should be and as a place to note items like names and email addresses. It also functions as a personal diary to note your thoughts and reactions to what and how you've studied, help you chart the processes and procedures you've been through. If you had a good essay mark and another not so good, you can look back through your learning diary for any significant differences in the processes that you underwent for each to help you understand why one essay was better than the other. It is not easy to be aware of the processes and changes that happen during learning, and it can be surprising to see where you were even a month ago, and how much you have learned (or changed) since. The Learning diary encourages reflection, as in the rush to get things done, it is easy to throw out the baby with the bath water. Reflection can include notes on how long things took to do and what the payback was, increased confidence or help you to see when to ask specific questions and who to ask. Putting what's inside outside makes it easier to take a long, hard and more dispassionate look.

Everyone is different, but the following are some possible points to include in your learning diary.

- **Work to hand in today:** You need to note what it is, the time it has to be in by, and where to hand it in.

- **Pre-class preparation:** Where and when you're doing it, and with whom

- **Questions and comments relating to reading and preparation:** Anything you've noted from the reading you've already done for today's classes, including anything that is not clear.

- **Expectations of what the class will cover:** Jot down your ideas based on the lecture title, say, and the recommended reading.

- **Comments and impressions after class and after reflecting on class notes:** How far the class answered the questions prepared beforehand, any other points to raise in a seminar or with a tutor.

✔ **Comments and impressions of classmates in after-class or reading group discussions:** How far these add to the points you have raised yourself and whether there are still problems. If problems do still exist, note what you can do about them.

✔ **General evaluation of the topics studied so far and possible ideas for essay or other assessed work on the topics:** Note points which might link to exams or other ideas or links. Comments on books you have read and very importantly, record the bibliographical details, page, and chapter numbers for future reference.

✔ **Reminders of resources you need:** These include books to reserve, collect or return, websites to check, people to contact and journals to read (these usually can't be taken out of the library). Also, you could remind yourself to ask your subject tutor if you can borrow copies of texts from her.

✔ **Reflections on what you've learned today:** Note any impressions which were very different from what you expected; anything exciting and warranting more research, perhaps for assessed work; anything interesting about the methodology or way of teaching, or perhaps how you learned from a classmate. Include any new ways of doing things you tried out – whether useful or not – and any study tips you learned which saved time.

✔ **Reflections on value-for-time of various ways of learning:** Decide whether you had any preferences, (for example, working alone or in a group or pair). Note what was good, what was difficult, what was usefulor interesting. Keep a record of how long certain activities took.

✔ **Records of formal feedback:** Note any grades or assessment comments received today and where they are filed.

✔ **Updated information:** Note the email address and phone numbers of any new members of the seminar or study group.

Some subjects of study may, in addition to your own learning diary, ask you to keep a separate learning (or learner) diary, for that particular subject to be part of the formal assessment procedure. You may be asked to write up your diary notes into a report of your experience of attending a particular taught course. As this experience is a process over time, your diary notes may record how at first (with dates) you disliked a subject because you were not confident of your ability, but how you asked more questions and became more confident and your marks improved. Then you enjoyed the subject more. (The diaries are intended to be truthful records, so if you really hated the topic you are not penalised for that. You are penalised for not keeping the diary or asking for help – in other words, you can't suffer in silence with a learning diaries.)

Give Me a Break! Using Your Downtime

Mens sana in corpore sano – a healthy mind in a healthy body: The Romans were quite sure about the importance of that. Of course breaks are important, that's why we need to sleep, to regenerate, repair and create. The same goes for students, and even true if you are young: you are probably still growing, so some of your energy will be channelled into doing that. The difficulty is getting a balance. Just as the learning diary works on a daily basis in conjunction with the timetable, which basically works on a weekly basis, you may need to juggle at two levels – daily and weekly – to satisfy your overall break needs, that is, non-study time.

Taking daily breaks

Things to remember when organising daily breaks are:

- **Respect the law of diminishing returns.** Anything over two or so hours without a break means the time required to learn is much longer. Thursday on the example timetable could be a difficult afternoon. It's worth asking for a short break in the middle of a two or three hour class, especially if you know your tutor hasn't given up smoking yet.

- **Apportion your break time sensibly.** If you have a heavy lunch, you will be digesting for a few hours, so if you can't have a break or siesta, use this time to do routine things. If you are in class, it's probably best to focus on your notes rather than try to be wildly creative. Do that by all means, just not on a full stomach.

- **Take screen breaks.** If you are working on line, Health and Safety at Work guidelines recommend at least hourly breaks of a few minutes. This means focusing on things at a different distance to your computer screen, not taking a break to bid on Ebay or watch Youtube. Get up, walk about, go outside, watch the birds fly, look at something farther away than fifteen inches from your nose that moves.

- **Take proper food breaks.** Relax by making a super spaghetti Bolognese. If you live on chocolate bars, you'll get surges of energy then feel flat. And you'll get spots.

  If you jog to the supermarket or store to get your Bolognese sauce (mind how you carry it) and you'll have a great screen break, exercise and more oxygen in your lungs, a better appetite and you won't want chocolate ten minutes later.

- ✔ **Bribe yourself.** It's easy to sit book in hand and daydream. When you need to concentrate, set yourself a target, something obtainable, like reading ten pages or writing up some results in an hour. Promise yourself a quick trip to the pub thirty minutes before closing time, and to jog there and back. You know which buttons to push. Not concentrating means being in a kind of limbo, suspended animation. If you are tired, take a nap.

- ✔ **Get to bed early:** The story that every hour you sleep before midnight is worth two hours afterwards is a bit silly, but if you are asleep by 11.00 p.m., it is easier to get up an hour earlier than usual, do some work and be more productive.

- ✔ **Have a chat break every day**: On the phone, over a meal, to the lady in the corner shop – so that you are anchored in reality and have your feet firmly on the ground.

Overall, it's not really about how long breaks are, it's about when and how you take them.

Working out weekly breaks

Weekly breaks take the slightly longer view. For example, you could spend five hours running a marathon one day, and then have three days without exercise. Non-study things to build in breaks for on a weekly basis include the following.

- ✔ **Take a break for weekly chores.** Breaks for cooking, shopping, washing, cleaning – the physical necessities of life – not all have to be done daily, but at least weekly to avoid permanently matted hair (unless you're Russell Brand) or eggy jumpers.

- ✔ **Give yourself a once-a-week treat.** Everyone needs at least one treat bigger than going to the pub (unless it's to watch the big match) to look forward to each week. Cheap diversions can be local markets (with perhaps cheap free range eggs or cabbages) boot fairs or jumble sales. The college itself may have a weekly market. Outdoor markets, better still, walks or bike rides for a few hours work wonders. Build treats into the programme, preferably with a friend and outdoors at least part of the time.

- ✔ **Focused exercise.** Many swimming pools sell cheap tickets for early morning swims. A free hour may be long enough to go to the gym, but may cost more. For cheaper alternatives, team sports, like football, basketball or netball, played a few times a week, will get the adrenalin going.

✔ **Keeping your weekends free:** Weekend breaks can take some planning. You can keep your week-ends free of study by making your weeks a little more dense in a *work hard, play hard* system. If you have light days during the week, make sure you take advantage and fill them up with study, not sleep. Unexpected invitations or treats tend to come at week-ends, so don't leave the week-ends to catch up with everything. Work fairly solidly through the week and take advantage of week-end fun time.

If you take paid work while studying, keeping the week-end clear for work is probably more manageable than trying to work and study during the week. Even if you work as well, try to have one clear day that isn't planned so that you can be flexible and respond to the unpredictable.

Chapter 2

Tutors and Student Support

· ·

In This Chapter

▶ Wising up on welfare

▶ Checking out your tutors

▶ Sorting out your study support

▶ Recognising your responsibilities

· ·

Going away to college or university is a big step and probably the first time you've been totally responsible for sorting out three big areas of your life: your welfare, your studies and your finances. Sound a bit daunting? Things aren't so bad. The other side of the coin is that going to college gives you a tremendous opportunity to become truly independent, and you have access to free advice from various sources – not just from your tutors, but from the Students Union, welfare and financial services and careers advisers among others – something to take advantage of for now and in the future as well.

Whereas parents and grandparents tend to have mantras like 'Neither a borrower nor a lender be' or 'Live today because tomorrow we die', the advice and support you can get on campus relates to your current situation. For example, the financial advice available takes account of the savings market and your individual needs and priorities, rather than a set of rigid principles to live or die by. This in itself can be disturbing, and it's important to remember that, unlike in the outside world, no one can benefit from the advice available except you. Advisers aren't going to meet their sales targets or receive a bonus because you've taken their advice, so they have nothing to gain personally. In most cases, you can ask for advice from more than our source and then make up your own mind. You don't have to accept all, or indeed any of it.

Working Out Your Welfare

University or college welfare services are in place to support your physical and mental health needs, help you find accommodation or learning support if you have a disability, and provide financial advice. Many campuses have resident dentists and opticians as well as doctors and nurses in a health centre, and a pharmacy, so you can fit in appointments in between classes.

Getting Set for Student Life

Although help is always available, you need to be proactive and ask for it. You don't need to suffer in silence. As well as the advice in your information pack or student handbook (see Chapter 1 for more on these), you can find information about different kinds of help on notice boards in public places all over campus, and some tell you how you can make anonymous requests.

You're now an independent adult and authority figures don't check up on you on a daily basis. They respect your privacy but are ready to help if you ask them to. If you miss a few lectures they'll probably notice and try to find out why, but won't chase you up immediately after you miss one. If you have to miss lectures because you're ill or have to go away on family business, call the school office staff so that they know your situation. And if you need help, let them know. They do care about you but at the same time they try to give you space.

Few of us are mind readers. Some people find certain subjects difficult to talk about whereas others find them easy, so it's important that you find the right person to help you. You may, for example, prefer to talk to a woman rather than a man. Don't let any worries of this kind stop you from asking for help sooner rather than later. Try talking to someone you feel comfortable with first – a fellow student, or perhaps a Student Union officer – they can help you express your worry. You can always write it down, or even draw it if this helps.

It's quite normal to be a bit homesick at first and nothing to be ashamed of. It takes a while to make new friends, but be proactive and join a few societies, buy a cake and knock on a few doors and offer some in your hall of residence.

Using the Student Union

The Student Union notice-boards can be particularly helpful. The Union looks at things from the student perspective and often has direct involvement in welfare service provision as well as being an adviser to the university on student affairs. Student Union staff have all been though the student experience, so they tune in to student needs pretty quickly. You can usually find someone in the Union office who can help (or who'll get the right person to call you) and you don't need an appointment, so they can be very helpful in the first instance. They can refer you to the appropriate person to advise on financial matters – loans, grants, savings and banking for students, debt management, single parent and housing support, if appropriate.

The Union has links to help you find accommodation (as well as the university accommodation office) and can advise you on the rights and responsibilities of both tenants and landlords. For instance, if your landlord refuses to return your deposit when you leave your accommodation, or if there is inadequate heating and such like.

Employers often advertise short-term posts of many kinds (for instance, baby-sitting, paid cold-cure or psychology experiments, clerical work within the university) with the Student Union, who prescribe minimum rates of pay and try to make sure you are fairly treated.

Childcare and nursery places for students with children are also concerns of the Student Union, who will also have links to local schools, after-school clubs and transport arrangements for children to be taken and picked up from school when parents are in class or studying. Students normally get priority over staff for on-campus nursery places for pre-school children.

Student Union advisers know the procedures for obtaining study support (for instance, if you think you might be dyslexic), counselling and welfare. Union members often man crisis centres with an emergency phone number, in some cases 24 hours a day. They can help with other welfare matters such as confidential free contraception and abortion advice independent of the student health service, if that is appropriate.

Finding help, support or counselling

Most Student Unions also run a Student Helpline which is run by students for up to 24 hours a day. They can help with practical concerns like morning-after pills or pregnancy counselling as well as other worries – they've been there too perhaps, as they're students like you.

A Health Service student counsellor can be a starting point – a person who can also direct you to the best person to help you. For instance, if you feel a bit worried or anxious, a counsellor can help you find the underlying problem. For instance, your problem may be mainly linked to concern about your financial situation. She can then suggest who to talk to and help you make an appointment to sort out the practical aspect of the problem.

Many student counselling services have an open appointment book in a reception area in which you can pencil yourself into a gap when you're free and make your own appointment without having to go through a receptionist or other formalities first. You don't even have to give your real name until you feel confident about doing so.

It's good to talk, and problems are better out than in. Most worries diminish when you have someone to listen, take you seriously or discuss things with. A second opinion is always useful, and students and professionals alike on campus have had some training in giving you help and support. They also have a back-up support line themselves that they can go to for advice as to how they can help you, if necessary.

Living on campus

Most universities offer accommodation to first-year students on *campus*. The campus is the main area occupied by the university and often includes the main teaching buildings as well as at least some of the purpose-built university accommodation. When you live on campus you're in some ways in a sheltered environment, but you still need to think about a number of everyday issues.

Security

If you live on a big open campus and have a long walk to your residence, when returning late at night or early in the morning make sure that you know what's available in an emergency. Emergency phones may be positioned round the edge of the campus that put you directly in touch with the security officer on duty. Find out where these are in the daytime so that you know the nearest to your route home. In some cases you may be able to make a call from the university entrance and ask for a security officer to walk with you back to your residence. These services are designed to make you feel safer rather than to suggest any potential threat.

If you think that you have an intruder or there's a loud, drunk and disorderly student who can't be persuaded to leave, call security and ask for help. Tipsy people tend to lose their balance and crash down stairs so you're probably doing them a favour by asking for help as you're less able to prevent falls and possible injury if you try to solve the problem alone.

In case of fire at night, make sure that you follow the fire regulations – you'll be drilled once a term in your residence and on campus, in a lecture room. Very often there's a small, rapid-response fire unit on campus and a direct link to the nearest fire station on an emergency link as soon as an alarm is used. This means that if you smoke in a prohibited place (this includes your room in most residences) and the unfortunate happens, you can be in real trouble.

Your residence has to pay a fee each time a fire engine responds to a call, which has to be paid whether the fire is real or not. Be careful, and don't mess around with fire alarms. It's not in your interest to bankrupt your college!

Health emergencies

A student residence mentor is usually on duty at night in student residences, so if you're taken ill, you can call her or knock on her door. She usually has a supply of extra blankets and basic medication in her rooms. If you just need some aspirin, try to call in the evening, not the middle of the night. Night calls should be reserved for real emergencies, like suspected appendicitis. Similarly, if you need a reassuring chat, make it at a reasonable time. The mentors work in conjunction with the porters and security, as well as the Student Welfare Service, so are able to judge the best action to take in most situations.

Solving other problems

If you live in a campus residence, a porter is usually available in the daytime, so report your dripping tap and the radiator that doesn't give any heat or the fused electrical system during the day. You can leave a note at the porter's lodge in the morning on the way to lectures. Be specific so that the porter, using a pass key, can identify precisely the problem and fix it while you're out.

Various complaints procedures are available if you encounter problems, for example, with noisy neighbours in your residence or if you feel bullied in areas where you have to share facilities, such as the kitchen. If possible, try to talk to the individual yourself but if this doesn't work, your mentor can arrange a meeting between you.

If you lose something on campus, report the loss to the residence porter and the porters in the buildings where you had lectures, or elsewhere. Also inform the lost property office, usually within campus security. Keep a record of the date and time and if the item was valuable. You may want to report your loss to the police as well. These records are necessary if you want to claim a replacement on the campus (if appropriate) or claim on your own private insurance.

Getting Help with Health Issues

When you arrive on campus visit the Health Centre if there is one, and register with the doctor, dentist and optician (if you need one) unless you are living at home and are already registered with Health Service Professionals in your area. You don't need to live on campus to register on campus. It is quite difficult to register with a National Health dentist these days, so a campus dentist is a bonus. As well as being convenient and time-saving for appointments, if you have any special health needs or concerns, it is good to have a health specialist on campus who is aware of this, for instance, if you are diabetic. It is also useful to be able to get repeat prescriptions easily through the associated pharmacy. The Health Centre often runs 'giving up smoking' and other clinics and staff dedicated to young persons' needs and concerns and are very difficult to shock. Also, you aren't likely to meet your Auntie Molly in the waiting-room.

Facing financial matters

You're likely to find several banks on or near the university campus and even in these hard financial times they may still offer various inducements for you to deposit your grant or loan with them, for example, £50.00 or an MP3 player. The main thing is for you to be wary of any credit cards banks may offer and the repayment terms. All the banks have leaflets detailing their student accounts and what's on offer, and you can probably ask for a more detailed discussion through their information desk. If you already have an account, you may have gone through the decision-making process. However, the Students Union or the main administration building have an independent Student Financial Adviser who can help you find your way through the mass of information. It's well worth making an appointment with the Adviser. Some points to consider are:

- Although interest rates aren't high, make a little money by putting your grant or loan into a savings account and then transfer what you need to a current account each week.

- If your granny gives you some money, save it, and spend your loan instead. Even in bad times, the repayment rates for student loans are less than the interest on savings (unheard of otherwise) so make a little more money when you can.

- If you're offered a credit card, be aware that interest rates are always fairly astronomical if you don't repay what you owe each month. You may find a card that offers cash back on purchases. This is worth considering as long as you pay it off each month, and so avoid having to pay interest.

- Check out the special rates offered to students in bookshops, hairdressers and so on. Not all provide a better deal than otherwise, but theatre or concert tickets are usually cheaper.

✔ If things start getting out of hand or you don't know where the money is going, make an appointment to see the Student Financial Adviser as soon as possible. She helps you to make a list of your outgoings so that you can see what's happening to your money and make changes. She'll help you to make a budget plan to get your finances back on track and in control of how and on what you spend your money. It's particularly important to get help with your budgeting before you decide that you must get a job, on the grounds that a penny saved is a penny earned. If you just take on a job without working out where you're currently wasting money or how you can best use it, you can end up wasting even more and not be much better off – and tired to boot!

Advice costs nothing; it can help to put you in control and you don't have to take it. It's always preferable to be in a well-informed position rather than one of ignorance before you reject advice!

Coming to Terms with Tutors

Tutors come in two main varieties. *Personal tutors* look after your general welfare and ensure that you aren't drifting off course in your university life in general and your academic work in particular. *Subject tutors* are specialists who teach different subject areas in your degree. For instance, within a History degree you could have a subject tutor for Medieval History, another for seventeenth century European History, another for the Industrial Revolution and post-1948 Chinese History. When you have to do written work or exams in their subject areas, they are the experts to call upon. Some will give you tutorials to advise you on your written work.

Personal tutors

You probably have a year tutor or personal tutor who's notified of any absences and reasons for them by the faculty or school office or by her secretary. This tutor keeps a record of your work and exam marks and generally has the information about you she needs to keep an eye on things. A subject tutor may inform your personal tutor if you have missed a lot of classes, for instance, and the subject tutor has not been able to contact you or is not happy with your reasons for being absent. They do talk to each other! Subject and personal tutors have formal and informal meetings to check on progress and any problems. Your subject tutor will probably only suggest a meeting if she thinks that you have a problem with your grades or exam results or unexplained absences. There may be a once-a-term meeting for all personal tutors and their tutees just to keep in touch.

Make sure that your personal tutor knows who you are, as she's the most likely person to give you a character reference when you leave and the one to call on first if you find yourself in a spot of bother. If you have any concerns about your course, your work or personal matters, she's the person to contact, sooner rather than later. Personal tutors don't go looking for trouble, so be proactive. You may find that she was aware of potential problems but wanted to give you some time to work things out for yourself and didn't want to push you. You can visit your tutor during her office hours and if she feels you need more time together or she needs to contact other people for help, perhaps a subject tutor, she'll organise this and arrange another meeting with you at an appropriate time.

A social gathering with staff and students usually takes place once a term, so use this to have a chat with your tutor in order to get to know each other if you haven't had reason to seek each other out beforehand.

If you want to switch courses, or even go to another institution, then your personal tutor can help you negotiate this and support you. You'll have to provide a reasoned argument for why you want to transfer and consider the practical problems – will you have to repeat a year, can you extend your grant to another year, or can you catch up the lectures you've missed without re-doing a year? She talks through the pros and cons of various courses of action with you.

If you have problems concerning the conduct of the course you're currently attending – for instance, cancelled lectures or lack of feedback on written work – your personal tutor is the person to talk to if you find approaching the relevant subject tutors difficult or unsatisfactory. To help your personal tutor find the cause of the problem and sort it out satisfactorily you need to provide her with details such as the number of cancelled lectures and their dates, the hand-in dates for work and so on. If you have a learning diary, you need to record this information in it.

Subject tutors

You may have several subject tutors for the various sub-areas of your course of study. Those who set you essays or other assessed work often timetable – in some tutorials to help you through the various stages of the process – they need to approve the title, objectives, methods, help with finding appropriate resources and so on. Tutorials of this kind may take place fortnightly or at regular periods in term time and continue through part of the holidays, especially the summer. Office hours are for those who don't have timetabled tutorials and for emergencies.

Taking a break

If you've been ill or had personal problems it may be possible for you to suspend your studies for a year – take a year out – so that you can recover properly and regain your energy. Again, your personal tutor can discuss this with you. She wants to feel reasonably confident that you're motivated enough to return to your studies after taking some time out as this involves holding a place for you at the same level next year. Personal or year tutors want their students to be happy in their courses and to do well, so they do their best to make sure that this happens.

If you need an extension to complete your work, talk to the subject tutor in question sooner rather than later, that is, not the day before or a few hours before the hand-in time. Acceptable reasons for an extension include:

- **Being ill during the research or writing-up period.** This is why it's important to contact the school office when you're ill so that the office has a record of it.

- **Unavoidable delays in obtaining data.** These can involve postal strikes, people at the other end of an arrangement being ill or unable to help at the time they thought they could, delays in information being published, posted through the inter-library loan service or getting lost, and so on. If you've kept a record of your efforts to pull everything together in your learning diary it can help you explain any problems and show your plans. (If you made no plans or efforts to calculate the time needed, it's more difficult to argue your case. If you're a postgraduate, you'll have formally submitted your plans for your dissertation or thesis, which you can ask to update in view of circumstances – but, again, do it in good time.)

Subject tutors should also supply you with detailed feedback so that you can improve your written work and presentations. For longer assessed work, they give feedback and advice on the process as it goes along. Final pieces of work may receive less feedback. If you need to discuss your feedback because you don't understand it, it seems inadequate or irrelevant, or you'd like more detail because you want to do further study into the subject of your dissertation, make an appointment or email your subject tutor. Even if she's on a dhow in the Nile delta, she'll have her laptop with her and can respond to email. Make the subject of the email pertinent and snappy to ensure that you get her attention and a response.

Academic accountability – duties and responsibilities – apply to students and tutors alike.

Most institutions have an approximate turn-round time in which students should get their marks back from tutors – it's usually about two weeks for undergraduates. This information may not be recorded in your student pack, but it's reasonable to ask for it. You then know whether your expectations in terms of time are too high or if you have a problem with your subject tutor or the system.

Examining Study Support

Study support is separate from the subject you are studying, but is anything that can help you with the process of studying, from general study skills classes, extra time to complete assignments, right through to, in special circumstances, a free computer. It also covers special tutoring or extra classes in particular skills you need for your course. Because it comes in various forms, study support is often provided from various places in the university other than your own school or department . If your department provides support, this is probably in the form of workshops explaining and helping you to develop questionnaires, write up results or data in an appropriate way or develop summary or other skills you need for your course. There may be more general support available for writing, presentation and other skills needed for studying and perhaps a mentoring system where students in the year above can help you through their experiences and the training they received. Mentors are more likely to be used in courses with a deal of abstraction, for example, maths or computer science.

In some cases, if your department doesn't provide more general or basic skills such as tips for essay writing, you may need to ask your personal tutor to agree to your request for support through attending a general study skills programme provided centrally by the university. This is normally free to students, but your department may be charged for this service, so permission may be necessary for you to attend.

If you have a diagnosed problem like dyslexia, then special support exists for you. You may be given longer in exams and more time to write essays. You may be able to borrow a computer or laptop if you don't have one. The Student Welfare and Health Service (they're normally located in the same building) are the best places to find out what specific support you can get for your particular needs and also can help you with any paperwork or applications you need to make.

Make sure that your personal tutor is aware of any applications for support or help that you've initiated, so that she knows what you're trying to do and can help.

The Student Union may also run support classes with the help of the Student Welfare service. These classes may be more concerned with the psychological (rather than the straightforward practical) approach to study, and may include aspects of yoga or meditation designed to clear the mind and open it up to ideas and creativity. Support classes can be useful as a general background to study and if they're free and you enjoy yoga or meditation they can help you feel calmer and more in control. Other sources of support may help with the specifics of how to tackle a particular piece of work – including your subject tutor.

You can sometimes find additional valuable help and support 'through the back door'. Some so-called community volunteer literacy programmes – possibly part of adult education – run tutorial programmes to support individuals where eligibility for support is rather woolly. Tutors are often retired teachers or professional people who volunteer their time to help individuals with their written literacy or numeracy. The tutors may welcome the opportunity to read and discuss essays to improve punctuation, self-expression or general presentation at a level of personal detail way beyond what is normally within the time and student number capacity of a general study skills programme at your college. For the tutors, it may be a more interesting experience than their usual work and, as they're unpaid, they're free to decide their approach, and who they help.

If you have a learning difficulty, you may be eligible for access to these volunteer tutors. You can find such helpful people through the public library service or in volunteer skills swaps. For instance, you can swap some DIY, washing or dog walking in return for editing work on your essay. Retired professionals are quite good substitutes for the educated person or academic who's not a specialist in your subject who you need to keep in mind when planning your writing or presentations.

You can find a good deal of online study support, possibly from your institution, and it may recommend other sites to visit. Some sites provide useful examples of referencing systems, exam questions or tips on how to write essays. Some may appeal more than others, depending on the level and depth of the information they contain. Some are very specific to the systems in the institutions they were written for; others have a more general relevance.

Check where information comes from. The email addresses of UK higher and further education institution colleges end in *.ac.uk*. You can check levels – undergraduate or postgraduate – usually within the study skills or support pages. Australian and European study practices are generally closer to UK practices than American ones. Online study skills pages can be useful for finding the answers to specific questions such as how to construct a well-written paragraph. Alternatively, simply Google your question for the quickest way to find a possible solution.

Tim Johns' University of Birmingham Kibbitzer pages (`www.eisu2.bham.ac.uk/Webmaterials/kibbitzers/indexes/indexchron.htm`) are helpful for general academic vocabulary and easily confused terms. The examples are drawn from the British National Corpus, the biggest collection of both spoken and written British English, so the examples show how words are used in real sentences and phrases taken from the samples and word substitution exercises help illustrate differences in meaning.

Behaviour and Responsibilities

'There are two ways of doing things,' according to Duck the Great Western Engine, 'the Great Western Way or the wrong way'. Well, it's not quite as black and white as that, and rules aren't always precise, but you need to bear in mind that although you do have to look after number one, you should also be aware of how you can help other people help you best. This means avoiding behaviour that causes problems for other people, as this can mean that they can't or won't help you – which isn't in your best interests. Think about the long-term implications, not just the short-term ones of 'a bit of fun'.

Disciplinary issues aren't just individual concerns but affect the well-being of the whole college or university community.

Knowing your responsibilities

Your college has a definition of misconduct, which generally covers any behaviour which disrupts the work, social or sporting activities of any student or member of university staff or concerns indecent behaviour or use of indecent or abusive language, including that contained in posters or other printed material. Serious cases may go as far as the *university court*, the administrative body responsible for dealing with infringements of university rules – a bit like a magistrate's court. As in a court of law, a student has the right to a defence. Your personal tutor, who's in the best position to give a character reference, often acts in defence of a student, but you can ask whoever you like to represent you. Tutors can also refuse.

Preventing plagiarism

Plagiarism is the most serious academic crime because it can mean you're not allowed to continue your studies. In front of most assessed written work is usually a statement you have to sign saying that what follows is your own unaided work. If you're accused of plagiarism and you feel this is unjust, you can defend yourself and the case may be heard by the university court.

Crossing the line

'A bit of fun' means different things to different people. On one occasion, a student rather the worse for wear found himself near the car of a porter he'd recently had a row with and promptly decided to take his revenge against the car. Unfortunately, he'd forgotten about the nearby CCTV camera, and equally unfortunately, he damaged to the car. Luckily, the porter enjoyed the fact that the student had been caught on camera as well as being angry about his car, so he agreed to let the student clean up the car and have the damage repaired and then to forget the whole incident. Not so lucky was the student computer hacker who faced prosecution and had his degree withdrawn. Be aware of how other people may see things.

Tutors often check for plagiarism by typing a phrase from your work into Google. If the identical phrase comes up within a text appropriate to your subject, but which you have not acknowledged, this may suggest plagiarism to them.

However, common technical terms are considered 'public' or 'common' knowledge and don't have to be referenced each time you use them within a longer phrase, terms like *governance, radiation therapy, the hunkering down of the economy, relevance theory, judicial review, collateral damage,* although they should be defined when you use them for the first time.

Remove any technical terms from the offending phrase and Google the rest. Several texts may come up from several different subjects. This is because English is a phrasal language and five, six and even seven-word phrases are commonly used as if they were a single word.

Phrases like these are considered to be 'packages' that can't really be split up and so form part of common usage. They're glued together as one unit of meaning. Examples are:

- ✔ 'According to the received wisdom of that time'
- ✔ 'In fact, the opposite was true'
- ✔ 'In the best interests of all concerned'
- ✔ 'Each case should be judged on its individual merits'
- ✔ 'All is not lost'

If you manage to find several examples with different words in the slots left empty by technical terms you've removed, this suggests there's no plagiarism. Plagiarism also has to be shown to be intentional.

It is still safest to make sure that you reference everything very carefully. If you feel you've made too many references, ask for some help with summary skills, rather than leaving out a citation reference. It's better to have a skills problem than an honesty problem.

Chapter 3

Becoming a Critical Thinker

· ·

In This Chapter

▶ Grasping the meaning of critical thinking

▶ Advancing an academic argument

▶ Evaluating evidence

▶ Developing an academic voice

· ·

This chapter talks you through the main reasoning concepts and skills you need in order to evaluate what you read and hear in lectures, plan your own work – whether essays or presentations – and make constructive criticism. The critical thinker is an *analytical thinker*. An analytical thinker carefully checks information to make sure the details fit together logically and that no contradictions exist. She also looks for patterns and systems in data or information so that she can make predictions or create hypotheses.

Along with the formal requirements of your course – the lectures you have to attend, the amount of assessed written work you have to do, the examinations you have to take – you have your own priorities for what you want to achieve. You may want to study for a higher degree, be more interested in the all-round university or college experience, be concerned about achieving high marks or be willing to experiment. Your personal interests influence the amount of time and effort you spend on different activities, but critical thinking helps you get the most from all or any of them. Critical thinking is also perhaps the most useful transferable skill from the world of education to the world of work.

What Is Critical Thinking?

A *critical thinker* brings her own knowledge, experience and judgement to consider the accuracy or value of any information she is presented with. She also knows that how good information is depends, to some extent, on the person who gives it and the qualities they bring: in other words, their expertise. A bi-lingual Russian and English speaker is likely to provide a more accurate translation into English of a Russian newspaper article than an English person who has been learning Russian for six months. The critical thinker understands the usefulness of statistics, but also knows they can be used badly. Critical thinking establishes patterns between events. The more times an event happens in relation to another event, the more likely there is to be a connection between the two. For instance, the number of children who catch measles increases as the number of children vaccinated against measles falls each year. The critical thinker checks the questions which data – and the researcher's interpretation of those data – answer. She accepts nothing (in academic terms) at face value, without evidence and evaluates everything, including her own work, within this framework.

Scoping out the skills of critical thinking

Various sub-skills exist within critical thinking, most of which you use on a daily basis but may not be explicitly aware of. They include:

- **Reflecting on what you're told.** Reflecting on information you're given means taking time out to consider your reaction to it. Do you agree with it, are you surprised or excited by it, do you think it links to other information you have? If you disagree or disbelieve it, why? What would it take to convince you? Reflection helps you to find where you stand in relation to a piece of information. If you record this in your learner diary (check out Chapter 1 for more on this), you can see later how you developed and changed, or retrace your steps if you need to rethink ideas.

- **Observing how information is presented.** Is it in a paragraph, a table, an illustration, a graph, a map or a chart? What kind of information is presented in each form? What is the clearest or easiest way to present different kinds of information – a description, a large amount of data, to make comparisons? Can you think of ways to improve the way information you have read about is presented?

- **Comparing new information with previous knowledge.** Does the new information extend or confirm your previous knowledge, by adding more instances, or contradict it because the results are different? What changes are you going to have to make in your evaluation of it and the earlier knowledge if there are contradictions? Are there differences in the methods, physical location, length of study, what was studied and numbers involved which can explain the differences in results? If the new information confirms the old, what's the next step? What aspects of difference should you look for?

- **Considering the status or reputation, skills and abilities of the people who give you information.** What's in it for them? For instance, a politician who wants your vote may be prepared to be 'economical' with the truth to fit his purpose. For this reason, any government's information is best compared with another source of data. An independent researcher, not paid by a pharmaceutical or other big company, is more likely to take a neutral attitude to her research results, although this doesn't mean her research is necessarily good.

✔ **Distinguishing between fact, hypothesis, and opinion.** Not always easy, but very important. Facts are what there is evidence for. Some factual statements, like 'all men are male', don't tell you much. Others, like 'the sun rises in the east', we take for granted. Collecting large amounts of evidence over several years, however demonstrates the fact that there are more suicides over the Christmas and New Year period than at other times of the year. Many *hypotheses* – theories or ideas which need to be tested by academic enquiry – prove to be correct, and so become facts within a research framework. *Opinion* is personal. Based on impressions, experience, and perhaps limited research, you can't demonstrate opinion objectively. An opinion can, however, be the start of an idea, develop into a hypothesis, with research and evidence collecting and then perhaps become fact.

✔ **Identifying the conclusion of an argument.** Conclusions are what you are left with (or meant to be) after a discussion or argument. The conclusion of an argument is sometimes but not always stated. For example, your girlfriend might tell you that her favourite perfume is *Angel* and expect you to draw the conclusion that that's what she'd like for her birthday. Conclusions, like the truth, are not always simple.

✔ **Identifying the stages in an argument.** The stages in an argument show the links between the information given and the conclusion. They are not always stated. For instance, a holiday price comparison website may argue they give you the best choice of holiday (the conclusion) because they compare more holidays than any other price comparison site (the premise). The missing link in the argument is 'more holidays means being able to choose the best.' This is not necessarily so, because the meaning of 'best' is not certain. The best holiday could be the cheapest or the one in the best location, and even if the website compares more holidays than any other, the 'best' could still be found on another website.

✔ **Evaluating the quality of the evidence presented.** How good is the evidence? Where and who did it come from? How was it acquired? For instance, in an extreme case, information given under torture or threat would not be reliable. Information given by someone who might gain from it should not be regarded as 'good' evidence and not enough on its own to make a case. Always ask who gains and who loses.

✔ **Being aware of what hasn't been discussed and wondering why not.** Sometimes data is missing in a data set. For instance, if a government produced data for flu deaths every year from 1995 to 2005, with the exception of 2003, then why did they miss out that year? Were no statistics kept or were they in a bureaucrats stolen laptop? Sometimes what is missing and why it's missing is more interesting than what's there. If 'school discipline in secondary schools' is a general government discussion paper, but it only refers to the state sector, does that mean the private sector has nothing to offer or no discipline problems, or no one asked them . . . or what?

✔ **Analysing and evaluating the argument presented.** As soon as you have analysed and checked out the logic of statements and made sure there are no contradictions either in the information or in the real world, you can *evaluate* the argument or conclusion. (You may also have checked the data sources, methods, research tools and results.) Evaluating data means giving it a value – not quite marks out of ten but sufficient to answer these questions: Is the argument or conclusion good? Does it explain all the circumstances or only some? Does it have flaws, or leave awkward examples out? How could I make it better? Evaluating includes making suggestions for improvement.

✔ **Making inferences, decisions and judgements.** Making an inference is when you draw a conclusion from what is suggested but not explicitly stated. Newspapers that print stories of two famous people seen in the same place at the same time encourage us to *infer* that there is some connection between them without saying so directly. Equally, research can present data in such a way as to encourage this when the evidence is weak. *Decisions* usually involve choices, and come after you have evaluated the different possibilities. *Judgements*, similarly, come after evaluations and usually state a preference for one thing – usually a methodology or a theoretical view-point – over another after you have investigated both.

✔ **Weighing up the evidence and presenting your own argument.** Weighing up the evidence includes evaluating and judging it, and it could be that none of the theories or arguments given seem to work in all cases, so you may have an argument of your own to present.

A very simple practice to keep critical thinking on track is to keep asking 'Why?' after every claim or statement that is made. This covers everything, from technical information, such as 'Why is the gap between the glass panes 6 centimetres?' to motivational ones, for example 'Why is the customer praising the product?' As Socrates observed, if you keep asking 'Why?' you find the answer to all the important questions in life from within yourself.

Although emphasis is often placed on the 'content' of subjects, or subject knowledge, in fact a large percentage (probably over 60 per cent) of any subject involves applying critical thinking skills, although subject teachers rarely teach these skills explicitly. It seems to be assumed that 'good' students automatically have these skills. Indeed, we all used them as children, but we may need to be reminded of how to use them as adults.

Making an academic argument

Academic reasoning is the basis of academic argument. Good reasoning means that anyone in a similar situation, with similar information, would come to the same conclusion. The reasoning has its own internal logic, quite separate from whoever does the reasoning. The logic of the reasoning is like an abstract equation: if $a = b$, and $b = c$, then $a = c$.

Using critical thinking in the real world

Think of a double-glazing salesperson. He represents a well-known company and phones first to book an appointment. The company's reputation and the politeness of the salesperson encourage you to let him into your home as you're considering buying double-glazing. You have some degree of faith or at least a neutral stance in relation to what he wishes to tell you.

The salesperson presents well-rehearsed 'facts and figures' and probably a model window. He's not an engineer or designer, so the model makes up for lack of knowledge and allows you to examine the double-glazed unit. The honest salesperson passes your technical questions on to an appropriate expert. For instance, if you want to know how the 'facts and figures' were calculated, the salesperson won't have been involved. His role is to pass on information uncritically.

If the claim is that double-glazing will reduce your heating bill by 20 per cent, you can challenge this conclusion on logical grounds alone. At this point it's impossible to compare your current heating costs with heating costs after installing the company's product, so you've no evidence upon which to calculate savings. The basis or premise of this argument is missing. If a local customer attests to the 20 per cent claim, this evidence may have some value for you. However, if the customer was offered a financial inducement for endorsing the product's claims, this affects the quality of the customer's evidence and thus the argument to persuade you to buy the product.

Another argument may be that new window units will increase the value of your property. An estate agent is a better source of evidence to support or challenge the likelihood of this, but it's only a likelihood, not a fact. The guarantees offered, the price and comparisons with the charges and quality of other products may help you create your own argument and negotiate a good deal if you decide to buy.

For example, say you have three parcels, labelled a, b and c. If *a* and *b* each weighs 10 grams and *c* weighs the same as *b*, then *c* also weighs the same as *a*, that is, 10 grams. Or to put it another way:

Parcels *a* and *b* both weigh 10 grams,

Parcel *b* weighs the same as parcel *c*,

So parcel *a* weighs the same as parcel *c*, which is 10 grams.

This three-part argument is called a *syllogism*. The first and second statements constitute the *premises* and the third is the *conclusion*. The conclusion can only be correct if both the premises are correct. If the logic is sound, the argument is sound. In this example, the link between *a*, *b* and *c* is the comparison of their weight. In the double-glazing example in the nearby sidebar 'Using critical thinking in the real world', it's impossible to compare heating bills with and without double-glazing before double-glazing is installed. This means the premises are faulty, so the conclusion – that double glazing can give you a 20 per cent reduction in heating bills – is meaningless.

The logical pattern for a syllogism is to go from general to particular and compare a specific example with a general example or principle:

> All mammals feed their young on milk.
>
> The mouse is a mammal.
>
> Therefore the mouse feeds its young on milk.

By contrast:

> All birds can fly.
>
> Bats can fly.
>
> Therefore, bats are birds.

is an example of faulty reasoning and poor evidence. The underlying questions to ask here are:

> Can all birds fly?
>
> Are all animals that can fly birds?

As the answer to both questions is 'No', then what follows is faulty because the basic statement (premise) is flawed. No further analysis is needed in this instance. Sometimes the syllogism is misused, especially in spoken argument, because there is no general to particular pattern, so the conclusion is meaningless or nonsense. Somtimes both premises are factually correct, but the conclusion is not. For example:

> Some Americans are rich
>
> Some poor people are Americans
>
> So some poor people are rich.

If you can spot the flaw in reasoning or see that like is not being compared with like (comparisons are really big in the academic world) then bingo, you don't need to go or read any further in the argument, because it follows that any other arguments or conclusions derived from the same premise are faulty. Much of academic enquiry is about asking questions, not supplying answers or solving problems. Spotting flaws in reasoning *is* important, not destructive. No amount of time or examples can improve faulty basic reasoning, just as, if its foundations aren't sound, a building falls. Academics are human and can be so seduced by the beauty or seeming symmetry of their research that they miss basic inconsistencies. Remember, it was a little boy who spotted that the Emperor was naked!

Re-awakening your critical child

Ironically, most children are excellent critical thinkers before they have to work together in groups at primary school. They have to conform to school rules for the smooth running of classes. You can listen to small children in supermarkets any day arguing with their parents. 'If you don't buy me that, I'll scream, and you don't like screaming', I heard an articulate three-year-old threaten, her logic based on past experience.

Recapturing the logic structures you instinctively used as a child and applying them to the knowledge or facts you're presented with is the most powerful and fruitful tool for your studies and life. You do know how to be a critical thinker – you may just have forgotten for the moment.

Analysing Claims and Evidence

Logical reasoning is the benchmark, but to extend knowledge requires making guesses and having new ideas that must then be tested. These new ideas are called *hypotheses*. A hypothesis is a possibility – something that you think may happen, or be the case. The point of academic enquiry is to search for evidence to support hypotheses, the facts that need to be true for their hypotheses to be correct. Academic argument consists of reasoning and then finding and linking the evidence to support hypotheses. The quality and amount of evidence they find to support a hypothesis increases the likelihood that it is acceptable. Sometimes, researchers have a *null hypothesis*, which is sufficient to explain most of the data they have, but where the results could be due to quite different reasons. They may investigate by using two or more hypotheses (including the null hypothesis and an alternate hypothesis) to see which explains the data they have best. Other academics analyse their evidence and then the claims made and the conclusions they have come to. Sometimes they draw different conclusions from the same evidence, or can even suggest another hypothesis to explain the data.

For instance, even as recently as about 15 years ago, climate change was not accepted as a reality by all scientists, or indeed, politicians. Those who supported the climate change hypothesis set about searching for evidence to support it – what needed to be true if climate change and global warming were indeed happening. That was the first stage.

Climatologists noted the hole in the ozone layer, the rising temperature of the sea, the melting ice caps, the more frequent storms and floods in some places and droughts in others. Biologists noted the relocation of some sea mammals searching for food, the reductions in the numbers of some species and the increases in others. Evidence from different disciplines all combined together to support the climate-change hypothesis, making it more likely to be a reality.

Of course, if global warming was indeed happening, then the next question was 'Why?'

Some scientists claimed man-made carbon emissions were creating an overall greenhouse effect and triggering the other changes. The change was happening too rapidly to be attributable to natural causes and so they argued that carbon emissions had to be cut to slow down or reduce the effect of the climate changes, which they perceived as negative.

Other groups of scientists, although accepting global warming was happening, argued that there were just as many positive outcomes. For instance, Canada would gain economically, becoming the biggest supplier of wheat as the grain-growing areas shifted north.

Still other groups of scientists, while not disputing the evidence for climate change, did dispute its interpretation and the conclusion – that man was responsible. Often supported by politicians, they argued that climate change is a natural process and the current changes were not happening as quickly as some scientists feared and so were not directly linked to man's industrial processes. However, as evidence continues to mount, global warming, still a hypothesis 15 years ago, is now accepted by most people as a reality. Some argument still exists about how to tackle the problem.

Necessary and sufficient conditions

Necessary conditions have to be present for something to be true or take place, but on their own, aren't enough. With necessary and sufficient conditions in place, then something is true or can take place.

For instance, being a mammal is a necessary but not sufficient condition for being a man. Plenty of mammals aren't men. However, being a mammal and a human and of the male sex and over 18 years of age satisfies the necessary and sufficient conditions for being a man.

Necessary and sufficient conditions provide very useful concepts and tools. Very often, when something goes wrong or something unexpected happens, it can be explained in terms of the conditions being necessary, but not sufficient. You can use this tool to critique other people's work and even your own. A tutor sometimes asks you to do this at the end of a piece of written work or after a presentation to show what you have learned from carrying it out. For instance, when you evaluate your own work, you might say that something was missing, so that the conditions, though necessary, were not sufficient. This could be because you didn't have enough data to generalise from, or because you didn't cover all possibilities, so need to extend the research. How to make things better next time is important to add to the end of your work to show what you learned by doing it and using necessary and sufficient conditions is a useful way to help you find some useful self-criticism. Chapter 1 introduces you to learning diaries.

In the academic system, being right or wrong isn't really the point. The point is to be aware. If you've attempted to do something and it hasn't quite worked, that doesn't matter if you honestly evaluate:

- **What you did:** Your research questions, research and methods

- **What happened:** Did you get the answers you expected, what problems did you come up against, how did you solve them?

- **Why you think it happened:** could you have prepared better or foreseen problems?

- **What you should have done:** were you too ambitious, did you miscalculate the time you needed, should you have used a different method?

- **What you now know and could use to make improvements next time:** For instance, only about one third of questionnaires get returned – unless you put everyone in a room and go through them with the respondents and answer any questions, though most will not give up more than 20 minutes or so for this.

You receive credit for your analytical skills if you do this. A good bet for improving your understanding and your ability to communicate this to your tutor is to analyse what happened and why it comes within the framework of necessary and sufficient conditions.

Evaluating the evidence

Imagine you're a detective and have just received an urgent phone call. A woman has returned home to find a broken kitchen window, the kitchen door open, and her purse missing. On the way to the scene, you may anticipate a robbery.

However, an altogether different picture emerges: it turns out that the woman's son lost his key, broke the kitchen window to get in, went out again through the door to find a glazier to fix the window taking his mother's purse with him in case he had to pay.

Evidence often gives rise to several possible interpretations. Be open to other possibilities and consider what other evidence is necessary to support a hypothesis, and look for it. If you feel the evidence you have read about or found (so far) is weak, then say so. Offer alternative explanations or hypotheses to illustrate your analytical and evaluation skills. Don't make or support claims based on weak or circumstantial evidence. Instead, offer them as possibilities. *Claims* in academic terms are very strong and require very powerful evidence to support them.

However, it's always better to obtain or unearth as much evidence as you can. Sometimes statistics can help through providing large numbers of examples to give results above what would happen by chance. In the social sciences, for example, where qualitative or case study research (where the numbers involved are small) is often preferred to quantitative research (involving large numbers), another way to improve the quality of the data or evidence is to use triangulation.

Triangulation is when you look for the same information using three or more different methods. For example, in classroom research, the researcher may observe a class, interview the teacher, interview the students, give both the teacher and students a questionnaire, use exam. results, homework, the subject syllabus, the teaching guidelines provided by the school. This variety of methods is very important where relatively small numbers are involved and also because what people are told to do, or what they say they do, quite often differs from what they actually do. Such research may result in different answers to the same questions from different sources. If you read about small case study research that didn't use more than one method, then it's worth wondering why, and if, had this happened, the results would have been different.

So, evaluating the evidence means considering its quality as well as quantity and the usefulness of methods used to obtain it – plus considering anything that would seem logical to do but wasn't done, and wondering why not.

Having an academic opinion

In every day life, we say 'Everyone has a right to their opinion – even if we disagree with it.' Although this is also true in academia, you have to work a bit harder! An academic opinion is the conclusion you come to when you have evaluated all the evidence you were given in a lecture or read about or researched. It doesn't come 'off the top of your head'. You reason and support your conclusion by evidence.

However, coming to a reasoned conclusion doesn't mean having to support or choose one claim rather than another. You can have an open opinion, recognising merits and faults in more than one argument or equally, feel that none of the solutions really addresses a particular problem.

From the 1940s to the present there's been a relatively and comparatively high number of teenage pregnancies in the UK and US. Strategies to reduce the number of pregnancies, such as sex education, repression of sex and sex education, access to contraception and abortion at different periods, have all been tried and produced similar negative results. The number of births continues to rise. In June, 2008 (BBC 1. Breakfast news) 17 girls aged 16 and under from one school in Massachusetts were all found to be pregnant, raising suspicions of a pregnancy pact and that there may be – in this case – strong social factors influencing young pregnant girls.

Having an academic opinion can also mean that you believe, for example that:

✔ Some evidence is more relevant, more clear, more tangible than other evidence.

✔ Some evidence is only useful in a supporting role.

✔ All the appropriate research has not yet been carried out.

✔ The most useful evidence is not available.

If you can suggest different methods, different questions to ask, different groups of people to research (in age, gender, age, occupation, location), different places and times, at the end of an essay or presentation or seminar, this is where your academic opinion counts most. Your conclusion is the outcome, the culmination of your reflection, analysis and evaluation of what you've read, been taught or prepared as assessed work.

Just a few lines of suggestion at the end of the conclusion of an essay indicates that the process of learning how to handle information has taken place. It should be there. Too often people have done all the hard work, but don't put their reasoned suggestion, the outcome of their academic opinion, at the end of an essay as they would when speaking. That's where the marker looks first, before they read anything else, to see what's been learned. Make a good impression in your conclusion, and the rest is relatively easy.

Developing your academic voice

Having an academic voice is related to having an academic opinion. Everyone is allowed to have a voice and an opinion, which, in both cases, must be based on reasoning and evidence. If you want your academic voice to be listened to, it must follow the rules of logic and present evidence to support it. Seminars and presentations have a social aspect, so much of the language used – including pronouns – is relatively informal in order to communicate well with the audience.

In written language, the introduction and conclusion to essays are personal to the writer and pronouns like 'I' or 'my' are fine. However, in the body – the data, description, analysis and evaluation – these pronouns should be avoided to make it clear these parts contain 'objective' evidence and data. ('We' should also be avoided as it can suggest your work was not independently carried out, but is collaborative.)

Four general principles that work well to keep your academic voice in tune are:

- ✔ **Honesty:** Only say things you can provide evidence for and always say where you got them from. Hearsay and personal experience, while interesting, don't constitute academic evidence.

- ✔ **Relevance:** Make sure that what you say is relevant to the topic under discussion and keep to the point.

- ✔ **Clarity:** Make everything clear to the reader or listener to help him follow the proceedings. Assume he's an intelligent non-expert in your subject. Provide headings and a framework – a 'how to read' or 'how to listen' so that he can follow the stages in your argument.

- ✔ **Reality:** Explain what needs to be explained. That means give definitions or explanations of ideas or processes that may not be known to the non-expert intelligent reader. However, don't explain that which is common knowledge.

By keeping in mind these 'rules' your academic voice becomes honed and a voice to be reckoned with. Watching 'Question Time' gives a flavour of whose voice is respected and backed with evidence and whose doesn't work so well for its owner. Sometimes, the best voices come from the audience.

The skills discussed in this chapter interconnect and support each other. An awareness of them and the academic system can help you decide where your time and efforts are likely to be most fruitful.

Chapter 4

Embracing ICT Skills

In This Chapter

▶ Understanding what technology you need

▶ Connecting to the Internet

▶ Using Systems Learning and Support

▶ Accessing online material

▶ Watching out for pitfalls

*I*CT (Information and Communication Technology) pervades all aspects of modern life. Information is electronically stored, received, transmitted and manipulated, by computers, mobile phones and even watches. Many young people have had access to computers at school, and over half have had computers at home, though they may have had to fight with other family members to be able to use them!

Computer literacy is now probably essential for studying at college or university, and in most jobs it's not only useful but necessary. If you have been shy of ICT in the past, now's the time to get better acquainted to make life easier both for the present and later on.

Understanding the Technology You Need

You can't avoid the fact that you need a computer at college. This section takes you through what you need – both the computer itself and the software applications you run on it – and how to get hold of them.

Handling the hardware

If you're buying a computer or laptop for college, make sure that you choose one that's up to the job. As a general rule it needs 256 megabytes of random access memory (RAM) and a processor of 750 Mhz in order to run the software you're likely to be using at a reasonable speed. A PC should be able to run the Windows XP operating system, or OS X if it's a Mac.

If you don't have your own personal computer or laptop before you start further education, you may find that your college has quite a fast turnover of computers and may dump them or sell them cheaply to students after a couple of years. This often occurs because the maintenance costs of computers soon become higher than their value and computers become outdated quite quickly. Nevertheless, monitors and computers discarded by colleges are often better than ones bought second-hand from a shop or through advertisements. If you have to pay for a college computer you should have it checked over first, so ask if it's been serviced.

If you need more temporary storage space, you can always buy extra capacity (RAM, or Random Access Memory) for your computer and save things you definitely want to keep onto a hard disk, which is also useful as back-up. Alternatively, you can use a memory stick which, like a hard disk, can be carried in the pocket and then inserted into a computer connected to a printer so that you can print out your work. You can probably survive without owning a printer!

In some cases your tutor may allow you to write by hand short essays and other work that requires hand-drawing or the working out of calculations on the page . In most cases, and almost certainly for assessed work for a degree, you need to use word-processing. If your word-processing is slow, it will soon speed up with practice and it provides several benefits over handwriting your work. Word processing skills allow you to:

- ✔ Correct and reorganise your writing by cutting and pasting.
- ✔ Save your time and energy with pagination (page numbering), word search, spell check (but be careful) and other facilities.
- ✔ Make sure that your work is legible!

Most institutions will set up computers to use Microsoft Word for word-processing and related office tasks, or may use Apple Mac computers, which have their own document and word-processing packages (usually the iWork suite).

However, you don't need to purchase an Apple Mac even if it is the preferred computer in your subject area because if the software offers some advantages in presenting the subject material, you will have access to it on campus. The computers in computer laboratories dedicated to a particular subject are the best ones to use and you will have access to them for usually at least 12 hours per day. The computer laboratories run like a library, with a technician on hand to help instead of a librarian.

You can also find *computer clusters* – groups of computers – in the library or language centre that you can use, usually set up to use Microsoft Word. The groups of computers on site will have computers and printers set up to serve them , so you can plug in your memory-stick, computer disk or laptop to get a print-out. Most work still has to be handed in on paper.

Technology support for learning

If you have a recognised learning disability, you may be eligible for a free or subsidised computer from your local education authority (LEA) to help you learn. Your LEA can advise you about this. It may be possible to request a test through the LEA or your college counselling service to establish whether you need support or not.

Another technology support is voice-recognition software. You speak through a microphone and your computer produces the written, word-processed form – punctuation as well! Microsoft Office XP includes inbuilt voice recognition but you still need to use the mouse and keyboard to some extent. Dragon Naturally Speaking Voice Recognition and IBM's ViaVoice Software operate completely hands free, so you can move about a bit and wave your arms to get your creative juices going.

All the voice-recognition systems need some training to be able to recognise the rhythms and cadences of a particular voice and you need to check for accuracy the word processing they produce. But for those who like to speak their thoughts out loud or can't use a keyboard, these systems are powerful tools. They may be available on campus for use with computers in the Language Learning Laboratory – earphones are available there so that students don't disturb each other. It's worth trying out voice-recognition software and checking its availability on campus before you buy it.

Check the word processing produced or ask someone to check it for you as the software may not be able to distinguish between, for example, *I ate blackberries* and *I hate blackberries,* though this isn't easy for people to differentiate either. The punctuation is usually quite good.

Find out which is the preferred system in your area of study – basically the choice comes down to Microsoft or Apple Mac. On campus you normally have access to that system in a dedicated lab or in the library so that you can view online, use or print out any special features of the system used specifically to teach aspects of your course. It doesn't matter which system you use for word processing.

Surveying the software

Find out what version of whichever software application your college or university uses is acceptable – for example, documents composed in Microsoft Word 2007 cannot be read when you're running Word 97–2003, but you can save your work as Word 97–2003 documents if the computer you use has this more up-to-date version of Word. iWorks for Apple Macintosh computers dates from 2007 and may not be compatible with some earlier AppleWorks systems for Apple Macs.

When you buy you computer or laptop, it may not come with a word-processing package already installed, so you need to consider what's available and the costs. Your first step might be to bargain with the retailer to get a free word-processing package, or at least a price reduction!

Microsoft Office Word 2007, is not normally provided already installed. It is probably the most sophisticated package and has all the word-processing functions you need (including PowerPoint for presentations, graphics and dialogue boxes) and some you may never use, so you might consider Microsoft Works word-processing software, which includes spreadsheet and database facilities, and a more basic word-processing package. It costs about a quarter of the price of Word (about £30 as opposed to at least £120) and it is compatible with Word, so you can safely receive documents written in Word. Some companies provide Microsoft Works free of charge when you buy a computer.

'Open Office' is a free word-processing package you can download from the Internet that is also compatible with Microsoft Office Word. The package contains word-processing, spreadsheets, presentations, graphics and databases. You can find hints and suggestions to help you get started on line.

Security is a big problem these days, so it's important to protect your computer from viruses, spyware, hackers and other computer infections through anti-virus and anti-spy software and a firewall, which are usually sold as a combined package in a 'security suite'. Norton and Mcafee are well-know software security suite programs, though less well-known ones like Kaspersky are also reliable.

You can often save money by downloading security from the Internet, especially the previous year's system, which will usually be offered at half price when the new system comes out.

Free Internet security checks are not advisable as some have been know to infect a computer in order to charge for the removal of a virus. Sometimes free security systems are offered, online but see if you can find feedback on their efficiency from someone that can recommend them.

Other computer software packages that are useful for study purposes include:

- ✔ **Spreadsheet programs:** These include Microsoft Excel and Lotus 1-2-3. They allow you to keep records, make calculations and plan schedules. (iWorks provides similar functions.)

- ✔ **Presentation software:** The most commonly used presentation package is Microsoft PowerPoint, which allows you to make presentations using a computer screen or a data projector. You can also send your presentation in digital format by email or over the Internet.

- ✔ **Graphics software:** A range of packages exists, such as Adobe Photoshop and Illustrator, Macromedia and Fireworks, which allow you to create and edit pictures and drawings for use in your work.

✔ **Desktop publishing (DTP)programs:** DTP programs such as Adobe Indesign, Quark Express or Microsoft Publisher provide page layout and other publishing requirements, so that you can lay out your thesis or dissertation in a neat and organised way.

✔ **Internet browsers:** Internet Explorer is normally already installed on computers set up with Windows. However, Mozilla Firefox is free, easier to use, and is frequently updated. Other good browsers include Safari, AOL Explorer and Google Chrome.

✔ **Email:** Your college or university will give you an email account to contact you and for you to use for college business. Email programs download emails to your computer and have good built-in filters to direct advertising and unsolicited mail to a Spam folder, a kind of holding facility or in-tray separated from you main mailbox. They have built-in spell checks when you compose emails.

You will probably want a separate email account to keep your social and private life separate from study business. Hotmail is probably the most popular email program, followed by Yahoo, while other email programs are linked to Internet providers, like btinternet.com. Mozilla Thunderbird email is strong on security, while Microsoft Outlook (currently part of the Office suite) can set up an email to respond to an email address you find on a website without having to close the website window.

If you're a language student or want to self-study a language, use the Language Learning Laboratory computers that are set up specifically for word processing or practising exercises in a particular language. Students of Russian, for example, can use a Cyrillic keyboard. (You can also find other learning support in the Language Laboratory enabling you to access news or television programmes in your chosen language.)

Connecting to the Internet

You can study without owning a computer by using the public ones on campus, but it is not possible to study today without using the Internet.

The Internet is a vast resource for maps, the weather and world news as well as subject-related articles, some of which you will probably be asked to read, and many other things, not all useful. You may well be given a tutorial on how to evaluate a website – to decide whether it is reliable or not.

Two types of connection to the Internet exist, *wired* and *wireless*, both using the signals coming down a telephone line. A wired connection only serves a single computer, which has to be physically connected (wired) to the telephone. There are various packages available, from a dial-up connection which costs the same as a local call, to a monthly fee, which gives access at any time and where there is little or no restriction on the amount of time spent online, to faster, broadband connections. Most providers insist on a minimum contract of one year, which usually makes wired systems too expensive for students, unless they can share the costs. If you are staying in lodgings, it may be worth asking if there is a computer connection.

Most colleges which use a wired system have a special user agreement for educational purposes and so can connect many computers into their wired system. Wired connections are used for teaching in the computer labs. The teacher can control what is displayed on the computer screens to the students using them as part of a class, from a central console.

Some lecture theatres provide sockets so that you can use your laptop for note-taking. This will save your battery, but there is no connection to the Internet.

On the whole, if the system is wired to the Internet – in most formal teaching areas, the library and computer labs – then there will be computer terminals wired to the Internet for your use.

However, most colleges now have wireless free routers around campus, providing more freedom for students to move around and easily connect to the Internet using their laptops. They can also connect their PCs to the Internet through the wireless routers in their halls of residence.

Working out WiFi

Wireless network adaptors are pretty much standard equipment for laptop computers these days. Most tertiary level education establishments have wireless router broadband connections, which allow several devices to connect to the Internet at the same time. The wireless routers convert and broadcast the signals coming down the telephone wires in a specific area – such as a lecture theatre or halls of residence – and work in the same way as a cordless telephone. Public or commercial establishments normally broadcast within a radius of around 100 metres. The area covered from private homes is smaller, but even so, you may find that you can pick up a wireless connection on your laptop in the street or in a park because you're within the broadcast area of the signal.

WiFi hotspots (the areas in which you know that you can get a wireless Internet connection) are often provided by businesses for their customers, so use by other individuals would be seen as poaching. However, as wireless broadband is now more common in residential areas you sometimes find signal overlaps, making it difficult to know whose private wireless signal you're using!

If you do use a WiFi hotspot, you won't know what security measures the owner of the wireless router has put in place, so it may be possible, for instance, for a third party to sniff out your password for your email account. So make sure that you have taken steps to safeguard your system by installing an Internet security system. Some anti-virus software is freely available on line, for example, `free.avg.com`.

As PCs aren't generally mobile, manufacturers assume that Internet connection is through a wired system and so PCs come supplied with a wired Ethernet adapter for this purpose. If you want to connect a personal computer to a wireless system, for instance, so that you can use the free wireless facilities in your room, you need a wireless adapter. This can be in the form of an add-in expansion card in one of the available slots in your PC and can be a permanent installation.

Alternatively, wireless adapters come in the form of a USB plug-in that you can plug into any available USB port on your system. These adapters are usually quite small and not expensive.

If you have a PC and free access to wireless broadband, it's probably much cheaper to buy a wireless adapter than to pay for wired Internet connection: if you don't have a phone line already, having to wait for one to be connected can take up valuable time. Alternatively, you can arrange to do all your work on campus. Most parts, including the library and computer clusters are likely to be open till at least 9.00 p.m. during the week and during the daytime at the week-end.

Browser beware: Restricted access material

The most useful support you can find is often the online material produced to go alongside your course. This often consists of a summary of the course lectures and seminars with reading lists, worked examples of problems, names, emails and contact numbers of key personnel, coursework submission dates and exam dates, as well as web references that have been screened. Sometimes tutors publish lecture notes online for those who missed the lecture or who had a timetable clash. There may even be a chat room or you may have access to a student mentor through this link. As well as overall course information, there's usually a notice board to tell you of postponed or cancelled lectures due to illness, and also to remind you of interesting visiting lectures, where your attendance is not mandatory but which you may find interesting. In short, it can include a course magazine or news-sheet so you probably need to log in to your course website several times a week.

The information may be on a Local Area Network (LAN) associated with a particular building or area and set up specifically so that particular hardware and software facilities and information can be shared, for instance, in a dedicated computer cluster.

The information you need is more likely to be generally available on campus but is often only accessible through a password, so make sure that you note it down in a safe place – your learning diary? (See Chapter 1 for more on keeping a learning diary). The info may also be accessible only on campus and not from home, so this is something else to check so that you plan your on-campus time to include accessing online course information and keeping up to date – something else to add to your learning diary.

The library catalogue and other resources may also only be accessible through use of a password and may not be accessible off campus, so find out how your particular system works and whether it's possible to make online requests for inter-library loans,or reservations, to enable you to work out the best time to do these things.

Sampling Systems Learning and Support

You don't need to understand how digital software works to be able to use it, but some help mastering the system as you practise is useful. You may find support is available through your college's computer or study support centre. There may be free short courses, in-house online tutorials written specifically for the needs of students in your college or expert advice available for particular problems. You can also find free online tutorials that you can work through at your own pace: for instance, a selection of PowerPoint tutorials is available at `www.quasar.ualberta.ca/edit202/tutorial/PowerPoint/PowerPoint.htm`

Most colleges offer short courses on using the library online that's important to attend as each institution operates its own particular system. In addition, courses may include some to help you master particular skills relevant to your course of study, such as the use of graphics, so take advantage if you're offered them.

General ICT housekeeping skills and good habits you need to develop include:

- ✔ **Regular file saving:** Try to backup all important files at least once a week. For word documents this can be as simple as e-mailing them to yourself. For bigger files, either back them up onto recordable media (CD/DVD) or use a portable hard drive independent of your machine to save them on.

- ✔ **Consistent file-naming:** Try to use filenames that allow you to easily access what you need, There's no point, for instance, in saving a History essay as 'Document 1', because you won't be able to relocate it easily without a more identifiable title. Also, try to keep your files organised into folders, so you do not have to go through 3.000 to find the one you are looking for!

- ✔ **Using email effectively:** E-mail is only effective as a means of communication if you check it regularly, at least once every day. Also, try to keep e-mails as concise as possible, especially to your tutor. Remember, he or she may have to read several hundred a day so you need to get you message across effectively and without wasting unnecessary space and time.

Take courses for the use of software that you aren't familiar with early in your student life so that you benefit as much as possible and have a greater effect on your student career. Blocks of time become more difficult to find later on as you progress through your course. Courses are usually offered in the late afternoon and early evening (even at week-ends) over a week or so, with the same course repeated at different times to take account of those who have to miss some to attend lab sessions or similar.

Your Student Union office can probably give you information about free courses available on campus for those who aren't so familiar with computers as tools for study – perhaps you have used them mainly for playing games. Courses may include basic word processing, using search engines and other skills.

If you happen to be a computer whizz-kid, you can often find opportunities for part-time work, like being available at certain times in a computer cluster to troubleshoot should the need arise. You can get on with your own work until such times as you're needed. See the Student Union for rates of pay and acceptable conditions.

A good idea is to join the local library near where you live. As well as being a good alternative source for reserving books you can also use the computer facilities. Librarians tend to be very supportive and helpful to those using basic functions.

Some local adult education and night school classes also offer basic courses in computer familiarisation, perhaps in using Excel and PowerPoint, as these tools also have business applications and therefore courses are quite popular (and cheap – ask for a student discount).

Assessing ICT Pitfalls

A number of common problems do occur when using computers. The important thing in dealing with them is not to panic. Frequently-encountered issues and how to deal with them include:

- **Freezes and hang ups:** Moments when your PC just won't do anything. The best strategy is to give your computer a minute or two to sort the problem out, before using 'control-alt-delete' (or the equivalent procedure on a Mac). If all else fails and you have to turn your PC off, then you can use a system restore in Windows to recover where you were. However, always save documents regularly as this recovery is not always guaranteed.

- **Virus problems:** If you have a virus that your Internet security virus scanner tells you it cannot remove (but can isolate) a useful procedure is to Google the name of the file, as somebody in a usergroup will often have written a file detailing how to remove it. For really persistent viruses, seek professional help.

Being wary of automatic correction

Never trust any word processing program's built in systems for auto-correction or auto-formatting. They are not infallible, so check everything for yourself. Word hates the passive voice, for instance, though it is sometimes necessary. As for formatting, always make sure the document looks the way it needs to, and if it doesn't, change it.

Most word-processing systems have a spell checker, which checks the spelling and punctuation of your work. In terms of the spelling, you can set the checker to British English or American English. In most cases, either is acceptable if used consistently, but not a mixture of both. For example, using *color, tire and check* (American spelling) and *colour, tyre and cheque* (British spelling) in the same piece of writing can be not only irritating but confusing to the reader.

American spelling gives fewer choices, so some people find it easier to use, but there can be ambiguities. For example *tire* can mean become tired as well as what goes on the wheel of a car, so British English spelling tends to be more precise in making these distinctions in the written form (though not in the spoken). Another common example is the two forms: *program* (computer program); *programme* (events, television or theatre programme) in British spelling, where American spelling has only one form, *program,* used for both meanings. Both topics can be discussed on the same page in written work, so the distinction made by British spelling is often helpful to make clear which you're referring to in a particular sentence – without having to guess.

In general, if you feel uncomfortable using or understanding certain aspects of technology, get some human help where you can. For the most part, technology can make things easier or quicker, as long as you keep a wary eye open for the occasional anomaly.

Part II
Becoming an Active Learner

In this part . . .

If you thought that being a student was simply about absorbing information, think again. Academic life is active and outgoing, requiring you to adopt an active and outgoing approach to your studies.

This part is where to come if you want to find out about the different sorts of learning experience you have available to you as a student, and how to respond positively to them so as to maximise the benefits you receive.

If you want to know how to embrace an active learning lifestyle, whether it's by taking great lecture notes or running a successful seminar group, Part II is the place for you.

Chapter 5

Learning Actively in Lectures, Seminars and Tutorials

In This Chapter

▶ Preparing for a lecture or tutorial

▶ Looking at how lectures work

▶ Sizing up how seminars work

▶ Testing out tutorials

Active learners take control of their learning. They bring the knowledge and experience they already have to help them understand new ideas. They use the information they are given to create their own meanings and understandings, and so they remember better what they have learned. They form categories to store similar information, standards to help them consider how possible, probable or certain claims are, how good evidence is and so forth. They never passively accept information, but always ask questions about its accuracy, the methods used to get it, the people who gave it and whether it is likely to be as useful in another part of the world or in ten years' time.

Active learners are not empty vessels waiting to be filled. Being an active learner is a bit like being a gardener who carefully prepares the soil for the plants she has chosen to grow. She plants the seeds in the best environment for their survival, and because she has chosen them, she has certain plans and expectations for how they will develop. Of course, some seeds scattered randomly will grow, but are likely to provide a poor harvest and many will not survive. Active learners are very good at using what they know to find out what they don't know.

Preparing for a Lecture

You get so much more out of any class, any class – whether it's a lecture, seminar, tutorial or workshop, or any group learning situation – if you put in a little preparation beforehand. For most lectures, you receive some preparatory reading to get you ready. If you've planned ahead, you've reserved the texts from the library, perhaps to share with fellow students, and used the title of the forthcoming session to suggest some questions that you want the group or the texts to answer.

It really is good to talk with your fellow students, because that sets up more networks in the brain than reading and writing alone. You can share the reading, with everyone reading a different text. Organise a pre-lecture chat with fellow students or a mentor and report back on the text you read. Even if the chat is ten minutes in the pub the night before, it prepares the ground.

Important questions to consider can include:

- ✔ What do I know about this already?

- ✔ How does it relate to the previous lecture and/or the next?

- ✔ Is it mainly factual, concerning events, research or experiments?

- ✔ Is it about theoretical viewpoints or perceptions?

- ✔ What do I need to take away from the lecture – a general understanding of principles or concepts, how something works, or detailed and specific information about an event?

- ✔ Can I obtain the same information without attending the lecture?

You need to note the answers to these questions and the views from your discussions with your fellow students in your learner diary so that you can compare them to your reactions after the lecture. Your diary is an important account of your development, where you were and what you learned. It also tells you a lot about your own work habits and favourite methods, which can be very helpful if at some future time you need guidance. Favourite questions at job interviews are about self-knowledge of strengths, weaknesses, ways of working and so on. Your learner diary tells you all about these, provides you with examples and gives you the chance to respond in a much more confident and interesting way.

The first question in the list is worth pondering before launching into reading, because it sets up a framework. If, for example, you studied the same subject at an earlier stage in your education, it may be that you now have to consider the issue from a different perspective or in more detail. Use what you already know as a good basis on which to graft new knowledge.

It is foolhardy to miss a lecture because you feel you already know a lot about the subject. The way a lecturer links material to other topics, or the new perspective he brings to the topic can change your ways of thinking about it. These new angles may be difficult to find elsewhere. Fifty minutes or so attending a lecture may be time well spent.

The second question encourages you to think about the overall objective of a series of lectures and how the parts are linked. It also encourages you to make your own links. If links aren't clear this is definitely something to check out with fellow students before the lecture, if possible. If they too are unclear about the rationale, then ask your tutor for an explanation.

For the most part, lectures are mainly about theoretical models, experiments or abstract concepts, their internal logic, how they came about and some evaluation of their strengths and weaknesses, or about very important events, their causes and their impact on later events – with various opinions and evaluations of this. In both cases different opinions and evaluations – the academic arguments – are the aspects of the lecture most difficult to find elsewhere in the same form. Your subject tutor can summarise these for you and name sources (that you can read in depth later).

However, the summary and views the tutor provides merely set a framework for comparing other views – including your own – agreeing or disagreeing and looking at more evidence or better ways of approaching issues and better theorising. This framework provides a set of tools and examples, a starting off point for your consideration, a stepping-stone, but is certainly not an end in itself.

Looking at Lectures

Lectures normally involve relatively large groups of students – at least 25, and sometimes more than 100. They're the traditional way of passing on large chunks of information to a large group of people. Very often, students with different major subjects share the same lectures on core areas.

Lectures are a good way to make new friends from different disciplines. They have a slightly different 'take' on things and you can contribute to each other's post-lecture understanding and increase your knowledge base.

The structure of lectures is similar to the organisation of academic written work. Both are formal – lecturers usually have prepared notes and don't speak 'off the top of their heads', except perhaps in answer to a particular question at the end, because they don't have evidence to hand. Both are largely monologues, though some lecturers accept interruptions and there's usually space for questions at the end. What is special about lectures is the 'breathing spaces' built in to cope with the average individual's attention span of 10–12 minutes. The plan of an average 50-minute lecture probably looks, in very general terms, something like Table 5-1.

Table 5-1	Structure of a typical lecture
Section of lecture	*Description*
Introduction (12 minutes)	Recap on last week's lecture, context of this lecture within the lecture series, summary of main points in this lecture (often three, with some subsidiary points)
Break	Joke, aside, comment on the weather/ news, ask if everyone can hear, if it's too hot or cold, or similar
Section 1 of talk (10 mins)	Link to previous work, point 1 main features stressed, reference back to the introduction – possibly invites questions
Break	Comment, aside, some moving around, pacing, checking overhead slides are clear
Section 2 of talk (10 mins)	Link to Section 1, main features stressed, link to Introduction, possibly invites questions
Break	Asks how the course is going, possible reminder of hand-in dates, other 'housekeeping', jokey comment
Section 3 of talk (10 mins)	Link to previous sections, main features stressed, perhaps invites questions
Break and so on	As previous breaks or similar
Concluding summary (10 mins, average overrun of 2–5 mins, depending on questions)	Refers back to Introduction, recycles main points. Summarises main arguments and main theoretical positions, gives own view, invites questions

The breaks for jokes and asides take less than a minute, just enough time for you to take a big breath, relax and get ready for the next part. The times for the components are, of course, approximate, but the breaks and the patterns of three seem to be fairly generally hard-wired into humans. Some lecturers make breaks by involving the audience and asking them to guess outcomes or predict what comes next at approximately the same points in the talk – every 10 to 12 minutes. In each case, breaks are a way of dividing up the talk into bite-sized chunks – and lecturers need a breather as well!

If the lecturer is very organised and time conscious, then the parts to really concentrate on are the introduction so that you know what's coming, and then the last part of the lecture, which should crystallise everything – as long as the lecturer doesn't run out of time. If he does, this important review normally comes at the beginning of the next lecture.

If you find yourself getting fidgety in a lecture, this may well reflect the lack of a break. The talk may have gone past your 12-minute attention span. It's quite likely that someone may interrupt at this point to ask for a window to be opened or make some similar request, thus giving everyone a break – you'll probably feel better after that!

What you noted in the lecture depends on your preparation questions, your preferred system for note-taking and the form it took. Check out Chapter 7 for the low-down on note-taking in lectures. The first thing you need to review quickly as the lecture draws to an end is any question (in your learning diary, or previously discussed with the other students) that the lecturer didn't answer. If it still seems relevant, now is your chance to get noticed and ask, because:

✔ It's good for you to identify yourself as someone who both prepares for lectures and listens to them.

✔ It's going to put a memory marker in your brain so that recall of this talk makes exam preparation and essay writing easier and the answer can help things slot into place or give you something to challenge or argue about.

✔ It's good to give the lecturer feedback on how his talk was perceived before and on any gaps or misconceptions that persist. If he hasn't got a ready answer, you'll have helped his preparation of the next lecture (or any seminar follow-up).

After the lecture, spend a short time – over coffee with your fellow students, for instance – reviewing your impressions of the talk, whether you agree with each other, whether your views have changed, any links with other topics you've noticed and so on. It's a good time for a for everyone to jot down what they have understood from the lecture on a large sheet of paper so that everyone can see and compare it with their understanding. This could be a group mind map (see Chapter 7 for more on mind maps).

Any talking is useful. Some people remember what they hear better than what they read and any explanation of your views to someone else helps you to organise your thoughts and discover any information gaps, enabling you to put them right.

Sizing Up Seminars

In the higher education hierarchy, if you have a clash, tutorials take precedence over seminars, which take precedence over lectures. While lectures are clearly a mass market tool – some lecture theatres can hold more than 300 students and most hold up to 100 – seminar rooms are smaller and can usually hold between 15 and 35 students, so seminars are less formal and more friendly than lectures. Questions are easier to ask in a seminar and much more discussion develops, which can gives everyone the chance to have their say.

Sorting out types of seminar

Seminars can have different purposes. In some postgraduate courses, all the teaching can be done by seminars, usually because the group size is relatively small, perhaps less than 25 people. However, the functions and procedures are different from that of a lecture. Seminar types fall into two basic categories with the following functions; you can have both types during your course:

✔ **Follow-up seminars:** These seminars cover and reinforce the core information from a lecture series. Those who attended the lectures are divided up into smaller groups so that:

  • Important points can be reviewed and more detailed examples given or worked out – for instance, specific examples from economic history.

  • Points raised in the lecture can be extended or linked to other areas of work.

  • Students' understanding of the main features of the lecture can be checked and more explanation given where necessary – so you can raise points you're not sure about.

  • Students can argue with some of the claims of the lecture if they seem illogical.

A follow-up seminar gives you a great opportunity to check your understanding, ask questions and discuss the issues raised in the lecture. Any questions you didn't manage to ask at the end of the lecture can be raised here, though the seminar may not be taken by the same tutor. It's even more important that you 'make your mark' by asking a question, commenting and so forth to show you've prepared and to confirm your existence.

✔ **Small-group teaching seminars:** Seminars can be the vehicle for giving new information to smaller groups of students, especially postgraduates. Because the number of students is small, seminars allow teaching and learning to be more collaborative. Undergraduates may also have small group teaching seminars if they can choose a special topic to study or a project to work on, for which the lecture format is not suitable. In small-group learning, the responsibility for teaching and learning is often shared. Students may choose, or be allocated, topics to research and present to the rest of the group, while the tutor works with part of the group and checks, explains and extends what the students present. Usually about half the group devotes itself to the presentation of the topic and the rest to discussion and input from the tutor. In the early part of courses, the tutor often does the presentation until the timetable for the input from the students has been arranged.

Although it can be quite scary, volunteer to give your presentation early on, because:

- You get brownie points for doing so and the tutor always looks favourably on the person who goes first.

- It gets the ordeal over with and stops it hanging over your head.

✔ **Work-in-progress seminars:** These are for both undergraduate and postgraduate students to report back on their project work to date and get feedback and suggestions, especially from their fellow students. Doctoral students may get few chances to meet with other students, so work-in-progress seminars are particularly important for them to network and make contacts.

Work-in-progress seminars are great in helping you get an idea of how you are doing with your own project through seeing what others are doing. You can get and make suggestions, consider new methods and approaches and practise defending your ideas and answering questions in a safe and friendly atmosphere. Undergraduates as well as postgraduates can have oral interviews to complete their degree requirements (see Chapter 19 for more on oral exams), so work-in-progress seminars give good practice in explaining your ideas.

If your group organises work-in-progress seminars, it is important to attend as well a present your ideas and make sure everyone has an audience. If the subject is not one you are interested in, the methods might be useful and you can always learn how about the problems of answering awkward questions.

✔ **Workshop seminars:** Workshop seminars (usually just called workshops) have a particular purpose or problem to consider and everyone is involved. Numbers can be as high as 30 participants, but the chair usually divides the group into smaller groups of four to seven students, with each group considering a particular aspect of a problem. The aim is to find a solution that is acceptable to everyone at the end of the time allocated – which may be to have another workshop to debate a new problem which has cropped up!

Workshop seminars are very good for practising lateral thinking skills or bouncing ideas off the wall. If you become involved, for example, in starting up projects, getting ideas for work placements or any student feedback forums to improve teaching or facilities, then the workshop format may be useful to you as well. Workshops are about which things to do and how to do them, so are not limited to academic subjects.

Preparing to participate in seminars

Relatively small numbers make up a seminar group, so it offers greater opportunities to communicate and interact with the other participants.

This also means that if you try to hide in a corner and keep your head down, you're going to be remarked upon as the person who didn't participate much. It's difficult to escape attention in a small group, you're likely to be noted for something, so it's better for it to be something positive.

Because seminars are small, a lot more social interaction goes on and who-ever leads the seminar is responsible for trying to make sure that everyone is involved and that the group's dynamics work. Although lecturers don't always take registers in lectures, they do in seminars, so they note your presence or absence. You should know the names of all or most other participants, and can greet them at the beginning of the seminar. The tutor is also likely to greet you by name, making the whole atmosphere less formal than in the lecture, but you may feel more visible.

You're almost certainly to have been given readings to prepare for your seminar. They may be the same as for the lecture if it was a follow-up, in which case, your seminar preparation follows on from your lecture preparation and post-lecture discussions and notes. In particular, you should note anything you found unclear, either in the lecture or the preparatory readings, as the seminar is the ideal place to ask for clarification, and you'll probably not be the only one who needs this.

If your seminar is based on small-group teaching, and you're not involved in the presentation, you should still consider the seminar questions and do the readings – perhaps share them with other participants and have a pre-seminar meeting. Follow the same pattern of preparation as for lectures. You can also ask more detailed and specific questions in seminars and equally, if you can't quite pinpoint your concerns, you can appeal to the cooperative spirit of the seminar for help.

If you've already been preparing for lectures, sharing readings and having discussions with your fellow students you'll have had good practice in cooperating and taking part in seminars.

Knowing who does what in seminars

Seminars, like any meetings of a similar size, take on their own character according to the dynamics of the group. The livelier and more cooperative the group, the more successful the seminar and the more learning that takes place. Seminars are more democratic than lectures, because less distance exists between the tutor and students, and comments can be more direct and pithy, so expect occasional fireworks. At the same time, both students and tutors can learn from each other, not only factual information about the course, but also about human behaviour.

In formal terms, the participants in a seminar are the *chair*, the *presenter* and the *audience*. The chair may be the tutor, but he may hand over this role to a student, possibly rotating each week, especially in postgraduate seminars. The tutor may be both chair and presenter, especially for undergraduates.

- ✔ **The chair:** Responsible for the general organisation of the seminar – the topic, the time spent on presenting the topic and the time available for questions. The chair is also responsible for ensuring that as many people participate as possible, that no one dominates all the discussion and for keeping order. Most questions should be asked through the chair, otherwise the chair decides which participant can ask the speaker a question.

- ✔ **The helper:** The right-hand person of the chair, who you can appeal to for practical help, for example, turning off the lights, as well as strategic or tactical support. The chair and presenter should also be prepared to act as helpers.

- ✔ **The presenter:** Responsible for preparing and giving a talk in a well-organised way on a particular topic to a group of people who share the same interests. The presenter needs to keep within the time allocated to the presentation and questions and can ask the chair in advance to organise the supply of particular pieces of equipment, such as overhead projectors. The presenter can ask for the chairs and the room to be arranged in the best way to suit their presentation – for example, in a circle or horseshoe. See Chapter 6 for more on the presenter's role.

- ✔ **The secretary:** Most people take notes for their own use in seminars, but in any situation where the main group is sub-divided into smaller groups, for example in workshop seminars, and the small groups report back to the whole group, one person in each small group is usually asked to record their views and act as secretary.

✔ **The audience:** Prepares for the seminar by reading and identifying questions to ask, points for clarification and so on. The ideal member of an audience leans slightly forward, with open chest (rather than folded arms), smiles and makes encouraging noises to the presenter. (a form of encouragement called *psychological stroking*) and raises a hand to catch the attention of the chair when he wants to ask a question or make a comment.

In seminars, individuals may adopt other roles or behaviour patterns that arise from how the group operates. The relationship between individuals in the group is important and sometimes, someone has a bad hair day. You can probably recognise some of the types – they crop up from time to time, but aren't usually a permanent fixture. The main point to remember is that when people are negative, *they* have the problem not you, so keep smiling!

Perusing personality types in seminars

Psychologists who study the behaviour of people in meetings, especially business meetings, use the following terms to identify particular behaviour patterns.

The facilitator

In an ideal world, all the participants in a seminar would be facilitators. Facilitators help and encourage other members of the group. They help explain difficult points by offering examples and step in to help avoid arguments, in the mildest of ways, without trying to take control.

The silent type

The silent types say very little in seminars and may appear withdrawn from the group. The problem is that the group doesn't know if the reason for their silence is nervousness, diffidence, feelings of hostility or superiority. Other members of the group feel uncomfortable and silent types often cause others to argue. The silent type generally evokes a negative response – at best impatience, at worst aggression. It's often suggested that introverts are silent types and don't speak in seminars but this is neither necessarily true nor an excuse for not getting involved.

If you're a silent type, then try to behave like an ideal member of the audience to raise your profile and be seen in a more positive light. If you find eye contact difficult, aim for the middle of the forehead. Practice psychological stroking by saying, 'Yes, I agree' and 'Me, too' and make other, similar positive noises and comments. If you do have a problem, then you can ask for clarification by saying things like:

'Can you go over that again, please?'

'That concept is not quite clear to me, can you explain?'

After a time, you may feel confident enough to give your own view or criticism. If you're taking part in the second type of seminar, this sort of practice and familiarisation with working with the group is even more important as you'll be under the spotlight at some point when you give your presentation and make your contribution.

If you have a silent type in your seminar – and most seminars have one – this gives you the chance to be a facilitator. If you can, do some of your pre-seminar preparation with him to give him confidence, and refer to what you did together in preparation in the seminar. This can certainly gain you brownie points and respect from the group and your tutor.

The aggressive type

Aggressive types can be loud, noisy and impatient, feeling that the answer to a problem is obvious and there's no more to say on a topic, and that time is being wasted because everyone else is a bit slow. They tend to miss important details and can be a bit scary to other members of the group. The chair can use their comments positively – though more gently – if things really do need to be moved on.

Again, you can practise your skills as a facilitator and try to involve the aggressive type in pre-seminar or even post-seminar discussion. His aggression may be to cover up insecurity or other problems and your concern, rather than an aggressive reaction to aggression, may turn him into a pussycat! In any case you've nothing to lose by trying to be helpful and everything to gain for you and the group. Even failure is seen as a positive action.

You can also encourage aggressive types to change their body language by leaning back in their seats with their hands held loose and taking some slow deep breaths and notice how the people around them relax as a result. This allows them to be seen in a more positive light. You can suggest they give themselves and everyone else a bit more space by being a little less self-conscious and listening to other people so that they can pick points to ask about or put questions about what's just been said, or at least count to ten before interrupting. Helping them cultivate a little patience in this way also helps them to see they're learning – but it takes patience.

If you're the chair, make sure that the aggressive type doesn't sit next to the silent type, and isn't in the silent type's direct eye line. Changing where people sit can make a big difference.

The rambling type

Ramblers tend to miss the point, get distracted and often confuse two separate or different things. Everybody has met one or been one at some point. They usually have a story or anecdote to tell that they believe is universally true based on their experience alone. They can be very entertaining, but need to be more disciplined. Others in the group can find them a bit frustrating and boring, especially if the chair doesn't step in and stop the seminar going off the point. The chair needs to politely interrupt and explain that, although the rambler's comments may be interesting, they're not evidence and don't relate to the subject under discussion.

Ramblers need more focus and again, if you're presenting or chairing the seminar, you can encourage them to share pre-seminar reading preparation and discussions so they can relate that to what they hear in the seminar – rather than their last visit to Thailand.

The abusive type

Abusive types are relatively rare, but can be quite rude to the extent of being abusive – about the course, the tutors, other students, life in general – and give plenty of reasons why things won't work or can't be done. They can be dispiriting to other students and staff alike. Although a person may be having a really bad hair day, you may need to remind him to put aside whatever is annoying him, but try to learn from it. Remind him that he's basically a lovely person and he'll get more out of life by being positive and looking for solutions, rather than looking for the worst in everything. Ask him to imagine things working out the way he wants them to and see how good he feels about that.

Again, as a facilitator, you can encourage him to try some lateral thinking and show him how to use a mind map or a table of possible solutions derived from pre-seminar readings or discussions. Find out his favourite form of physical exercise and if he doesn't do much, suggest learning to salsa or kickbox.

If you're the chair and find you have an abusive type – probably a temporary mood – then you may have to ask that person to wait until he has something constructive to say or ask him to restrict his comments to very specific areas.

The sniper

The sniper doesn't appear very often, but if someone has a bee in his bonnet – however justifiably – about another member of the group and allows this to turn into a witty but cruel repartee, it may be quite funny but not helpful to the individual or the seminar group. In the same way, if a sniper doesn't like the topic, he may make witty, but derogatory comments. It may be that the sniper hasn't prepared for the seminar, so snipes at those who can be a smokescreen for his guilty conscience.

If you're the chair and you have a sniper, sit him near you to make it difficult for him to make comments without swivelling in his chair. Many snipers snipe sotto voce, under their breath, so you may perhaps offer him a throat sweet or ask him if he needs a glass of water, and having given him attention, then focus on the rest of the group.

A facilitator can encourage a sniper to apply his creative energy to making reasoned criticisms of the preparatory readings or theories under discussion. Criticisms of ideas or theories is part of academic life. Public witticisms at the expense of others is not. If he finds sitting duck targets irresistible, then suggest he pinch herself and count to ten. The momentary thrill of getting a reaction isn't worth the long-term resentment he may be building up in his targets. What takes seconds may take years to recover from and may never be forgotten.

You never know who you'll be facing across a desk at an interview decades from now, so it's always a good idea to avoid making enemies. Even if a sniper's target has forgotten the incident, the sniper may remember and so compromise his performance at the interview.

Testing Out Tutorials

Tutorials are usually one-to-one, though occasionally you might share a tutorial with another student or a small group if you have similar needs. The subject matter of tutorials is more specific to your needs than that in seminars or lectures. If you are carrying out a project in a small group, you may get some tutorial help for that particular project. If you are working on an essay or presentation, your subject tutor may offer you some suggestions, or you may have a meeting with your personal tutor once a term or so to check your progress. As most tutorials consist of a dialogue between you and your tutor or supervisor, it's important that you work together to establish a good relationship in which you can be honest with each other. It's important for you to be able to question constructively what you're told, in case there's a communication problem or a misunderstanding, and to be comfortable about doing that. You don't have to agree with your tutor's viewpoint nor he with yours, but you do need to understand each other's position. It is equally important for your tutor to criticise your work constructively or prompt you if you've been remiss without being afraid of upsetting you, otherwise he can't give you the guidance you need. This isn't helpful to you in the long run, so be prepared to take constructive criticism.

Personal tutorials

Undergraduates usually have a personal tutor and perhaps a tutorial once a term, unless an important issue comes up. Personal tutors may not teach you. Their concern is your general welfare. If you are ill or have some difficulties in your private life, or anything else that may affect your work, they are there to help. If you are ill or going to be absent from class, you or a friend should normally phone the office, and the information will be passed on to your personal tutor so that they can keep an eye on you. They will also have a record of your course marks.

If you have any concerns, be proactive and ask for a meeting with your tutor. If you are worried about your marks and need more feedback or suggestions about how to do better, then ask sooner rather than later. Tutors may get official feedback from exam boards or departmental meetings after term has ended, so there can be quite a long gap before they are able to catch up with you.

A personal tutorial is your chance to contribute to the agenda and clear up any problems, uncertainties or general questions you have about procedures, the organisation of your course, the facilities available, or even your accommodation. You can inform you tutor in advance of any points you'd like to discuss, so that they can prepare and find out any necessary information to pass on.

Your personal tutor is often the one approached for references later on and a good co-operative relationship is in everyone's interests. In the event that you get into trouble with the university authorities – for a prank that went wrong, or unpaid library fines, for example – then your tutuor is the one who gives a character reference.

Subject or project tutorials

Students at all levels can have subject tutorials, usually to support longer or important pieces of written work, research or experiments. If you are working on a group project or with a partner, then you may share a tutorial as your interests coincide. The difference between important pieces of work at different levels is partly length – though some undergraduate written work may be 10,000 words or more, so longer than a Postgraduate 5,000 word term essay, but shorter than a postgraduate dissertation – and partly the amount of research involved. The last assessed undergraduate work often involves some original research, which allows students to spread their wings and have a taste of working for a higher degree.

You must prepare for these tutorials, even if you cannot decide on a topic. You should try to outline your dilemma, if possible, in advance in a note. For instance, you like topic A but you haven't been able to find much useful information, or you are not sure whether the theory you have chosen fits the situation well enough. Your tutor will be able to help and save you time and energy. It is important not to miss these tutorials as life can be a lot more difficult without them and if the tutor has set aside time at a particular point, he may not easily find time for you later on. It really can be a case of use it or lose it.

It is particularly important to keep a record of specific project tutorials in your learning diary as this will help you identify points to raise and note down the tips and suggestions you get in response. If you are working on a project with partners, then you can help each other out by planning what you want to get from the tutorial.

Supervisors go on holiday or on conference or research trips during the summer. Find out when your supervisor is going to be away and try to see him as much as you can beforehand. Don't let his absence become an excuse for delaying the firming up of your framework. In any case, later on, you want him to read a draft of a least part of your work, and you're going to miss out on that if you haven't got to first base by the time he disappears. Also ask who you can call upon to help in your supervisor's absence and send his stand-in, along with your supervisor, a copy of your outline plan and a note about what you think you may need help with later on.

Doctoral students agree a contract with their supervisor that sets out the rights and responsibilities of both parties. For example, there's normally a tutorial meeting every three months to formally document progress with a written report or minutes agreed by each party. Some supervisors meet their students less formally on a weekly basis to keep their fingers on the pulse. Every student and every student/supervisor relationship is different, as are the requirements of each area of study, but the agreement between the supervisor and the student regarding the frequency of supervisory tutorials is held to be a formal agreement. You may, of course, have more than one supervisor, but you make your agreement with the main supervisor.

Always keep all your supervisors up to date with what you're doing – just a short weekly record of work and plans for the next week helps. You don't need to send bulletins weekly, but you should keep them weekly. Records of your supervisory tutorials and what you agreed there are particularly important.

If your main supervisor is unavailable, this record can help your second supervisor take over. If ever there's any dispute between you and your supervisor, your record is also evidence of what you agreed, the work you did, to show to the postgraduate programme tutor.

If you're a doctoral student, you have less structure in your studies than other students. You may have work-in-progress and methods seminars as well as tutorials in your first year but you probably don't have to physically present yourself more than a day or two a week. It's important to establish and maintain your work programme and record, especially if you're isolated doing fieldwork later on and can only keep in touch by email. If you haven't already set up a pattern, it can be quite difficult to find one that works for you and your supervisors at a distance. Supervisors can also leave and go to the other side of the globe, so make sure that you take responsibility for the structure of your research so that you can slot your supervisors in as resources, rather than be dependent on them as individuals.

Lectures, seminars and tutorials all involve interacting with other people. You don't have to like them to work with them, but you do need to respect them and their right to an opinion – which you don't have to agree with!

Chapter 6

Grappling with Group Work: Workshops, Seminars and Presentations

In This Chapter

▶ Benefiting from group work

▶ Making use of workshops

▶ Giving presentations in seminars

▶ Appreciating audience feedback

*W*orkshops and seminars provide interactive ways of learning. Whereas lectures consist mainly of monologues from expert tutors in particular fields who pass on information to an audience, workshops and seminars involve much smaller groups working together. A chair helps manage the organisation and contributions of group members and generally sees that things run smoothly and amicably in workshops and seminars. One member of the group is also responsible for presenting new information or questions or problems for the group to discuss. Workshops normally involve the leader setting tasks for the group to perform, often in smaller sub-groups. The small groups then report back their findings – what they've learned, discovered or discussed – to the group as a whole.

This chapter takes you through the detail of group work, and shows you how to make the most of its benefits.

The Benefits of Group Work

Many benefits exist in group work, not least having others around you to talk with, listen and react to. At a very basic level, words live for fractions of seconds then die, but during that brief period, they actually create sparks and neural links in the brain of both the speaker and listener. If a dialogue takes place between two or more speakers and each is able to make an approximately equal contribution, then a chain reaction begins, like a ball batted back and forth in a game of tennis. Each comment links to another idea, and then you may recreate the dialogue – by telling an absent friend of your discussion and so bring them into the loop.

Of course, the uncritical passing on of comments, like Chinese whispers, can lead to misunderstandings. Each comment needs to be examined in the light of your knowledge, understanding and beliefs, so that you can ask the next question or look for contradictions.

In a group, you can ask a question and get an immediate answer. In this sense, group learning involves mutual learning and is dynamic, continually being added to, amended or redirected. It can also be very fast.

Sounding out Socrates

The Socratic method of learning consists of asking a series of questions to help individuals and groups identify their underlying beliefs and the extent of their knowledge or understanding. Socratic dialogue includes building up each individual's self-confidence in her own thinking, and the search for answers to a particular problem can become the common pursuit of the group.

Socrates (469 BC–399 BC) passed down to posterity the interactive dialogue or discussion form as a method of learning. Indeed, Socrates practised his dialogue methods in the market and workshops of Athens, as there was no formal organisation for advanced learning at the time. However, his learning system worked so well that his student, Plato, founded the Academy of Athens, the first institution of higher learning in the western world. In turn, Plato's student, Aristotle, founded his own school in Athens. Socrates, Plato and Aristotle are regarded as the founding fathers of Western Philosophy and each made their own different and varied contributions to learning and education as well.

Socrates wrote nothing, but Plato wrote down many examples in his *Dialogues* and other works of the interaction and questioning between Socrates and various citizens of Athens in their workshops. Plato was also a mathematician, while Aristotle was interested in logic and created the syllogism argument form, which proceeds from a general idea to a more specific one and then a conclusion.

Working Out Workshops

If you need to find out a lot of information in a short period of time, then you'll find the workshop format very useful. You can divide up a task into parts and have groups of four or five people look at each part. (Around about these numbers seems to be the most successful in achieving a set task .) Within a given time frame, the groups debate the question or identify the problems you've asked them to look at. This involves them first examining the issues they must consider, their beliefs and attitudes to them and deciding the principles upon which they're going to base their investigation. They state these principles or ways of working (modus operandi) when they report back to the whole group, who may well ask for further explanation or justification for how they've tackled the problem. One member of each group can act as secretary to record how the group worked and reached its conclusions.

Some of the general benefits of the workshop are as follows:

- It fosters cooperation between members in small groups and then the larger group.

- Small group dialogue and discussion generates a lot of ideas and can be very creative.

- Four or five people are usually enough to generate a variety of opinions, but if not this can usually be remedied at the reporting stage to the whole group stage where a wider range of views is heard.

- Seeing problems from someone else's perspective means re-evaluating your own views and beliefs.

- Hands-on learning by activities and learning from each other has a bigger impact on understanding and memory than reading for example. In addition, it sets up possible frameworks for understanding written texts or lectures, so it's an aid to learning in other ways.

- Participants can have a great sense of achievement from what they've done and discovered in a relatively short space of time (usually 1–3 hours).

- Workshops like this also allow you to practise transferable skills – skills that are useful in the work place. For instance, the ability to listen, have confidence in expressing your opinion, be open to other points of view, to realise that there's more than one method or way of carrying out a task (or skinning a cat), to work under strict time limits, to work cooperatively, to develop 'people skills' and so on.

Table 6-1 shows the format of a typical workshop. For the different roles within a seminar group, check out Chapter 5.

Table 6-1	A Typical Workshop Format	
Task	*Activity*	*Outcome*
Introduction (of topic, goals, time spent on activities, forming groups)	Leader/facilitator notes important information on OHP transparencies or whiteboard so that everyone can see	Students understand objectives, methods and time allowed
Form small groups	Groups organised according to task or rotation of members	Groups know members and arrange seating to allow easy communication
Task sheets or instructions prepared by helper	Facilitator – ensures at least one copy of each per group	Groups distribute sheets among themselves or arrange to share them
Method of group feedback decided by facilitator	For example, OHP transparencies and pens or flip charts provided for note-taking. (High tech not so workshop friendly)	Secretary uses selected method – flip chart, OHP transparencies, to make decisions, information, changes of mind and so on visible to small and whole group later on
Task one debated by group, then task two and so on Whole group feedback	Small group facilitator or if group very cooperative, unnecessary, but organise so everyone has a chance to take part Secretary collects findings of group to display	Secretary notes opinions, beliefs, findings, things to consider, questions to ask, problems and so on Small group findings presented to whole group, usual visual representation as well as spoken (OHP or other)
Facilitator summarises viewpoints	Facilitator possibly uses check sheet on OHP written during small group feeding back to whole group	Notes points of similarity, difference, unexpected outcomes, new questions – general group summary

The hypothesis may be that British press reporting of overseas news is mostly restricted to Europe or the USA. The workshop leader gives each small group one or two newspapers of the day to investigate this claim and then to report back to the group as a whole so that a larger comparison table can be made. Each group needs to discuss how they're going to measure the reporting of overseas news (for example, pages or columns as a percentage of the whole paper) and categorise it – in terms of country, region or whether, for instance, sports news counts as overseas news.

Using workshops for self-study

As you become familiar with the workshop format as one of the methods used in your course instruction, you can then adapt it relatively easily to as a method to study together as a group. The workshop format can be particularly useful for courses which involve experiments – psychology, linguistics or education, just as much as engineering or the applied sciences – or where students can be each other's guinea-pigs. If you and your classmates are working on separate but related areas, awareness of what each other are doing greatly increases what you learn and what you can contribute to. The most important thing to remember is that while preparation, testing, suggesting and so on are often best done collaboratively, writing up of anything must be done individually, and be your own personal work. That said, almost any topic can be tackled using the workshop for self-study.

The workshop leader or chair has a fair amount of planning to do, but much of it is practical, like deciding the timing or providing overhead projector (OHP) transparencies (usually available through your school of study office). Once planned these can easily be repeated or handed to someone else to organise. The rewards are more than can be achieved by an individual in the same amount of time.

One of the main points in favour of using the workshop format for group study or revision is that the group can achieve a lot more than individuals in the same amount of time. You can probably book a room in your college at a precise and convenient time to hold your workshop and this gives the whole exercise a more professional aura and can help your participants take it seriously and turn up on time. You can also sell it as empowering – which it is – and once you've set up a workshop it can then tackle many other tasks or negotiate as a group – perhaps an extra class in a difficult topic, or more time to complete a task.

Using workshops for preparation

Even if your numbers are limited and you have to work in fewer groups, you can use a workshop to discuss the meaning of essay titles or exam questions. As long as you have two or more groups, you can find out more in less time than by working on your own. With essay titles, it's useful to discuss with one member of the group as the devil's advocate, so that other members of the group can think up counter arguments to defend their positions.

The workshop format is very useful for reading preparation before lectures and seminars. It's highly practical where there aren't enough copies of certain key texts for everyone to read. In this case, summarising or reviewing a text for the group at least gives everyone a chance of having some knowledge of it before a lecture or seminar. If this is balanced by everyone having access to a preparatory reading (preferably at least two people should read the same text to provide more than one viewpoint), then this establishes a give-and-take organisation, with everyone having equal responsibility and equal benefits.

At least two people reading a text also provides some security if one is ill and can't attend the workshop. Another fall-back position is for readers to record their thoughts, reactions and views on tape or disk, so that the group can play them if, for some reason, a personal appearance isn't possible. As a general principle, some readers may find making comments and recordings as they go along more immediate and less time consuming than taking notes – so recordings would always be available for themselves or others, in class or for self-study.

Getting the workshop organised

Organising the workshop can be like trying to herd cats – and we all know how uncooperative cats can be – so setting up workshops requires a certain amount of structure and energy. However, arranging workshops has some major plus points:

- ✔ It looks marvellous on your curriculum vitae.

- ✔ You impress your tutors (you can invite them along to relevant workshops and encourage them to participate).

- ✔ You develop a lot of people management, time management and organisational skills in the process.

- ✔ You contribute to the learning on your course and make it more fun.

To organise a workshop effectively, you need to be a good facilitator. See Chapter 5 for more on facilitators. The main points to bear in mind when organising a workshop are the following:

- ✔ **Find days and times that work for everyone:** Sometimes 5.00–6.00 p.m. or thereabouts – followed by a pizza or drink in the pub or a swim – works quite well because it uses 'dead' time creatively and productively without intruding into the evening.

- ✔ **Rotate partnerships in the sub-groups:** This makes each workshop a new experience for each student, with new partners.

- ✔ **Plan collectively the tasks you want to do together and the goals you want to achieve:** Ideally, do this some weeks ahead, but with flexibility, as new concerns are likely to crop up as the term goes on. Collective planning encourages both cooperation and taking individual as well as group responsibility. It also discourages any negative traits.

✔ **Make sure that the goals set are achievable within the time frame:** You may have to subdivide workshops over two or more sessions or focus on a particular aspect so that goals and tasks are clear and can be understood.

✔ **Stick to the time you've allocated for completing the tasks set – in groups and collectively:** Timing means that a chair or facilitator needs a watch. It's very tempting to allow what seems to be interesting to go past its allocated time but in workshops, achieving set goals within a time frame takes precedence, which sometimes means moving on. The group feedback mustn't be ignored. It's the cohesion for the workshop, when everyone finds out what the others did or thought – the pay-off for their investment. If a group has very interesting things to say, it may continue outside the workshop, perhaps raising points in a seminar. In this sense the workshop is the prime mover, the starting off point for new ideas, but you need to maintain the structure of the workshop so that everyone feels a sense of momentum and that targets set have been met.

✔ **Encourage participants to keep learning diaries:** This ensures that they have notes of any pre-workshop preparation, their collective group notes and information from the workshop itself. To encourage future participation it's important that everyone gets a sense of learning and achievement.

✔ **Be sure to inform people in good time of any housekeeping:** Notify any changes to the time or place of the workshop well in advance. You need to remind everyone of the topic for discussion and ask for any new sources of information they've discovered. Once the workshop format has been firmed up and works well for everyone, give yourself a break and rotate the role of facilitator, so that everyone has experience of that as well.

Use email to keep in touch with the group. Emailing is informal and uses the same forms as spoken dialogue. One email copied to the group takes a lot less time than a series of phone calls and you don't have to worry about when to send them whereas phone calls at the wrong time can be disturbing.

The online communication can turn into a chat room or discussion forum, but can't replicate the multiple face-to-face interaction of the workshop, so although it can be an extra learning support, it can't substitute for the live workshop.

Workshops are the most democratic form of learning because all the participants put in more or less the same work and time, so each person is equally important and valuable. Each participant takes responsibility for her own learning and for that of the group – learning from others and informing others. Workshops offer highly practical hands-on learning by doing and learning by discovery within a structure and time frame that intensifies the learning process. The practical nature of a workshop also means that learning is quite measurable and explicit, which gives participants confidence in themselves and in what can be achieved.

If you can't find a workshop to join or are wary of starting one, the closest activity is to join a debating society or perhaps a political group. You're not joining for the information (or if you are, that's a bonus) but to experience the methodology and organisation, the problems and pitfalls and to see how much better you can do in organising a workshop. Joining a similar type of group can be very useful for improving your self-confidence and can empower you.

Giving Presentations in Seminars

Less formal than lectures, seminars aren't generally organised to include small-group activity as the main focus, as workshops do. Nevertheless, seminar presenters are nearer to their smaller audiences than lecturers and the relationship is more intimate, so involving the audience and making seminars interactive is always an advantage for the presenter for various reasons:

- It takes some of the pressure away from the presenter and also gives her feedback from the audience to help her proceed.
- It involves the audience, so they become active learners.
- It creates a lively atmosphere and makes for a pleasant experience.
- Everyone learns something, including the presenter.
- It can help with the organisation and control of the seminar.

Kinds of seminar

Aside from where you give the seminar and whether it's for students that you know or people you don't, most seminars fall into the following categories:

- **Report seminars:** Jointly given, with each speaker dealing with a separate section of the report. Report seminars are usually based on experiments or research results or they can be work-in-progress seminars, linked usually to research.
- **Work-in-progress seminars:** involve individual students reporting back on their work to date so that they can get feedback and suggestions from the audience about any changes to make and how to continue their work. Any individual project, experiment or research work at any level – undergraduate or postgraduate – often includes work-in-progress seminars.

 ✔ **Information-based seminars:** Different class members tackle different topics and share their findings with the group. Information-based seminars can take place at all levels of study.

Engaging your audience

How much you can involve the audience depends to a certain degree on the type of seminar you're giving and how long you've got – 10 minutes or 50 minutes, for example. However, it's always useful to engage the audience, which makes it clear that you're talking to them rather than at them. The following list suggests a few ways of engaging your audience; the first manages things for you if your time is limited.

 ✔ **Ask a question at the very beginning of the presentation:** Write the question down so that it can be seen by everyone and ask the audience to note their response. The presentation title itself can be in the form of a question that you can use, but a more focused question or set of questions is better. If it is a yes/no-type question, you can do a head count to see how opinion is divided. It helps if the question is provocative. Tell the audience you'll ask the same question at the end of the presentation to check opinions again, as in a debate.

 ✔ **Show the audience a photograph or picture:** Ask them to think about where it was taken or where it came from or who was involved, what was happening, and why.

 ✔ **Show the audience a substance or something they can touch:** Pass the object around and suggest what it is. For instance, fossil dinosaur poo is not immediately identifiable. You can ask them to guess the weight of something (a bag of rice) not because that is the topic of your presentation but to illustrate the range of guesses the audience may suggest, or about different people's perception of the same thing.

 ✔ **Play pre-recorded sounds:** Ask the audience to identify them or particular characteristics of them.

 ✔ **Present certain symbols:** You can try, for example a swastika, an Ankh, a Celtic cross, a lion rampant or the saltire (Scottish flag) and ask the audience to note down their immediate reactions and what these symbols suggest to them.

 ✔ **Use smells to conjure up impressions:** Driftwood, for example, usually retains some sea-salty smell – an appeal to the audience's imagination.

 ✔ **Ask the audience to guess the answers to questions as you go through the seminar:** For example: 'Which country held the most executions in 2008?'

✔ **Pose the bodies of members of the audience or ask them to adopt certain positions to demonstrate body language:** What is visible to them in some positions and not others. You can ask them to role-play certain characters or situations as a demonstration to other members of the audience. Make sure that you respect boundaries if you do this and reassure your audience, but it can be very effective, as the demonstrators can 'feel' the situation.

This list is by no means exhaustive but is a reminder that you can appeal to the senses as well as abstract reasoning. The objective is to gain the audience's attention – promise to reveal all at some later point – and involve them in the proceedings.

Avoid being gimmicky – just use one or two techniques, not all of them in one seminar. However, don't be afraid to experiment, because that's how you learn techniques. At worst your audience may be bemused, but if you've given them a sensory memory cue it may help them remember your presentation. You can ask them a few weeks later for the answer to a question where you used a sensory prompt and they'll be surprised how well they remember.

Managing the seminar

One of the scariest things about giving a presentation for the first time is worrying about how the audience is going to treat you – apart from if you're tongue-tied, forget why you're there or fall flat on your face. If you know your audience, if they're fellow seminar attendees and you have listened to their presentations before giving your own or shared lectures with them, you have a fair idea of what to expect. If your audience is unknown to you, it's even more important for you to establish a relationship with them. Check out the preceding section on 'Engaging your audience' for some ideas.

In either case, as presenter, you can organise the room space to help you manage the proceedings, as Figure 6-1 shows.

Find out when the seminar room is free so that you can arrange it to your liking. If you have only a few minutes to arrange it, call in the cavalry, and do the same for them when it's their turn.

If the room is rectangular, you can place yourself and any equipment in the middle of one of the longer sides (which side depends on where the door and windows are and any power points that you need) so that you can be as near to your audience as possible, with fewer but wider rows. If you place yourself at one of the shorter sides of the rectangle it allows a greater depth of rows, which creates more distance between you and the audience at the back, as in the traditional 'chalk and talk' classroom manner, which is not appropriate for a seminar.

Provoking a response

Within reason you can use an opening question to stir up debate, such as the following yes/no-type questions:

✔ Should public money be spent on supporting failing financial institutions?

✔ Does every woman have the right to terminate a pregnancy?

Yes/no-type questions are the type normally used in a debate. Questions can also require an answer. For example:

✔ What form of renewable energy is potentially the best answer to UK energy needs in the 21st century?

Remember to avoid anything which can be interpreted as racist, ageist or sexist or which mocks a certain group and avoid topics like religion or politics. Your discussion should be based on evidence, not opinion. It's perfectly acceptable to say 'women between the ages of 18 and 25 spend the most on make-up compared to other age groups (26–34, 35–50. 51 and over)' as long as you show the evidence.

Fairly formal seminars with twenty or more in the audience are sometimes organised in two or three curved rows, which is at least better than straight rows facing the front. You may have to stick with the curved lines if the audience is large but make sure that the rows have the right degree of curve so that the people at the end of the rows can see you and any OHP projections or other aids you're using.

Sometimes, seminars are arranged 'in the round' with the presenter at one side of a circle of desks, which gives the impression of equality, as in the Knights of the Round Table. However, the desk can 'trap' the presenter, and sometimes make the use of seminar aids awkward, as with overhead transparencies, as these can't be seen easily by the people on the immediate left and right of the presenter.

Probably the best arrangement is the horseshoe. This can be seats alone or with desks in front of them, but the important point is the open part. The presenter can set her table or desk and aids in the open area, a little behind the two ends of the horseshoe and with enough space on either side to allow her to move around inside the horseshoe and interact and maintain eye contact with any of the participants. The horseshoe gives all the participants as near as possible the same vantage point and access to the speaker.

Making eye contact and being able to move around inside the horseshoe helps you to control the proceedings. You can also physically put yourself as a barrier between two participants who are giving each other a rough time, and blank one out from the other.

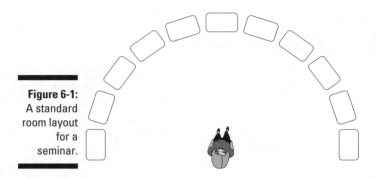

Figure 6-1:
A standard
room layout
for a
seminar.

Once you've established the organisation of the room, the seminar aids – handouts or any props that you think you need, – the seating arrangements and so on, try to enlist the support of some friendly faces to act as facilitators for you. This is especially useful the first time you have to give a presentation. If you don't know your audience because you're presenting at a conference or meeting outside your institution or area of study, try to import a couple of friends to give you support.

Place your two lieutenants at approximately 10 o'clock and 2 o'clock on the horseshoe (see Figure 6-2), so that they can catch your eye with a nod, a smile and provide some psychological stroking, so you know where to look when you need a bit of reassurance. They can also help maintain a positive tone with those on either side of them. Just knowing they're there can be an enormous boost to your self-confidence and allows you to get on with the job rather than worrying about it. It also seems that this kind of positive balancing draws more positive engagement and responses from the audience.

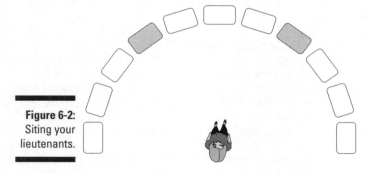

Figure 6-2:
Siting your
lieutenants.

Handling questions

Normally the chair of the seminar introduces you and discreetly informs you how much time you have left, and you need to allow time for questions at the end of your presentation. It's good to have questions, because that suggests that the audience were attentive, you gave them something to think about and so on. No questions suggest that the audience were asleep or you put them to sleep, so questions are a good thing.

Prime your lieutenants with a question each that you think fits the context of your presentation well. Ideally, they're only in a fall-back position: they should only ask questions if no one else does. This is again mainly to reassure you that your presentation prompts a question or two.

Questions are put through the chair, who normally repeats them for you. This gives you a little time to think of your answer – if the questioner isn't one of your lieutenants. If the question is the result of a misunderstanding and the chair is your tutor, she often helps out – or other members of the audience may do so – in your defence. If you need a few moments to form your answer you can begin your response with a phrase that allows you a bit more time to think, such as:

> 'That's an interesting point, thank you for raising it.'

If you think that the question is a bit loaded, you can turn it back on the questioner and ask:

> 'I'm not sure about that – what do you think?'

Or you can even put the question to the whole audience. If you're asked a question that you can't answer, be honest about it. Some of the following responses may be appropriate:

> 'I think that's outside the scope of my talk, but it's certainly something to think about.'

> 'I don't know the answer, but I'll try to find out and get back to you.'

> 'I can't tell you, I'm afraid – does anyone here know?'

The essence of the seminar is that there's very little distance between presenter and audience, either physically or in power terms (aside from the organisational aspects – anarchy isn't an option) so an expectation of cooperation and mutual help exists, particularly in the 'open' part of the seminar, the questions. Be honest, expect mutual support and you'll probably get it.

When you're part of the audience in a seminar, remember the importance to the presenter of being asked questions. You've probably prepared your questions and others may arise during the presentation, but if, for whatever reason, none arises, a positive comment is equally appreciated. Even 'thank you' or 'that was useful/interesting' or 'it has made me think' boosts the speaker's confidence and ends the presentation on a positive note.

Audience feedback

One of the most important aspects of seminars is for presenters to get feedback from their audience. Although this may be in terms of the general support and encouragement mentioned above, presenters, particularly of report or work-in-progress seminars, need critical feedback to help them develop their ideas, methods, hypotheses and so on. In this sense, the seminar is a trial, a testing place, more a public brainstorming at the beginning of something or perhaps looking for suggestions as to how to analyse data or improve methodology at a later date.

The main purpose of the report-type seminar is to seek an active response from the audience, that is, to get feedback. If you're presenting a report seminar, you need to think of the best way of presenting your problem or dilemma, or indeed solution, if you just need confirmation that you've done the right thing. Given that your aim is to get useful feedback, you need to present your work in such a way as to encourage it. You need to consider bite-size chunks and built-in pauses or gaps to give the audience time to react. Report seminars are often ongoing, so you can probably present another some months later with an update of your progress and possibly comments and thanks for the effectiveness of the previous advice given. With this in mind, you need to give a brief account of your long-term aims but focus mainly on the immediate feedback you need.

The scheme of a report seminar may look something like Table 6-2. The three-point rule still applies – three main points or a main point with three sub-points makes it more likely that your audience take your points on board and respond to them – as in liberty, equality, fraternity, faith, hope and charity. See Chapter 5 for more on the three-point rule.

Table 6-2	The Structure of a Typical Seminar	
	Content	*Objective*
Part 1: Presenter to audience		
Introduction	General aim and ultimate objective	Orientate audience to general issue
Specific report aim	Particular issues raised in this report	Identify specific concern to audience

	Content	*Objective*
Part 1: Presenter to audience		
Issue 1,2,3 (or issue 1, sub-parts a,b,c)	Specific point or further detail	Raise issue/ question to get feedback
Summary of general needs	Identify specific feedback or comments needed	Request for feedback
PART II: Audience to presenter (role-switch)		
Questions and feedback	Responses to issues raised	Provide feedback, criticism, suggestions
PART III: Presenter to audience		
Response to feedback	Explanations given, ideas clarified	More feedback, different opinions, different suggestions

Of course, the feedback to the points raised by the presenter can come after each issue raised and not just at the end of the presentation, although this is more usual. In a work-in-progress seminar, the presenter makes certain points that she wants the audience to bear in mind while she explains the next point or decision she took and the work she did, so that the audience can understand the logic behind her actions and identify any flaws or anything that she should have taken into consideration but didn't, in order to bear these points in mind when giving feedback at the end of her presentation. Table 6-2 shows that there's a certain amount of role reversal, because the time allocated for questions extends and becomes a discussion between the presenter and audience. Members of the audience aren't only invited to participate, but they can actually take the floor. It shouldn't surprise you to discover that the audience in a work-in-progress seminar is likely to include tutors, supervisors and academics as well as fellow students.

As the presenter can give the audience the floor, this type of seminar can look more like a dialogue. Although the main objective is for the speaker to learn, the method tends to be through experts giving their opinions and advice, that is, those who've already jumped through the relevant academic hoops and who therefore speak from a position of authority. However, fellow students can help the presenter reflect and encourage this aspect of learning through their feedback. They can be more Socratic and ask why the presenter did what she did and if she now thought it had been a good idea.

It's always useful to attend a work-in-progress seminar as a member of the audience if you're studying at a similar level.

Observing the kind of points academics raise can give you an insight into what, individually, they think is most important. Questions always tell you more about the questioner than the person questioned. One of them may be your potential examiner or supervisor at some point, so it's useful for you to know who is good at certain types of advice. For instance, one may feel that a research topic needs refining and suggest how to go about that; another may recommend some reading sources to the presenter.

If the subject is not of interest to you, concentrate on observing the methodology of the presentation, the methodology of what the presenter is reporting, and consider how far it makes sense to you. You can evaluate these procedures.

If the subject is of interest, then it's even more important to attend the work-in-progress seminar as you and the presenter may be able to help each other or share resources and you definitely need to know the parameters of the presenter's work so that you can make sure that yours is quite distinct. You may even be able to cite her work in your work – or vice versa. It's always good to be referenced.

From the feedback and discussion section at the end of the seminar you can pick up tips such as the preferences that particular external examiners have, who the best supervisors are and the best time and place to find them, and so on. You can also get a nose for what to avoid. It's always good to have your ears pricked.

Make sure that you check out the accuracy of any opinions or gossip with other sources. As long as you do this, these opinions can often set you off on new and interesting paths you may not have considered before.

Workshops and seminars are participatory. It may be quite difficult to escape participating in a workshop, and although it may be possible to do so in a seminar, if you've taken the trouble to attend and aren't a presenter, you may as well have your presence there remembered by making a positive contribution to the session. The smallest supportive comment, offer of help, illustration or example puts you on the map and makes your presence felt.

Chapter 7

Taking Notes During Lectures

- -

In This Chapter

▶ Examining your expectations

▶ Heeding handouts

▶ Exploring ways of note-taking

▶ Organising your ideas

- -

*T*he notes you take during lectures are for your personal use as a record of the lecture for future use and they should be in a form you find both convenient and efficient. You have to make sure that you record what you really need. Many people worry about missing something and record information they don't need while ignoring, for instance, the lecturer's evaluation of the evidence presented, which is likely to be valuable and not necessarily available elsewhere.

The person sitting nonchalantly through a talk, arms loosely folded across his chest, is often the one who asks the most devastatingly pertinent question without a note in sight! How does he manage to do this? He's almost certainly come prepared by considering what he already knows about the subject and what the title suggests. Even that knock-out question may have been prepared beforehand, all of which allows him to sit and watch as well as listen to the talk. Two senses are better than one! Asking questions helps to make you memorable in a positive way. Most people benefit from some memory support in the form of handouts or notes for longer-term reference. Lecturers are also often willing to allow recording equipment in their lectures, so if you have a particular need or preference for aural learning support, do check with the lecturer or school office for permission beforehand.

Matching Your Expectations Against Reality

Think of a lecture as a film. Most people going to the cinema or theatre have some idea of what they're about to see and hear. The words of the title conjure up certain expectations. The film or play may be based on a book they've read. The actors or director may be associated with a certain style or type of performance. Part of the experience is comparing expectations with what actually happens. Lectures are the same. Active learners identify what they already know then use that to guess or predict what will happen in class and so create a framework for new information.

Your predictions may be way off or quite accurate. It doesn't matter which. If the unexpected occurs, this can be a good prompt to find out why the prediction wasn't accurate. It may be because the title or description was unclear or misleading. It may be because the prediction was based on an earlier misunderstanding and this is an opportunity to clear that up. If the prediction was correct, it builds confidence as the foundation for the next step. It's a win-win situation and is what human beings have learned to do to survive, though students don't have to worry about whether the crocodile will get them before they've hauled in the fish they've just caught! Playing detective can help self-motivation through less-than-inspiring lecture-room experiences.

Preparing the Ground for Great Notes

Before each lecture (the night before if possible, so ideas are bubbling away while you sleep and do other things), look at lecture titles for a few minutes and note down – perhaps in your learning diary – what they suggest to you. This means calling to mind what you already know or think (you may be surprised at how much you do know). Form questions that you expect the class to answer. Use these to compare against the information you actually get and to question it and identify any gaps in knowledge or logic. The course programme, in addition to the topic of each lecture, gives some questions to consider, and may suggest readings or links to the general reading list in order to put the lecture in context. Even a few minutes looking at this can improve your general understanding of the overall programme and give you more confidence.

Identifying different types of lectures

The title of a lecture often suggests what type of lecture it will be. Lectures fall into three broad categories.

- ✔ **Introductory lectures:** Often give an overview or a history of a particular topic, highlighting the major debates 'in a nutshell' – a great help in avoiding masses of background reading, which isn't always productive.

- ✔ **Methodological lectures:** Focus on the debate against competing theories or methods in a particular area of study.

- ✔ **Sequential lectures:** Each lecture in a series considers a particular aspect to compare with the previous and following week's lectures. In this case it's very important you review previous lectures as well as preview the next in the series. This doesn't take a lot of time and can pay big dividends. Knowledge really is power.

Taking your place

Choose a good place to sit – where you can see and hear easily, near an exit if you feel claustrophobic, next to the best note-taker or the person who disagrees with you most – whatever makes you feel most comfortable or animated.

The early bird gets more choice about where to sit. Arrive in plenty of time for your lecture.

Handling handouts

Many lecturers provide paper handouts for use during lectures. These usually give the main sub-headings and references to the theory or books they're using, and the main arguments, so that you don't have to worry about noting these. However, you don't want to spend time reading a handout during the lecture, so it's good to get there a bit early and skim the handout to see what it tells you. If the handout has gaps between the headings, or printing is only on one side of the paper, you can add your own comments and ideas to these notes or 'star' points of interest. By adding your own comments you have the advantage of keeping the information – handout and notes – together in one place. Paper handouts mean less writing and more opportunities to watch as well as listen and be an active participant. You can note other people's reactions and learn from these as well.

If the speaker uses overhead transparencies and you think that you've missed something vital, you can ask to make a paper copy after the lecture or ask the lecturer if he can make the information available online.

Weighing Up Ways of Note-taking

The form that notes take is largely a matter of personal preference and convenience. Overcrowded lecture theatres may mean there's limited space and elbow room, making it difficult to take notes. In this sort of situation l ecturers often give out good handouts which may make extensive note-taking unnecessary, so you don't have to worry about having enough space to write. The advantage of this is that this frees you up to pay more attention to the lecturer. When you need to make extensive notes, two main options exist:

- Making notes on paper.
- Making notes on a laptop computer.

Whatever kind of notes you take, make sure to note on the top righthand side of the page, the following basic information:

- Date of lecture
- Title of lecture
- Who gave it
- The course number if it's part of a series
- The overall course title
- Any other identification that is useful to you. For example, you may want to colour code the lectures belonging to a particular series, or each lecture and its associated seminar, preparation and follow up notes in your learning diary.

Highlighter pens are also useful for highlighting important points, things to check up on or topics which cut across lectures from different lecturers. You can change the font colour on your computer to similar effect.

Highlighter pens (or changing the font colour) can be particularly useful when you read over your notes later. You may consider some points made earlier in the lecture more important and relevant than you originally thought. Using colours is also a useful memory aid.

Making notes on paper

The main advantage of paper notes is that you can make drawings or symbols. Writing notes also helps you to concentrate and engage fully with what the lecturer is saying – and stops you from falling asleep. Paper notes certainly help the brain create new memory associations and links.

Many people use their own personal shorthand, and the ones you use to text messages will work equally well for taking notes in class. It is also worth considering other signs or symbols that can save you time. Table 7-1 shows some examples.

Table 7-1	**Some Technical Symbols to Borrow**	
Symbol	*Meaning*	*Example*
+	And, in addition	Fish + chips
	Positive, a good thing	+ Interesting
=	Equal to or the same as	Time = money
≠	Not equal to, not the same as	Laugh with ≠ laugh at
<	Less than	EURO 1.00< £1.00
>	Greater than	£1.00 > $1.00
%	Percent, for each hundredth	90% wool, 10% nylon
~	Roughly, about	9ct gold is ~ 60% copper
→	Leads to, implies or suggests	Carelessness → accidents
←	Results from	Pneumonia ← virus
×	Multiplication, times	5× as expensive as
±	More or less, error margin	± 1 in 10 men are colour-blind
&	And	Tea & toast
@	At	Back @ 2.30
!	Surprising fact	Hitler was a vegetarian!
?	Question, debatable	Full employment ? economic decline?
#. No.	Number	#. 15 (++ for cross-referencing)
∴	Therefore	I think ∴ I am
∵	Because, because of	3 million died ∵ starvation

These are the most common symbols and if you create your own, this can add some fun and satisfaction to the art of note taking.

Making notes on a laptop

Some lecture theatres have plug-in points for laptops – find out before-hand by contacting the room bookings office or visiting the lecture theatre. Otherwise, if you intend to take notes on your laptop, make sure that you've charged up the batteries.

If you're a proficient touch typist, you may find that you can take notes and also watch what's going on. The problem is finding a framework for your notes. You may be able to add to online course notes. Decide how you want to organise your notes before going to the lecture. Frustration with technology can add to stress. The feeling of having missed something shifts your attention away from what's being said to coping with what's on your screen.

However, if you're comfortable with laptop note-taking one big advantage is that you can more easily incorporate your notes into other work, especially written work, later on. For example, you can refer to laptop notes quicker – as information, opinion or to argue with – than paper notes when word-processing. Remember to note the title, speaker and date, and you can also refer to any questions at the end of the lecture, as long as you acknowledge everything in your writing.

You can speed up your laptop note taking by using abbreviations. Many abbreviations in Table 7-2 will be familiar, but check you understand their meanings. For instance, 'i.e.' and 'e.g.', are often confused, so using these correctly in your notes will both save time and ensure you use them appropriately in your writing. The list is by no means exhaustive, and you can create other abbreviations to suit your purposes and the subjects you are studying.

Table 7-2:	Some common abbreviations	
i.e.	Id est, (Latin) that is	What I like best, i.e. chocolate
e.g.	Exempli gratia (Latin)	Water mammals, e.g. dolphin
Etc.	Et cetera (Latin) and so on, and other things	Poverty → poor health, housing, malnutrition etc.
ASAP	As soon as possible	Return library books ASAP.
C	Century	I was born in C20
c.	*Circa* (Latin): About	The first oil shocks were c. 1973
v.	*Versus* (Latin): As opposed to	Traditional v. herbal medicine

cf	*Confer* (Latin): Compare, consult, especially another author's work	cf Smith, (2007)
Re.	Regarding, about	I need to see you re. your essay
Q&A	Questions Answers	questions and answers
w/o	without	Tea w/o sugar
B4	Before	B4 WW2 (World War II)
P, pp	Page, pages	Read pp 39-53
Govt,	Government	The responsibility of local govt.
m/f	Male/female	Exam results for m&f were about the same

Organising Your Thoughts

No matter what method of note-taking you use, the basic way to organise your thoughts is to check what you expect to learn against the information you actually receive and add any unexpected information (see Figure 7-1). This 'unexpected' information may include the view of the lecturer. Measuring the change in your views or the accuracy of your predictions – probably a bit of both – is very important. These measurements outline your personal learning and growth.

The lecturer's job is to first to pass on factual information and then its interpretation according to the main theories. Near the end of the lecture, he's likely to give his own view after weighing up the arguments and evidence. If he's done his job well, you may be surprised by his view. The relatively short time that he spends evaluating the arguments and giving reasons for his view is very valuable as an example of evaluating ideas and presenting a rational opinion. You can obtain much of the factual matter of the lecture elsewhere, but not the rationale that the lecturer presents for his views. It's therefore particularly important to note his rationale down as an example of academic thinking. If you disagree or can't follow his thinking, this give you an excellent opportunity to ask a question – it doesn't have to be one you prepared beforehand.

The end of the lecture may leave you with more questions to ask. That's good. It indicates an active response and that your learning process is continuing. People who ask questions are always remembered as active learners, which is good for *you* when you need to ask for a reference later.

When and what to note

The most important thing to note from lectures may be the reasons the lecturer gives for his considered opinions. He's likely to give a small number of main reasons (three or four) with keywords, which probably involve comparisons. The lecture introduction outlines the main points (often, but not always, about three in number with some sub-points), which the lecturer expands, examines and justifies with examples. He then summarises his findings in the conclusion – including his opinion. Any handouts tend to include the main points (facts), any references to books or journals, and links to previous and following lectures, but not the lecturer's view in any clear way, so it's important to catch this. For the basic structure of lectures check out Chapter 5.

Find out from the school office if the lecturer gives class handouts and if not, whether there are class notes that you may be able to download. In the unlikely event that there are no notes of references or other support material and nothing available online, then a useful strategy is to note with a friend. One of you can be responsible for any references to source material – books and online references, for example – and the other for explanations and examples. You can leave gaps in your paper notes and fill then in later when you exchange information with your friend. If you are using laptop notes, you can easily insert new materal.

Overall, attending a live lecture gives you information through your eyes as well as ears and if your head is constantly down taking notes you can miss a lot of the action. The raised eyebrow, the smile, or even the little jokes that can act as markers and help you remember details, pass you by. Notes should be helpful and not a burden. Sometimes, noting a lot of detail in one area can mean missing something else, as writing up the notes can intrude into the next section of a talk.

At the end of each lecture, a good habit is for you to note down the interesting ideas and main concepts you remember without looking at your notes. This is good practice in summarising ideas and makes another memory marker for use later in revision or as a prompt to ask for clarification. Put these notes in your personal diary and compare them with the thoughts you had before the lecture.

Linear note-taking

Linear note-taking is the process of writing down information in the order in which you receive it. Paper is itself two-dimensional so linear notes follow the natural sequence of time: page 1, 2 and so on, beginning, middle and end. Time order and page numbering can help you check something quickly later, as your recall prompts are going to be in terms of time or sequence and position on the page. However, your brain is multi-dimensional, and the more links you can make to existing knowledge (by preparation, for example) and creating other links as you listen, the better you'll have captured knowledge and made it your own. This also gives you multiple access points to that knowledge, instead of just two – time and space.

Handouts rarely contain interesting anecdotes or examples, but they can be valuable as mnemonics, so a keyword or marker in your notes to remind you of an anecdote or example can be useful to help you recall the information or point with which it's associated.

If the lecturer doesn't give out handouts, he's likely to give the main points in the introduction of the lecture and then expand upon them with examples. If mind maps (see the section 'Non-linear note-taking' later in this chapter) are a step too far, you can note (or type) each main point from the introduction on a separate page and fill in the key points for each as the lecturer introduces them. Another way is to note down the key topics from the introduction and give each a number or letter to use later when they're discussed in more detail (see Figure 7-1). Doing so avoids repetition and saves time.

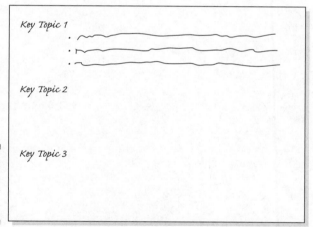

Figure 7-1:
Organising
your
information.

Non-linear note-taking

Non-linear note-taking involves using *mind maps* or *spidergrams* (shown in Figure 7-2) that start with notes in the middle of a page, usually in an oval representing the subject, and then spread out with 'legs' making links north, south, east and west. You don't organise such notes in time sequence but in terms of meaning, similarity or hierarchies of importance or association. They reflect the internal workings of your brain, rather than the external event, the lecture. Each time you get a new idea, your mind makes several links to your existing ideas, links that have not existed before. The more links you can make to existing knowledge (by preparing, for example) and then create as you listen, the better you will have captured knowledge and made it your own. This will also give you multiple access points to that knowledge, instead of just two – time and space. Occasionally, we make bad links, for instance, if we mishear something the lecturer said – Napoleon's mysteries or Napoleon's mistresses, say – but we are more likely to spot the problem and correct it if we use mind maps rather than linear notes.

In order to take non-linear notes or mind maps you have to use additional sheets of paper at the top, bottom and sides so the notes extend onto them giving a holistic overview, which is easier to understand. Notes produced in this way usually look nothing like the lecturer's overheads or paper handouts. They're the interpretation of the writer, truly representing his understanding of how what he's heard fits in with what he knows. He'll also recall the lecture well for future use because he's set up his own system of links and connections rather than using the time and space system of most lectures.

However, they can take up a lot of space and can sometimes work better as a group project after the lecture, when everyone can contribute their understanding of the main points, and areas that are not clear.

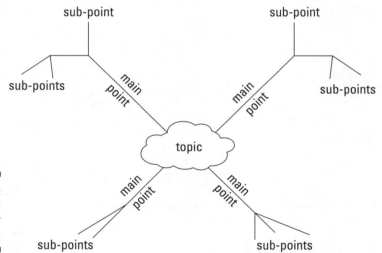

Figure 7-2:
A mind map, or spidergram.

Some lecturers encourage participation in class by using mind-map and brainstorming methods, usually with one person noting the ideas of a group – a great way to try them out. Such notes can take up a lot of horizontal space, so it helps to have small writing and be neat! If you see someone using mind-map note-taking techniques in a lecture try to sit near him and perhaps compare his notes with yours over a coffee and chat. You'll probably see he's noted down less than you and can give a summary of the lecture without much head scratching.

Notes aren't a substitute for learning! But if you make notes creatively, and try different ways of taking information down, you're more likely to find the method that best helps you to remember information when you need it later.

After the Lecture: Adapting and Reflecting on Your Notes

Lectures usually provide you with additional references to those in the general course notes, especially if someone has asked a particularly interesting question that's prompted the lecturer to provide a reference.

Your written work must relate to theories, hypotheses or issues discussed in the lecture or talk programme, so some of the references you've been given must be used in your writing. You need to build up a working bibliography with notes to help you later on.

Building a bibliography

Use an old-fashioned card index with author, date, title, place of publication and publisher on one side of each card, with any comments or links to other books. You can put quotations on the other side – most lecturers include important comments from key theorists. Card indexes are easy to shuffle into alphabetical order, easy to carry in the pocket to the library to search for or reserve books, and weigh a lot less than a laptop. It's particularly important to build a bibliography for topics that you're thinking of writing about.

Another advantage of making an index is that you have a quick reference from which you can see if there are other publications online by the same authors – more up-to-date journals for instance – or find their home pages and their current interests or even email addresses to ask them questions. Accurate references are a good way to check out the respectability of online publications.

If you are making laptop notes then keep references from a lecture series, associated seminars and your own research together in a folder appropriately labelled for you to find easily. You may want to record paper note references on your laptop or pc later on to prepare references for an essay or presentation. Word 2007 has a facility to help you create bibliographies. What you must do is ensure that you have correctly recorded the information you need to refer to another author's work within your written work or presentation and give a full reference in the bibliography. This is so that anyone has the information necessary to find the same information as you.

Whatever system you use (and your student notes will guide you on this) you need to record the following information, though the order or presentation may be a little different from the order given here (known as the Harvard system).

- ✔ Family name of the author
- ✔ Initial of the author's given name
- ✔ Date of publication
- ✔ Title of book
- ✔ Place of publication
- ✔ Name of publisher

You then need to produce the whole bibliography in alphabetical order, as in this example:

> Black, R. and Koser, K. (1999) *The End of Refugee Cycle? Refugee Repatriation and Reconstruction*, New York and Oxford, Berghahn Books
>
> Bohner, G. & Wanke, M. (2002) *Attitudes and Attitude Change*, Hove: Psychology Press
>
> Boyden, J. & Ryder, P. (1996), 'Implementing the Right to Education in Areas of Armed Conflict,' `meltingpot.fortunecity.com/ lebanon/254/boyden.htm`, accessed 27/09/08
>
> Boyden, J. (1994), Children's Experience of Conflict Related Emergencies: some implications for relief policy and practice, *Disasters*, Vol. 18, No. 3, p. 254-267

The first two references are for books with joint authors. The author that comes first is the same as on the book. The third reference is to a web address: Note that the date of access to the website must be given at the end of the reference.

The last reference is to a journal, so the volume number and edition number are given to identify the specific journal, while the page references as there are several articles in the journal. Articles in journals are identified by italics, while the titles of books or the names of journals are normally underlined.

If an edition number exists in a book you are using, you should also note that. It is very frustrating – not to say time-consuming – if you have forgotten to note down one of the details of the book and have to try to find it again.

This is an area where accuracy is very important. The *Honesty Principle* of communication states that you must say where you got something from and give a complete and accurate reference. Apart from that, it you don't record things carefully, then when you remember in year three something from year one that could be useful, but you haven't recorded enough information to find it again, you'll kick yourself! It's basically the practical thing to do.

Notes from lectures and any associated references can have various purposes outside the timeframe of the lecture. They can help you prepare for an essay or presentation or an exam question based on some lectures. A course in year two may be a follow-on from a year one course. Thinking ahead can help you adapt your notes and how you organise them to your needs, save you time, make your written work more pertinent and interesting and make you less likely to fall victim to problems like plagiarism.

Following up on lecture notes

Another safety net, apart from the possible availability of downloadable notes or lecture handouts, is to get a perspective different from your own. Discuss lectures afterwards with classmates. You should never worry about admitting something wasn't clear – you won't be the only one – and asking someone else to explain helps that person clarify his own ideas and realise explicitly if he has gaps in his own notes or understanding, something he may not have otherwise realised. Note swaps are more interesting than re-reading your own notes as they offer a different 'take' on the subject. Other people's interpretations and techniques can help build up your own store of internal references and encourage you to discuss or think about these differences. It's all about making comparisons and reflecting!

If you are making laptop notes then keep references from a lecture series, associated seminars and your own research together in a folder appropriately labelled for you to find easily. You may want to record paper note references on your laptop or pc later on to prepare references for an essay or presentation. Word 2007 has a facility to help you create bibliographies. What you must do is ensure that you have correctly recorded the information you need to refer to another author's work within your written work or presentation and give a full reference in the bibliography. This is so that anyone has the information necessary to find the same information as you.

Chapter 8

Making Use of Feedback

In This Chapter

▶ Understanding formal feedback

▶ Wising up on the marking system

▶ Getting early feedback

▶ Taking note of what tutors say, want and think

*F*eedback is any response to your work or ideas from another person. Formal feedback includes the marks for your assignments or your exams marks. Discussion and constructive feedback are crucial parts of studying. Think of any study activity as communication, part of a dialogue with an audience. The process of discussing your work and receiving feedback on it helps you check your own understanding as well as the message you've communicated to others.

Finding Out About the Formal Feedback System

Formal feedback includes the marks for your assignments and your exams marks. Some marks are part of your degree classification, so they help you check your progress. How much information you get back apart from a mark depends on your subject or tutor. Some tutors give back exam papers and go over exams so that you can see what you did well and where you went wrong. This is usually in subjects where the next topic is based on the previous one, so that a certain level of understanding is required to continue the course. If you have to resit an exam, you can ask to see your exam script again and ask for comments and suggestions for improvement. The resit exam will cover the same material, but will not be the same exam, so make sure you cover the material. (Chapter 18 deals with exams.)

Knowing what you get feedback on

Some coursework will count towards your degree each year. Most year three undergraduates will have to produce an extended research essay or dissertation or write a report of their own experimental work or similar project, where they have some choice of topic as do postgraduates. Formal feedback and assessment with comments comes after work has been submitted, but feedback during the process of preparing and planning your work is much more useful. Your subject tutor or supervising tutor should comment and advise on your work-in-progress, but you can get feedback and suggestions from your friends and classmates less formally through discussion.

Undergraduates as well as postgraduates can choose a topic for major projects from those studied during the year or term. However, the title has to be agreed to by your tutor. Take their advice very seriously if they suggest you change it. If you don't, and it all goes horribly wrong, they won't be very sympathetic, especially if they are the marker. If you are very committed, and in extreme circumstances, you may be able get a second opinion or help from another tutor.

The process may take some time so you may have already started on your next piece of work by the time you receive feedback, so be unable to benefit from it immediately. This is another reason why it's important to get early feedback and find out about the formal system.

Feedback can be very brief or quite lengthy, depending on the practice where you're studying. Sometimes feedback is given under a number of formal headings such as:

✔ **Subject treatment:** Is it accurate? Have you shown you understand it? Have you chosen the right books or passages to quote?

✔ **Logic and argument:** Is the question, argument or issue raised answered in a logical way, with reference to data or examples?

✔ **Layout/structure:** Are all the important parts there? Is the layout and structure clear and has the organisation been stated in the introduction? Are the pages and sections numbered and the paragraphs well-structured?

✔ **Language and style:** Is the language formal and impersonal and free of bias? Is the style and punctuation clear? Is the grammar accurate?

This can be very useful for showing you your strong points and what may be letting you down. If two markers mark your work, then each writes separate feedback, which gives you the benefit of two sets of feedback and two opinions. Sometimes, feedback is only a few words or a sentence or two and is a general impression, which isn't so helpful.

Ask the college office or tutor for an example feedback sheet if there isn't one in your student pack. If the headings are similar to those listed above, they tell you what to focus on, as these are the points the markers consider when they assess work. If you're not given an itemised feedback sheet or guidelines for understanding feedback comments, then it may be useful ask your tutor if it's possible to have some, especially if they're used in other subject areas in your institution. Feedback headings or guidelines are useful for markers as well as students and allow comparison between different pieces of work at different times at a detailed level to show progress (or not), so most tutors welcome them as a useful tool. Ask your fellow students and Student Union or group representatives to support the idea.

Sometimes a first piece of coursework isn't graded but is commented upon. Where no feedback comment sheet with headings exists, this is an excellent time to suggest introducing one to give tutors practice in using them. Students can also give feedback on the helpfulness of the headings. If you can get an example from friends in another subject area, this really helps make the point.

Understanding the marking system and minimum requirements

Check your course information or find out from the departmental office what symbols the college uses to grade assessed work. You need to know:

- ✔ What your grade means, (whether it's high or low).
- ✔ How the scale works.
- ✔ What the minimum pass level for coursework is.

For example, if the scale is A to E and A is the best mark and E is a failure, then the pass level is usually around C or C–. However, it may be that over the whole of your course more than one E, or an E and D, or two Ds count as failing the whole course – or that no more than one C– is acceptable. You need to know. The same goes for numerical scales. You also need to know how many pieces of assessed work go towards calculating your chances of making good. For example, if four pieces of assessed work are required, and you already have two D grades, then two C+ grades are the minimum necessary to make a borderline pass in most courses. If you're given a low grade you may have to work really hard to improve your other grades by enough to get you through, so again, early feedback is important at the outset to help avoid such difficulties.

Bouncing back from a low grade

If you get a low grade you need to know what it means and what your situation is. Many subject areas don't have tutor meetings to discuss students' performances until late in the second academic term, so may not pick up problems before then. Getting detailed feedback a short time after submitting work or being assessed in class or the laboratory is very helpful whereas delayed feedback is not. It's important that you make an appointment with your tutor to discuss your best plan of action and how she can help you. You get 'brownie points' for being proactive (though not aggressive) and by taking the initiative can certainly help yourself.

Being given a low mark is a wonderful opportunity to show how much better you can do next time. Tutors are interested in individual progress and effort. Get them onside and they'll support you in helping you focus on what you need to do to achieve better marks. The academic process is a dialogue and you're a very important participant.

Getting Early Feedback on Coursework

In most instances, your tutors need to formally approve the topic and outline plan for written work, research or presentations, or you can ask them to comment on your early outline plans. The same goes for projects or lab. experiments. If you are not sure what you are meant to do, ask. With luck, you will have a friendly lab assistant as well who's seen it all before and can help you out before the fruit flies escape.

Give tutors something concrete to comment on to get the most out of them. They don't usually respond well, if at all, to 'What shall I do?' or 'I don't know what to do'. If you put your ideas and plans down on paper or by email (assuming you're allowed to contact tutors by email) no matter how simple they seem, then they have some idea of what you're trying to achieve and also they have time to reflect on what you've written before commenting on it face-to-face or by email.

Most tutors are pleased to be involved in the early planning stages of your work – even if they don't have to be – because it makes life easier for them too. Giving early feedback helps avoid problems later and provides some individual guidance and support to students. Your plans provide feedback to them insofar as they can detect from them your responses to certain aspects of the course or their teaching and see what needs more clarification. In other words, plans and feedback are integral to academic dialogue.

Getting early feedback is important. Avoid wasting time on topics that are too broad for you to cover adequately in the time and space allotted or too vague and unfocused or even irrelevant to the core issue you need to consider. Your own work – written or presentation or experimental – needs to relate to the coursework for the same term or year, particularly the theoretical aspects. Tutors' comments can help you make those links more clearly and in addition, they often suggest reading references to help you.

Discuss your plans with fellow students or course mentors if you have them. Sometimes housemates studying a different subject can be even more useful as they're the 'intelligent non-specialists' in your subject and can give you feedback about the coherence or logic of your plans – whether they 'make sense' to them, what you need to make clearer or explain in more depth and what you can assume is 'common knowledge' and doesn't need expansion. 'Common knowledge' can be difficult to pin down, but concepts like 'university', 'hospital', 'supermarket', 'film' or other aspects of daily life can usually be assumed and don't need explanation.

Acronyms such as GDP (Gross Domestic Product) are commonly used by economists for example, but if you're an economics student, it's important to show you:

- ✔ Understand what the acronym stands for, so put the full form in brackets the first time you use it (as shown above).

- ✔ Know what it means – this is where feedback from a fellow student can help by asking you to explain or define what something means.

Early feedback helps you:

- ✔ Focus on the topic, what is relevant, and what you need to find out.

- ✔ Consider the organisation, framework and logical links of your work.

- ✔ Make adjustments to your work and keep on track.

- ✔ Avoid last minute panics.

- ✔ Practise taking criticism informally and using it constructively.

After the Event – What Tutors Say and What They Mean

Your tutor's feedback on your coursework may be in the form of a comment sheet with sub-headings. If you have any queries, it's easy to ask your tutor for clarification as you have a specific point to refer to. If her comments are general or an overall response to your work, it can be difficult to pinpoint what changes you need to make. If the comment suggests you need to do more of something, this is another situation where a learning diary is useful, because you can refer back to your preparation, what you did, and have a fair idea of how long you spent doing particular things. This can be an important negotiating point between you and your tutor, as her comments may not identify an underlying problem if she's made certain assumptions. If you do need to discuss your feedback in depth it may help you to consider it within the framework below – to help you and your tutor pinpoint more clearly how to resolve any problems.

Table 8-1 shows a few common comments from tutors and tips on how to tackle problems. Many of the examples are relevant to presentations as well as written work or essay-type exam questions.

Table 8-1	Typical Feedback – and How to Respond
Subject treatment comments	*What you should do*
You haven't stated the problem or theory you're investigating, (problem with clarity)	Be direct, explicit and specific, especially in the introduction. Say what you're going to do and do it. Write the introduction last and make sure that it refers to what you actually wrote. Consider adding a sub-heading to your title to make the focus clear. For example, to the original title 'The relationship between poverty and school dropout rates in Ghana' add ': a study of Year 3 children in two rural and two urban primary schools between 2002 and 2006' specifying time and place to narrow the focus and set up a comparison between rural and urban to provide material for analysis and suggest the information you need to find
You've used up too much space for description and background information, (problem with balance)	Calculate the number of words (or time in a presentation) available for each section and make sure that the balance between the parts – background description, theoretical discussion, analysis and evaluation and so on. is reasonable. Analysis and comment make your work individual and are where you get your marks. The rest is there to support them. A collection of detailed factual information may be too general, not focused enough and not have enough input from you. You need to demonstrate your voice

Subject treatment comments	What you should do
Your information is inaccurate, (problem with honesty)	Cross-check information from two or more sources to make sure that it's accurate, including information from two or more sets of lecture notes. State where you got your information so that your audience can find the same information from the same sources. Don't rely on your memory. Give (surname and date) in the text or on the OHP transparency and so on, and a full reference – surname, initial (date) title, place of publication, publisher, or as appropriate, in the bibliography/reference section
Most of the information is irrelevant to the argument. You don't answer the question, (problem with relevance)	Always devise a set of research questions to answer in your work. For instance, for 1. (above) : ✔ What percentage of children enrolled in each school drop out by Year 3? ✔ What is the average income/work of parents in rural and urban schools respectively – who are considered poor (definition needed) ? ✔ Does parental income/work correlate with drop-out rates? ✔ Is there any difference between boys' and girls' dropout rates? and so on. The research questions guide the information you need to find
Logic/Argument comments	
Your treatment of the subject is superficial	Make sure that you understand and demonstrate that you understand the main issues involved. This means referring to theory and reading material, and probably lectures to support your ideas. Develop research questions and give definitions for key ideas/theories that you use
You give little or no evidence to support your argument	You may know about the appropriate evidence but if you don't demonstrate what you know and your understanding of it, then you won't get credit for it. Argument without reference to evidence has little value. Your own experiences are part of your development but no substitute for evidence. Make sure that you provide evidence in support of your ideas and give sources

(continued)

Table 8-1 *(continued)*

Subject treatment comments	What you should do
Your argument is emotional rather than factual	Use your emotions to choose a topic to be passionate about and then create a hypothesis/research questions and look for evidence – or lack of it – and ask why. Your ideas have to be rooted in fact, theory or logical hypothesis
You make emotional rather than factual comments	Avoid applying 'value' terms like 'the government's action was *unforgivable'* or 'the government acted in an *unacceptable* or *ridiculous* way' when making comments as these adjectives are emotive.
	'African members of the Anglican communion said they found the ordination of gay priests unacceptable.' (*Times*, 16/6/08) is a factual quotation, not your comment, so there's no problem with using *unacceptable* here.
	Logical comments based on fact and may be used to infer other information, for example:
	The National lottery claims that 1/3 of prizes are won by consortiums and encourages people to group together to increase their chances of winning. However, 2/3 of prizes are won by individuals, so further information is needed, like the average size of a group and prize won and so on, to calculate the best odds
It isn't clear whether concepts are personal or part of a theory	Make sure that you give references for theoretical ideas. Put theoretical discussion in a different paragraph (or section) from personal comment, so that it's clear which is which. Beware of plagiarism (honesty problem) by accident and always give your sources
This is collection of sentences with no clear purpose	You have to provide a framework for your work and links between sentences and sections so that your reader or listener knows why you're giving certain information and for what overall purpose. Your sentences may come from your notes but need to be ordered, structured and linked to some purpose
You don't define the concepts you use in your work	Definitions of a concept vary according to different theoretical perspectives. Define which one you're using and why, and relate this to your argument to demonstrate your understanding. Dictionary definitions can be helpful benchmarks to compare with other definitions

Subject treatment comments	*What you should do*
The methodology is not explained well, nor are the results clear	As well as what you're doing, you need to say how you're doing it, using what methods and why. You may use several methodologies, like a literature search, interview, questionnaire, observation, experiment and so on. If the methodology and research questions aren't clearly stated, the results or what they mean won't make much sense to you or your reader/audience
Layout/structure comments	
Your structure obscures the meaning	Make sure that your sentences don't ramble and that you change paragraphs when you change topics. Use sub-topic headings to show the reader/audience what to expect in each section. Don't make paragraphs too short (one sentence) or too long (more than a page). The average length is about 2.5 to a page with 1.5 spacing
It was difficult to put your paper together again after I dropped it	Make sure that you secure your work firmly and don't forget to add page numbers. Don't put your marker in a bad mood by causing her extra work
I don't know where you got your tables from	If you created the tables yourself, say from where you got the information (*source author, based on . . .*). If you're using someone else's tables, refer to the source, (honesty problem, beware of plagiarism)
You've put description, analysis and comment all under one heading	Separate out these areas to make it clear which is which and distinguish analyses and comments from other authors (by using correct citation references) from your comments, which should come last. For example: 'From the evidence discussed, it seems likely that . . .'
Language and style comments	
Your style is not appropriate to academic written work	Academic writing style is formal rather than familiar. Words like *don't* aren't normally abbreviated. Sentences should be direct and technical terms used where appropriate. Presentations are less formal and more familiar forms can be used

(continued)

Table 8-1 *(continued)*

Subject treatment comments	What you should do
Your punctuation is non-existent	Punctuation is a form of road map to show meaning. Use the spell check to help with punctuation as well as spelling. It doesn't spot all problems so ask a classmate to read through your work as another check
The language you use is too strong for the evidence	*Must* and *is* imply strong claims. It's safer to use forms like *suggest, may, might/could, possibly, probably, likely* and so on. For instance: 'The evidence from the survey *suggests* girls are *more likely* to drop out than boys as they have domestic tasks in the home.' Your reader/audience is less likely to challenge this than 'The evidence *shows . . .*'
You've made too many spelling errors	Use the spell check. Either British or American English is acceptable, but avoid a mixture of both, especially on the same page. For instance, British English distinguishes between *program (as in computer program)* and *programme (as in TV programme)*, whereas American English has only one form for both, *program*. If you use both *program* and *programme* to refer to a series of planned events, this confuses the reader. Keep a checklist of words you know cause you difficulty
You use any old word to refer to academic views	*Claim, state, imply, mention, indicate* and so on aren't interchangeable and have different meanings. The most common and least controversial reporting verbs are *say* and *suggest*. When in doubt, use these

Tutors can be very good at telling you what's wrong but not so good at telling you how to improve matters. Overall, clear layout makes a good visual impression and makes it more likely that your work will be warmly received, so give yourself the best possible chance by paying attention to these areas:

- ✔ **Paragraphing:** Each paragraph should have a topic sentence to tell the reader what the paragraph is about (see Chapter 10) and each paragraph should have one main subject.

- ✔ **Section headings:** Show the reader what the sections are about. If you are not allowed to use section headings for some reason, then it is even more important that the first sentences of each paragraph shows what the topic is.

- ✔ **Page numbering:** Make sure the page numbering is accurate and clear.

- ✔ **Correct referencing:** Ensure the references are clear, complete, and follow a consistent pattern. See Chapter 7 for more on referencing.

Putting yourself in your tutor's shoes

You may be able to get hold of sample essays from previous years of your course from the college office or the Student Union, or by asking friends in the year above you. Grades aren't normally written on the scripts but any sample written work passed on by the school office or Student Union normally have a good pass or better grade. If you can get three or four or more, rank them in order (best, next best and so on) and ask some fellow students to do the same to see if you agree. You can discuss why you thought one was better than another and so on. It may be that you and your colleagues use different criteria, but it's useful to discuss your views of what a good piece of writing is in the context of your studies and which you'd prefer to read if you were the tutor, and why.

Analysing, assessing and evaluating others' work are key skills for any student and you can learn and practise a lot of skills in this way in a very short space of time.

Understanding how tutors think

Some subjects are assessed through worksheets which lay down certain procedures to follow. The tutor mainly checks the accuracy of readings or calculations put in boxes. Most subjects, however, require at least one piece of assessed extended writing to ensure that all students have experience of writing – as part of their all round education and before they enter the world of work.

Imagine marking 20 or 30 (and it can be more) essays on the same topic. What do tutors look for and what do they do first? There's a common procedure, which goes something like this:

- ✔ **Assessing the length:** The tutor jiggles the script in her hand to get an idea of its weight and hence length – too long, too short (there are penalties for both) or about right. She makes a hypothesis before checking the last page number. The essay's possible mark range may already be decided!

- ✔ **Checking the conclusion:** She reads the conclusion to find out what observations, suggestions for the future or conclusions the writer has come to and what she has learned from doing the research and writing. If this is missing, the slope gets more slippery, unless it's a maths essay, where no conclusion is required.

- ✔ **Matching the conclusion to the title:** The tutor checks that the conclusion refers back to the title and the introduction, which she then reads. She checks to see if the writer has given instructions on how to read the work, that is, has the writer made the organisation of the parts clear as well as the main question or questions she's discussing.

✔ **Skim reading:** The tutor skims through the work (or looks at the contents page, if there is one) to look at any section headings, tables or diagrams to get an idea of the balance of the work – background, theory, specific case/experiment, results, tables and so on, and analysis. Without reading anything more she now has a good idea of the potential mark and whether or not the work is balanced.

✔ **Detailed reading:** She then reads in detail to firm up her impressions. She notes whether references to the appropriate authority have been made through the citations in the text and whether they're linked to the lecture programme. She checks for errors in understanding or claims that are too strong or lack evidence or logic.

✔ **Checking content against section titles:** She re-checks by referring back to section titles after reading sections to see if they fit and to the introduction to see if the actual structure is the one promised in the introduction.

✔ **Detailed checking:** Finally, she checks that the references in the text have been expanded in the bibliography or reference section, that the appropriate system is used (depending on the subject) and that references to web pages and journals are appropriate, or at least give enough information for her to locate them. She then allocates a mark and/or a rank position, which are possibly provisional.

Although the ideal may be that nothing should be judged by appearances, it's clear that this isn't the case. The most brilliant ideas can be lost if paragraphing is poor, or if they're placed in an inappropriate part that means they're hidden and can't be recognised without the expected layout/structure prompts. Although there are some cultural differences between subjects, these expectations provide a framework or set of boxes to fill, and what sort of things they can be filled with. This, then helps frame the questions you pose, your research and where you look for answers, and the final product – your writing.

Making feedback a two-way process

Communicating academic requirements and the clarification you need is a two-way process. Don't assume everyone understands and you don't. If you don't give your feedback to tutors, they remain unaware of your needs and make false assumptions about your learning. Learning takes place by asking questions, so ask for and use feedback and see it as a positive support and tool for you to use.

Part III
Gathering Your Evidence

'I've come to collect the books I orderd the other day.'

In this part . . .

One of the biggest challenges to any new student comes from the amount of research you have to do. You're in charge of your own learning now, and this part equips you to take on all the resources out there.

Here I cover the range of research methods and tools at your disposal. Reading and taking notes skilfully, using the Internet with discrimination and handling and illustrating data efficiently – it's all here.

Chapter 9

Research Methods and Tools

In This Chapter

▶ Putting together hypotheses and theoretical frameworks

▶ Devising your research method

▶ Exploring data sources and access

▶ Understanding research tools and methods

▶ Avoiding pitfalls

Studying is not just about being told things, but about finding things out for yourself, and putting two and two together in new ways. It's a creative process. When you go to the library to find answers to a problem or confirmation for an idea, you are doing research, and if you compare two or more things which haven't been compared before, you are being creative and developing new ideas. This chapter looks at the whole process of research, from developing a hypothesis through to anticipating and avoiding problems.

Generally speaking, you're not going to compare chalk and cheese but things which have a good deal in common, so you are likely to find small differences between them when you embark on your research, but these can have large effects, especially when combined with other research. Equally, you may find new things to say about data that already exists. If you take care of the pennies – the little things in research – the pounds, the big things, take care of themselves.

The hallmark of good *empirical research* (research about real life events) is that it can be repeated under similar conditions but perhaps in a different place and by a different researcher, but obtaining similar results.

Developing Hypotheses

A *hypothesis* is basically a statement – or sometimes a question– to which you can only answer 'Yes' or 'No'. Hypotheses need to be tested, which means finding evidence to support or dispute them.

For example, once scientists knew that both animals and plants stored their genetic information in the nucleus of cells, they created a general hypothesis that they could add genetic animal material to plants. This hypothesis was confirmed when they successfully added certain fish genes to strawberries. This also improved the fruit's ability to resist frost. (Apparently, the fish genes allow the strawberries to produce a kind of antifreeze). Whatever your view of genetic engineering, this is a highly imaginative way of putting two things together and creating strawberries with attitude.

In this case the hypothesis was:

> The addition of the fish gene to the strawberry DNA allows the strawberry to resist frost.

This hypothesis had in turn developed from earlier hypotheses, namely:

> It is possible to add genetic material from animals to the nucleus of plant cells.

> Adding animal DNA to plant cells can improve the performance of plants.

In order to test this hypothesis, scientists grew strawberries containing fish DNA and subjected them to frost to see what happened to them, probably over time and in several different places. More detailed issues include defining more precisely the temperature parameters (exactly how many degrees below zero), as frost is anything below the freezing point of water, and over how many consecutive days of frost. In other words, following the hypothesis come questions like 'How much frost?' and 'Over how many days?'

Even when evidence exists in support of a hypothesis, certain conditions usually need to be fulfilled or certain circumstances have to be in place or *fixed* so that you can be sure that the results are not due to some effect other than what you are researching. Equally, if the experiment was unsuccessful, then research to discover why is just as important, because you don't want to throw the baby out with the bathwater, but use what you learned to make a better or different experiment by knowing what to avoid next time – even if the original idea seems a bit crazy. One way of looking at research is as a series of hypotheses to test, with the outcome of each framing the next, together with the related questions about the circumstances and conditions.

Devising a Theoretical Framework

Once you have a hypothesis in place (something that is either true or not true, which you aim to demonstrate) you need to think about the theoretical *framework* you need to use in order to find out whether you hypothesis is correct. The theoretical framework first considers what the problem is and then what the feasible solutions for solving it are. If you're a plant geneticist interested in producing frost resistant tomatoes, you may use the strawberry theoretical framework and apply it to a similar experiment with tomatoes. In general terms, the theoretical framework is based on previous research; previous knowledge is used as the basis for creating new knowledge and each researcher adds her own twist or interpretation. This is similar to the way clothes designers use fashions from an earlier era, but add their own special something to create a new style.

Choosing a theoretical framework

Which theoretical framework you use depends on where you're coming from – your subject of study. In the social sciences, a pool of theoretical insights often exists that can be used in many areas. For instance, research in development studies may borrow a framework used in education. As well as the general theoretical framework, you can also use an additional analytical framework to discuss the results of your research.

The *analytical framework* is how you decide to present your findings to help you interpret your results. It could be a statistical framework, where you convert you data into a table, graph or diagram so that you can see links and connections between your results that would be hidden in a purely verbal account, and thus analyse and interpret them to your reader in the light of your original hypothesis or questions. Another way of thinking about the analytical framework is as a tool to help you make a summary and put all you results in one place so the reader can see them as pure data or information,. She can then see very clearly the basis for your analytical comments and data interpretation which follow.

Similarly, a particular topic may be of interest to several disciplines from different perspectives. An agricultural student may be interested in the eating quality of the frost-resistant strawberry – its taste, texture, size and the response to it from the strawberry-buying public in comparison with more conventional varieties. An economist may be interested in the effects of the frost-resistant strawberry on the consumption of other strawberries, the price of strawberries in general and on the livelihoods of farmers in Central Africa who export their strawberries to the UK.

Relating framework to hypothesis

Your hypothesis and theoretical framework are in a chicken and egg situation. Either can come first as your initial idea for your work. You might, for instance, be intrigued by a theoretical framework you learned about in class and would like to apply it to a different situation, as in the example of applying the strawberry framework to tomatoes. Usually, you're expected to use the core or main theories you've studied in class and apply these in term exercises to a hypothesis or questions that you create in order to have practice in using and understanding a particular theory, including when it fails to adequately explain events. For important essays and dissertations or theses, you're free to choose your own theoretical framework. You can start with the theory and consider what particular context to apply it to, or you can start with a hypothesis and then look for the theory. In many ways, starting with the theory makes life easier.

If you start with the idea, hypothesis or question, then discuss the theoretical framework with your tutor early on, to make sure it fits. She'll also advise you whether to tweak the question you seek to answer in your essay slightly to fit better with the theory or she may suggest alternative or additional theories as well as research frameworks. This can save a lot of time, effort and grief later on.

Always ask yourself what the problem is (what you want to find out) and what feasible ways exist for solving it or finding an answer.

Got a theory, dearie?

All subjects have 'classical' theories, which are then challenged by other, newer, competing theories. Academics often fall into schools or camps supporting one theory or another. Sometimes older 'classical' theories can be added to or modified to offer a better explanation of events – and better guidelines for achieving certain aims than newer, more radical theories, so there is often some recycling of ideas. Other theories are unlikely to resurface (we hope), like the Victorian theory that women are only capable of lower order thinking so should not be educated as this causes them too much stress. The evidence for this theory is that women have smaller brains compared to men, which is generally true. The hypothesis, which seems to have got left out of the argument, was that brain size is related to intelligence, so no one tested it. The scientists of the day just assumed a smaller brain meant lower intelligence. Wrong!

Choosing Your Research Method

Research is usually broadly divided into two types, *qualitative* and *quantitative*. In practice, a lot of research projects combine both. Table 9-1 shows key comparisons between the two methods.

Table 9-1	Comparison between Qualitative and Quantitative Research Methods	
	Qualitative research	*Quantitative research*
Interests	Human behaviour – why+ how decisions are made, problem-solving	What, when, where things happen
Methods	Case study, recorded interview, participant observation, focus groups, action research – triangulation of information where possible	Scientific method, empirical data collection, control of experiment, manipulation of variables
Objects of study	Targeted/selected groups	Random samples
Role of researcher	Central to the research – has to examine own motives/bias and so on	Objective, stands back from research
Data analysis	Looks for categories and patterns	Measurement using mathematical models, standardisation
Results	Not generalisable	Aims for statistical significance and generalisability
Outcomes and Evaluation	Hopes to find insights for further work – can possibly lead to more quantitative research later	Empirical evidence, for example, find main causes of traffic accidents, or assess public opinion, (online questionnaires) as the basis for law or policy-making and so on

Qualitative research

Qualitative research is used in many disciplines, especially the social sciences, and studies human behaviour in areas like decision-making. It focuses on detailed investigations of particular groups through case studies, observer participation, interviews with individuals and focus groups. For example, a class teacher may study her students in the context of her teaching. She may ask them to debate a certain issue – the amount of homework they should have at weekends – as a focus group, and report back to her. She may ask the same question of their parents and other teachers as part of a questionnaire. (If she reports the number of answers to the questionnaire, the percentage of parents and teachers in favour of increasing weekend homework, this aspect of her research would be quantitative.) Because of the small numbers being studied, the qualitative researcher tries to use several methods, perhaps three or more, to find out the same information – for example, interview, observation and questionnaire – to lend some weight to the results and make them more reliable. This form of checking is called *triangulation*.

The researcher must be rigorous in reporting information from those she studies and note any possible bias or influences on herself that may affect her research. She must also formally ask the permission of those she studies and protect their identity by reporting their remarks anonymously. This requirement is practical as many people would be too afraid of losing their jobs or of being ill-treated, to talk to researchers. The analysis of qualitative data can be particularly difficult, involving the search for key words or ideas in interview or discussion recordings, which are natural and spontaneous, as the researcher does her best not to interfere or ask leading questions.

Quantitative research

The advent of telephones, computers and mobiles has greatly increased the range of possibilities for quantitative data collection. Everyone can participate and vote for their favourite pair on *Strictly Come Dancing*. Quantitative data, once stored, can be compared over a number of years – voting patterns – for example. Data on bird flu from various parts of the world can be mapped, as can weather patterns, and both are used to predict future patterns. The researcher defines very specifically the data to be collected and the method, but can leave the actual collection to others or even select from within data that's already stored. The power of quantitative data is in the numbers involved and their statistical significance. Care needs to be taken though, to compare like with like. It's perhaps preferable to see these methods as part of a continuum, rather than as different ends of a spectrum. Pilot (first- try or preliminary) studies often use qualitative research methods in preparation for larger quantitative research later on.

An alternative research method is to look again at someone else's data and reassess it. This can save you time, because you already have the data, and you might be able to rescue earlier work by showing, for example, that the data collection methods and results were fine, but the interpretation of the data was inadequate.

A new student looked at the results from equipment which a research team hoped would diagnose early signs of deficient sight, but which seemed to fail to do so. A link exists between diabetes and blindness (diabetic retinopathy) and early diagnosis means a patient's sight can be preserved. The new student researcher found a different way of interpreting and analysing the data and found that the equipment was indeed making the predictions required of it, but in a slightly different way and performing at a much higher level of accuracy than anyone had anticipated. The evidence was there but had been not seen. The project was thus rescued and the student showed that the earlier work was not wasted, the design of the equipment was highly efficient and further research should continue along the same lines.

Longitudinal studies

Longitudinal studies are when a researcher observes the same things at different times over a long period. For instance, biologists can observe and record variations in the wing patterns of generations of fruit flies bred in laboratories. These creatures produce new adults every two weeks, so the most appropriate method for studying their genetic inheritance is a selective breeding programme and two weekly observations of the new adults.

Longitudinal studies are also used a lot in psychology to monitor the progress of patients, or in schools, to monitor children's development and behaviour over at least a year in most cases.

Sampling 7up

Perhaps the most famous longitudinal study is the *7up project*, started in 1964. 14 children from different social backgrounds were filmed as a study of British society. The project was commissioned by Granada television for their *World in Action* series and the rationale was the Jesuit idea *Give me a child until he is seven and I will give you the man*. Although originally a 'one-off', the project was extended and filming (directed by Michael Apted) has taken place every seven years since. The last film was in 2005, *49up*. Although two of the original 14 dropped out in their twenties, the very different lives of the remaining children – some suffering from alcoholism and obesity – link back to their situations in the earlier films with each successive new film.

With longitudinal studies, you're in for the long haul, so you need to set up the experiment very carefully and try to predict any possible problems. In the *7up* case mentioned in the nearby sidebar, the programme makers were very lucky to lose only two participants. Long-term, people-based projects risk dropouts, so you need to involve more people than you think you need.

If, however, you're doing laboratory based experimental observations, you're likely to have strong computer technology support, and a much clearer routine.

Delving into Data Sources and Access

Computer technology means you have access to huge resources – you can even access them through your mobile on the bus going home. If you're doing higher degree research, you're duty bound to keep up to date with everything in your niche area. Everyone uses the Internet to access at least secondary data or background information during their studies.

It is a close-run thing at the moment whether news gets onto the Internet on television or radio first. In the same way, new ideas are often published on the Internet before they get into a journal or a book. However, there are still good reasons for checking out paper publications:

✔ **Their contents are peer-reviewed, edited and checked.** No universal way exists of doing this on the Internet, though some sites are very good, especially those connected to paper publications.

✔ **Internet articles can sometimes be ephemeral:** Certain types of Internet article are here today and gone tomorrow. not all news reports for example, can be easily accessed at a later date, though a selection of items and many journal articles are archived. Paper publications persist over time.

✔ **You can check the background and experience of the authors of paper-based publications:** You can't always do that with Internet articles or find out how data found there was collected.

However, many reputable publishers offer Internet versions of their publications in addition to the paper-based ones. The Internet also gives access to invaluable sources of local, national and even international government or non-governmental organisation data and statistics, and the search facility within documents means that you can pinpoint key words quicker than by scanning paper documents. Books and paper document can be not only heavy to handle, but expensive to print.

Not all Internet sites give free access, so if you find a potentially useful one that you have to pay to use it's worth asking if your library subscribes to it, or at least read some reviews of it before paying out hard cash.

Even *field research*, where you observe and research people, animals or projects in their own environment, uses computer technology to analyse results, so it's difficult to imagine coping without a computer. In addition to public and college library computers, if you don't own a computer you can use your college computer labs and other clusters (computers grouped together). Colleges and universities upgrade their equipment fairly regularly and often just skip computers and monitors or sell them very cheaply. The Student Union is likely to know of any good deals and you can probably find some computer service personnel to advise you about servicing second-hand computers. Universities usually have good quality equipment, especially monitors, which they scrap despite it still having a good deal of life in it.

As well as published material, university libraries also contain paper, microfiche or disk-based copies of the research dissertations and theses of its own students – so-called unpublished research. This can be very helpful in your work, as not many people may know of its existence. You can use and refer to it in the same way as published work, adding 'unpublished' in brackets at the end of the reference, and in doing so you open it up to a wider audience.

Your tutor or the librarian may know of other useful unpublished research that you can request from its author. Much research is eventually published, but it takes some time to happen and may not be in the original research degree form: 'Unpublished' is not a comment on its quality.

Reviewing Your Research Tools

Research tools include things like questionnaires, interviews, observation and data or information that already exists. *Research tools* and *methodology* are often referred to together, although the research tool is what you use and the methodology is how you use it. For instance, using a questionnaire means following a theoretical framework to decide the type of questions to use and how they should be framed to avoid bias. You also need to consider the analytical framework for discussing and grouping the answers, to make sure the questions allow you to compare the answers (probably with tick boxes for speed of marking) and so that don't forget to add questions about the gender, age, job description and so forth of your respondents, so you can analyse the responses according to age, gender and so on. So the tool relates to a theoretical framework and also the analytical framework. The methodology is about how and when you administer the tools. For instance, you might use a questionnaire first and then choose some people who gave interesting answers to interview – your second tool. The Internet can also be a research tool to give you access to information or conduct email interviews, for example.

Most research involves several research tools. For background reading, literature reviews and literature-based research, many websites provide their own extensive research tools to help you use the site effectively and find what you need. Tools include archived material and links to other archive material in subject or alphabetical order, for instance *The Economist* www.economist.com/research/; *Intute* for the social sciences www.intute.ac.uk/socialsciences/researchtools/, and the Library of Congress, which offers a range of legislative and other resources and links, at www.loc.gov/rr/tools.htm

Research tools also serve as a useful reminder of the need for clarity in the contents page, layout, support material and illustrations in your own paper-based dissertation or thesis – how to be helpful to the reader.

The tools for your empirical or experimental research depend on the subject, your methods of data collection and whether the research is generally qualitative or quantitative, although, as already mentioned, it can have aspects of both.

Developing research questions

You can have a main research question or hypothesis, but in addition, you can find probably several subsidiary questions all linked to the main topic. As the research becomes more specific – sometimes after it has begun – you may need to change or modify the main or subsidiary research questions. It is important to note these changes in your learning diary, as they can be used as part of your evaluation of your own work in your writing and a reminder of what to do more or avoid next time.

The research questions guide the research; they're questions to which the research needs to find answers or explanations. The research questions make a framework for the research and suggest which particular tools are appropriate to your needs.

In the example of the experimental strawberry research, possible further research questions after the hypothesis was proved to be correct (fish DNA added to the strawberry DNA does help the strawberry resist frost) may include:

✔ **Question 1:** Does the fish DNA affect the taste of the strawberry?

✔ **Question 2:** Does the fish DNA affect the texture, colour or size of the strawberry?

✔ **Question 3:** Does the fish DNA improve the shelf life of the strawberry?

The same research tool may not be appropriate for all the questions.

For Question 1, you can set up an experiment for human tasters to compare the taste of at least two kinds of strawberries, one with fish DNA, and select the strawberry they think tastes best. This requires a fairly large number of volunteers to be statistically significant, so would be quantitative research. The volunteers can answer in *tick box* form (methodological tool) by computer – easier for analysis and to combine with other tasters' responses – or on paper.

Which strawberry tastes the best? Please tick your preferred answer:

a) Strawberry A

b) Strawberry B

c) No difference

d) Neither tastes good

For Question 2 you can make the comparison objectively by weighing and measuring the fruit and comparing it with standard varieties of strawberries. If there were significant differences, this may lead on to a further research question: does it matter? Again, human volunteers would be necessary, so the most economical method would be to anticipate this and add another three questions for the human volunteers to answer, using the same format as the first. (*Which strawberry's texture/ colour/size do you prefer? Strawberry A, B, there's no difference, neither*). There would thus be two research tools to answer the second question – objective measurement and the subjective responses of volunteers. Both would be quantitative methods.

Question 3 concerning the shelf life of the strawberry can also be measured experimentally and objectively in comparison with standard strawberries – by measuring the time between picking and mould developing under controlled conditions – it's wiser not to involve human tasters in answering this question!

Research questions, especially second- or third-level questions, are very important in helping you to select the most appropriate tools for your research.

If you discuss your ideas with your friends , they can help to think up research questions to anticipate possible answers, it's easier to notice, for example, that Question 2 can be answered using two methods – objective and subjective – and that it's easy to add the appropriate extra questions for the human volunteers who are needed for research Question 1. If you don't think through your questions and possible answers you can miss some great opportunities.

Constructing case studies

Case-study methodology is used mainly in the social sciences and is the focused, in-depth study of a particular situation or case over time. In other words, case studies are basically qualitative and longitudinal, like the *7up* series. Case-study research is often combined with other research tools or methods.

For example, if, like Jamie Oliver, you want to find out what primary school children eat in their school dinners, you may choose a case study for part of the project. It's always a good idea to compare things, so your hypothesis may be that children from a wealthier background eat food at school dinners that's nutritionally better for them than do children from a poorer background. Select two schools from the same town, one in a poor area and the other in a richer area. Because in any research, you want to keep things as similar as possible, the only difference being the thing you want to research (the nutritional value of the food eaten for school lunch by the two groups of children) then the groups (school classes) you compare should be of the same age, number, and the same balance between boys and girls, with approximately the same number eating lunch at school. Ask for class lists from each school and choose the classes that most resemble each other (providing the school has agreed to your research, of course).

Always make sure that you know the profiles of the members of the group you're studying – age, gender, where they live, parents' occupation and so on. (You can include this information as part of a questionnaire or from school records.) Make sure that you can link this information to your observation notes of the children. It may be, for example, that you find greater differences between what boys and girls eat (and the hypothesis is false), but if you've forgotten to find background information or link your observations to the children's profiles, then you won't be able to show this.

Your case study can include finding out what the children are offered at lunchtime over a period of time (the longitudinal aspect). This means defining what's nutritionally good (or not and why), what choices each school menu offers over the school week, and whether the children can make good nutritional choices from the menus offered. This information can come from documentary evidence or menu-planning by the school cook, depending on who supplies the school meals – a local authority caterer or the school kitchen. The researcher then observes and notes what each child chooses over a number of weeks, to find out their nutritional choices.

Interviews with the children can help explain why they chose or reject certain food. The questions should be standard – ask each child the same questions about their choices and so on, but leave the answers open (not just *yes* or *no*) as far as possible, to allow the children to express themselves – this is the qualitative aspect of this case-study research. Give parents and teachers a questionnaire, with a choice of *tick box* responses, concerning (for parents) eating habits at home, whether they read food labels for salt-content and so on. Ask teachers about health and nutrition education at school – in school cookery lessons, for example. Where these exist, the researcher can observe classes and the children's responses to them, which is another qualitative aspect of the research.

Once you have an idea or hypothesis, brainstorm to think about what background information you need and how to obtain it – documentary evidence, questionnaires and so on – and how to eliminate all variables (differences) other than the ones you're interested in.

Querying with questionnaires

Questionnaires consist of a series of questions where all possible answers are provided and the respondent (the person filling it in) only has to tick boxes or circle answers. Questionnaires provide a good way of getting basic factual background information and where answers are limited to a few alternatives, respondents can tick boxes. Questionnaires also make analysis quick and easy. They're a quantitative method but can very often be used alongside qualitative methods. Questionnaires can ask for opinions and views, but the quality of the information you receive depends on the form and quality of the questions you write.

Responses to opinions can be in the form of 'strongly agree', 'agree', 'neutral', 'disagree', or 'strongly disagree'. Items can also be ranked – 1, 2, 3 and so on – to show the order of preference. Some questionnaires have a few questions at the end that allow the respondents to express their views – a more qualitative aspect. Questionnaires can easily be sent by email thus avoiding postage costs, which used to deter both senders and receivers.

You may need to make questionnaires group-specific. Those sent to parents, teachers, dinner ladies, local authority catering, children and so forth may have many questions in common and some others specific to each group.

You should definitely test your questionnaire before using it. Ask your friends to help. Are any of the questions biased? Do the possible responses give enough choice? Are you going to get the answers you want in the form you want? Don't forget to add the profile information. You probably want to keep the respondents anonymous but you still need to know their age, gender, nationality, perhaps qualifications, job title and so on. This information helps with cross-referencing and organising the data later. For questionnaire examples, see `www.ltscotland.org.uk/curriculumforexcellence/onlinesurveys/index.asp` or join YouGov and be paid for doing surveys as well as experiencing a range of questionnaire and survey questions – and seeing how you like them!

People give up their time to answer questionnaires, so make them clear and simple.

Outlining observation

Observation used to be referred to as *fly on the wall research* and people thought that observers could report what they observed totally objectively and could float around offices or sit-in on meetings, be quite invisible and have no effect on the proceedings whatsoever. Researchers today have to take account of:

- ✔ What they bring to the observation – their experience, background and belief system and how they report events.

- ✔ How they may affect those they observe, in terms of gender or status problems, inhibitions, non-cooperation or abnormal or atypical behaviour in the presence of the researcher.

In other words, researchers don't just have to be highly aware, they have to record explicitly any emotional or social responses they have to the research and any responses they evoke among the researched, including arguments, distress and so on. This means that although the observer may not take part in any activities she is nevertheless part of the research and has to take account of and be accountable for her contribution to the research. The *fly on the wall* is thus considered a myth and an impossible one at that.

That said, the observer in a classroom or boardroom, for instance, normally sits at the back, avoids eye contact, takes notes and records the proceedings (after having first asked permission) and is as unobtrusive as possible.

However, if the role of the observer extends – as is often the case in qualitative research – to conducting informal interviews, working with focus groups, helping the group under study to produce documents or records of their discussions and is generally more involved in the daily lives of the researched, then this is normally referred to as *participant observation*. This term fully acknowledges the observer-as-researcher effect on the research.

If you anticipate conducting participant observation, make sure that you have permission for what you want to do – or tailor that to what you can get permission for. Make clear what it is you want to do and how you want to do it and state that the information you gather is to be anonymous. If you can, show how what you want to do can benefit those from whom you need to get permission (but not as a spy for them – occasionally, those in power get the wrong idea.)

Evaluating experiments

Experimental research is not confined to the laboratory with fruit flies and fishy strawberries. The key word to understanding experiment is 'test', that is, experimental research is not dealing with events as they happen in a normal or natural way but under 'test' conditions. It should be possible to repeat an experiment and obtain similar results under similar conditions. A good example of an experiment is indeed a test.

Exam boards that offer the possibility of taking English language tests every month have to have a huge battery of reliable and valid tests in order that each one is of a comparable standard to the others. This means that all exams must be pre-tested. The students selected are at just below, at the same and at a higher level of the exam – based on their class and previous exam work. They take a test that's new to them but which has been pre-tested and found to be acceptable and a week or so later they take the new test, which the exam board hopes is of the same standard.

The hypothesis is that the new, pilot test is of the same standard as the older test. As with all research, especially experimental, everything should be controlled except for the one variable that's being tested – in this case – the test. This means both tests should be done at the same time of day, same room, in the same length of time and so on. The students are the same, the standard is set by the old test and the results of both compared.

Ideally, each student should get approximately the same marks on both tests for the hypothesis to be correct. If this is not the case the exam board needs to know where to make adjustments. If an overall pattern of higher marks for the pilot test emerges, that suggests it's easier; if the marks are overall lower, then it's more difficult. If, when compared to the first 'standard' test, the marks of the good students are low and the poor students high, a big problem arises – definitely back to the lab.

With experimental research, the choice of (quantitative) analytical tools is also important. Tests results are often displayed as a bell curve, with standard deviations. However, the analysis also needs to look out for 'rogue' questions, which when removed may make the bell curve more as expected. These then are the questions to rewrite or eliminate.

Experimental research can be a very useful way of collecting empirical data and a good way to practice using analytical tools. In language research, for instance, there's a claim that women use different or more modal verbs than men when giving instructions. As shown in Figure 9-1 You can draw a triangle on top of a square and ask an approximately equal number of men and women to instruct equal numbers of the same or the opposite sex to draw this (make sure that they sit back to back and cannot see the drawing) and record what they say, on paper and tape.

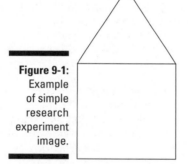

Figure 9-1:
Example of simple research experiment image.

The expected result is that men tend to give orders - 'Draw this, do that' or use strong forms like 'You *must* do . . . ' and check saying 'Have you done what I told you?' Women tend to give more information by locating the drawing on the page and tend to see the exercise as co-operative, saying 'We *have to* do . . . ' , and use softer forms like '*Can* you draw/do . . . ?' and check by saying ' It *should* look like . . . ' 'Was I clear?'

You'd need to set up parameters for the experiment – making sure you had instances of males instructing males, females instructing females, females instructing males and males instructing females –, to cover other possible differences if the hypothesis wasn't proved. Additional records of age, occupation and marital status, can also be useful for your analysis.

This would be quantitative research, so the more the merrier. Your results research data sheet can identify the four parameters and note the occurrence of modal forms, something like Table 9-2. (You can add another column for swear words – or even make that a separate experiment.)

Table 9-2:		Example Research Data Sheet			
Modal form	*Male to male*	*Male to female*	*Female to female*	*Female to male*	*Total number*
Could	X number	Y number	Z number	P number	
Should					
Ought to					
Have to					
Must					
Can't					
Couldn't					
Shouldn't					
Must not					

Try to think through all possible variations and possible results to make sure that you include all the data you need to explain all aspects of your experiment. If you think what your final data sheet may look like, this can help you work backwards and set up your experiment precisely. As you are only interested in the modal words, with this kind of research, you don't need to transcribe the tape, just identify and count the modal forms. Bingo!

Approaching action research

Action research is often connected with education in the UK and, in general, is associated with the social sciences. Teachers may ask themselves what aspects of their teaching are most effective in terms of test results, or most enjoyable for their students, because they want to improve their teaching and the classroom experience of the children they teach. Action research involves a process of reflection and then using this to bring about change or improvement – the action bit.

However, to build a fuller picture, teachers also need information from the students they teach, in order to work together to plan ways of changing things – more of this, less of that, and so on. Teacher and students working together within the social unit of the classroom to bring about change is referred to as participatory action research. The methods used may include discussion and feedback slips, but also the trialling of teaching methods and designing teaching methods that suit the needs of all the members of the class. Different students learn in different ways – some may prefer abstract logic, others analogy, or visual or aural representations. One teacher recorded her classes so that the students were able to re-run them at home. This appeared to give some support and a level of confidence to some, so that they were less stressed.

However, action research can also take place in companies (another form of social unit or social community) with employees working cooperatively or through using an outside researcher to support or organise activities to help improve their work strategies, sales and customers services and so on.

If you're thinking of undertaking action research, you need to find ways to gain the support and cooperation of the others involved in the research. For instance, all are equal in action research – bosses and workers – but you may have to find ways of encouraging participants to have a voice or listen to others, possibly through small, mixed-group project work. The difference in status between members of the group may have to be overcome.

Investigating interviews

In research you use interviews to elicit responses from individuals that can't be covered in questionnaires or other methods. It's important that you ask all the interviewees the same questions, so that you can make comparisons. Don't forget to record a profile for each person: age, gender, occupation and so on. Interviews are normally recorded (with the permission of the person being interviewed) and the interviewer takes notes as well. The setting should be relaxing so that the interviewee isn't stressed and you should assure her of her anonymity. Interviews are part of qualitative research, and designed to tease out nuggets of information or insights that cannot be got from questionnaires. Questions are normally mainly open-ended to allow people to express themselves freely.

Interviews can also be conducted using the telephone or through email. Telephone interviews are easy to record and email ones are already written down for you, you don't need to transcribe them! However, email responses aren't as spontaneous as face-to-face or telephone ones so you may need to take that into account in your analysis, especially if you use different interview methods – phone, face to face, email.

Try out your interview questions and your interview technique on a helpful guinea pig. You'll soon see if you're not getting at the information you want and you can make the appropriate changes. Rather than transcribing everything, look for key phrases as a way to organise and analyse your results.

Assessing storytelling

In this area of qualitative, case-study research, the researcher encourages the subjects to tell their life histories, usually in written form, up to the research period, which can be a period when they're studying or doing some work-related training. They then record their feelings, reactions and attitudes to events during the research period and afterwards, when the period of study or training has ended, they reflect on what has taken place and their attitude to it.

Storytelling as a research tool is usually used within the social sciences: the researcher is a participant observer and often a confidant and supporter of the researched. It's often used alongside other methods (interviews, questionnaires) and compared with data such as exam results or performance at work data. The research questions may be to do with the expectations and motivation people have for taking certain actions or making certain decisions.

The research questions often seek to find out why people do things – study in another country, change job frequently – what their expectations and motivations are and whether what subsequently happens comes up to their earlier expectations. It seeks to discover the underlying reasons for actions or the situations people find themselves in, which storytelling can reveal, and which may not even have been clear to the subjects themselves. It attempts to tease out information that cannot easily be obtained in any other way. For example, some storytelling research revealed certain female students applied to a particular university because it was within easy reach of a very famous university and offered them access to what they perceived as highly suitable husbands. Subject of study was irrelevant and yes, they did meet and marry superior husband specimens, in their view, and never used their degrees. However, that was not what was recorded on their CVs or anywhere else.

The researcher works very closely and confidentially with the researched, so observer bias need extreme care. If respondents drop out and the story remains unfinished, the researcher is in difficulties. Taking on a few extra cases as insurance is a good idea: ensure that the respondents are a clearly identifiable social group and have enough in common to work well and support each other. They need to be motivated to cooperate with the research as attending meetings and keeping diary records takes time. As far as possible, try to get a gender balance The analysis and categorisations of the stories can be quite difficult, but also fascinating.

Avoiding Pitfalls

Research can be great fun, but, as they say, it's all in the planning. The following is a list of things to consider. There's no such thing as failure, only learning. However, we don't always have enough time to be that philosophical.

- ✔ **Keep an eye on the time:** Yes, time is public enemy number one again. Don't be overambitious unless you can give up sleep for a month. Do spend time refining your research questions, also your interview and questionnaire questions and make sure that you allow enough turn-round time in which to get questionnaires back. Email format should make that easier. Remember, the longer the interview, the longer it's going to take you to transcribe it (two minutes of interview take about 30 minutes to transcribe) so try to develop categories with key words to avoid transcription – or have shorter interviews! Make sure that you allow yourself enough time for analysis. Pick out the most noticeable items if time is running short, and analyse them well and forget the rest. You probably wouldn't have space for it anyway. Better to do a little beautifully and in detail than a hotchpotch, because now you've gone to the trouble to get all that information , you want to use it. Don't worry, it'll probably come in useful later.

- ✔ **Triangulate data as far as possible:** This helps make the data more reliable. By using different ways of collecting information and comparing the views of different researchers, if they all come to similar conclusions, you've done your best to ensure that the results you have found are as reliable as possible. You also need to ensure that the data are internally valid, that is, the results are due to what you think they are and not something else. This means making sure at the outset that no other possible variables are present that can interfere with your results. Think of all research as an experiment – it's easier then to think of what you need to control in the research situation.

- ✔ **Evaluate your research:** Don't worry about picking holes in your research – if you don't someone else will, so get in there first! It shows you've learned something and you'll be given credit. Reliability and validity and the steps you took to ensure this are important: mention them. Remember, something must first be reliable before it can be valid. Much social science is case specific and so the validity is internal. Experiments, on the other hand, may have *external validity*, which means they are *generalisable* and can be repeated elsewhere with the same results.

✔ **When dealing with respondents, the people you're studying, ensure that they understand what you want them to do:** Make it clear to them that you'll make sure that they're to be anonymous and ask them to give written permission to let you use their responses.

✔ **Always have something up your sleeve:** Send out twice as many questionnaires as you need, interview more people than you need but only use the most interesting. You usually have one or two unhelpful interviews because people haven't been in their job for long or have just moved to the area, and so on, so build up some slack but use ways to avoid large chunks of transcription.

Overall, be honest, clear, relevant and stick to reality in your research, just as you do in your writing and presentations.

Chapter 10

Finding Answers: Reading and Research

In This Chapter

▶ Recognising the functions of reading lists

▶ Refining your reading and research skills

▶ Homing in or how texts are organised

▶ Discovering different types of media resources

▶ Sharing resources and reading groups

*R*eading documents – whether books, journals or on the Internet – is probably the main way to find information you need outside of lecture time. Case study or research results and reports may be the main ways to support your arguments in writing or presentations, but a review of the literature and theoretical perspectives also form the background to arguments or tools for analysing research and results. With so much information available literally at your fingertips – in some areas of biochemistry, for example, new papers are published online every 6–7 hours – even if you did nothing but read all day, seven days a week in your subject area, you'd barely scratch the surface and have no time left for anything else, not even to write essays, let alone eat, sleep or party!

For this reason alone, the best strategy is to be selective about your reading. The best way to do that is to create questions to which you need to find answers, and use different reading strategies for different purposes. Most importantly, you must not feel guilty if you never read another text starting at page one and finishing on the last page. Research reading – reading to find answers – is not the same as reading for pleasure, where to follow the plot, you do need to read each page in numerical order.

Reviewing Reading Lists

Reading lists provide essential and recommended reading to support and extend class work. They're also your first port of call for finding possible texts for your purposes – reading to prepare for an essay or presentation, for example. More specifically, reading lists:

- ✔ Give you an outline of the topics and related reading for the term or year.
- ✔ Provide you with a range of views to read about.
- ✔ Help you prepare for the term's work in vacation time.
- ✔ Help you reserve books or journals in the library when you need to use them.
- ✔ Provide back-up resources in case the main texts are unavailable.
- ✔ Help you plan your reading before and during term.
- ✔ Suggest extra resources if you want to pursue some areas in more depth.

You may feel a bit overwhelmed when you receive the reading lists for your course, but they have several purposes and you don't have to read every book (or even part of every book) on the list. In practical terms, most tutors try to ensure that at any given time there are at least enough relevant resources for half the students on the course, that is, at least one text to share between two students. The number of resources suggested in the reading lists can link to the number of students on the course, though key texts may be photocopied so everyone has a chance to read them. The books or articles that appear at the top of the list are the most important or relevant, so it's a good idea to reserve them. Most libraries – departmental or the main university one – have four-day loan periods for key books to give as many people as possible a chance to read them, as there are only likely to be four or five copies of each text, at most. The list is likely to contain references to articles online as well, where they're freely available.

Identifying what you really need to read

You usually get two reading lists: one for preparatory reading to do over vacations and one which tells you the weekly reading that your course draws upon. Each list may have sections for *essential* reading and *recommended* reading. Essential reading generally takes priority, though holiday reading often includes some background texts that cover a topic in more general terms, but are well written and fun to read.

Use vacations for any general background reading because you'll be too busy during term.

If you cross-check your general reading list with the weekly reading texts, you find some appear in both and these are the ones to concentrate on as they're probably the most important. You can then plan to reserve library books or journals so you have time to read up on topics before studying them in lectures or seminars. Cross-referencing also makes the lists shorter as you can eliminate any duplication. You may find that the weekly reading texts refer to specific chapters, further narrowing down the selection for you. These texts tend to be linked to questions or particular causes to investigate, and can frame your purpose in reading them, the kind of questions to find answers to in the text and the kind of notes to take as you read. Generally speaking, the first four or so books on each topic are the most important for you to get hold of.

Another way of checking the relative importance of texts is to look at the date of publication. More recent publications usually have more up-to-date information to argue against or to support the main or current theoretical perspectives.

Balancing your reading

The tutors who contribute to write reading lists try to represent the main theories and perspectives within each subject area. Tutors don't limit their recommendations to texts that represent their own viewpoints, but try to suggest a range of perspectives to give you a balanced overview.

Tutors have a duty to guide you to enough information to help you make up your own mind and not impose their views, though you may come to share them.

Comparing and contrasting various interpretations or theories about the same event helps you to understand how they came about, how they fit into the historical time frame of the subject and how they contribute to knowledge.

For example, some sources may be written from a feminist or Marxist or classical economic perspective. These perspectives provide a framework for considering the topic within a different analysis based on a particular theory or way of interpreting the world. Sometimes reading resources track how perceptions within a general framework have changed, or how new branches that have roots in the past have developed.

Study groups often compare the same problem from a different perspective over some weeks. Perspectives or theories often criticise the one that went before, so each becomes more understandable in terms of the other. Similarly, reading lists often relate to this sequence of comparing alternate views in the recommended reading sources.

If you find some reading material difficult to understand, the best way to make it clearer is to read other material about the same subject written by different authors. Comparisons help clarify issues whereas reading from one author's perspective only can be both difficult and restrictive.

Reading as Research – Finding Answers to the Right Questions

Considering all reading for academic purposes as research shifts the balance of power from the writer to the reader. As a reader and researcher, you have particular needs and aims, and particular information that you want the text to provide. You're not so interested in what the author wants to convince you of, but more in how you want to use the information the text provides – or you hope it provides. This is important as, if it seems logical for information to be included but it's not, then it's worth asking 'Why not?' What is missing from a text can be as important as what is stated.

The best way to find out if something is missing is to read and compare several texts on the same subject at the same time.

Creating research questions

If the main purpose of reading is to find answers to your questions (and not to be told what is what by the writer), it follows that being clear about your purposes before you begin reading helps you select the most appropriate texts or parts of texts. The easiest way to do this is to formulate some research questions to focus your reading. Research questions for reading are particularly useful because:

- ✔ The research questions and the answers you find, especially if you compare and combine the answers from more than one source, can be directly used in your own work.

- ✔ Creating research questions means creating your own note-making framework. Your notes form the basis of your own work rather than merely a reflection or summary of the text you're reading – they're one step removed.

✔ Using reading texts in this way helps you create your own texts from your perspective or judgement of the evidence presented to you by your reading, stamping your identity and voice on the texts you then create.

In many cases, you can start by looking at the questions asked in essay titles, or the seminar or lecture questions for your course, as you will probably be reading in order to answer these. However, these can be complex, or there may only be statement, so it's always a good idea to start with the basics: Who, what, where, when, how and why?

For example, 'How successful was the first crusade? Who was involved? What was it? Where did it take place? When did it happen? How was it organised? Why did it happen?'

If you read to answer these questions, you will get a fair idea not only of the events but the reasons for them and the problems, to help you develop your own view.

Refining your reading and researching techniques

You always have a lot of reading as a student, and if you don't keep your objectives clearly in mind, you can get sidetracked by some interesting but irrelevant information which is outside the focus of your topic. You can always make a note to read it later when you have more time. Searching for and finding keywords tells you that there is some potentially useful for you on the page.

Scanning for keywords

A basic reading research technique is to formulate keywords – the topics, theories, names of researchers, places, methods and so on– that you want to find out about. Using a keyword search in the index of academic books tells you if they cover your topic, the number of pages devoted to the subject and which they are. Recommended reading on the topic is likely to be a profitable source, but it may be surprising to find what a small proportion of the whole text you need to read to find the answer to your keyword question.

The abstracts at the beginning of journal papers contain keywords in heavy type, referring to the topic, location, methods, important institutions like the World Bank and so on, to tell you what is contained within the text. 'Googling' keywords also throws up possible lines of enquiry.

Searching or 'scanning' for keywords means looking for them in the text and when you've found them, reading what comes before and after. The quickest way to find keywords, apart from using the index if there is one, is to look in the topic sentence of paragraphs as described in the section above.

Scanning can be particularly useful for finding definitions.

If you feel that your topic should be included in the work you're reading, but you can't find it, try another keyword that means the same thing or is linked in some way. For instance 'gender' if 'feminist' brings no results, or 'classical economics' if 'Adam Smith' brings no joy.

If you feel really perplexed that your topic is not included, then perhaps the time has come to ask 'Why?' This is worth checking out with your tutor. You may have found a focus for your own critique.

Skimming for general information

You sometimes see expert skimmers in old-fashioned bookshops flipping through the pages of books to get a general idea of what they're about, reading more intently when their attention is attracted. Of course, the publisher's blurb on a book cover can substitute for an abstract, but you, the wily reader, won't rely on that alone because it's written for the general public and you have individual needs, so you'll do a bit of skimming research, particularly before paying out hard cash.

If you're attracted by a particular book or text and want to see what it offers in general terms, then skimming can give you some clues about the type of text it is. In a book, a descriptive or scene-setting chapter may be food for thought. You may be attracted to the style and layout or use of pictorial illustration as a model, rather than the content. Skimming is a way of generally evaluating a book's usefulness.

You can also skim to find out about the content after you've identified a useful topic sentence. Really fast skimmers focus on the centre of the page and let their eyes glide down the middle of the paragraph.

This type of scanning can work as a way of checking out a paragraph that looks potentially useful from the keywords in the topic sentence.

All reading techniques are intended to save time (and sanity) and keep you focused. You probably do most of them already – think how you read a newspaper. You probably scan the headlines to find a subject that interests you and then maybe look at the topic of some paragraphs or skim through to get a general idea and perhaps read the introduction and conclusion carefully. You can do pretty much the same with academic texts.

When to read every word

All words may or may not have been created equal, but some certainly are more equal than others, depending on how you use them and where you find them. Scanning sees keywords as more important and skimming sees all words as having limited, general value. Both these methods are speed techniques to save time and help you keep focused. They also have distinct values. However, you're also likely to be stopped in your tracks by something potentially great. As already suggested, it's a good idea to read conclusions and introductions carefully because they provide a summary of the whole piece. They can also be the basis of a critique if they don't 'match'. The following areas are generally also worthy of a bit more of your attention, where every word may count.

- ✔ **Definitions and potential quotations:** You need to read these carefully and equally carefully note them down, including the punctuation, in order to use them in your own work. You also need to note the full reference to put in your reference or bibliography at the end, and put the author's surname, the date and page of the publication in brackets after using the quotation in your text.

  You may well want to compare definitions or quotations from different authors, so be sure to note down the references correctly as you can waste time looking for or trying to reconstruct references later on. A card index is useful for this, organised according to author or topic, as suits best.

- ✔ **Data and how it is presented in tables, diagrams, graphs, charts and so on:** These need to be read carefully to understand how the presentation of the data encourages a certain understanding of it and whether this is deceptive or illuminating. This is another instance of checking out what's missing. See the nearby sidebar 'Questioning the data' for an example.

- ✔ **The steps of arguments, especially in official documents:** You need to be read these carefully to make sure that they're logical and don't make presumptions. With careful dissection, you may write a whole counter argument of them as your essay – a great way to use reading.

- ✔ **Writers quoting other writers:** A potential source for the critical reader, especially if you're familiar with the quotation. Read carefully to see if they've quoted in context (particularly newspaper quotations) or if they've misapplied it.

- ✔ **The analysis and evaluation parts of texts:** Generally, originality and value lie in these parts. The rest of the text is set up to support them, though of course, can be criticised for failing to do so. These parts can be worth reading carefully to critique or gain ideas from. Analysis and evaluation usually come in the sections (usually two) immediately before the conclusion. The conclusion will summarise them as explanations and comments on outcomes, so you can use key words in the conclusion summary to find the analysis and summary sections earlier in the text.

Questioning the data

Always question any assumptions and omissions in a set of data. For example, say that you have some data on convictions for dangerous driving. The age-group categories for the data are 10–16, 17–25, 26–35, 36–45, 50–70, and 75 and over. You may not worry too much that the under tens aren't represented and assume the 10–16-year-old group of underage drivers includes joyriders remanded in institutions for young offenders. However, why are those between 45 and 50 and 71 and 74 not represented and is the category 75 and over a bit too wide? As it stands, is the data very informative? Could it be separated into categories to show the difference between male and female drivers, convictions related to alcohol, and so on? Can it be given a context by comparing it with data from previous years, or different countries, different times of the year and so on? Could it be more useful than it is now (simply a comparison between age groups)? Careful reading of data can release a host of analytical questions or evaluations and suggest paths the critical reader can then follow.

Homing In On How Texts Are Organised

In general, academic texts present information in a particular order and with a particular function to guide the reader through the text. This structure tells you where to find certain items, like the literature review or the theoretical background or the research results, as all these tend to appear in a certain order. If, for example, you are interested in comparing your results with results published in a journal, you can go straight to the results section. The structure also suggests where to find more detailed information at paragraph level. Understanding how these features work can save you time and keep you focused. This order and function are common to most academic writing – essays, dissertations, theses, research and journal articles, book chapters, books, examination answers, presentations and even abstracts. How long the piece of writing is doesn't matter. Books are sometimes collections of articles by different authors, with each contributing a chapter. Each chapter, in this case, would follow the same structure described here.

Section organisation, function and usefulness

Sections usually have headings with keywords to give you a good idea of their subject content. However, understanding the function or purpose of each part of a paper, essay, report or chapter in a book is equally important. The online version of a published paper looks very similar to the paper copy, so the same principles apply, except that you scroll through pages on screen rather than flip paper. The functions outlined in the following list do not all follow the order that texts are presented in. The conclusion, for example, comes last in a test, but it is the part of the main text most useful to read first, especially if no summary or abstract exist to help you find out what the text is about. In general, it is most useful to move from the general to the particular, so that is the order of reading I suggest. A useful order for reading the parts of text to find out if they're any good to you is below.

- **Abstract:** This is a formal heading that appears before a journal article or conference paper (or on the cover of an important essay, dissertation or thesis written by a student). Abstracts are more specialised and shorter than summaries and particularly useful in academic conference papers or journal articles, where there is no indexes. They highlight keywords in bold type – topics, theories, methods, name of places, key institutions and so on, and tell you both about the structure and content of what follows.

- **Summary:** The summary comes before conference papers, journal articles, before online papers or important student essays, dissertations and students or books and provides a more general overview of what is to come and how it is organised to help you judge the usefulness for your purpose. Books often have a short text at the beginning, on the inside flyleaf or on the outside of the dustcover, which may perform the function of a summary, if it is written by the author.

- **Conclusion:** Has the function of summarising the text and giving the writer's view about the particular research, theories and methods (and their particular usefulness), recommendations or what to be wary of, based on the outcomes of the work. Conclusions can be very useful sources of quotations, because they often give the writer's view 'in a nutshell'. If you just need a writer's viewpoint, the conclusion is a good place to look. If you need more detail, then the conclusion will give you a good idea of where else to look in the text.

- **Introduction:** Gives brief indications of purpose, research questions, methods and context and most usefully considered as complementing the conclusion.

- **Background section:** Discusses the geographical or political contexts, and give information about population size, climate, local industries or social factors such as live births. Engineering contexts give, for example, technical specifications. Using the same references as in the work can be a good source of more details – or comment if more up-to-date data has become available and changes the picture.

- **Literature review:** Provides definitions and short summaries of the key theories or guidelines used as well as criticisms or analyses of them.

- **Specific objectives section:** Poses research questions, hypotheses or aims in more detail, arguments for choosing the topic and theoretical or other framework.

- ✔ **Methodology section:** Provides a rationale and description of the chosen methods and why they're useful for their purpose. This can be a good source of definitions or criticism or can help you choose your own methods. The form of words used to protect informants is also helpful.

- ✔ **Experiment, case study or test situations:** Describe how the methodology was applied in practice and may be useful as a model or for spotting loopholes in it and then critique.

- ✔ **Results section:** Can be compared to the hypothesis, research questions or expected outcomes. The methods of analysing research may provide useful models or something to criticise. Examples of tables, charts, diagrams may be particularly worthy of consideration, especially for Arts and Humanities students who may not automatically consider such techniques.

- ✔ **Analysis sections:** Largely relate to how the results are presented. If the results are put in comparative frameworks ('before and after', for example) then they're likely to reveal more interesting analysis and comments. Sometimes you can reuse badly presented data or inadequately analysed data in your work to reveal more information.

- ✔ **Evaluation:** May come at the end of the analysis or partly in the conclusion. Again, it's worth looking at as researchers have been known to stumble upon a gold mine without realising it. You may be able to do better.

- ✔ **References or bibliography:** Can be useful for finding sources you can use for your work. Check the dates of publication to find the most up-to-date and probably more useful.

- ✔ **Appendices**: Can be useful if they contain raw data, which may be a good source for you to re-use in a different way. There may also be sample questionnaires and other forms that can be good models. Check how the writer evaluated them in the text.

Whatever kind of information you obtain, always say where you obtained it and give it a reference in your bibliography and on the page of your text in which you use it. As well as being useful to you, it's evidence that you did some preparatory reading!

Paragraph structure

If you have decided to read a particular section which has a number of paragraphs, then the same system of reading the last paragraph first (as the summary or conclusion paragraph) gives you the general objectives and conclusion of this section, while the first paragraph gives the general objectives and organisation of the section. Paragraphs in academic texts also tend to have a particular structure, which you can use to your advantage. This is a particularly useful strategy if you have to summarise the main points in a section and chapter and get bogged down in detail.

In more than 90 per cent of cases the first phrase or sentence in the paragraph indicates the topic of the paragraph, that is, it's a summary sentence. In most other cases the topic phrase or sentence comes last. In a few cases, there's no topic sentence as each point has equal value – these paragraphs are quite easy to spot from their layout.

Exploring Other Media Resources

Information doesn't have to come from written resources. Your school subject library or central university or college library may have audio-visual resources of digital recordings of various off-air education programmes, including:

- ✔ Recorded lectures, for instance, from the Open University

- ✔ Interviews with important world figures by skilled interviewers

- ✔ Classical films and commentaries on them by renowned film critics or historians

- ✔ Recordings of natural history programmes, or good quality documentaries

- ✔ Talks given by important visiting speakers, or recently created doctors of philosophy or professors and recorded by university technicians. These can provide information straight from the horse's mouth!

Using audio-visual resources

If your preferred learning mode is through the ear or if you simply want to have a change of method, these resources can be very helpful.

You need to modify your strategies, but the fast forward or stop buttons can be a great help. Begin by listening to the concluding remarks to evaluate how useful listening to the rest of the talk is likely to be, or, better still, if anyone asks questions at the end of the talk, these may usefully point out omissions, criticisms and interest in the argument presented, all of which can make your antenna quiver and provide you with a benchmark for listening to the talk.

You can also quote from recorded material – the stop/rewind system can aid this. You need to note the name of the speaker, the title of the programme or talk, the date of the recording, the approximate point on the recording where the quote happened and, if it's a television programme, name the producer. You should also note the date you listened. All of this fits well in your learning diary.

If you're lucky enough to find some recorded material by one of the authors of some recommended reading, this material can make the ideas clearer and explain bits you 'missed.' Another advantage is that you know exactly how long a recording is. This can help you plan your time, although you won't know precisely how much you want to listen to or in how much detail by rewinding and so on. However, it's easier than guessing how long you'll want to spend reading a book or journal article.

What you learn through your ear and subsequently note and make use of is more thoroughly integrated into your mind and memory, so using audio-visual material can be particularly useful for topics for which you have to sit exams.

Television

It's always worth checking out Open University programmes or documentaries on BBC 1, 2 and Channel 4 as these are likely to be of reasonable standard. The History Channel also shows some excellent re-enactments, but do cross-check any information you note with a reputable source. If you're studying politics, 'Question Time' or transmissions from Parliament may give you some insights into argument, the importance of body language and so on. If you record programmes, use them in the same way as those in the audio-visual digital library.

The BBC website for instance contains a vast number of links and in many cases, after the transmission of a programme, you can find the written text of the commentary, which makes it easy for you to find references or give accurate quotes. You can also find links to related material in the archives – other programmes on a similar topic or material that can be read online. Keywords come in handy for searching the archives. Green issues and global warming are particularly well represented from several and quite unusual perspectives.

BBC iPlayer allows you to download programmes to watch on your PC. You need to check which are available and for how long. In addition, the BBC website has blogs and interactive message boards (as do other television channel websites) where you can contribute your views on topical matters and find out other people's views.

With so much of interest to distract you it can be time wasting, if entertaining, to log on to blogs and chat rooms without having a specific purpose. Be tough with yourself!

Radio

Radio current affairs programmes (especially on Radio 4) also offer useful and up-to-date information on international relations, comparative cultures and so on. The featured journalist gives you some idea of the likely quality of the content and you can check his profile on line.

You can subscribe to BBC podcasts and have your selected programmes sent to your PC: with some free software they can be transferred to an MP3 player, enabling you to listen anywhere. Once you've downloaded programmes to your MP3 you can keep episodic programmes or, by checking to see forthcoming topics, create your own archive for possible future use. Again, the advantage of using your MP3 player is that you can stop or review when you want to and even listen while doing something else.

Note down in writing the official broadcast date of any material you want to use – you can check dates on the BBC website – and don't forget to note the name of the producer, who replaces the publisher in audio or visual formats in your reference section.

We are so used to considering radio and television as entertainment – even serious, factually based programmes – that it's easy to be sloppy when referring to broadcast media programmes in essays. All the formal references must be given as you would from written texts. Another safeguard is to cross-check any information you want to use with another source, preferably a print source with a different journalist or a written academic source, to make sure that the information is accurate and also to get a more balanced perspective. Indeed, you may want to argue that the broadcast media piece is unbalanced, specifically because it's produced for a mass audience. In this case, it's even more important to compare it with a piece from the print media or an academic source to support your argument.

Even if you don't use any broadcast media information directly in your work, listening to and watching programmes on the same topic that you read about nevertheless sharpens up your critical reflexes and gives you a more rounded view of the topic. You'll be accessing more parts of your brain, increasing your memory storage and making more links as you go about your daily life without even being aware of doing so!

Other print media

In addition to the uses of the print media mentioned above, newspapers and other magazines and supplements can be the most up-to-date sources of information along with broadcast news. Some of the quality newspapers like *The Guardian* or *The Independent* give emphasis to particular topics on specific days (*The Guardian* on tuesdays contains an education supplement). It's worth becoming familiar with the sections of newspapers and the subject headings at the top of each page – Home or Overseas News, Politics, Economics, Sport and so on.

If you're studying a subject that touches on politics, history, peace studies, economics, the EU, Anglo-American relations and so on, you should consider buying one of the quality newspapers as they cost less for students, some as little as 10p a copy. Alternatively, the papers are available in your common room or library and you can always photocopy an article that catches your attention, though this may be more expensive than buying your own copy. Ideally try to read at least two versions of the same news story. Articles relating to a specific topic rather than current news stories may not appear on the same day in more than one newspaper, but are likely to receive comment in several sources within the same week.

Weekend newspaper articles usually comment on and review the events of the previous week, and these overview articles can provide useful summaries of ongoing events.

You can cut out interesting articles from quality newspapers for future use and create your own archive. Many of the authors are respected journalists with experience in particular fields, or academics and politicians who occasionally write articles for the quality press. Alternatively some articles may provide good fodder for criticism.

Articles written by leading or guest journalists show the author's name. Some news articles don't mention the writer, but whatever it says – name or 'foreign correspondent' for example, be sure to cut that part out and note the date, the newspaper's name and the publisher's name for your bibliography or reference section, as you'll need this information if you refer to it in your work later on. You can apply similar techniques to reading print media as you would to other written sources, as mentioned above.

Online newspapers

Online newspapers like *The Guardian*'s www.theguardian.co.uk look very similar to BBC news online, not surprisingly as these two online media forms are in competition with each other. The front 'contents' page shows a range of 'click on' topics, some illustrated with photos, making the layout clear. The articles are relatively shorter than corresponding print media ones and the online structure and presentation has more similarities with the popular print media, or magazines, perhaps reflecting the intended readership. The online layout (short, one-sentence paragraphs) of articles isn't the best model for the layout of essays, but works quite well for reports.

Online newspapers and BBC news online search pages can perform a similar function to indexes. They provide quick sharp access to dates, times, names and so on, which you can have some confidence in (and can cross-check with other online news sources). They're a little ahead of Google in this, being specialist news sites, and list references by the most recent.

Continuing the theme of comparison, ideally it's best to check information against a different media source. For another perspective, you can also access overseas newspapers online such as *Le Figaro* International at www.lefigaro fr. the home website page of which is in French, or the German weekly magazine *Der Spiegel* International, online website `www.spiegel.de/international`, which is in English.

Comparing other (inter)national newspapers reveals what each considers to be lead or national interest stories: what one leaves out, others may include, giving food for thought.

Most online newspapers are subscription free and quite different from their print-media counterparts. You can find websites selling downloads of printed media newspapers, but you're better to avoid these.

Sharing Resources and Reading Groups

Although your college may have fairly few copies of recommended or essential readings, other resources are available. You may find online articles on a similar topic by the author of one of the readings, but check the date in comparison to the printed article as he may have had a change of perspective. If he has, he should refer back to his original position and explain what's changed. Recordings of lectures, radio talks and all the other resources mentioned above can contribute to giving you a wider and thus more memorable range of inputs and complement other material. This can also help if your preferred learning mode is aural or visual rather than mainly by reading.

The resources available should give you choices, not headaches, so if you still feel a bit overwhelmed, it's time for teamwork.

If you have a mentor for your course, a student in the year above who meets your group on a regular basis to offer support or advice, you can ask his help in organising a reading group. Your mentor may have reading tips remembered from the previous year or may know of secret caches of material. He can help organise the reading group and allocate tasks during the mentoring period.

If you don't have a mentor or a formal place to meet, you can ask room bookings or the use of a lecture room to hold a reading group class. You may find a white board or overhead projector useful tools that help formalise the situation and help everyone to feel a sense of responsibility to the group so that each person prepares a contribution.

A group of between six and eight is probably the most manageable, as the hour or so for which you can book a room won't be long enough for any more contributions. Ideally each participant should study two resources, at least one of which should be essential reading. If possible two people should study each of the resources to provide two views of each, certainly of the essential reading. The study questions on the reading list or the weekly class notes on the reading should provide the topics or heading guidance for the questions to be answered through studying the texts.

Why should people bother to come to a reading group? There's a simple economics of time, effort and pay-back argument. If they read and prepare information from two sources and attend the reading group, the effect is that:

✔ Built-in planning of this kind helps everyone organise their time so that they can contribute.

✔ They take responsibility for their learning and have responsibility towards others.

✔ For whatever amount of time they spent on their sources, for an extra hour or so they have access to three other sources (if there are six in the group) and lots of cross-fertilisation of ideas.

✔ Student self-help groups impress tutors and everyone who attends gets brownie points. It's also the kind of activity that tutors use when giving references as evidence of leadership potential.

✔ Once you're set up and have been running independently for a while, and if there's a particularly tricky problem, you can invite your tutor along to help. There's a good chance he'll accept as you have the organisation in place.

Explaining to others helps you learn

Everyone benefits from sharing ideas, especially in a reading group, because every comment sparks off a link. The speaker needs to vocalise what he's read, making it necessary for him to think about it more and helping him to check his own understanding. Others in the group feed back to him in some form their understanding of what he's said, so constant checks and balances take place that benefit both speaker and listener. Everyone takes on both roles in a reading group. Those who become particularly animated can carry on the discussion afterwards. Reading discussion groups also provide useful practice for giving presentations.

 Use the white board or OHP transparencies to write up each person's short or keyword responses to the reading questions in columns under headings. This then give you a summary of the group's responses, providing a visual memory aid to add to any notes you've taken. You can photocopy and distribute OHP transparencies, which can be adapted or used later in written work – acknowledge the source of the information in the normal way so everyone can officially credit their reading group work!

Reading past essays

Reading past essays on similar topics has various benefits. In the context of group reading they can provide useful models for the structure of essays using the formal qualities outlined above. They can also be used to see how students have used source information, of the kind the group has been comparing, in their own work.

The same is true of reports. Are the required sections there, the appropriate definitions and explanations, specifications and methods, conclusions and recommendations? Does the group agree on how they evaluate the work?

The overriding benefit of reading and comparing previous good essays or reports and so on in a group is to see how the writers have integrated reading and other resources into their own work for their own purposes and in what form they've done this. Have they used reading information to create their own comparison tables, graphs and so on, to define concepts or use as benchmarks?

Any essays written the previous year may be out of date, so references to sources may now have a different spin, but the form won't have changed much.

Chapter 11

Taking Notes for Your Purposes: Not the Book's

. . . .

In This Chapter

▶ Establishing the essentials of note-taking

▶ Getting credit for reading

▶ Developing note-taking skills

▶ Analysing information

▶ Noting references

. . . .

*E*very author – and that includes you – has a specific reason for writing. This is particularly so in academic writing, in which the writer selects the time, place, actors, rationale and theoretical perspectives to fit her purposes.

Once a writer completes a book or paper, the reader is then in charge. It's important to remember this and not feel compelled to follow the writer's agenda unless you choose to and it fits your needs.

Your main need is to gather information to use in your coursework and for revision. That's why effective note-taking from books is so important. This chapter shows you how it's done.

Knowing What You Need from Your Note-Taking

Most readers read an academic paper or book, or most likely, part of it, for one or more of a variety of purposes, including:

✔ To quote a definition or key comment, especially if the writer is a key academic in her field.

✔ To check details like a date, the title of a book or a reference or the spelling of a name.

✔ To find the writer's evaluation of her own or another's research, or the methodology she used.

✔ To consult the literature review and the insights it may provide.

✔ To adapt and use or criticise the author's methodology.

✔ To gain insights from how the writer presents her findings – tables, graphs or diagrams.

✔ To see if the author's source material or data is useful.

✔ To see how far she agrees with another author, or a group or 'school' of academics.

✔ To consider the author's critique of another researcher's approach.

This means that any academic or non-fiction text is, in essence, a reference book. You don't read the chapters in sequence like a crime thriller, but in any order you like, and you take notes on as much or as little of it as you as decide you need.

Getting Credit for Reading

There's no direct way of getting credit for your reading. The quantity or number of books or papers you read is irrelevant. Whether you read a hundred texts or ten, you're not going to get better marks on the grounds of numbers alone, especially if you add a lot of books to your bibliography that you've not actually referred to in your writing. Every degree course has an external examiner from another college or university to check the course is of an acceptable quality and that the marking of the examinations and course work is fair and accurate. Part of their job is reading a selection of exams and assessed work and they are particularly good at spotting the problem of items in the bibliography that are not actually mentioned in the written work!

If you really have read many more books and articles than you refer to in your own writing (why have you read them, then?), you can put a subsection such as 'Background Reading' in your bibliography and list the texts not directly referred to in your writing, using the Harvard system or the one you're asked to use, in the normal way. This gets you out of technical difficulties and may gain you some credit for being organised and honest. See Chapter 7 for more on compiling a bibliography.

Choosing the right sources

Relying on only one source in a particular section of your work can create problems for you. You need to compare information from at least two or three other authors to show you have a rounded understanding of the subject. This can be done by checking factual information – dates, times, places, events – or contrasting different theoretical views or different explanations, analyses or interpretations of the same event. It's important to show that you're aware of these differences and take a balanced view because you may need to explain any differences as part of your analysis. For this reason it's important that you organise and target your notes.

The main way to get credit for reading reflected in the mark for your writing is to choose the most relevant and appropriate sources and to integrate them well with your own writing. That means commenting on any sources you use and linking them to what goes before or after on the page, as well as your essay or section title, research questions and so on, as appropriate.

Using quotations or references that you don't comment on or link to your own ideas can even reduce your marks. The reader may see them as there simply to bulk up the number of words. A link may seem obvious to you, but you need to say it 'in black and white' to demonstrate to your reader (marker) that you've understood its relevance. This follows the principles of clarity: (making everything clear), and relevance (explaining what needs to be explained).

The use of reading in your writing is to build a framework of legitimacy for the subject that you're writing about. With a longer piece of writing – a thesis, dissertation or long essay – the writer supplies a literature review to do just that. A longer piece of writing gives details of the main theories and research in the area and you, the writer, chooses a 'niche' – a space or gap which allows you to add your bit. If you want to criticise author A, authors B and C may aid and support your criticism through their different evidence or experiences, even if they don't criticise author A directly. This can be your niche, your addition to knowledge. It's a kind of academic circle of life. A new idea may have many parents, but you're the midwife – you bring it out into the world.

Understanding your purpose in reading and note-taking

Read for your purpose, but first identify what your purpose is. If you can only find one text on your subject or you can't get hold of the texts that are available in time, then redesign your research questions (Check out Chapter 9 for more on research questions). Maybe the research questions were too specific, or assumed plenty of information was readily available, or included certain information that are only possibilities and not actually facts. For example, choosing to write about the lifecycle of microbes on Mars assumes that there are or were microbes on Mars. At the moment, it isn't clear whether the 'evidence' for microbes on Mars is indeed biological in nature – it could be mineral – in which case, there may have been no microbes.

Before you start detailed reading, you need to check out what's available in your area of interest. You need to use:

- ✔ Your course notes
- ✔ Suggestions from your tutor
- ✔ The library catalogue
- ✔ Internet sources

If you find some sources that look interesting but not useful at the moment, note down the reference in your learning diary for possible future uses. If you tend to use dates as memory aids, then put the reference in your diary for that day. If you prefer to have a 'possibly useful' section at the back of the diary, then note the details there. If you take the trouble to note something, note it in a place where you can easily find it again, say, six months from now. Have a strategy for finding notes again, otherwise references tend to get lost and your efforts will have been for nothing.

Developing Your Note-Taking Skills

Note-taking for your purpose means finding questions that you hope the text can answer. This means devising research questions to guide both the form and content of your writing and also the smaller and more detailed questions contained within the bigger ones.

You may have as an essay title 'Will China's 1979 one-child policy pose problems for the care of the elderly in China?' As the essay writer you need to review and consider the evidence and use it to give your view. You need to find texts to give you the answers to questions such as:

- ✔ What percentage of China's population is below working age, or retired? (More detailed questions may include: what is the age of retirement, average life expectancy, the average age of starting work? What is the proportion of workers to non-workers in the cities and the rural areas?)

✔ What were the proportions of the different groups in the population in 1979? (The questions above can make comparisons between 'then' and 'now'.)

✔ How were the elderly cared for in 1979 compared with now? If there's a difference, why? Is it possibly anything to do with the one-child policy or what are the other possible reasons? Is there a mixture of reasons? Are there differences between the towns and the countryside?

Always cross-check information, even if you find an article on just this subject. Country statistics may not be the most reliable, depending on how they're collected and what 'face' that country wants to present to the world. The World Bank and other international organisations' websites can often provide useful sources of data.

Generally speaking, it's best to read the most up-to-date material – that is, not more than a few years' old. One exception to this is past statistics used to compare with the present. However, quite often you can find historical data referred to in a recent book, so you may not have to go back to the original source.

Don't jump to conclusions. You can use several ways to skin the proverbial cat. An increase in the elderly population can be a sign of social welfare improvement. A decrease in the birth rate may also be an indicator of development because women are taking more control over their fertility. The decline in the number of workers (following the fall in the birth rate) suggests there may be economic difficulties, with those in work supporting a larger, non-working population than before. But this is to consider the situation from a western viewpoint. Other social factors like family support for the elderly in China may mitigate against this situation, or there could be a decline in traditional values and the adoption of more western-like work or social practices. Some articles you find may consider the problem from an economic perspective, others consider social or political aspects or compare several countries' care for the elderly in their populations. Your angle may not be the same but you can still use some of their evidence at the more general, background level, probably by looking at their statistics.

Once you've found good sources and answers to your first-level questions, try to create a new set of questions to probe deeper. If you can't find the answer you expect from a text, then think why, and consider the possible reasons why something you expected is missing. Socrates said that if we keep asking 'Why?' we can find many answers within ourselves. Some successful writing simply consists of asking 'Why?'. If you can show a hole in the logic, you've made your contribution to knowledge. Suggesting some possible reasons and possible research can set you up for your next piece of work or even your D.Phil!

Tabulating notes from several sources

Reading several sources dealing with a similar topic at the same time to find answers to your questions gives you several advantages:

- ✔ If one text is difficult to follow, reading similar information from another may make things clearer than re-reading the same text several times over.
- ✔ It can help you see what's generally agreed upon and where there are differences.
- ✔ It can give you different interpretations or analyses of the same information.
- ✔ It can raise your awareness of particular issues you may not have thought about before.
- ✔ It can help with summary skills.
- ✔ It can give you confidence to probe further when your logical guesses have come good.
- ✔ It can give you confidence as it acts as a checking system.
- ✔ It reduces any temptation to plagiarise.

However, reading is nothing without making good notes. The most thought-provoking way to start is to note the answers to your questions from several sources at the same time, in table form. This allows you to check what information is easily available and what isn't, and compare different sources by reading your notes horizontally as well as vertically. No single text is likely to answer all your questions, so making notes in this way also identifies information you need to look for and you're less likely to leave important questions out. It can help you decide what looks promising and the form in which you want to present the information.

You control operations more effectively than if you just jot down notes in a notebook based on the structure of the original text – if you do the latter, you're still playing the game by the author's rules, not yours. You may even be able to transfer your table notes directly to your written work. In any case, the notes you take should be closer to the final product – your written work – than they are to the source of information – the reading text.

Table 11-1 gives you an idea of how this works. Write the answers to your questions on A4 sheets so that you can compare the answers from several sources side by side on the floor or on your bed, to give you an idea of:

- ✔ The most useful texts.
- ✔ Where answers are thin or non-existent and decide what to do about it.
- ✔ The range of information or general agreement.
- ✔ Any problems with the available information.

Table 11-1 compares information from four sources about the percentage of the population in age groups: 0–14 (below working age), 15–64 (working age) and over 65(retired) in China, in order to help answer the question: 'Will China's 1979 one child policy pose problems for the care of the elderly in China?'. For each population age group, the nearest available data to1979 (when the one child policy was introduced) and to the present day is given. From this, it can be seen that the information from each source is slightly different, but that the trend to an increase in the percentage of retired people is shown in all sources.

When comparing data, it is often difficult to find a complete match in terms of the dates of information or numbers, but as long as the trends are the same, then this strengthens the idea here, that, yes, there may be a problem for the care of the elderly as their numbers are increasing, while the number of future workers is falling with the birth rate.

Table 11-1	**Example Noting Grid for China Essay**			
	Source			
	`www.china daily.com. cn/china/ 2006-09/01/ content_ 678901.htm`	`www.cia. gov/ library/ publica tions/ the- world- factbook/ geos/ ch.html`	*Wikipedia*	`www.all countries. org/china_ statistics /4_4_ basic_sta- tistics_ on_ national_ population .html`
1. Population aged 0–14 (2008)		20.1(2008)	20 (2007)	22.89 (2000)
2. Population aged 0–14 (1979)				40.69 (1964) 33.59 (1982)
3. Population aged 15–64 (2008)	70 (2005/6)	71.9 (2008)	67.7 (2007)	70.15 (2000)
4. Population aged 15–64 (1979)				57.65 (1964) 33.59 (1982) 66.74 (1990)

(continued)

Table 11-1 *(continued)*

	Source			
	www.china daily.com. cn/china/ 2006-09/01/ content_ 678901.htm	*www.cia. gov/ library/ publica tions/ the- world- factbook/ geos/ ch.html*	*Wikipedia*	*www.all countries. org/china_ statistics /4_4_ basic_sta- tistics_ on_ national_ population .html*
5. Population retired, 65+ (2008)	7.69 (2005/6)	8 (2008)	11.7 over 60 (2007)	6.959 (2000)
6. Population retired 65+ (1979)				3.56 (1964)
				4.91 (1982)
				5.57 (1990)

Information for 1979 (the year the one child per family rule was introduced) was impossibleto obtain, probably because there was no census in China in that year. This doesn't have to be a major stumbling block. You might decide to use the 1982 data from www.allcountries.com as a baseline, when there was a census, or use 1964 data as a 'before' baseline as well – after all, it would've taken a while for the one-child policy to have an effect on the working population age band (logically) and you may want to check on how effective the implementation of the one-child policy was.

Some statistics use different age bands (over 60 instead of over 65, for instance). The statistics available from four sources vary, as do the dates they refer to. From the census data there seem to be trends, so you may decide to present the information in a graph and include future projections, as the essay title refers to the future. A falling birth rate and a rising retired population would theoretically, at some point, become critical. When that happens may be another question to ask the literature. This gives you a possible theoretical perspective or base-line calculation to use.

Notes like these set you off on your next line of enquiry.

Often, no precise agreement exists over numbers, so the safest way to describe them is to use adverbs such as *approximately, about* or *roughly*, using an average or summary of the numerical data. Realising that numbers are flexible, approximate and not fixed in stone, is a useful lesson to learn. It's always worth questioning any number that doesn't seem to make sense, just as you would at the checkout in the supermarket. It would be surprising if all the sources did agree on exactly the same number, unless they were all quoting from the same base source. The differences may be due to the methodology used. This is another question that may be worth noting for your analysis or comment section later.

Studying is about learning by thinking, asking questions and thinking again – or you may say, pondering and reflecting. Note-taking – and what and how you do so – is a core skill in this process. This is how you bring your unique contribution to learning, which you show in the end product, your writing (or presentation.) If you use the strategy I've suggested, it then leads you to the next strategy, level of questions, answers (or lack of), analysis and comment.

Summary skills

The ability to summarise information is an important skill and attracts credit in your writing. Taking table notes (as in Table 11-1) helps you to summarise information from several sources by reading horizontally across. The answers from the literature to question 5 ' What percentage of the Chinese Population is over retirement age ?'are shown in Table 11-1, point 5, but the data uses different age bands (over 60 and over 65), but the figure of 8 per cent for 2008 looks well supported by the earlier figures from the other sources. A range of information to summarise also helps you to choose the appropriate language to use. For instance, stating *approximately* 8 per cent of the population were over 65 and had retired from work in 2008, would be a reasonable statement. If you went on to investigate why Wikipedia uses the age range 60+, then one reason may be that retirement ages differ in different provinces and between the sexes. For example, in Shanghai, women can retire at 55. In view of this, you may say *at least* 8 per cent of the population are of *retirement age*. In any event, always compare data from difference sources.

A summary can be about a range of information. In question 5 the summary would be 'from *about* just under 7 per cent (6.959) in 2000, to 8 per cent or even more in 2008, showing a *steady increase*.

The index pages at the back of books or a keyword Google search can often help you locate precise information to note in a grid form (as in Table 11-1) to use as the basis of your summary.

Mixing books and the net

You're most likely to find the most up-to-date – even up-to-the-minute – information on certain topics on the Internet. For example a keyword search on the British economy may give you a range of expert opinion from economists, institutions such as the Bank of England, OPEC, the quality newspapers, and so on and may even provide you with a ready made summary of schools of thought. Likely topics within the general economy include the reasons for price rises, falls and future projections in the housing market, consumer goods, currencies and so on. For example, according to the Nationwide and Halifax building societies respectively, house prices fell in August, 2008 by 1.9 and 1.8 per cent. Current social science and education topics are also likely to provide a range of opinions to summarise. Check out Chapter 13 for more detail on using the internet for research.

The nature of texts means that the best places to find ready-made summaries of information are:

- ✔ The last chapters of books, especially the last few (three or four) paragraphs.
- ✔ The last one or two paragraphs of a chapter.
- ✔ The last one or two paragraphs of a section or subsection.

Check all the above against the introductory chapter, section or paragraphs of the piece to find a partial summary, but normally without the concluding comments.

These summaries reflect the writer's view, but they're nevertheless a good source for making general comparisons with the views of other writers and provide insights or suggestions for making your own analysis.

Comparing and contrasting

In some sense, everything maintains its existence through comparison (or contrast) with something else – male and female, hot and cold and so on. In a nutshell, comparing two or more things means showing what's similar and what's different about them. Contrasting things means focusing on the differences between them.

The ad men have for decades had us taking the Pepsi challenge, seeing which powder removes the most stains, telling Stork from butter and comparing the road-holding and acceleration capability of several desirable vehicles . We compare political parties and the prices of almost everything. Comparison does seem to be pretty hard-wired into us. You're a natural at it, you were making a comparison when you screamed at nine months' old because you thought your brother was given a bigger ice cream than you!

Some of the common units for comparison/contrast are:

- ✔ **Time:** Two or more dates or periods, or before and after something happened (as implied in the China example).

- ✔ **Place or geographical location:** Insights from research in one place can suggest possible ways of doing things in another. An education or production system from one part of the world may be possible to use in another part. This means you have to compare what happens in each place first, and then find the differences.

- ✔ **Social or economic factors:** Rich and poor or bourgeois within a country, the Gross Domestic Product (GDP) of various countries, that is, their incomes and outputs, social indicators – birth and death rates, education levels and so on.

- ✔ **Traditional and modern:** For example, traditional and modern medicine, or farming methods.

- ✔ **Religious, ethnic, language:** Such comparisons often go together, for example, China's 55 ethnic minorities, UK's indigenous languages, English, Welsh and Gaelic.

- ✔ **Town and country (urban and rural):** Often within the same country, as conditions vary.

- ✔ **Capacity:** For example, of different engine sizes or referring to measurements of physical or manpower resources. Capacity is a common unit of comparison in reports of various kinds.

Units of comparison are very useful at the next layer of note-taking. You can use the same system of an A4 sheet for each area of comparison or contrast.

First comparing what is similar between two projects or experiments helps you consider what possible reason there could be for the outcomes being different. For example, a seed supply project to farmers was very successful in one place but not in a second. The climate and soil conditions were similar in both, and the men in each household collected the seed, as the project specified. In the first place, men were responsible for planting seed, so the project went well. In the second location, it was the women who plant seeds, and didn't know how to use them well. The researcher didn't check who was responsible for planting in the second project, but simply copied the first. All the differences you can find between two or more situations provide potential reasons for analysis. You also need to compare your own aims in writing with what you have and have not achieved. This self-criticism and analysis from reading your own work is a mark-winner!

Comparison and contrast are central to reading and note-taking in order to create an argument or theme for written work or presentations. However, when you set two situations side by side, they should share many of the same features, that is, you must compare like with like. The exciting part is the differences that you then reveal. For instance, if you compare two cars that are identical, except that one has a petrol engine and the other a diesel engine, the engine difference is the general variable (what they don't share in common), and it generates several other differences to discuss as a result:

- The cost of each type when new.
- How far they maintain their resale value.
- Greenhouse gas emissions and green credentials.
- Fuel consumption and fuel costs (efficiency).
- Noise levels, the effects of cold weather, maintenance costs, engine life and so on.

The discussion may lead you to suggest an alternative, like converting the petrol engine to duel fuel in order to use Liquid Petroleum Gas (LPG) – a cheaper and greener fuel.

A common problem is to read widely rather than specifically and with an aim. This results in finding too many differences at a very general level. For example, if you try to compare a formula-one racing car with a horse and cart at a general level, they're both wheeled vehicles, but beyond that similarity (a *constant*) there are so many differences (*variables*) that there's very little to learn or conclude of any interest. Something similar can happen if your reading has very little focus or no well-considered questions to find answers to. What you've read may not be very useful or usable, but more importantly, lack of focus may mean you've not read some appropriate texts and consequently have missed some important information – a waste of both time and opportunity!

Analysis

Intelligent note-taking isn't just a matter of finding the right texts, which are the ones suitable for your purposes. Once you've made notes from each reading source for each question you want to find the answer to – ideally on single sides of A4 or similar so that you can compare them easily – and found differences and similarities, the next question is 'Why?'. This is where the key skill of analysis comes in.

Where sources disagree, you need to consider the background or context of those making the different claims. Use your reading to dig around and feed your notes on this aspect. This is also a comparison exercise but at a deeper level and entails some logical deduction as well. For example, Greenpeace and the US government are likely to have very different takes on the impact of fossil fuel power stations on the environment. As well as considering the factual basis for claims of pollution (and these are normally about the degree of pollution or in comparison with another energy source) you need to understand where the two sides are starting from. The following example gives some of the possible reasons for differences in data or in the interpretation of data:

Greenpeace is likely to take a more extreme environmentalist view that an American government for four key reasons:

✔ **They have different power bases.** The American Government depends on votes from all sectors of American society, including many with a vested interest in polluting industries.

Greenpeace is an independent charitable organisation supported by donations whose aim is to 'defend the natural world and promote peace by investigating, exposing and confronting environmental abuse, and championing environmentally responsible solutions'. See `www.green peace.org.uk/what-we-do`.

✔ **They have different time frames.** An American government has to bear in mind that congressional and presidential elections take place every four years (half at the same time as the presidential elections and the other half two years into the presidency) and for the Senate, every six years. As with any elected government, planning tends to give consideration to short-term needs, like being re-elected, because without an elected power base, it can't put into practice any long-term plans.

Greenpeace is concerned with the long-term future of the planet and with opposing any action in any part of the world that it believes is detrimental to the environment. *Greenpeace* isn't answerable to voters. As well as having a long-term perspective, it also has a *rapid response* perspective, and doesn't have to wait for the approval of the Senate or any elected authority for its actions.

✔ **They have different attitudes to the law.** An American government has to justify its actions in terms of both national law – to the electorate – and international law– to its allies and the wider world – and be aware of how its actions will be perceived.

Greenpeace activists are prepared to break national and international law, for example, the law of trespass, to expose actions that they see as environmental abuse.

> ✔ **They have different missions.** The American Government has many areas of concern – the economy, defence, social services, education, the environment and so on – and has to balance many needs, including that of being re-elected.
>
> *Greenpeace* has the mission statement quoted above and no external electors or other stakeholders to answer to. It has a single focus and objective.

When considering different views or interpretations, it's always worth you asking where they come from, who put them there, who pays the piper, what their likely motives and mission are and so on. Another way of looking at interpretations is to consider bias. Everyone has bias due to their past experience such as where they live, their social background and so on. It isn't possible to be totally free of bias, although we may not be aware of it.

Some reports openly acknowledge bias in a certain area. Don't relax too much, as they can be quite biased in another area that they don't acknowledge. If a text claims to consider two sides of an issue – the arguments for and against the legalisation of cannabis – then a quick numerical account of the number of pages, paragraphs or lines devoted to each side of the argument gives you an idea of how balanced or not the text is.

Gender bias and the wide use of gendered pronouns for all actors – *he* – is still quite common, often arising from the culture of the writer rather than deliberate choice. However, it also assumes that all the important things are done by males. Consequently, legislation, access to education and social services and so on may all be organised from a male norm point of view and be hostile to female needs, for traditional or cultural reasons, rather than the deliberate exclusion of female needs. They simply aren't perceived.

Critiquing and text analysis

Critiquing and text analysis involves even more detailed reading and note-taking, possibly at the word-by-word level. If you find a good source, this can be a very fruitful as well as quite an easy note-taking exercise to transfer to your written work.

For instance, if you suspect a gender bias in a particular document, you can scan it for the use of male and female pronouns and simply note and compare the numbers for each. An example of this is from a student (thanks to Earl Kehoe) who was looking at the history syllabuses of three different junior year groups in Rwanda and, through counting pronouns, noting how many references to male and female each contained. He then extended his search to looking for named males and females and considered their status.

For example, a named woman mentioned as the wife of somebody may be given little status on her own account in the text. If you find a gender or other imbalance using this simple method, it may well give you plenty to comment on – as an example, if most males referred to are soldiers this creates a social imbalance in the documented history).

You can also choose to analyse the particular claims a text makes. For example, if the history documents described above claimed to represent the history of the nation, you can challenge this if you found a large imbalance in the number of male to female pronouns and names used in favour of males. The document would represent part – the male part – of the history of a nation.

Gender bias is still worth checking as a starting point for detailed reading, note-taking and analysis and for asking 'Why?'. Ageism is another bias worth looking for in official documents, work-practice documents and so on.

Detailed text analysis means looking at a text in great detail to try to find underlying meanings that relate the text to events in the real world or to other parts of the text. You can adopt numerical counts for pronouns (as above) or set up other categories in a table, for example, positive or negative references to people over 65. You can also examine the use of *overgeneralisations*, statements which make wide-ranging claims about a subject based on limited evidence.

One example is the association between hoodies and bad behaviour.

A head teacher in Wales in 2005, reportedly said, according to BBC Wales (`http://news.bbc.co.uk/1/hi/wales/south_east/4605667.stm`)

> 'We are particularly concerned as hooded tops are reappearing and the hood is being used to hide pupils' identity during unacceptable behaviour. All hooded tops will be confiscated and only returned at the end of each half-term.'

This statement is an overgeneralisation. *Some* pupils may be using the hood to hide their identity during unacceptable behaviour, but the statement suggests that all pupils who wear hoodies do so for this purpose. In this case, reading at word level means noting the missing word 'some'.

If your studies include aspects of law, governance, international relations or similar topic areas as part of your course, then you may find document analysis – detailed text analysis and interpretation – particularly fruitful. It's worth remembering that a text may tell you as much about the author's attitude (whoops!) as it does about the topic, and this may well affect the treatment of the subject.

Citation/quotation and note cards

Whenever you read a text, it's most important to note down the author, date, title, place of publication and publisher for a book, and add editor, journal title and volume number for a journal article and web reference and date of access for a web-based text. Check with your course notes to see what their specific requirements are. You must also write down the page number if you make a direct quotation and perhaps a range of pages – pp5–11, for example – if your comments summarise these pages, or perhaps a chapter. See Chapter 7 for more on noting references.

These references allow your tutor to find the references you used. Some books may have different editions – hardback and paperback, for instance – so it's important to note the edition (and the date of publication) and the page numbers. The page numbers for a particular reference may well be different in another edition. Basically, noted references are a kind of 'proof' or evidence that you've read or at least consulted certain texts.

I've suggested that you use a card system for quotes based on the author's name so you can easily shuffle the cards into alphabetical order for your bibliography or reference section. Some people prefer to keep their reference cards with an elastic band round them for each topic or keep their references online. If you like reading on the bus, as I do, then cards are useful as dealing with a laptop on a bus is not recommended! You can keep references in your learning diary on a topic or date basis. The decision is yours to use which-ever method or combination of methods works for you.

Whichever method or methods you use, make sure that:

- ✔ You've noted all the necessary reference details.

- ✔ You keep your notes systematically so you can easily find them in future.

- ✔ You quote any direct quotations accurately – spelling, punctuation, and so on, and no words left out.

Nothing is more frustrating than realising you've made a mistake in copying down a quotation. This can be a double whammy when time is short as you may have to leave it out, thus negating your earlier effort and the chance to get credit for it, or waste time re-doing something that just a few extra seconds of checking would have sorted out.

Chapter 12

Using the Internet as a Research Tool

In This Chapter

▶ Making good use of the Internet

▶ Avoiding plagiarism

▶ Using online research tools

▶ Accessing useful websites

▶ Approaching e-learning

The Internet is a huge and wonderful resource as well as a tool, something that would have seemed unbelievable to our grandparents. It holds not only old and respected wisdom, but up-to-the minute web publications that can reach the public quicker than their printed versions. Broadband widths are being extended to cope with the increased use of the Internet for watching films and television on laptops, which can also be study resources. It's difficult to conceive of studying today without using the Internet. If you don't have your own PC or laptop, you'll certainly have access to them on campus, probably up to 9 or 10 p.m.

Online Dos and Don'ts

So much information literally at your fingertips can seem overwhelming as well as tremendously exciting, but dangers exist.

Be aware that the Internet is a free medium and anyone who's connected to it can use it to express themselves. The content of pages posted by individuals isn't monitored or checked in the same way as paper publications, so:

✔ Check the source of any information you find and don't use it if you're unsure about it.

✔ Cross-check Internet information with other sources as far as possible.

> ✔ Always note the date you accessed the web as well as the URL and other details, like the names of authors.

Protect your eyesight by taking screen breaks. Look at and do something different every hour for a few minutes. A short walk outside is best.

Browser beware: inappropriate web pages

Online information can be very seductive particularly if it isn't available elsewhere. Before using any web information for your own studies or indeed reading in detail any information, use the URL and home page to find out:

✔ Who wrote it.

✔ For whom it was written.

✔ What its purpose is.

✔ At what level it is written in terms of detail and authorship.

✔ When it was written.

For example, a description of the workings of condensing boilers for installation engineers may be too detailed for a report comparing the cost, efficiency and green credentials of different types of boiler. The information used in essays and reports must be selected to reflect the objectives of those pieces of work. More appropriate sources of information may be technical comparison sites giving costs, energy outputs and carbon footprints, consumer feedback on the practical use and efficiency of different boiler types.

Similarly, if you search by topic and find an online essay example on a topic related to one you're interested in, it may treat the topic too superficially if the author is a primary or lower secondary student. It can be useful as a summary or checklist of the main points, but that's all. Any online essay should be treated with extreme caution as it may be written in accordance with a different writing culture and therefore have different requirements, even if the level seems appropriate.

Accommodating balance and bias

An online account of an event – just like a newspaper – can reflect the personal or political viewpoint or even prejudice of the writer, so should be balanced against accounts of the same event from different sources. For example, the Russian Federation presence in Georgia in August 2008 is described in quite different terms in Georgian, European Union, Russian Federation, US, Turkish and Chinese sources. Rather than doing a paper search it's much easier to use a search engine to find online views that agree with your own search because of your choice of keywords which may have a particular bias, so make sure that you check out other sources and views so that you balance your work well.

The Internet reflects a range of opinion and information, not necessarily facts. To be on the safe side you need to cross-check information and consult a range of sources. This shows your reader that you're being open-minded in your reading as well as professional in your research.

It's also important to check when a piece was written. Generally, information that's more than five years' old needs to be treated with caution as subsequent events, breakthroughs in knowledge, research or methods can make earlier information redundant and thus reduce its value except, perhaps, from a historical perspective or because the information relates to core theories or paradigms that still form part of the mainstream.

It'll be obvious to your reader (marker) if you haven't taken the bias into consideration when selecting material from the Internet: you need to provide evidence or support for your work. Be both wary and aware.

Avoiding Internet plagiarism

With all that the Internet offers, it's tempting to think that the last word has been said on many subjects or that you can't possibly express an idea as well as an Internet source has.

The Internet is a tool and Internet resources are there to be used by you as long as you acknowledge them. You're in the driving seat. Your needs and reasons for consulting texts aren't the same as those of the authors of the web pages . For one thing, you're looking for information on a web page that's already been written, so it may benefit from being updated by you in some way. You may be able to add information or link information in it to another source and create a whole new text in your own words. Identify your needs and reasons and then select sources that help you, but adapt them to your requirements.

As well as using search engines to find books, authors, or a topic, you can type in a few words or a sentence. For example, if you want to find the whole of Portia's speech at the touch of a button, you can type *The quality of mercy is not* into a search engine and in seconds you have a link to the whole speech and other information about *The Merchant of Venice* as well.

This facility to match a few words to their origins is one reason why it isn't only dishonest but foolish to copy down sentences or even phrases from the Internet and use them in your own work without acknowledging them. You marker won't have to work very hard to find the likely source if he suspects that's what you've done! The Internet is there to help you but isn't a substitute for your own thinking or consideration of a subject. By all means use it for your purposes, but say where the information came from.

For this reason as well, don't buy online essays, although they can be bought on many subjects at a price. Buying essays is a foolish idea because:

- ✔ They may not fit your topic very well as they've probably been written for a more general purpose.

- ✔ They may not be written at the right level.

- ✔ The length may not be appropriate.

- ✔ You don't know how accurate the writer has been about referencing and acknowledging.

- ✔ You'll be responsible for any mistakes.

- ✔ The essay may have been written years ago and is now out of date, as are the references.

- ✔ The essay may be badly written, biased and not written within your academic culture.

- ✔ It's possible that your tutor has already been presented with the same essay by another student or by a watchdog academic system that's spotted the use of bought essays and passed on this information to faculty members.

Above all else of course, the purpose of education is to develop your learning potential to the full. Research and writing and other academic tasks are meant to be an apprenticeship to this end. Copying from the Internet or buying essays doesn't contribute to learning in the academic sense.

The best way to avoid plagiarism from the Internet is to:

- ✔ Create questions to find answers to on the Internet – identify your purpose.

- ✔ Make sure that you note down all the URLs with potentially useful information and your date of access.

- ✔ Cross-check and note information from various sources (for more on this have a look at Chapter 10).

- ✔ Summarise in your own words the information that you don't want to quote directly.

✔ Discuss any difficult parts of the material you've found with friends, your tutor, explain it to your mum (usually a good listener) or say it out loud and record it on a CD. Speaking means your brain has to process information, and you find out what you did or didn't understand or what you took as 'read', but which is really full of holes. Prepare to be surprised!

The Internet as a Life-Saver

The big advantage of the Internet is that it's available 24 hours a day. You can use it in the middle of the night (providing you have access) or whenever you get inspired to write or have an idea to research. If you're an insomniac, it can be ideal and no worries about working in your pyjamas or alternative night attire! If you have poor eyesight you can magnify web pages to help you read them. Some people find reading from the screen easier than from a paper source, though don't forget to take screen breaks!

Sourcing books

The Internet can be particularly helpful in sourcing recommended or helpful reading texts. Try these ways of finding what you need:

✔ **Using your library online:** Access your college library's catalogue online to check the availability of recommended books, certainly on campus. If a book isn't held in the library you can normally fill out an inter-library loan request slip online to borrow it from another library. This may take a week or two. The Internet can thus be used to give an up-to-date status report on the availability of material so that you can consider alternative action.

✔ **Using the Internet to buy books:** Find copies of books that are hard to get hold of, perhaps because they're out of print. www.amazon.co.uk for example, is probably the best source of second-hand books through its private seller system and the books are often quite cheap. Buy from a UK seller to cut down transport costs and time. Books can arrive within three days – check whether the seller posts first or second class. It's worth bearing this in mind when you compare sellers and prices.

You can re-sell any unwanted books on Amazon when you've finished with them. If they were useful to you, there'll be someone out there who needs them, as long as they're still readable (avoid underlying in ink and that sort of thing). You may even make a profit!

✔ **Accessing author's work direct:** If you can't get hold of a book by a particular author, try searching for an article or paper he may have written on a similar topic. A good place to look is his home page if he has one, as these usually include a list of publications with their dates, and links to any that are available online. If you can't locate a book or paper there's no harm in going straight to the horse's mouth and emailing the author – his email address will be on his home page. In addition, academics may well be happy to send you an article by email attachment, if you ask them nicely. They may even have a more recent conference paper on the topic which hasn't yet been published, and which they're happy to share with you.

✔ **Asking your peers' opinion:** If you've joined an online chat room to discuss your study interests, you may find someone there has a copy of the book you need or can help you. This is particularly useful if you only need a page or two as they can be electronically scanned and then sent to you as an email attachment.

Online chat rooms are particularly useful for philosophers, but they can become a substitute for other work and an avoidance strategy, a bit like taking lots of baths. It's important to talk to real people – in the pub or wherever – and not spend your break time in chat rooms. Use them only as a tool for your immediate use.

As well as getting information about your topic, the Internet can also help you find out about methodology. If you key in a search for a particular research or analysis method, you can almost certainly find not only some definitions but also some examples of the method in use. This can help you develop your own methods. Equally importantly, it can help you to understand how the methodology was used or misused in someone else's research, in terms of its appropriateness to the subject, its interpretation and its analysis.

It's useful to find out the names of the well-known academics in your subject area and use an Internet search to find out where they're currently working. They may well have put their course outlines and maybe even their lecture notes so that their own students can access these off campus. You can take advantage of this as well as gaining another viewpoint or more detailed information.

Online research tools

In addition to the research methods mentioned earlier in this chapter, a number of general tools exist to help you get started on the quest for information from the comfort of your chair. As with everything else, it's a good idea to keep a record of all the websites you access, with dates and a note of their possible use, in case you need them in the future.

Bibliographies

If you read a text with no bibliography it's probably a newspaper or non-academic account, so be wary. Online journal or published articles normally have a bibliography or reference section at the end.

It's a good idea to look at bibliographies as the dates of the publications they refer to can give you an idea of how up to date the article is. Some articles may be published on the Internet some time, even years, after they were originally written. Check to see if they've been revised.

As well as telling you something about the date and range of subject matter of an article, even if you decide the article doesn't look promising for your purposes it may be that one of the references in the bibliography is more focused to your needs and can help. For example, you may find an up-to-date journal article in the bibliography that you didn't know about, plus some indication of the subject matter from the reference made to it in the article. You can always check with your tutor if you're concerned about using it. However, if the publisher is well known, the article will have been vetted, even if the writer is not so well known (check them out on another web search). In general terms, online articles provide a good source of up-to-date research and articles. These in themselves may not be enough to base your work on but they can certainly be used to supply supporting evidence.

The bibliography is one area where another student's work can be very helpful. Many students, especially at Master's level, publish their own essays on the Internet.

You don't know what the mark is, so be wary of referring to the content. You can quote some unpublished research from an M.Phil or D.Phil (with the writer's permission, of course), but reference is normally made to 'received wisdom', that is, academics or others who aren't at the 'apprentice stage' as students are.

Students at Master's level and above often do sterling research on their bibliographies and include online references that they've used that can save you time and hassle.

You may find that some of these referenced web pages are eventually taken off, which is why it's important to remember to put the date you accessed a web page to show that at that time it was in existence.

Bibliographies from other university courses or course programmes that you can access also come in useful for finding references that you may find handy when you're writing essays or reports where you have to extend and expand on the work you've done in lectures or seminars on your course.

Again, find out the names of eminent scholars in your subject area and then their homepage and list of publications. Looking at the bibliographies of the most up to date of these can direct you to useful sources or tell you what's 'sexy' – the topic of the moment – in a particular subject area. You should also note the purpose for which any of these references were used in the eminent scholars' articles. It may be they criticised a methodology that you were thinking of using or a piece of research or analysis, so this can be useful information.

You can benefit from such criticism. It can provide you with a theoretical framework through which to analyse other work, or you may be able to use other work to show that some criticism wasn't justified. In either event, a reference can provide the jumping off point for further work – justification or criticism – that's how the building blocks of education are made.

Google

Google is probably the widest-ranging search engine, with billions of entries. It can save you a lot of time (and maybe agony). As with any search engine, the more accurate the information you give it, the better the results. However, it's better than most at interpreting misspellings, and asks you *Did you mean . . .?* through its automatic spell checker and offer alternatives.

Google has many useful features, including world weather, world time zones, stock market results, but the most useful for students are probably the following.

- ✔ **Fill in the blank.** Put an asterisk (*) into the part of the sentence you want finished or the question you want to ask. 'Will you still need me, will you still * . . .'. This can be really useful if you didn't manage to write down all of a quote during a lecture.

- ✔ **Google books.** If you type 'Google books' into Google, press 'enter', and then type the author or title of a book into Google books, Google then returns any pages with that content. This is very useful for tracking down titles or quotations (as well as spotting plagiarism).

- ✔ **Definitions.** Type 'define' then space, then the word you want defined and you get a dictionary definition.

- ✔ **Synonym search.** If you type ~ (tilde) in front of your search term (~carbon neutral) Google displays related terms.

- ✔ **Calculator.** You just have to type the calculation you'd like done in the search box, for example, 20 per cent of 357982165.

- ✔ **Unit converter.** This can convert many measurements – height, weight, length and other quantities into different units. Type in the conversion you want, '27 kilometres in miles', for example, and Google provides the conversion.

Overall, Google at the moment seems to offer the simplest and most comprehensive searches, saving time and effort.

BBC online and other television archives

The BBC website, www.bbc.co.uk, is a vast resource, offering not only up-to-the-minute news, online radio and television broadcast information, podcasts of programmes to listen to on your iPod, but also a range of really useful resources for students.

The BBC and other online television web pages offer television or audio clips, a different learning medium and a welcome change from text learning.

Of particular interest to students are the History, Science and Nature and Society and Culture sections though it may well be worth checking out others such as Health. Each topic's web page signals television or radio programmes that fall within these wide parameters, as well as links to websites that have related articles or factual information sheets.

The BBC online archive contains a collection of photographs, documents and clips from television and radio programmes from the last 60 years, classified under various topics such as the birth of the National Health Service or Survivors of the Titanic. It's worth a look, as the BBC continually adds to this archive. The Science section has interactive links and links to illustrated articles about space travel and time warps.

Much of the content of the BBC, Channel 4, and other television web pages related to education, is aimed at a young audience, although they often provide links for research in greater depth or detail. Some of the content relates directly to broadcast programmes, and extra information that's not broadcast is available online. The interactive information includes simple experiments, tasks or questionnaires that can serve as models for your own work or start you thinking. The layout and style is generally clear. If you find any difficulties, you can comment on them.

You can also find various blogs written by journalists, which you can respond to, providing another chance to ask direct questions and get answers from 'the horse's mouth'.

Overall, www.bbc.co.uk web pages offer three main benefits to students:

- ✔ A user-friendly guide to some core concerns and topics illustrated through audio or audio-visual clips, photographs, diagrams as well as text – a multi-sensory learning experience.

- ✔ Factual references from the archives – there's a useful time line to consult – and resources that illustrate the mood or passions of a particular period.

- ✔ Suggestions for simple experiments or research, some of which may interest teachers or may be adaptable for other purposes.

Channel 4 and other networks also have education resources, especially good interactive ones, mainly aimed at school students. Channel 4's archive footage of World War I, for example, is of general interest.

Television channels' web pages offer visual images and sound to complement the written word and documentary, history and natural history. Programmes are often made by experts in their fields or have academics as consultants. In addition, they often include a commentary and invite opinions from experts with different perspectives.

Online newspapers

Online newspapers like the *The Guardian*'s www.guardian.co.uk or the *The Independent*'s www.independent.co.uk have a similar layout to television web pages, with news on the home page and links to topic pages like science and technology, the environment and education. Online newspapers can provide up-to-the-minute information and have links to more detailed information in archived articles. *The Guardian* and *The Independent* online contain particularly useful education sections, including e-learning pages, with helpful hints and links to useful websites.

Check out *The Guardian* and *The Independent* for what's hot in particular subject areas and for helpful e-learning hints.

The *Financial Times*'s ww.ft.com/home/uk can be useful for economists, *The Times*'s www.timesonline.co.uk for world news and comment and *The Daily Telegraph*'s www.telegraph.co.uk for culture and business.

Also available online are American and European newspapers such as *The New York Times*'s www.nytimes.com or *Der Spiegel*'s international edition in English, www.spiegel.de/international , which can provide a different perspective on economic or political events. Le Figaro has an international edition in French. www.lefigaro.fr/international.

Wikipedia

At the time of writing, *Wikipedia*, the free online encyclopaedia, had 2,517,264 articles in English and this number is growing. It's published in at least 262 languages. Jimmy Wales and Larry Sanger started Wikipedia in 2001 with the aim of assembling all human knowledge. Wikipedia is 'collaboratively edited' and provides an online tutorial for would-be 'Wikipedians'. Since its birth, it has grown steadily in popularity as well as in size. If you have rare or specific knowledge about the origins of a field, for example, here's your chance to add a new topic, albeit anonymously!

Various schools of thought have considered the merits and demerits of this collaborative editing. On the one hand, there's no editorial board to check the accuracy of the content, so it's worth checking any information you want to use from another source. Also, as the contributors are unknown, you can't check their credentials.

On the other hand, incorrect information can be edited and corrected, and this undoubtedly happens in popular topics. Some entries actually contain appeals for help in providing greater accuracy and more detail and point out shortcomings in the entries. Some entries are highly detailed and others sparse. Some are complex and assume a fairly high level of background knowledge of the subject, whereas others are more basic.

However, on a Google search for a topic or definition (unless you specify a Google definition) Wikipedia is likely to be at the top of the list. Readers quickly become accustomed to the Wikipedia layout, key words and statistics for each topic.

The page layout makes Wikipedia entries relatively clear and easy to grasp. Wikipedia is a good port of call for initial enquiries, but, as is always the case, information should be cross-checked with that from another source.

As the 262 or more language contributions operate more or less separately – not translated from one language to another – it may be interesting to compare a topic that appears in two different languages. This may reveal different ways of looking at the subject, though there's no way to check that the same contributor did not, in fact, write both contributions, that is, translated his own work or wrote a separate entry in two languages on the same topic. For further information on the operation and philosophy of Wikipedia, see www.en.wikipedia.org/wiki/Wikipedia#Reliability_and_bias.

Other useful online sources

Many useful online sources of help are available, organised on a topic basis.

If the website address includes 'ac', then the source is a university and you can feel reasonably confident about using it. If the address says 'edu', then it's a bona fide education site but the level may not be appropriate. Equally, some very good sites (examples below), don't have 'ac' or 'edu' in the address but good ones are often linked to an academic source of some kind. Useful free sites for web education and research resources that don't require a subscription include:

Intute

Intute, www.intute.ac.uk, is a free online service giving access to various web resources for education and research that have been vetted by subject specialists from a consortium of British universities and partners. Intute organises subject matter under general topics:

- ✔ Arts and Humanities
- ✔ Health and Life Sciences
- ✔ Science, Engineering and Technology
- ✔ Social Sciences

You can also browse by subject and there's also tutorial support in using the site. The target audience is lecturers, researchers and students in British higher and further education.

The Intute site covers a useful range of topics at a higher level than, for example, the BBC. Nevertheless, articles on the same topic from these two resources can mutually support each other and help you read them critically.

1PL

The Internet Public Library at www.ipl.org is a good way to find academic publications on a range of topics. The site also provides tips and suggestions for making searches. Originally started in the University of Michigan, the site is now run by a consortium of universities. The Frequently Asked Questions (FAQs) give a flavour of the site and gives help with writing references to web pages and other support.

Science topics

Up-to-the-minute Biological Science information for a general audience is available from the online version of *Nature*, www.nature.com, *Science Daily*, www.sciencedaily.com, reports up-to-the minute news on a range of science and technical topics, including medicine, and *Science Direct*, sciencedirect.com, offers some free access to current issues and is well worth a look for scientists.

Check out with your subject area or library to find out which online journals you can access through a general university subscription. If you like Science Direct, for example, you may be able to persuade the powers that be to pay for a subscription. The online articles generally appear before the paper-based one. JSTOR, www.jstor.org, is a subscription-based source of a wide range of articles, so check to see if you can gain access through your college library subscription. Once a year, libraries usually ask for suggestions for new journals to subscribe to.

Business, Economics and Statistics

Quick MBA at www.quickmba.com is a good source for the discussion of theoretical models and the Radical Statistics Group, www.radstats.org.uk, provides statistics on a wide range of subjects. Greg Mankiw's blog at www.gregmankiw.blogspot.com lets you into the inner workings of the mind of a Havard professor, while more professors join in at www.http://blogs.wsj.com/economics.

History

For medievalists, www.fordham.edu/halsall/Sbook.html is a great site for eye witness accounts and contemporary documents and www.luminarium.org contains biographies and source material as well as medieval to Restoration literature.

International and European law

The Archive of European integration, `http://www.aei.pitt.edu`, is a good source of EU published green and white papers as well as legal research information and `www.asil.org` is a helpful guide to law resources on the web.

The BNC can provide support and help you feel more confident about the appropriate use of new phrases in a more extensive way than a newspaper. It's also very useful for studying English.

Media and Culture

`www.theory.org.uk` is run by David Gauntlet, Professor of Media and Communications at the University of Westminster, so his credentials speak for themselves. The University of Aberystwyth's `www.aber.ac.uk` media and communication page contains a range of topics with links to articles and archive material, including film and visual images.

Philosophy

For philosophers or those wanting to understand the rationale behind different concepts, Stanford University's `www.plato.stanford.edu` provides explanations and essays concerning key philosophical issues, all vetted by philosophers, so the credentials are impeccable.

British National Corpus

The British National Corpus (BNC), `www.natcorp.ox.ac.uk`, incorporates a collection of over 100 million words from a wide cross-section of both spoken and written English. Using the free online search engine, you can key in words or phrases and the engine provides up to 50 samples of the most common uses of them. This can be very helpful for using newly acquired vocabulary in your own work and showing you the other words or phrases likely to appear in the same context.

The BNC can provide support and help you feel more confident about the appropriate use of new phrases in a more extensive way than a newspaper. It's also very useful for those studying English.

Approaching E-Learning

E-learning – electronic learning – consists of any instruction that is partly or wholly delivered using computer technology. E-learning doesn't only refer to formal education. It includes the strategies companies may use to deliver training courses to their employees.

E-learning means that person-to-person interaction may be limited or there may be none at all. Some distance-learning universities deliver their courses entirely electronically, especially at postgraduate level. You'll almost certainly access some of your course-related material or information about your course of study through your PC or laptop and Internet resources are probably going to be an important part of your self-study or research activities. E-learning is certain to be part of your study experience.

Be careful when you do a search on any topic, but especially psychology or behavioural sciences. Check the origin of the information, as it may not be from an educational establishment. It's possible for you to refer in your work to company sponsored e-learning or research as long as you're aware that that's what it is and say so clearly: a good deal of high-quality, in-company work is available, some of it carried out by well-known academics.

Any research, testing or reports that come from companies has a specific purpose or agenda, often financial or economic reasons. University or college-based research on the other hand is supposed to be unbiased, although much research is supported by commercial companies, especially in the pharmaceutical industry. This support affects what is researched in universities, but shouldn't affect how it's done– for example, by influencing the results. Bear this is mind as a possible criticism when reviewing this kind of work.

Your tutor or course literature is likely to refer you to certain web pages that have been vetted. They're a good place to start your searches. Some recommended sites contain links to other sites, or have a reference or bibliography section that are probably reliable.

In addition to information that your home university or college sends you through the Internet, you may well be able to access similar information from other universities. Thousands of universities and colleges in the world use the English language (including courses in some European countries like Belgium and Germany) and most have online support materials for their students. You may be able to access some of these resources without a special password. Most education establishments like to provide online information about the content of their courses and methods of study to inform and attract potential students, so you can benefit from this.

Some postgraduate distance-learning courses have a range of discussion papers and suggested experiments to try online, but again, the best search method is to use your course name or the name of a well-known academic. A keyword search from your subject is also useful for finding references to academics in your area, especially if a search engine gives several different and reasonably recent references to the same person.

Many universities also provide study tips, for example, in 'Online Writing Laboratories' (OWLs), which usually have open access. These can be very helpful for science students in explaining the requirements of different types of writing, because these requirements vary relatively little between countries.

Humanities students, especially undergraduates, should be wary, as although Australia and New Zealand have a similar writing culture to the UK, US undergraduate writing requirements differ somewhat from those in UK. At postgraduate level, these differences are less marked.

Chapter 13

Tackling the Building Blocks: Numbers and Figures

In This Chapter
▶ Dealing with numbers
▶ Illustrating with diagrams

As a student of any subject, you deal with evidence. It won't always be good evidence, but academic work is evidence based. It's non-fiction.

Some evidence is quantitative, based on relatively large numbers. For example, the information gathered in a UK national census comes from every household with registered voters in the UK. It provides a good source of information about certain social trends such as popular first names or divorce rates or the occupants of particular houses. It's not very useful for information about migrant workers or temporary residents as the UK census takes place every ten years and most migrant or temporary workers aren't on the electoral role. Census information provides 'snapshot' information about a particular date every ten years.

Some evidence is qualitative. The emphasis is on the quality of the information, the richness of the detail about individual entities or relatively small groups, for example, eight-year-old children in a particular class or the pregnant women attending a particular clinic over a period of time or even the daily log book of a particular vessel, like that of the Starship Enterprise!

One of the important issues to consider is how to present information in your own work and how to understand (and criticise) the information that you read. They say a picture is worth a thousand words: a diagram, chart or graph may be clearer than words or words alone, especially if it can present related information side by side rather than on different pages. You also need to demonstrate a healthy scepticism towards any diagram, chart or table as it excludes, as well as includes, information, and what it doesn't tell you can be as important as what it does. This chapter gives you the low-down on handling and interpreting numerical data.

Dealing with Numbers

Many people distrust what they feel is 'number crunching' because they see numbers as abstract symbols – with little to do with real life or real situations and used, amongst others, by politicians for devious purposes. This is particularly problematic when opposing politicians use the same statistics and come to very different conclusions! Nevertheless, numbers, statistical data and percentages provide benchmarks for comparison and help provide a rounded and precise understanding of a topic from a particular viewpoint. The following basic arithmetical concepts are useful to understand and possibly use.

Statistics and statistical significance

If you ask people to think of the first word that comes into their head after 'Government', several say 'statistics'. Most academic disciplines use statistics in the collection, analysis, presentation, description, explanation and interpretation of data. You're unlikely to escape them completely. Many websites you access provide you with statistics of the number of 'hits' that day with maybe a graph of the hits for the past month showing peak times.

If something is statistically significant, it's probably true and the result isn't due to chance or error. You need a minimum sample size to assess statistical significance, and there are degrees of significance. For example, if something is significant at the 0.95 level, that means that it's 95 per cent likely to be true.

For example, when medical researchers need to make a drug is suitable for human beings, they give the drug to one group of patients and a *placebo* to the second *control* group of patients. The placebo looks like the drug – it might be a sugar pill or coloured water – but it contains no drugs. The patients don't know which group is taking the drug. The .researcher hopes to find an improvement in the patients given the drug, and she has to make sure that what she finds is not due to chance. Another way of saying this is that she has to reject the *null hypothesis*, which is that the drug has no effect on the patients The probability that any positive difference is not due to chance is called the p (probability) value. If the p-value is less than one in twenty (p-value <0.05) that means there is a 95 per cent probability that the difference in the results is due to the drug. Sometimes drugs trials are stricter and require a 97 per cent probability (p-value <0.03) or even a 99 per cent probability (p-value<0.01) that the improvement in patients is due to the drug. A very high level of confidence in a drug is necessary before it can be prescribed for the general public. The lower the p-value, the greater the confidence that the drug has improved the patients' condition.

Not everything that is statistically significant is important. As sample numbers increase, there are more likely to be blips in the results. For example, if 52 per cent of males and 48 per cent of females pass an exam in a sample of 100, there is no significant difference between the two groups. However, increasing the size of the sample will magnify the difference between 48 and 52 eventually to statistical significance. Statistical significance is not the same as having any practical significance so keep this in mind when you interpret results.

Various online calculators exist into which you can key your data to find out if it's statistically significant.

The calculator at www.prconline.com/education/tools/statsignif icance/index.asp can give you a simple yes/no answer about your data's statistical significance so it may be useful as a quick check rather than for more detailed analysis, whereas the downloadable calculator at:

www.statpac.com/statistics-calculator/ is more complex and detailed.

A statistical package is more likely to show you '0.05' to mean that the finding has a 5 per cent chance of *not* being true, which is the same as a 95 per cent chance of *being* true, so be aware of this if you download one and check whether it represents findings in terms of their likelihood of being untrue (0.05) or true, 95 per cent . Similarly, a value of '0.01' means that there's a 99 per cent (1–.01=0.99) chance of it being true.

Percentages

Perhaps you remember the old graffiti joke in the underground. Under the heading '80 per cent of Bishops read *The Times*', some wag had written 'The rest take it!' This is a useful reminder that percentages tell you about some, but not all of a population. The 20 per cent of Bishops who 'take' *The Times* may be more interesting than the 80 per cent who read it!

The question always to bear in mind is: 'What about the rest?'.

Per cent literally means 'in a hundred', so 4 per cent means four parts in every 100, a wonderful and efficient way of dealing with large numbers that would otherwise be confusing and error prone. Imagine all those zeros and commas, which you can avoid getting wrong by using percentages!

Percentages are often use to show how different countries spend their incomes. The importance they place on defence, education or social services can be compared in terms of the percentage of their overall income that they spend on each even though each country's income and currency are different. (I could define GDP as income here, but it's technically not quite that – so OK to keep it simple as 'income'?)

The currency used to compare the comparative wealth of countries is usually the US dollar (sometimes the yen in Asian economies). Sums in each country's currency are written first followed by the US dollar value, both for the exchange rate on a particular date. Annual expenditure on certain things can run into billions of dollars in rich economies, so it's worth remembering that a billion dollars US has nine zeros (1,000,000,000), while a European and British billion have twelve zeros (1,000,000,000,000) in case you have to carry out any currency conversions between US dollars and British pounds or Euros in billions. Make sure you put in the correct number of zeros when using a currency converter.

Percentages are often used on the axis for graphs, but do check what the numbers on the axis refer to, as very large numbers may be represented in terms of one 'per million' – for example, for large populations such as that of China.

You may come across the term percentile, which refers to the proportion of scores in a distribution which a particular score is equal to or more than. For example, if you have a baby, you can take its measurements – the circumference of its head, its height and weight – together with its gender and key them in to find out how your child compares with the general population of babies at the same age and of the same gender. If your baby's weight is equal to or more than that of 80 per cent of the babies of the same age, then her weight would be in the 80th percentile. See how this works at www.babycenter.com/baby-child-growth-percentile-calculator.

Fractions, formulae and decimals

Whereas percentage refers to a whole as being made up of 100 parts, fractions refer to any number of divisions or parts of a whole – $^{39}\!/_{47}$, $^{3}\!/_{111}$, $^{67}\!/_{82}$ – there are no limits. However, the lowest possible numbers should be used to make life easier and more elegant, so if both numbers in the fraction (the numerator on top of the line and the denominator below the line) can be divided by a third number with no remainder then do this. For example, $^{2}\!/_{10}$ is better expressed as $^{1}\!/_{5}$, or $^{28}\!/_{56}$ as $^{1}\!/_{2}$. Fractions are also used with percentages. For example, interest rates can be 4 ½, with ½ per cent representing one half of one hundredth part.

Decimals express parts that add up to one. The first place after the decimal point refers to tenths (0.3 = three tenths), the next to hundredths (0.03 = three hundredths) and the next place to thousands (0.003 = three thousands). Decimals are also often used alongside percentage rates. For example, the cost of living may haven risen by 2.3 per cent over the last month.

When you write up the results of an experiment, you may have to decide whether you're going to use fractions, percentages or decimal places to describe the results, and which is the most appropriate. Sometimes fractions become very clumsy, such as $-\frac{47}{328}$, but are commonly part of the algebraic formulae used in pure and applied sciences or economics to represent concepts for making calculations. If you're using fractions as part of formulae, you just have to put up with awkward numbers. Your calculator may provide you with some basic formulae and you can find many online to help you out.

However, if you have a choice, then decimals or percentages are often more elegant for describing data and the results of experiments. '55 per cent of boys aged 14 in UK have at least tried smoking and been drunk before their fourteenth birthday', for example.

Although fractions or decimals can be used along with percentages, it's not a good idea to use both when describing your data. This may seem a good idea to make things a bit more varied but the most important thing is to compare like with like. If you use fractions for some figures and decimals for others, then your reader has to do her own calculations to make the comparison, Basically, she has to do your job for you – which can be irritating, not to mention time-consuming and mark-losing!

If you find two sets of data during your research, but one is expressed in fractions and the other in decimals (or percentages) then choose one form and convert the other data to that form. Changing decimals to percentages is simple – 0.55 = 55 per cent but changing fractions to decimals (the first step in the conversion) takes a little longer, but if your calculator can't convert them, an online one like www.webmath.com/fract2dec.html can help you out and explain the process. $\frac{5}{27}$ written to 7 decimal places is 0.1851852 – the result of dividing 5 by 27. With decimal places, you have to decide how far you want to go – some literally go on forever. Most people throw in the towel after 6 or 7 or even fewer, and use the term *approximately* to describe the number they use for convenience. Large numbers of decimal places, in any case, are not always appropriate unless you are adding up large amounts of accumulated data or require a great deal of detail, perhaps for measurements. Maths exercises, however, often specify the number of decimal places you need to use, and it could be a lot.

A large number of decimal places is not suitable, for example, if you want to find the average score for a class of 37 pupils where the total of their scores is 313, and each score is a whole number. The average is 8.0400904 (and so on). The *significant digit or figure* rule is that the results should not be more detailed than the basic numbers used. Both the basic numbers are whole numbers – 37 and 313 – and no one actually got the average score. Using the significant figure or digit rule, the average would be 8.

The first significant figure or digit is the one that is not zero and zeros at the end of a number are not significant either. If the number following the last significant figure/digit is 5 or more, then the last significant/figure/digit will increase by one and if it is less than 5, it will be rounded down by one. For example, if you have to round 3,462.872 to four significant figures, the result is 3,463 while 5,463,254 rounded down to three significant figures is 5,460,000 (zeroes replace the numbers that are not significant figures). Very long numbers can be awkward and the degree of detail or accuracy neither necessary nor practical, so in these cases, using significant figures is more user-friendly.

On other occasions, fractions may make a point for you. However you decide to describe your data or refer to data you've researched, compare like with like – use the same system – and keep your reader or listener focused. She mustn't lose sight of your important message because she has to compute calculations to check out the information you present.

Mean, median and mode

Mean, median and mode provide ways of considering sets of numbers, often to compare them with other sets of numbers. One of the earliest times that most people encounter mean, mode and median is in school reports. They may also be used to calculate school league tables, compare data from previous years or data from other schools.

The examples here use much smaller sets of test results than is normal or desirable. The objective here is to illustrate the concepts of mean, median and mode and what they do and don't reveal.

Your school report for geography perhaps gave you the *mean* score for the class test to compare with your own test mark. If there were 15 pupils (A–O) in the class, as in the following example, the mean would be their combined scores (87) divided by 15 (the number of pupils), that is, 5.8. No one actually got the mark 5.8: it's the arithmetical average, the mean. If your mark was 6, you were just above the mean and if you got 3, you were well below the mean for the class.

The raw scores may be:

A	*B*	*C*	*D*	*E*	*F*	*G*	*H*	*I*	*J*	*K*	*L*	*M*	*N*	*O*	*Mean*
6	8	9	9	10	10	3	2	1	2	0	9	9	6	3	5.8

However, the average (*mean*) mark gives no information about the range of marks in this class – one pupil got 0 and two got 10. The total (87) can be the result of several different combinations of marks from 15 pupils.

Another way of looking at a set of results is to find the *median*. If the marks are arranged (or ranked) from lowest to highest, as below, the median is the mark in the middle, the 8th mark out of 15. In this example, it's 6.

Data set 1:

K	I	H	J	G	O	N	*median*	A	B	C	D	M	L	E	F
										m	*o*	*d*	*e*		
0	1	2	2	3	3	6	6		8	9	9	9	9	10	10

If there's an even number of examples, for example, 200, then the median is the score halfway between the marks for examples 100 and 101. If the score for 100 is 6 and 7 for sample 101, the median is 6.5.

Whereas the mean and the median are relatively similar, in this example, the *mode* (the most frequent score: 9 in this case), has a greater degree of difference. If all three – mean, median and mode – were very close in value, this would suggest most of the scores were within a relatively small range.

In general terms, mean, median and mode individually give limited information about a set of scores or how to consider an individual score within the context of other scores. Even those who have top marks or no marks at all, as in the example above, need the context of other scores from those taking the same test to better understand how their results compare with the rest of the class or other pupils in their year group. For example, the number of other people who got top or no marks.

The mode, which refers to the most popular choice (you can think about it as 'the fashion') can easily be applied to names, colours, films, number one chart singles – it's not restricted to being used with numbers. One important use of the mode is to identify popular selections in multiple choice questions. The most popular answer – not necessarily the correct one – or the most popular incorrect one can help test writers to assess whether the correct answer was too obvious or whether one of the incorrect answers was too distracting or confusing or perhaps the question was badly written. The strength of this information is increased quantitatively by the number of sample answer sheets analysed. Examination Boards often try out new tests on a sample of the kind of students the test is for, to discover this kind of problem before the test is used with real test-takers. Even so, some problem question may not have been spotted so the mode in the live test may indicate that a certain question was faulty and so allowances can be made for this when the official test results are calculated.

Weather forecasters often refer to the *mean rainfall* or *mean temperature* for a certain month or time of year in comparison with the same period in the current year. This gives us a broader view of whether we're experiencing really unusual weather or whether it's within the boundaries of 'normal' or 'average'. The Met Office has been keeping weather records for the UK since 1854, so the records accumulated over this long period provide more powerful information than a few examples over a short period – an example of the strength of quantitative data of this kind. In addition, the records for each period 'go into the pot' to continuously update the mean for comparison with specific periods in the future.

Standard deviation

The mean, median and mode all give you information about general trends in data. With small data samples, if you compare the mean, mode and median, you get a better insight into the data trends and spot larger differences. With large (quantitative) data samples, the mean and the mode as individual measures provide richer sources of information about trends. However, the median makes use of only a little of the available data.

In the example Data set 1 in the previous section, the mean is 5.8. However, a different set of fifteen responses but with different results and spread – as in Data set 2 – can produce the same mean (5.8) but a different median (5), a different mode (5) and a different distribution pattern.

Data set 2.

1   2   3   5   5   5   5   5   5   7   7   7   10   10   10

You need to make more calculations to reveal the differences between these two data sets. However, the mean provides the starting point for calculating the spread or distribution of the data to give a more accurate picture.

The *standard deviation* measures the distances between the mean and the individual scores. The standard deviation is useful for comparing the differences in the spread or deviations of two sets of data which have the same mean. It also shows you how spread out your data is and how consistent it is. A small standard deviation means your data is clustered around the mean, but if there's a large standard deviation, then the data isn't consistent.

For example, in the past, the minimum required height for male Metropolitan police officers was about 6 feet (1.83m) so the mean of heights would have been over 6 feet tall, perhaps 6 feet three (1.9m), with the heights of individual Metropolitan police officers clustered around this point. The difference between the mean and each individual's height (the standard deviation) is likely to have been relatively small. However, in the general population of men over 21 years old, the mean height in UK is around 5 feet 9 inches (1.75m), but the range of heights is much wider, so some individual heights will be several standard deviations from the mean.

You don't have to calculate the mean or the standard deviation yourself. If your calculator can't help, you can find online calculators to do the sums for you, for example, www.easycalculation.com/statistics/standard deviation.php. You just have to type in your data set. The results in Table 13-1 were generated for Data sets 1 and 2.

Table 13-1	Comparison of Data Sets	
	Data set 1	*Data set 2*
Mean	5.8	5.8
Standard Deviation	3.60951	2.75681
Variance	13.02857	7.6
Population Standard Deviation	3.48712	2.66333
Population Variance	12.16	7.09333

Mathematically, the *variance* is the standard deviation squared – or to put it another way, the standard deviation is the square root of the variance. Standard deviation measures spread or variation statistically, whereas variance captures the scale or degree of the spread – for example, the degree of spread in Data set 1 is greater than in Data set 2, but the difference in the standard deviation between each set is less striking.

The standard deviation and variance figures refer to each data set of fifteen samples. The population standard deviation and the population variance is an estimate for the overall population based on the sample. In other words, it's a scaling up of the results, an estimate of what the results would be if applied to the general population. This is a useful function for market researchers or opinion pollsters as they can only canvass a small percentage of the population but their results can be scaled up to give the population standard deviation and population variance. You can see that these are somewhat lower or more conservative estimates than for the small data sets.

You can also say – as maybe your school report did – that an individual score is one standard deviation below the mean, for example. If you want to know the standard deviation for each individual score (known as the z score), then you take the mean away from the individual score and divide the result by the standard deviation for the whole set. For example, students G and O in Data set 1 scored 3. The mean is 5.8 and the standard deviation for the set is 3.6 (approximately). The z score is the raw score (3) minus the mean (5.8) divided by the standard deviation (3.6), so the marks for students G and O were –.7 standard deviations below the mean. On the other hand, students E and F each scored 10, so 10–5.8 = 4.2/3.6, which gives 1.11 standard deviations above the mean.

The larger the number of examples, the better the data when the results are quantitative. However, it's important to remember how general or specific the input data was. Was it a subset of data like the height of male Metropolitan police officers or more general like the height of males in London of the same age as the police officers? Sometimes a clearer picture can emerge by removing and treating separately certain subgroups or areas. Bear this in mind when you read, as the inclusion of a particular subset can slew the overall figures. For example, if a bank has been doing very badly for each of the last five months but six months ago it had a good monthly result, the six monthly published figures give a rosier picture than it merits from more recent trends. Stock market and commercial companies – and governments – often 'shift the goalposts' by changing the timing for publishing their results or forecasts or by including or excluding certain factors to make things seem better – or calm the punters!

Illustrating Your Data

A picture is probably worth a thousand words in terms of what a diagram can do for you. Diagrams give visual representations of information. They can:

- Summarise information.
- Show the relationships between different pieces of information.
- Show processes and events.
- Show and share ideas.
- Give a lot of information in a small space – good when you have word limits.
- Be clearer and easier to understand for the many people who are visually inclined.
- Make life easier for your reader – less work for them, better marks for you!

Diagram is a general term for any device that visually illustrates data, including graphs, charts and tables. Diagrams represent abstract information at the cognitive, ideas, level rather than being literal, concrete representation of information. They can, though, contain both quantitative and qualitative information, for example, in tables. Numbers in a table can be quantitative, but the way the columns are arranged can show the relationship between different sets of numbers, and so be qualitative.

Venn diagrams

One of the simplest diagrams is the Venn diagram. It consists of two or more circles and where these interlock illustrates the common ground or relationship between them (see Figure 13-1). You can use it to tease out similarities and differences or to brainstorm ideas. You can also use two circles that don't touch in order to denote they have nothing in common in the present way of thinking. Finding a third circle with common ground that both the other circles can relate to and that can link the two is often an exercise in conflict resolution.

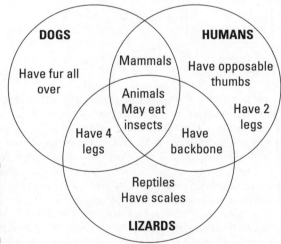

Figure 13-1: A typical Venn diagram.

Pie charts

Pie charts are also based on circles or ellipses. Figure 13-2 shows you one. They're useful for representing proportions or percentages visually, and hence are good at illustrating the size differences between different components. Pie charts often use different colours for each segment to enhance the message.

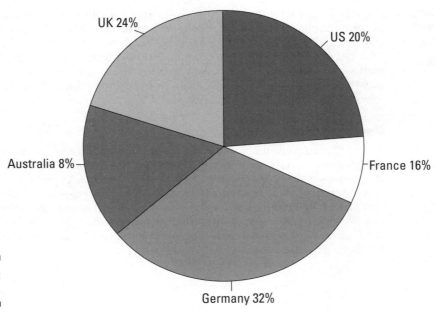

Figure 13-2:
A pie chart.

Bar charts

Bar charts compare two or more things proportionately, rather than in terms of percentage, and are made up of two or more rectangular bars, usually vertically represented, although horizontally is also possible. See Figure 13-3 for an example. The height of the bar shows the different proportions as all the bars are the same width. The example here uses coloured bars to represent three different types of university student (undergraduate, postgraduate taught and postgraduate research) while the horizontal represents different age groups and the vertical represents absolute numbers. This means that the three types of university student can be compared with each other at each age level in terms of the type of course they're studying and the number of students in each course as well as with the overall population of students at any other age level, giving 3-dimensional comparisons. Use bar charts to illustrate independent or discrete sets of information.

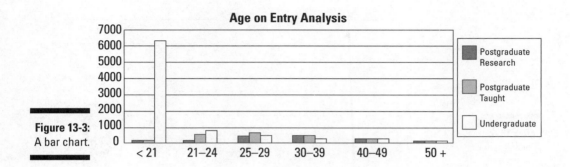

Figure 13-3:
A bar chart.

Histograms

Histograms look similar to bar charts, but the width of the bars can be variable, as it's the area that you compare, not the height. The bars represent variables that don't overlap and are next to each other. Histograms differ from bar charts in that they illustrate continuous data or data measured on a continuous number scale and they're only usually drawn vertically. Figure 13-4 shows a histogram drawn up from the data in Table 13-2.

The width of the bin (bar) depends on the frequency of the data, so they're very useful for simplifying large amounts of data. The raw scores below have been put into five data bins, giving the score frequencies on the right, which relate to the bar widths.

Table 13-2	Typical Data to be Plotted on a Histogram
Data range	*Frequency*
0–10 (3,7,10)	3
11–20 (15,16,19)	3
21–30 (24, 28, 29)	3
31–40 (32,32,33,35,35,36,36,37,38,38,39,39)	12
41–50 (41,42,44,46,47,48,49)	7

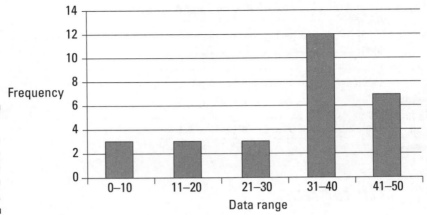

Figure 13-4:
A histogram
drawn up
from the
data in
Table 13-2.

If the frequency range had included 0–5, there would only have been one item in that bin, so it wouldn't have been very informative. You can choose the bin size that best fits how you want to present the raw data.

The visual representation of the histogram can thus change according to the size of the bin. Histograms present generalised information. They're not useful for depicting detailed information. Be aware of this in your reading.

Bell curves

Another way of presenting raw scores is in a bell curve diagram, which has wide use in various disciplines. See Figure 13-5 for a typical example. The mean is plotted on the vertical access and gives the location, and the variance (this is the standard deviation squared) on the horizontal, to the right (+) or left (−) of the mean, giving the scale. The mean controls where the 'hump' of the bell is and the variance controls how rounded or flat it is. If the bell shape is flattish, the standard deviations are larger, and if the bell shape is more pointed the standard deviations are smaller. Thus two bell shapes can be a quick way of comparing the similarities or differences between two populations or samples, for example, Data sets 1 and 2 above. (You can also plot raw scores around the mean and get a bell shape but the information this gives you is more limited.)

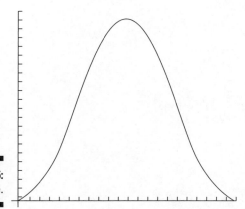

Figure 13-5:
A bell curve.

If the bell shape is badly skewed to the right, this suggests a problem, for example, a test was too easy, or if the shape is skewed to the left, perhaps it was too difficult. The visual form of the bell curve carries a lot of information on which you can then comment, and comment and analysis attract marks. The role of factual information is to give you something to comment on, to show what you understand and have learned. Bell curves and other diagrams provide a useful way of doing this.

You can plot the mean, variance and standard deviations of a set of figures on your calculator or an online calculator.

The bell curve is the common name for the Gaussian Probability Distribution. Yes, it does sound like something out of *The Hitchhiker's Guide to the Galaxy* and may well have been in Douglas Adam's mind as Carl Friedrich Gauss mapped astronomical data using this system and so became associated with it.

Flow charts

Flow charts illustrate step-by-step processes. They often show the different sequences that can happen after a decision point and the parts of the process are linked by directional arrows. Sometimes, you show different actions or activities in the process by using boxes of different shapes. Figure 13-6 shows a typical flowchart.

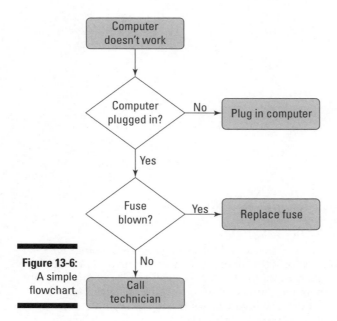

Figure 13-6:
A simple
flowchart.

Flow charts are often used as instruction manuals and can illustrate attempts to solve a problem or help to pinpoint where a sticking point was, so you don't throw the baby out with the bath water!

Flow charts can even be used as an overview of a project that you write up, or to show your tutor your thinking processes, so that she can appreciate you better!

Technical diagrams

Technical drawings or diagrams can illustrate architectural design material and components or can be blueprints for constructing buildings, boats, engines and washing machines. In all cases, technical diagrams illustrate the relationship between the sub-parts and components and the whole entity, whether this be a static 'machine' like a block of flats or a dynamic machine, like the engine in Figure 13-7.

Such diagrams give both an overview of a working system and of the relationship between the parts, and thus present a large amount of information. Figure 13-7 shows a simple example.

It's quite often useful to use a large diagram even when you only want to discuss part of the system, such as the piston, because the larger picture provides the context and location of the piston, which can be difficult and awkward to describe on its own. This leaves you to concentrate on your writing skills and intelligent comments on the sub-area – the piston – which is your current interest.

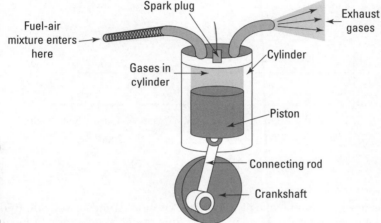

Figure 13-7:
A simple
technical
diagram.

Graphs

Graphs are basically lines drawn between dots, much like the ones you draw as a child to see what the picture would be when you had 'joined the dots'. One axis very often represents time and the other, quantity. Graphs are often useful for describing trends over a period of time and can map two or more variables on the same graph. For example, the general absenteeism from school of 5–9-year-olds can be plotted to compare with the figures for cases of childhood diseases over the same period. In Figure 13-8, two sets of data – the Retail Price Index and the Consumer Price Index for UK – are plotted over the same period of time in 2007. In this example, both indices follow a similar trend. If you're studying Economics, you use various types of graph.

Graphs can be very useful in supporting an argument. For example, trends in deaths from smoking-related diseases the year before and the year after smoking in public was banned in Scotland can be used to argue that the ban was effective in reducing deaths from smoking-related diseases. Relevant figures can often be obtained from local or national social indices. Of course, the cynical reader is going to ask if anything else coincided with the smoking ban that may have affected the figures.

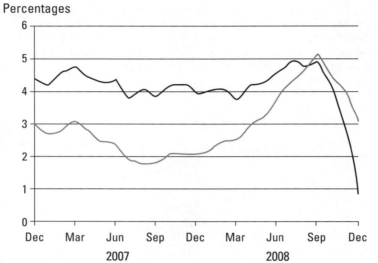

Percentages

As in the example in Figure 13-8, two or more trends can be plotted and compared over the same period of time on the same graph. A current claim is that with food prices going up, people are spending proportionately more on junk food and chocolate because they're cheaper, and less on 'five-a-day' type of food because it's more expensive and they can't increase their overall food budget very much to cope with this new trend in higher food prices. If you wanted to explore this claim, the four variables– food prices, overall food spending, the percentages of market sales for junk food and chocolate and the same for 'five-a-day' type food – can in theory be plotted over a set period of time to see if the trends are as claimed. Government statistics or those from the big supermarket chains would be useful here. If they're available, this gives you an opportunity to do the creative bit – to suggest why this happens or perhaps what can be done to offset the results of food price rises.

Tables

Tables give you a great way to summarise information and present the results of your own original research or to create your own comparison tables from someone else's data. For example, most universities publish detailed statistics about their students and what they study on a yearly basis. The one adapted as Table 13-3 refers to male and female students of some of the postgraduate taught and research courses in Humanities at the University of Sussex in 2007–8.

Table 13-3	Example Table Layout									
2007–2008	*Postgraduates: taught course*				*Total*	*Postgraduates: research course*				*Total*
Humanities	F	F%	M	M.%		F.	F.%	M.	M.%	
American studies	8	42%	11	58%	19	3	50%	3	50%	6
Art History	14	67%	7	33%	21	22	96$	1	4%	23
English	49	60%	32	40%	81	68	59%	48	41%	116
History	16	47%	18	53%	34	12	44%	15	56%	27

Similar information is available for other years, so you can create your own comparative table by selecting data for one subject over a number of years to make a new table about trends in the postgraduate study of Biology, for example, over four years as shown in Table 13-4.

Table 13-4	Trends in Postgraduate Study of Biology									
Biology	*Postgraduates: taught course*				*Total*	*Postgraduate: research course*				*Total*
	F.	F.%	M.	M.%		F.	F.%	M.	M.%	
2007–8	15	60%	10	40%	25	7	50%	7	50%	14
2006–7	14	67%	7	33%	21	30	49%	32	51&	63
2005–6	55	61%	35	39%	90	120	51%	110	49%	230
2004–5	24	57%	18	43%	42	44	67%	22	33%	66

You can use this new table information to create a graph of male and female student trends for the two types of postgraduate Biology course over a period over four years. For example, it seems that student numbers for both genders and both types of courses peaked in 2005–6. The interesting follow-up question is 'Why?'.

Tables can contain non-numerical data. For example, if you've learned a foreign language, you probably remember verb tables showing you the correct verb ending for each personal pronoun and each tense. Language tables can also group words according to how they're pronounced, or semantically, according to their area of meaning – for example, words associated with cooking.

You've probably used the Internet to research travel or car insurance or check the prices of electrical or other goods to find the best bargain and found a price and features comparative table to help you compare price, performance and what is included or excluded. You've also probably made your own work timetable or a duty rota table for who does which chores on which day. Tables are a great way of organising ideas and data or making plans as they allow you to make comparisons both vertically and horizontally. Tables can also summarise the raw scores from experiments or tests and be used as the basis for another form of diagrammatic information. Table 13-2 and Figure 13-4 show this kind of relationship.

Using diagrams can make things clearer for you and ensure that you don't leave things out and also help your audience or reader follow your argument easily. The diagrams here represent the most common ones. It's important to be clear about what kind of information a diagram represents and how specific it is. For example, histograms aren't the best source of accurate detailed information, but they're very good at dealing with large amounts of data in an impressionistic way.

Make sure that you choose the best way to make the most of your information. It's worth thinking again about the principles of communication, clarity and relevance, and making sure that everything is clear, and appropriate to your aims.

Part IV
Getting It Down on Paper

'And this is the patron saint of studying.'

In this part . . .

No matter what qualification you're studying for, you're going to need to write at some point. Academic writing has its own conventions and requirements, and this part deals in detail with them.

Here's where to come if you want to know how to structure your writing effectively and write with authority and style. I lead you through the basics of putting together written work, and show you that writing is concerned with demonstrating what you know and using that as a basis to find out new things – about yourself as well as your subject.

Chapter 14

Pulling Your Ideas Together in Writing

In This Chapter

▶ Sorting out the anatomy of academic writing

▶ Considering the elements of set titles

▶ Creating working titles

▶ Stamping your mark on your work

▶ Outlining plans

*A*cademic writing is non-fiction and bears specific characteristics. For example, the writer briefly mentions the end results in the introduction and devotes the rest of the text to explaining how the results came about. Agatha Christie wouldn't have got very far as a writer of detective fiction if she'd made Poirot explain in the first chapter who had been murdered, by whom, where, under what circumstances, and why. However, that, in brief, is more or less what happens in the introduction in academic writing. The reader isn't left guessing but is given a clear indication of what's coming and in what the order, a kind of route map. The reader – and that is you when you read other people's academic texts – can critique the work in some detail to see if it matches up to what was promised in the introduction.

Academic writing involves planning, reflection and reassessment over time. Writing up at the last minute with little planning rarely achieves good results.

Understanding the Anatomy of Academic Writing

All academic writing, whether essay, paper, report, dissertation or thesis, contains some common structural elements:

✔ The context and justification for choosing the topic.

✔ Previous work done in the area.

✔ Questions to research and/or respond to, hypotheses.

✔ A theoretical perspective.

✔ Research methods and tools.

✔ Research subjects/situations, including critiques of other people's work.

✔ Results and their analysis.

✔ An evaluation of the results/evidence.

✔ Conclusions drawn about the process of research and writing it up, and referring back to the introduction.

✔ Recommendations for future study methods or research to be undertaken.

You're assessed through the quality of your academic writing. Providing the structure is clear in approximately the order given above and you've obeyed the principles of communication in your writing, the outcomes of your experiments or research will have little effect on your grade. Part of the learning process is understanding what went wrong, so that you can improve next time. However, if you have marvellous results but do not write them up within the expected framework, then sadly this can affect your grade level.

The principles of communication are:

✔ **Honesty:** Always say where any ideas you use come from, whether they take the form of a direct quotation or a summary in your own words. Provide a short reference in the text (author and date) and a complete one in the bibliography.

✔ **Clarity:** Make sure everything is clear, from what your aims are to how your work is organised, including page numbers and headings, as required by your course.

✔ **Reality:** Explain what needs to be explained. Give definitions and explanations to show you understand key ideas in your subject area. Assume your reader has an understanding of the world and common or general ideas like 'exhibition' or 'cathedral' so won't need these explained.

✔ **Relevance:** Make sure that everything you choose to use and discuss is relevant to the topic you are writing about, including the reading you did. Always refer back to the title or research questions to make links to all the points you make. If you don't demonstrate how something is relevant, you won't get credit for it.

Paying attention to parts and functions

The structural elements listed in the section 'Understanding the Anatomy of Academic Writing' earlier in this chapter form part of academic writing in general and at all levels, and come in approximately the order in which they are listed. For example, all writing needs a basic theory or idea or claim and a hypothesis or question to answer and match the evidence against. Evidence can come from field research, experiments, observation or literature searches, including primary literary sources (like novels, plays and poetry). Secondary literature sources include data collected by other people or other authors' comments or analyses of case studies, experiments or novels.

All writing answers a question, and apart from in pure science or maths, the writer must say why they chose to consider a particular aspect of a topic and what conclusions they draw from the reading and other research they have done. This doesn't mean that you have to say that one theory or explanation is better than another. You can say both have merits (and say what those merits are) or that neither explains everything, or more work or evidence is needed. This may be no more than a sentence or so, but is a very important part of writing. It will come after the analysis part and could be part of the conclusion.

All the features must appear in your writing, and you must make the reader aware of them. It is very easy to read a lot and produce an essay which is largely a description of a situation or mainly a list of comments by academics – or both. There has to be evidence of you, the writer, in your writing. Part of that comes from the choices you make about which essay to write and which sources to consult, but you need to comment on and interpret these choices and tell the reader what you are doing and why. For example, if you have chosen a particular poem to study, explain why. If you quote an academic source, then why that one rather than another? Your presence in your writing is the thread running through the whole process – the order in which you do things, what you refer to, who you refer to and, most important of all, why. State it in 'black and white'. Even if your marker disagrees with you, if you have said what you aim to do in your essay or other work, have explained why and done it, you will get more credit for that than if you write an accurate list of information about the current popular theory or ideas, but offer little explanation comment of your own about them.

Exploring alternative methods

You don't need a lot of material on which to base an analysis and evaluation. A short piece of text can provide plenty of information. If you enjoy in-depth analysis at word level, then European Union, World Bank and Government sections of documents are excellent sources for critical analysis. Look out for concepts with no clear definition, contradictions between one part and another and suppositions that don't seem to be based on any evidence. If you've ever analysed poems or Miranda's 'Brave New World' speech from *The Tempest* for example, you can adapt those skills to looking at factual documents, except that in factual documents, the reader isn't supposed to guess or imagine. The meaning is meant to be clear – at least in the context in which the document was created. If it isn't, then why not? This can prompt you to find out who wrote the document and under what circumstances. If a civil servant with no teaching experience was mainly responsible for a government education policy document there would certainly be some problems with it, some of which would be revealed in the wording of the document, and others in the factual suppositions.

Using Models

A model is a piece of writing that gives you an idea of what a good piece of academic writing looks like. A model is helpful in three ways:

- ✔ **It shows you the general form, structure and presentation of a piece of writing.** Models demonstrate features such as the numbering of section headings, diagrams, tables and pages. They can show how to make references in the text and write bibliography or reference sections (check with you course notes for the requirements of your subject or find a model in your subject area), what Contents and Acronym pages are, and what summaries and abstracts look like. A model also gives you an idea of how much space is devoted to each section – background, results and so on.

- ✔ **It shows in more detail how to structure an introduction.** A model has section headings or paragraphs that fit the form the introduction, identify aims and the argument and evaluation.

- ✔ **It can provide you with suggested reading from the bibliography.** A model may give you ideas for sources which you had not previously considered.

Be clear about how to benefit from a model. Models aren't to be copied but can provide a framework of guidance. Essays on the same topic may give you suggestions for useful references or possible theoretical viewpoints. These are the only points you should note down for your purposes. You can also get an idea of the argument as a model, but you need to adapt it for your own uses rather than reproduce it.

Where to find models

The school office, library, or Student Union may well have some sample essays you can look at to get an idea of what's expected. These essays don't usually have their grades on them but should be of at least a good pass level. Your study documents should tell you of requirements specific to your subject and may include some examples. The university library holds copies of master and doctoral theses, which follow the same pattern as above, but in chapters rather than in sections.

Your tutor may suggest you read some journal papers, even some he has written, as general models. Some may well be comparable in length to what you have to write. The conclusion section is worth reading to see if you can identify the points referred to above, and it also gives you an overview of what the paper is about. You should be able to identify approximately the sections mentioned above and get some idea of how the structure works to support the argument.

Papers tend to be more up to date than books as well as shorter and more focused. Look for keywords in the Abstract to see if they fit your topic or theory needs and use the references at the end to help your research. You may find the description of the theory clearer in a paper.

Knowing what to be wary of

Tutors sometimes write model essays as examples, which can be a bit daunting as they have so much more experience. These essays can be good general models, such as papers, but shouldn't be taken as the expected standard. However, I do know of one student who dissected her tutor's model as an exercise in analysis (as described above) very effectively in her own essay!

Many students put their essays on the Internet and may even ask for comments. If an essay has been submitted as part of a university course and it gives the name of the university, that tells you a little about the quality of the work, but don't assume it's good. It's also important to check when it was written – time causes shifts in how people perceive situations and theories. British and Australian colleges tend to have similar writing cultures, whereas those in the US are somewhat different, so be aware of that. Online essays can be useful to read to get an idea of the structure of writing, but the content should always be yours alone.

Handing in essays that you can buy via the Internet creates several problems:

✔ They're not your own work and paying for them doesn't mean you're not plagiarising.

✔ They may not be of the expected standard or level. Your tutor will notice if your vocabulary changes significantly, or you suddenly become very proficient in an area where you had difficulty before. Equally, he may notice your sentences no longer flow as well as they once did.

✔ If you bought an essay in the past and got away with it, there may be great differences in style and expression between that one and another one as they were probably written by different people and your tutor is likely to notice something odd a second time.

✔ It's not impossible for two members of the same class to hand in the same essay written by neither of them!

✔ Bought essays don't guarantee that you'll get a good grade and, morality aside, may not be good value for money.

Buying or plagiarising essays from the Internet or anywhere else represents a basic misunderstanding about learning. You can only really learn by doing the work yourself. It's a process not a grade standard or hoop to jump through. Work that's your own, whatever its faults, has value, and you can't buy that.

Surveying Set Titles

In many cases, you can choose between three or four set essay titles. Most of them have a topic and a particular focus. For example:

Should we speak of religious flux rather than religious sects in the 1640s?

(From the University of Warwick Undergraduate History short essay titles, www.2.warwick.ac.uk/fac/arts/history/undergraduate/ modules/hi312/short_essays).

The topic is religion and the focus is 'flux' and 'sect' in the 1640s. Very often, essay titles also suggest any definitions that you need. In this case, you need to define 'flux' and 'sect' in the context of religion. The title already poses a research question, so you don't need to think of one. The definitions of 'flux' and 'sect' also supply the theoretical perspective and you can use these definitions to measure against the evidence – for and against 'flux' and 'sect'. Notice that the essay title also provides you with a comparison, a typical and useful feature to help organise your thoughts. 'Flux rather than sect' also suggests that the standard or older theory is 'sect' and that 'flux' is a relatively new idea.

You don't have to come to a 'Yes' or 'No' decision. The aim is to review the evidence and analyse it in terms of the definitions or theories. You may find that different parts of the country (where) or different groups or gender of people (who) behave differently (how), so it that the overall situation fits neither 'flux' nor 'sect'. You may suggest another alternative to 'flux' or 'sect' or way of considering the evidence or the need for more evidence to support either view.

When brainstorming essay titles, the following procedure is useful, based on the example above:

1. **Identify the topic, the main subject.**

2. **Identify the particular focus or aspect of the question. You need to look for dates or periods of time, and places or comparison between two different views.**

3. **Look for ideas that need defining as these are your main link to the theory or ways of measuring facts or what happens in practice.**

4. **See if there's a question in the title. If so, that also helps you to focus by providing a response, not necessarily a solution!**

5. **See if a comparison or contrast forms part of the title. That sets up your argument structure and analysis for you.**

If the elements referred to in the preceding list aren't obvious from the title, take a look at the other choices and see if they provide you with more structure for your work. Wherever possible, discuss essay titles with fellow students on your course to get different interpretations. If it turns out that a few of you chose the same title, then you can organise yourselves to share required reading and other resources.

Using what you know

As well as looking at the structure and form of titles, you also need to look at the content or topics they cover to see which you know something about already, and which appeal to you and so seem easier to write about. This is a good place to start but if the possible essay title is vague and has no obvious question, look at ones on other topics that are clearer and more direct (as above) and see if they can help you formulate a similar focus, question and comparison for the subject you prefer.

For example, if you were an English student you might be asked to write about 'Symbolism in the early poetry of WB Yeats' this is a topic, not an essay title, so you'd need to refine it. As all essays relate to class topics in lectures or seminars, your lecture notes or handouts will contain discussions around this topic. So, starting from what you know from attending class and doing preparatory reading, possible points to clarify first are:

- **What does 'the early poetry' mean?** What is the time frame and what are the early poems? (This is equivalent to defining 'early poetry'.)

- **What examples have been covered in class?** What reference to 'symbolism' was there in class, what were the examples?

- **What are the arguments or different views about the symbolism in relation to the poetry?** What is its purpose? What is its importance at that point in Yeats life and its relevance to his philosophical and other beliefs?

If you are writing an undergraduate essay then it will probably be between 2,000 and 5,000 words long, so you need to focus on a particular aspect and examples. Remember, two example poems are best (or two different view-points) so you can make comparisons. In essay-writing, you can either specify in a title your purpose or you can specify it in the introduction. Your focused title might be: ' Symbolism in the early poetry of WB Yeats; What are the main symbols used and to what effect?' or 'How far do the symbols reflect the poet's beliefs at the time? A comparison between two poems.'

Extending the title to include a focus (a more specific area – like 'which symbols' and 'to what effect') and a question (or the answer to a question like 'How does Yeats use symbolism to . . .) gives you a framework to begin your preparation and research.

Always try to start from what you know rather than taking on a marathon reading binge of discovery, which tends to confuse you and, almost certainly won't be sufficiently focused to be anything other than a waste of time.

Mind maps and initial ideas

Mind maps are a way of drawing information from different parts of your memory by not imposing a linear, rigid or pre-conditioned structure on your notes. The aim is to be free and let your ideas flow. The best method of creating a mind map is to note down the subject (topic) in the middle of the page and then see what ideas follow by writing down whatever comes into your head. For example:

Scottish Independence /who wins?/who loses?

Remain in EU? Isolation? Defence + Foreign policy? GDP per capita + expenditure increase/decrease? No more Scottish British Prime Ministers? Reduction in Scottish as well as UK power and influence?

The 'who wins?/who loses?' is another way of making a comparison and evaluating possible outcomes. (This was added after the initial brainstorm.) The first set of ideas usually contains several possible areas of focus and possible links between them. The next step can be to set out a comparison table like the one in Figure 14-1.

Who wins	Who loses
Independent Scotland = independent defence and foreign policy (e.g. Scotland was 90%+ opposed to the war in Iraq) – Moral stance?	United Kingdom lost, so place in G8 summit and NATO lost.
Increased revenue from oil from Scotland?	England may or may not have claim to North Sea oil – depends on angle of national boundaries and law of the sea – not clear cut
Scottish status in EU similar to Ireland or other small countries – may attract more overseas investment as gateway to EU, more jobs, etc.	Political status and voice lost in EU parliament as now minor countries, no UK

Figure 14-1:
Mind mapping.

There are many more possible points to add.

A further refinement is to group points – for and against or other comparisons – under the headings:

- ✔ Cultural
- ✔ Economic
- ✔ Educational
- ✔ Gender
- ✔ Political
- ✔ Religious
- ✔ Social

This works as a way of focusing down to a particular area and guiding your research and reading.

Guideline 'wh' questions

'Wh' questions – who what, where, when, how and why – are useful for providing the overall, in-the-round context for your work after you've narrowed down the comparisons and perhaps the focus on a particular area. They're a useful check to help you see any aspects you've ignored, particularly useful to consider when you're setting up research to make sure that you've covered all possible bases that may make for an interesting analysis of the results. For example, if you use questionnaires but forget to ask 'wh' questions to find out the respondents' age, gender, occupation, educational background, cultural background, migrant or resident status as appropriate at the methodology stage, you can't then separate out the results and analyse them under similar sub-headings to make interesting comparisons and contrasts. If the results show wide differences, it's be difficult to explain this without detailed information about the respondents and their circumstances, so for want of a little extra thought, you may lose a good deal of the value of your hard work because you can't explain the results. Being aware of what you've done and stating why you've had a problem redresses the balance to some extent.

'Wh' questions are at the back of the mind of the reader, and can alert him to missing content as well as what is there. The introduction to your work (after you've written the rest) presents the answers to the 'wh' questions of the reader in anticipation of him asking them.

Use 'wh' questions at all stages of your preparation and writing to help you focus and ensure that you leave nothing important out that you may want to rely upon later. 'Wh' questions also help you to be more objective in your work by considering all possible reasons or explanations and avoiding jumping to conclusions.

Creating Working Titles

If you have to produce your own working title, it gives you more freedom but it's easier if you consider your title within the same general framework as the example set title above – topic, focus, research question, comparison and/or contrast – using the 'wh' questions as general. You usually have to negotiate the topic with your tutor and then perhaps produce an outline plan with more detail of the focus and structure, or sections of your work. It's in your interest to consider this as carefully as you can to make the most out of the feedback you receive. For example, your tutor can suggest source reading for you or tell you that, although your plan is an interesting one, the data you need to support it is difficult to get hold of, inaccurate or outdated, or from unofficial sources with questionable reliability. If you can't get the data to explore or support your topic, you need to revert to plan B.

Plan B in the first example is to ask your tutor if she can suggest an alternative focus, where you can more easily find resources. For example, she might know of research, an experiment or case study in a different part of the world or using a different target population, but the same theoretical perspective. She might know of a little known study. If you are stuck for ideas, then ask her for a list of topics that previous years' students have written about. You might find something of interest and the resources they used will be available. You may be able to consult these and look at their bibliographies for resource ideas (as long as you acknowledge this in your work with a reference).

Your plan B may have to be to choose a different topic, so try not to be too wedded to a single idea.

Selecting three or four topics and doing a library search on each should give you an idea of what resources are easily available – ideally your preferred topic and a back-up plan B topic, in case you need one. If you have to do a quick search on more topics at this point to get a plan B topic, it's worth doing now, to give you more security. If you offer two topics to your tutor for consideration, she will also be able to point out any advantages in doing one rather than the other at this early stage of your work.

Always have a plan B. The greatest idea may not be the most practical, and you don't want to waste time on a wild goose chase.

When creating titles for projects or dissertations, it's important that you have a framework but not a straitjacket. You need some flexibility to take account of interesting twists or turns during the process of researching and writing and to avoid committing yourself to a dead end. The research question or hypothesis (or both) should be in place, but one way of keeping your options open and still being reasonably focused is to employ phrases like 'consideration', 'exploration' or 'investigation' of the topic and focus in the title, as this allows you to add later 'by doing x'. You can then narrow down the focus even more, depending on how things develop, which gives you some flexibility concerning the methodology you use (that can change according to what data is available) and the ultimate research outcomes. In 'by doing x', x may turn out to be:

- A comparative case study.

- An in-depth analysis of the internal logic of a document.

- An evaluation of the conclusions of someone else's work.

- Testing a hypothesis – it can be yours or someone else's – by seeing how it works in practice.

- Highly qualitative research into individual experience to suggest future areas of research and new hypotheses.

Considering Your Orientation

One way of stamping your mark firmly on a piece of work is by playing devil's advocate and taking an opposing stance to what seems to be generally accepted as preferable. For example, the UNICEF goal of universal primary education seems positive and to be generally acceptable. But, this aim may be in conflict with the need of some children to work and contribute to the family income in order to survive, so poverty eradication may be a necessary (but not sufficient) precondition for universal education in practice. More extremely, you may want to argue that compulsory education deprives children of choice, though the counter argument is difficult to deal with – children who complete primary education have greater life choices than those who don't (there's plenty of evidence for this). When you take a stance, play devil's advocate again and see what counter arguments you have to deal with from that perspective, and consider whether it's the best or clearest choice to make.

Your orientation and interpretation can also be closely linked to a particular theoretical perspective or contribute to showing the holes in, for example, Keynesian or Marxist economic theory.

Play devil's advocate as part of your in-depth brainstorming to consider your attitude or orientation to a particular topic and the feasibility of being able to argue successfully from that standpoint. 'Wh' questions are again useful here and 'who wins?/who loses?'.

Making Outline Plans

Once you've considered your options and done some basic research to find out about the availability of data you need to consider the feasibility of your research and estimate the amount of time you need to devote to each activity. The outline plan needs to focus on practical issues, the sequence of events and the time involved, in terms of:

- ✔ What you know so far and what you need to find out.
- ✔ Where you're going to find the information (for the literature review and data collection).
- ✔ How long it'll take to get it.
- ✔ What you're going to do with it once you've got it.
- ✔ How long that will take.
- ✔ How essential it is, and how far you can adapt your plan should time run out.

> ✔ Whether you're likely to get satisfactory results from the effort put in.
>
> ✔ Plan B.

For example, if you need to use the inter-library loan service, find out how long it takes to get hold of a book and plan how to use the waiting time or find an alternative source.

If you're using questionnaires, find out how many to send in order to get enough back to be statistically significant (or analyse and comment on if you're doing qualitative research), and how long people take to reply, on average. Strangers may take longer than colleagues or friends. Email questionnaires save the cost of postage but not everyone has access to email, so this may exclude significant groups. Suggest a date to return them by and keep the questionnaires simple so they take no more than five minutes or so to answer. You can always send a second set of more in-depth questions to those who respond early.

A general rule is that about one-third of questionnaires are returned. Don't get caught with no data or held up and so have to do things in a rush at the last minute. Consider alternative sources of information. The most abundant and easily available resources are your fellow students, often from a variety of backgrounds and differing experience.

The outline plan also needs to consider how much time is needed for:

> ✔ Background reading and noting.
>
> ✔ Writing up.
>
> ✔ Editing and checking.

This last is very important. A lot of work can be spoiled by basic errors or poor presentation.

Discussing your ideas with friends

Although it's useful to brainstorm essay titles with colleagues, it can be even more useful to discuss outline plans with them. They can be particularly helpful in solving problems. They may suggest alternative structures that are simpler and more dependable or they may have access to helpful professionals through their contacts or different chat room interest groups. You may well have students from a variety of backgrounds and nationalities on your course, offering very different perspectives and conceptualisation of issues, thus performing very well as 'devil's advocates' to help you clarify your own ideas.

You may have made certain moral assumptions, or not questioned some of the ideas you imbibed with your mother's milk, and friends can present different interpretations of things you've never questioned simply by telling things as they see them.

Always criticise on logical grounds, never on moral or religious grounds as these are personal, based on opinion relative to different periods and cultures and can't be proved.

Friends may be more 'streetwise' than you and know which are the best printers – the least likely to break down – or, for example, know of key ways and key words to wade through EU legislation and find specific information, or have other sources of information, short cuts or tricks.

Many people assume that if they know something then everyone else must know it as well. They may not realise they have information to share until they're involved in a discussion – so get discussing!

Discussions are win-win situations. If you give ideas, talking about them helps you clarify your own ideas as well as giving you a rosy glow. If you don't think much of it at the time, very often ideas percolate for a while and then come to the surface at a later date, often offering an alternative or interesting view you hadn't thought of before.

Seeking agreement from tutors

If you've had discussions with friends, you'll almost certainly be better aware of pitfalls and have avoided them or thought of a strategy to avoid them. Alternatively, if neither of these applies and the topic is still close to your heart, you can ask your tutor for help, in the knowledge that you've thought about the problem and can explain how far you've got with that. Your outline plan is then considered and aware. Your tutor may be able to suggest a framework or theoretical construct to help you, but is certainly better able to help because you've gone over some of the preliminaries with friends and thought through some of the issues. Tutors need as much information about your thinking process as possible, as well as the product of that process to orientate with your ideas and give helpful, specific, rather than 'standard procedure' comments. Help them do their job better. Your outline plan is both feedback and an aspect of the academic dialogue.

If you have a clear plan to use to negotiate with your tutor, you'll get brownie points for effort. More importantly, from a clear plan, a tutor can spot potential hazards, stumbling blocks and time delays more easily and so offer more specific warnings or help and support.

Everyone learns through making mistakes. Opening your plans to your tutor gives him the opportunity to engage with the issues you raise, to think about them, reflect, and come up with solutions, alternatives and sources you can't find in the library.

Discussion, suggestions and cooperation in the planning of academic work is part of the process as long as the final writing is the sole product of the person who's put his name to it as author.

Small, specific and beautifully formed essays, papers and even dissertations – shorter pieces of academic work – with relatively few points handled well and in-depth, are preferable to a wider topic focus in, simply because setting the scene and the background description for wider focus will almost certainly take up more than 50 per cent of the total available space!

Chapter 15

Grasping Writing Process Basics

In This Chapter
▶ Organising your writing
▶ Putting your information in order
▶ Presenting your information
▶ Using visual presentations
▶ Reviewing your work

*T*he hard work you've put into your research and preparatory reading is revealed (or not) through your writing. It's vital to do justice to your work, so make sure that you plan it, reflect and get feedback as you go through the process of writing up your work. This chapter takes you through the process of putting together a piece of written work.

Organising Your Writing

Some basic principles exist for putting together a piece of written work, and you need to take them on board:

- **Use your time sensibly.** Organise the writing up so that you don't have to rush it at the last minute.

- **Make sure that it contains all the relevant sections:** See that you achieve a reasonable balance between them. Written work normally requires some concluding comments or suggestions – this is true of reports as well as essay-type writing – so make sure that you include them because they can make a big difference to your grade. (The only exception is in purely theoretical work like pure maths.)

- **Ensure that you've analysed your results:** It doesn't matter if your experiment didn't work or your hypothesis wasn't confirmed as long as you've analysed your results, understand why they weren't what you were expecting, and say so. Your analysis and evaluation of your work in this sense can be more important than your results.

✔ **Make things clear to your reader:** Follow the main guidelines for good communication. Say what you are doing and how your work is organised in the introduction and use headings and section numbers to show this.

✔ **Ensure that you're honest in what you claim:** You can make use of hedging terms like *may, might* and *could*, and make the information you give relevant to the subject you're discussing.

✔ **Imagine your reader:** Assume that your marker (even if you know who it is) is an intelligent academic who's not familiar with the subject, in order to follow the *reality principle* – explaining what needs to be explained.

Assume your reader understands common knowledge ideas, that you don't need to tell her what a swimming pool is or how to knit, but you do need to give details about your research and the procedures you took. This isn't because she's not familiar with them but to show her that you know what you're doing. Otherwise, your work lacks logic and appears to take great leaps with no explanations.

Organising Your Information

Your essay, report, dissertation or thesis needs to contain different kinds of information in different sections or paragraphs. You need to draft your document as your general outline plan before you start your research, adding and amending it as you go through the process of researching and writing up sections and using it as a final check – in the form of the contents page is best – to make sure that you haven't left anything out and that the balance between the sections and different types of information is reasonable. It becomes difficult to jettison information that you've spent time and energy finding, so it's better to be more focused (or more economical in your use of time) in the first place and save your energy for partying.

Table 15-1 suggests the broad order and types of information in your completed written task. This isn't the most useful sequence for writing up the final draft (see the section 'Order of Writing' later in this chapter).

The description or 'not new' information forms the basis for the 'new' information you are going to add, so it must be relevant. Your selection and summary skills are important here. The other sections demonstrate your ability to argue for, or justify, your choice, the new information you've created and your analytical and evaluation skills.

Check the balance between the parts identified below in your own work. As a very rough guideline to keep in mind, description can be 50–60 per cent, new information about 20–30 per cent and argument about 10–20 per cent. The summary parts of the introduction and the conclusion can amount to about 10–15 per cent.

Table 15-1	Structuring a piece of written work
Section	***Description***
Introduction *Mainly summary*	Brief summary of the content of sections 1 to 5 of this table. Should show the reader how the work is organised, and what each section deals with
1. General background context *Mainly description, not new information*	Introduces the topic in general — where, when, who, what, how and why
2. Literature review/previous work in the area. *Mainly description, not new information*	Literature review/review of previous research, theories, views and specific topics or methods relevant to your work
3. Gaps in previous work and claiming a space or niche for your work. Explaining how your ideas are similar, different or extensions of earlier work or ideas *Argument for the relevance and importance of your work*	Limitations or restrictions of previous work Showing how/where your work fits in — fills a gap or adds to previous knowledge or asks new questions. Claim your space.
4. Hypothesis/research questions, questions you have created to help you tackle the topic. *New information*	Set out your explicit aims: what you aim to do, why and how.
5. Theoretical framework *Not new information, but you need to choose well and argue for your choice*	What theory or theories you're going to use to frame and guide your research
6. Description of your research context and your reasons for choosing it *Description, not new information, but you need to argue for your choice*	Background information to your experiment, case study or data search (location, particular features, issues or research needs, potential difficulties)
7. Research methods and tools How you're going to find out the information you want and why you have chosen that method. *Not new information, but you need to argue to support your choice.*	Data search, experiment and experimental methods, case study and tools (for example, longitudinal study, qualitative methods and so on as appropriate) including moral issues — for example, anonymity of respondents

(continued)

Table 15-1 (continued)

Section	Description
8. Results (possibly where tables, diagrams, other visual representations are useful) *New information, part of your contribution to knowledge*	This can be in various forms, but should be clear. Consider putting raw data in an appendix and selecting particular points to put in the main body to comment on.
9. Analysis of your work – and explanation of the tools – statistical or otherwise that you used. *New information, part of your contribution*	Refer to the hypothesis and research questions – what do the results tell you, how far do they answer them?
10. Evaluation of your own work – what you learned by doing it. *New information, demonstration of learning and ability to critique*	What parts you did well, what you could have done better, what you added to knowledge
11. Conclusion and more general reference to other work, other methods and other research in the same or related fields. *Summary, opening up the debatre more generally and making suggestions for the future*	Refer back to the introduction – quick summary of what you did and your findings and your suggestions for future work. These are also part of your contribution – new ideas or possibilities.

Just a sentence suggesting future work based on your experience of doing the research can make a big difference to your grade. This can be to make data, statistics, information from government institutions, pharmaceutical companies or other groups more freely available.

The relatively new area of evidence-based medicine involves a database of medical and pharmaceutical research balanced by feedback from patients and their carers about their experience of their medication, giving doctors and patients access to global information about the effects and outcomes of the medicine or medical procedures they're considering or have been offered.

Some institutions don't publish data because they don't consider it important or haven't the resources to carry out. For example, data about the impact on livelihoods of *tsunamis* or earthquakes or other natural disasters may be beyond the resources of the countries where these events happened. This information may be essential to understanding a situation or providing the appropriate remedies, but you may have to use data that is not as good as you would like, but was the best available to your study. You can point out this problem in your conclusion. Apart from purely theoretical studies, you work with the best data available, but this is often incomplete or rapidly becomes out of date; acknowledging this is important.

You can also make suggestions for including different methods or methodologies for studying the same phenomena, to get a more rounded picture (with better triangulation or better evidence) or ways to extend the methodology through new research. This can be added to the existing data base (more quantitative research) or the same principles applied another area . For instance, as an experiment, new methods of teaching girls maths and science in Ghana can be extended to South Africa.

You need to:

- Filter some information (background, context), which means identifying what is appropriate to your situation and summarising it.

- Explain some (your research questions, tools and theoretical framework and the research itself) and the logic behind them – justify what you're doing and why.

- Set out your results in a clear way, as objectively as possible, so that your reader can clearly see relationships, outcomes and any gaps.

- Analyse what happened and explain why.

- Evaluate what happened and where you could have made better choices, and what you've discovered – your reflection on the whole process.

- Expand from your work to the wider world and make suggestions.

Presenting Your Information

Your hypothesis and research questions have guided your research – your document search and literature review and any experiment, case study or other research. It's important to think of the final written outcome and the best format in which to present these different kinds of information. If you bear this in mind when considering the form of notes to take or the best way of illustrating your findings, in tables, diagrams or so forth, this in itself eliminates a lot of writing headaches. Tables and other visual representations can communicate with your reader better than verbal descriptions and can encourage you to comment more on them (as you should) because they tend to bring to your attention information that you were perhaps not directly aware of before in written form. Visual representations encourage your brain to make links. See Chapter 13 for more on using diagrams and tables.

In any case, as Alice said, 'What is the use of a book without pictures or conversations?' (Lewis Carroll, *Alice in Wonderland*). In this case, for 'conversations' read 'discussions'.

Using tables

I cover the general use of tables as a way of organising information in Chapter 12. See also the benefits of tables as discussed in the research section. Tables have these advantages:

✔ Ready-made information in table form can be a succinct way of providing the background to a particular situation. Tables can be clearer and easier to understand than a verbal description and use up less space. Always note the source of a table (in brackets) underneath it.

✔ Ready-made tables can be adapted to provide background information. For instance, if a table covers a period of five individual years, but only three of these are of interest, you can reduce the table as appropriate. Note the source underneath and add *adapted*.

✔ Tables provide a good way of presenting background profile information and research results, especially if you use human subjects.

You can organise tables according to age, gender or as appropriate to your research, as below. Note that in areas of research that may be sensitive you can protect identities by giving the subjects code names. Table 15-2 shows an example:

Table 15-2	Example Table Using Code Names				
Code name	**Gender**	**Age**	**Nationality**	**Occupation**	**Marital status**
Max	M	42	German	Journalist	Divorced
Jane	F	37	British	Accountant	Single

Tables are not only useful for numbers – you can use them for key words or codes, like F (female) or M (male). If the code words need explaining, then add, under the table, a key or *legend* explaining the abbreviations used in the table. For example:

Legend: M = male, F = female

Tables are also useful for categorising raw data so that you can comment on it and analyse it later. For example, if you were doing some action research to find out if a new way of teaching can improve the test scores of pupils with poor understanding of a certain topic and poor first test scores, you can try out a new teaching method (known as an *intervention*) and then give the same test again to measure the intervention's effect on the pupils' test results.

Table 15-3 is a shortened version of a possible raw scores table which in reality would have a lot more results – say about an average class size of 20–25. As part of the research, you can add a question asking whether the pupils preferred the second methodology to the first at the top of the second test paper, and include the answers in the table.

Table 15-3		**Example Raw Scores Table**		
Name (gender)	**Pre-intervention score (Test 1)**	**Post-intervention score (Test 2))**	**Preference for methodology**	**Comment**
Milly (f)	3	4	No preference	33% increase in score
Billy (m)	7	7	1	0% increase in score
Annie (f)	2	4	2	100% increase in score
John (m)	7	6	No preference	14% decrease in score
Fred (m)	3	6	2	100% increase in score
Mary (f)	6	8	2	33% increase in score

You can read the table scores horizontally and vertically and make several different comparisons. You have several possible ways of reorganising the table in the main text, by making possible sub-groups of:

✔ Those who scored under 5 in the first test and those who scored over 5.

✔ Only boys and only girls.

✔ Those who preferred the previous methodology to the new 'intervention' methodology.

✔ The percentage increases and the decreases.

Once you have a table of raw scores, various possibilities for the next step present themselves to you – what you want to focus on and where you need to ask some more questions or do a bit more action research. For instance, you can ask particular pupils some supplementary questions to find out why they achieved lower scores in the second test than the first.

If some pupils did better after the new methodology but preferred the first, this is something else for you to follow up. Most research of this kind has second-level questions following the first set of results. This means that your writing- up can follow the same pattern and show your reader how your research progressed and how each part led to the next in a logical manner. Any non-experimental empirical research throws up oddities – that's normal.

Using tables for raw score can help you suggest or theorise why certain things happened. If your analysis throws up another variable (like a different teacher for each methodology) that makes the results unclear and which you didn't foresee, you can always use your analysis in the evaluation section to show what you learned and how you would tighten up the framework another time. You get credit for doing this.

Using graphs and charts

You can use the same raw scores from the table to create a graph to plot, and so compare, the two sets of scores of each group. Figure 15-1 shows you how.

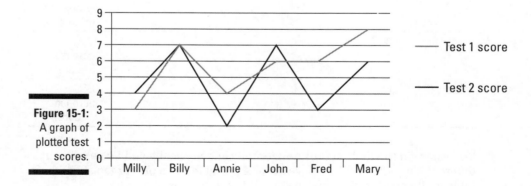

Figure 15-1:
A graph of plotted test scores.

The form you choose depends on where you want to put the emphasis. A bar chart using the same data would focus more on comparing the two scores of each individual child. Figure 15-2 shows this.

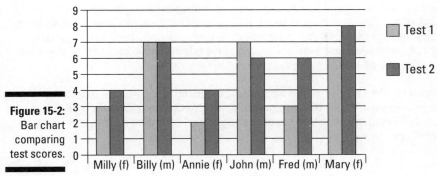

In selecting how to present data, consider which part you want to highlight and which tells the best story.

Using diagrams and other visual representations

Diagrams illustrating the components of machines do a far better job than a verbal description. For instance, you may want to compare and discuss two machines with a similar purpose that work in a different way.

Similarly, in a report, you can include architectural floor plans with possible variations to illustrate different designs, the use of different materials or variations in the placement of internal walls. You can't achieve the same effect by using words alone.

Plans or diagrams can also illustrate the outcomes of a discussion, that is, a new piece of information. For instance, people in Bangladesh made homeless by floods were able to identify their basic housing requirements as part of a participatory project (donor agencies provide the materials and technical expertise and the recipients of the houses identify their needs and provide the labour to build them). This information can be used to draw up plans for two or three different houses, according to the needs identified. Plans, pictures and diagrams are often the outcomes of participatory meetings between villagers, donor agencies and researchers – used to decide where to locate schools, village wells, or pathways – working in the fields of social science or development.

The first written communications were in pictograms – symbolic pictures. Think of the Egyptian tombs or Pictish symbol writing, or even Chinese script. Diagrams and pictures can communicate with your reader at a more basic level of consciousness – providing you label them and comment on them for the sake of clarity.

Diagrams don't have to deal with static information. You can use them to plot movement, as in this diagram of a car crash. Diagrams such as Figure 15-3 can also be used as a research tool to check or find out what an eyewitness saw.

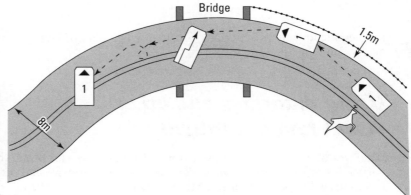

Figure 15-3: Diagram representing an event involving movement.

Photographs provide another way of conveying information, especially of something that's difficult to imagine without experiencing it. This information is often related to issues of scale. A photo of the skeletons of a blue whale and a white shark can illustrate that, although *Jaws* suggests that a white shark is pretty big, this concept changes when you see it next to a blue whale. In a similar way, a photograph of a Brazilian *favela* (slum) in Rio de Janeiro next door to a wealthy quarter conveys a wealth of information that words alone can't.

A picture speaks a thousand words – and Alice would approve.

- ✔ Choose visual representations that are clear and relevant – not because they're pretty. When they are, that's a bonus.

- ✔ Presenting information visually engages spatial concepts – relative sizes, locations, near to or far away. Visuals encourage comparisons, definitely a bonus.

> ✔ Visual images engage the imagination as well as the intellect, and that's good for helping analytical concepts.
>
> ✔ Visual representations, graphs and charts, do the job and make the point where a written description alone can't.
>
> ✔ Visual representations engage and stimulate more centres in the brain – yours and your readers – than words alone.

Reviewing Your Writing Order

The order in which you write up your work isn't the same as the order of the finished article you hand in. Computer technology makes it easy to 'cut and paste' material so that you can revert to the order indicated in the section 'Organising Your Information' earlier in this chapter without having to resort to scissors and glue. It's easier to start with the information you know and which you can get down quickly. This section gives the reasons for writing up the parts of your text discussed in Table 15-1 in the section 'Organising Your Information' in a particular order, with comments and tips.

Everyone worries about writing a good introduction, quite rightly, as it needs to make a good impression as the first thing to be read. However, as it's a summary of the whole piece of writing it's much easier if you it write last – it takes less time, is up to date and makes more sense.

1. **Start with descriptive text:** The easiest way is to start with the descriptions and factual parts of the piece of writing. These are unlikely to change very much and don't require too much head-scratching.

   The general background includes things like the geographical location of what you're interested in, health indicator tables, and possibly climate. Visual information cuts down the space used and the amount of writing you need to do.

2. **Put together the literature review:** This is the next thing to write up, as it's factual and unlikely to change, at least not during the time in which you're writing up your work.

   The literature review should be based around some of the research topics or theories you've discussed in your course and you'll probably compare different research methods and results.

If you haven't finally decided on the methods, theoretical framework or the research questions, this is probably a good time to touch base with your tutor. You'll have done enough writing up to show what a serious dedicated student you are. Your tutor may be happy to read your draft work-in-progress to help her give you the best advice.

3. **Write a description of your research context and your reasons for choosing it**. For instance, because it's under-researched. Include your research needs and any potential difficulties.

4. **Develop and write your theoretical framework:** This involves describing the theory or theories you intend using to frame and guide your research. Although you can write the theoretical framework at various points, before the research questions , you may find it helpful to have this section in mind before you tackle the next two sections below, which involve argument and the justification for your choices.

As you're likely to be drawing on a theory or framework discussed in class, this section is likely to be fairly familiar or 'known' territory to you, so it's good to get it under your belt sooner rather than later.

5. **Claim your space:** This is an argument section, where you justify your work and the way you want to do it. You may include some criticisms of work you referred to in the literature review and/or claims that your work is similar or different to it. It sets the historical framework as well as the framework for your ideas.

This is an important section, so a good idea to run through your argument with a friend or your tutor. You may find criticisms or critiques in the literature, but you need to make sure that you can apply them clearly to your situation. At this point, you may want to check with your tutor that you're focused and not trying to do too much, that you're comparing like with like and that you don't have the 'free radicals' of research – too many variables – buzzing about to mess up your results. Slim and narrow, with a 360 degree 'view in the round' is certainly beautiful in this context.

6. **Your hypothesis or research questions:** These come more easily after your argument for the appropriateness of your research and your secondary research questions need to be made clear now.

Check your research questions with your tutor, especially if the work to date causes you to reflect and make changes and you haven't discussed the argument section with her. The research questions can be sent by email, with permission, so shouldn't impose too much on her time.

7. **Research methods and tools:** This section sets out how you're going to achieve the aims set out in the previous section.

You need to state explicitly what information each tool or method provides and show that you've taken all possible precautions to safeguard the anonymity of any people who help you and have thought ahead to any potential problems and set safeguards or back-ups in place.

Try to pre-test some of your research, however informally, to help you anticipate any problems. If you can stagger your research, you may find problems half way and so write the last part of this section after you've discovered problems and put remedies in place.

8. **Present your results:** Think carefully about the best and clearest way to present results so that they speak for themselves and so that you refer to them in the analysis section. This is new, your contribution, so put your stamp on it. Results can be in various forms but should be clear. Results can be in various forms but should be clear. For instance, results can be what you find by comparing two pieces of literature written for the same age range, for instance, Enid Blyton's description of lacrosse and JK Rowling's description of Quidditch in terms of vocabulary range, sentence length and complexity, the number of characters involved in a scene and so forth. Consider putting raw data in an appendix and selecting particular points to put in the main body to comment on.

You hope your results support your hypothesis, answer your research questions or throw up some interesting alternative. If your data is quantitative, then you'll have numerical answers, if qualitative, you need to consider how to organise it in categories. Any raw data may be best in a table or perhaps an observation diary if you're doing an experiment. Once you've looked at the raw data and the patterns it falls into, you may tweak or firm up your hypothesis and research questions, because you've now made their boundaries clearer. You can put the raw results in an appendix and select the most important, or clear, in an organised form to appear in the text.

If you got a partial response like an unfinished questionnaire, and are doing quantitative research, it's probably better to exclude it. If your research is qualitative and it still contains valuable information, then you may include it in a question-by-question analysis, if you consider the answers to your questions are of value. You should state in your summary of results that a questionnaire was not complete, but included for certain questions, or that you excluded certain questionnaires because they were incomplete.

It's important, from an academic honesty point of view, to make all the results available to the reader in an appendix. (You can re-analyse other people's data – this counts as new research, although you must acknowledge where you got it from.)

Take a break from your results for a few hours or a day and return with fresh eyes. Patterns for organising them may then appear more readily.

9. **Analyse your findings.** The analysis section is very important. Having results is only the tip of the iceberg, the real work is knowing what to do with them and what they mean and how to organise them to show this. Another pair of eyes, like those of a classmate, can be extremely helpful here.

   Look at the analytical tools and consider from the results whether you need any additional ones. You can add a rationale for doing this in the analytical section and to the discussion of the research tools. If you don't have space to analyse everything, concentrate on what gives the most supporting evidence, then the next most and so on. This section can attract a lot of credit so be sure to state clearly the links between the results and the hypothesis, the research questions, research tools and methods and analytical tools.

   If you find some unexpected results or anomalies, acknowledge and make suggestions as to why. If two sets of results where there's a variable are virtually the same (for example, boys and girls), you can state that there's is no need to comment on them separately, unless your hypothesis was that they would be different, in which case you must.

10. **Evaluate your work.** The evaluation section is where you criticise your own work and assess what you have and have not achieved, and what you can do better next time. This section can retrieve your work by showing what you have learned by doing it.

   Mention anything that you hadn't anticipated and what steps you'd take to avoid this in future – any aspect, from the objects of the research, the framework, methodology and research tools and the analysis. For instance, you may have found it difficult to get up-to-date social indicators for Mali or were only to find one data source, so you can't confirm the reliability of the information you found. You may have found it difficult to get your respondents to fill in questionnaires, and so forth.

   This is the place to be up front and honest and demonstrate what you've learned from the exercise and what you now know how to do better. This demonstration of learning – not perfection – is what markers look for, providing you did as much as could reasonably be expected to lay good foundations for your work.

11. **Write the introduction and conclusion.** These are both summaries written at the end when you know about what should be in them. The conclusion should refer back briefly to the research aims, research questions and the results and analysis. It also has new information in your suggestion for future work, which will come after you've reflected on the whole process.

The aim of the conclusion is to locate your work within the general context of similar research – similar topics, research methods or both – and show how it fits in confirming earlier work, posing new questions about the methods or the theory. The final part of the conclusion looks to the future and to suggest new research areas, new research methods or tools, or general gaps in the available data that should be made public.

It's important to write a reasoned conclusion, even though it may be comparatively short. Even a single sentence opening up the topic at the end of the conclusion and showing how your thoughts are evolving can be enough, whereas nothing at all can make your marks take a plunge. It may be useful to take a break and write the introduction now to start some lateral thinking about it before writing your last sentence, to end on a high.

12. **Write the introduction.** Last, but not least, comes the introduction. You may prefer to draft it before you've finished the conclusion. The introduction summarises:

   • The general context for your research.

   • Your reasons for wanting to do it.

   • What you hope to achieve.

   • Why you think it important.

   • How you're going to do it.

   • How the overall work is organised, the sections and what they do.

Your introduction summarises briefly the parts of Table 15-1 numbered 1 to 5. Another way of thinking about the introduction is as a kind of manual to help the reader understand what the work is about and how it's organised.

Work can change and develop throughout the process of writing – as in the action research example – so the introduction, which tells the reader what to expect, should be written after you've completed everything else to make sure that it really does summarise what comes next, not what you thought would do so the month before. Introductions always have to be revised to fit the turns that work takes as it progresses – though not everyone remembers to do this!

In any event, you'll find the introduction much easier to write when you finished all the other sections.

Looking at overall logic

Following the organisation of information and reference links suggested in this chapter automatically gives an overall structure to your writing. Your student or coursework guide gives you the accepted style guide for using headings (or not) and the numbering system for headings and sub-headings.

Headings and sub-headings are like signposts to the reader, telling her where she's going and what to expect, just as you look for signposts when you drive to new places. These headings are normally listed in the contents page, which is like an overall route map to your work, a summary of the overall logic and structure.

The first sentence in every paragraph normally tells the reader what that paragraph is about. If your style guide doesn't allow you to use sub-headings or a numbering system, this is even more important. The first sentence of each paragraph in each section should make a summary of the section. If you produce a reasonable summary by doing this, the overall logic is probably working well, as in the earlier 'Organising Your Information' section.

Help your reader follow the logic of your writing straight away in the introduction. If you have a contents page, then all your headings, sub-headings and numbered sections can be listed to give the reader an overview of the contents (including appendices with raw data) and their page numbers. This tells the reader how long each section is as well as allowing her to dip into certain parts. If you do use a Contents page, check it against your final draft to make sure any changes necessary have been made – section numbers often have to be changed after revisions, so make sure to change those in the Contents if necessary.

The contents page started life as your writing outline, which you probably gave to your tutor, and even if you don't use sub-headings or a contents page in your area of study (or you're writing a short piece of only a few pages where headings aren't appropriate) continue using the contents page as a guideline and a check. You can see the relative size of sections and how much space you're devoting to each area. If the descriptive sections in 'Reviewing Your Writing Order' are more than 1.5 times as big as the results, analysis and evaluation sections, then there's probably an imbalance, not just in the space allotted but probably something missing from the argument section and thus probably the overall logic.

Various adverbs can be used to make logic links, like *hence, furthermore, in addition, however*. These in themselves can't make parts of your work fit together logically and, if used badly, only confuse the reader. They can add emphasis, especially if you're unable to use sub-headings.

When in doubt, leave out linking adverbs. Any organising word used once in a page is probably enough, because they tend to jar on the reader after that.

Getting draft feedback

Suggestions for getting feedback for your work in progress are in the 'Reviewing Your Writing Order' section earlier in this chapter. For feedback to work well for you, you need to organise your writing so that you can make steady progress and not leave everything to the last minute. This also provides spaces for reflection so that you can ask for help and support at the appropriate time, when you've prepared the groundwork well and can demonstrate the efforts you have made.

Feedback from your tutor

'God helps those who help themselves': So does your subject tutor. You're much more likely to get useful advice if you can narrow down your request to a choice between a couple of suggestions. Tutors are often happy to give preliminary feedback on written work as it allows them to see how you're doing and make any necessary adjustments to your plans and their teaching.

Ask well before the due date. A panicky email two days before the submission date about which theoretical framework to use freaks everyone out. Even if you don't have to, ask your tutor to take a look at your outline plan, and if you ask for help with a section, attach the outline plan so that she can see the overall logic of your piece.

It's difficult for your tutor to help if you give her a complete and finished draft a few days before the due date. If things need to be changed at that point, it's probably too late. However, if you check with your tutor at the various stages of your work, starting with your outline plan and then checking the research questions and the theoretical framework, you'll both get a lot more positive results. Even an email or a note saying what method you intend to use and asking for a comment helps keep you in touch.

Keep a record in your learner diary of requests for help and when you got feedback. This helps you plan feedback time into your next piece of writing and it's good to have a record in the unlikely event that you experience some kind of communication breakdown, like the loss of emails.

Feedback from peers

Whereas your tutor can help you with suggestions for the theory and case studies, earlier experiments, the expected form of your written work and suggest examples and sources, your fellow students are more useful as intelligent readers, especially if they're studying a different subject.

They can say whether:

- ✔ You've followed the reality principle and explained what needs to be explained to the intelligent non-specialist reader, but not what is common knowledge and requires no explanation.

- ✔ Your argument makes sense as a general concept.

- ✔ The examples, case study, experiment and other material seem appropriate (you may want to ask them before you talk to your tutor).

- ✔ They think that you've given too much information in one place and not enough in another.

- ✔ They're confused about what you're trying to do.

- ✔ They don't understand any of the key terms you've used or acronyms – these should be in an acronyms section following the contents.

- ✔ They find bits don't fit – especially the introduction.

Sometimes tutors aren't the best judges of how well your writing communicates because they're too close to the subject.

Try to get peer feedback as you go along. Law and philosophy students are particularly good at giving feedback from an overall logic and structure perspective and you'll be very good at returning the compliment with their written work.

Chapter 16

Looking at Form, Function and Style

In This Chapter

▶ Distinguishing between formal and personal writing styles

▶ Using references, citations, footnotes and quotations

▶ Making claims – and avoiding confrontation

▶ Brushing up your English language skills

Academic writing is different to fiction or personal writing in its form (the way it is presented), its function (what its objectives are) and its style (the way it is written and the vocabulary it uses). Academic writing is formal, so rather like a book of etiquette that tells you how to address a duchess and what to wear when you go to tea with the Queen, rules of behaviour exist. Your student handbook will tell you about many of the rules, like whether to use double or 1.5 line spacing between lines, what information you need to put on the cover of any written work and how they would like you to write the references to work that you quote from, On the other hand, there are certain features that identify writing as being academic that are not set down as rules or prescriptions, but which are just as important. For example, take a look at Chapter 14 for the structure and features academic writing should include. This chapter looks at the features that make your work formal and academic – and this generally means being taken more seriously.

Balancing Formality and Personal Voice

The style of formal writing includes the words you choose to express your ideas. These also give information about your attitude and how you see and understand academic notions. So-called 'knowledge' is not really definite or black and white and can change over time. Few people today think the world is flat or that the earth is the centre of the universe, but such beliefs were widely held at one time. What we call knowledge changes and develops as new evidence or new explanations appear. Many explanations account for some but not all of the phenomena they seek to explain, and the language you use must reflect this, and show, for example, what you thin the probability is of something being true. If you say something 'may be true', then you think it a bit more likely than something else you say 'might be true'.

All academic knowledge refers to the received wisdom of earlier scholarship, so as well as making sure you state where you got your information from, you have to consider the words you use to refer to other people's ideas. For example, if you say someone 'states' or 'says' something, this is taking a neutral position. 'Suggest' is not controversial either. However, if you state 'X claims something', this gives the reader the idea that you disagree and are going to criticise the claim. Just as questions tell you more about the person asking the questions than the answer, the words you use to report other people's ideas show your attitude to them. The reporting words used also demonstrate your academic voice, which is your attitude to what you are writing about.

Paying attention to the meanings and associations of the words you use forms part of the style framework of academic writing that protects and supports your ideas once you understand how to apply the rules of the game. When in doubt, use a neutral form (*say, state, suggest*) and if you say 'I claim', make sure you have plenty of hard evidence or prepare to be shot down in flames. 'I contest' indicates strong a criticism of someone else's claim, so again, you need hard evidence or good logic – as appropriate.

You show your personal voice and individual identity in your writing in several different ways. These mainly consist of your:

- ✔ Choice of subject.
- ✔ Research questions.
- ✔ Research methods.
- ✔ Choice of research and the academics to whom you refer.
- ✔ Evaluation of their and your own work.

 Be careful how you use phrases like 'I think' or 'I believe' and don't scatter them throughout your text. 'I think' or 'I believe' can indicate moral or religious views, whereas academic writing is concerned with evidence or hypotheses and logic, not personal feelings or emotions, valuable though they are as a motivating force to arouse your interest in a particular topic.

It is, however, possible to use similar phrases for a different purpose. You can give your academic opinion in remarks after you've evaluated the evidence you discussed in your work, probably in the conclusion. If your writing is an account of practical research you've carried out, then something on the lines of the following example, written at the end of the introduction, would be appropriate as an evaluation of your research that you're now reporting in your writing:

'Recorded abuse of old people in care homes has increased 30 per cent over the last five years and there has been little research into the qualifications or experience of care staff. *I believe* that this case study research into the background of staff employed in two care homes (one private, one local authority) can throw light on some of the reasons for abuse and suggest further areas for research.'

Check you've used forms such as 'in my view', 'in my opinion', 'I believe', and 'I think' only as concluding comments, as in the previous example. Comments such as 'I believe that moral values are more important than personal freedom' aren't appropriate in academic writing because, as beliefs, they may be difficult for you to provide evidence or a rationale for them, certainly not without going wildly off the topic. Avoid this danger.

It's sometimes appropriate to use personal possessive pronouns like 'my'. For example, if you repeat an experiment and come up with different results.

'Smith's' (2003) results indicate a link between thumb-sucking and cot death, whereas *my* own work establishes no such link' would be fine.

You also stamp your personality on your work through the way you organise it, the paragraphs and sub-headings you choose and the logical sequence of your ideas.

Using Citations, References, Footnotes and Quotations

When you refer to the words or ideas of another person – written or spoken the way you identify that reference is called the *citation*. For example, most subjects put the family name of the person followed by the year of the reference in brackets afterwards (Truss, 2003). That is the citation reference. At the end of writing, after the Conclusion, a full reference is given:

> Truss, Lynne (2003) *Eats shoots and leaves: The Zero Tolerance Approach to Punctuation*, London, Profile books

Most Arts subjects refer to this as the *Bibliography*, while Science subjects tend to call it the *Reference* section. They are both the same thing, and which name is used is a matter of the conventions of each subject area.

Other academics' work, or data from various sources, form the basis for your own arguments. You can refer to academics' work or the data they've used or quote their words in order to:

- ✔ Provide definitions of key ideas – different academics often give contrasting definitions that you can compare.
- ✔ Use their ideas as a basis for analysing evidence, or information.
- ✔ Evaluate or criticise data or the way it's presented.

Referring to earlier research and results anchors your own work to the academic framework. Such references demonstrate all the preparation and reading you did for your writing.

In order to have your preparation recognised and it obeys the principle of honesty, you must, if you use the ideas or direct words of another writer, state the source of your information. The same goes for the source of statistics or other data. A citation is someone else's words exactly as they appear in the original text but in quotation marks, or someone else's ideas that you describe in your own words, which you then use for you own purposes. Both require a reference, which means you must give the surname of the author, the date when the work you refer to was published and for a direct quotation, the page number on which it appears. If you use someone else's ideas but not their words, then a page or pages or chapter reference may be more appropriate.

Most Humanities subjects put the surname of the author and the year of publication in brackets immediately after the reference to a text or author. In an essay about energy conservation, the following background may be appropriate as to the essay writer's question.

'Producing energy from biomass has both environmental and economic advantages. It is most cost-effective when a local fuel source is used that results in local investment and employment.' (Bird, 2007, p.3.). The question then is, why is the uptake of biomass forms of energy so slow?'

If the next citation in your writing is to the same source (Bird, 2007) but a different page number (13) you can put 'ibidem' which is Latin for the same place or the short form 'ibid' and add the new page number, as in (ibid, p. 13). This can be useful if your citation is to two or more authors. However, you can only do this if the citation refers to the same source as the one before. If there is another one in between (Jackson, 2007), then you have to put the full name to the next reference (Bird, p.13).

Other subjects may use a different citation system. For example, some historians put numbers in the text after each citation starting from 1 on each page, with the references in the correspondingly numbered footnotes at the bottom of each page. Other subjects, like biochemistry or engineering, simply indicate references by a sequence of numbers in the text and then provide full reference details at the end of each chapter or section.

Check the referencing requirements for your course in your student or course study handbook. Make sure that you understand what you have to do. If you're not sure, the school or department office for your subject is probably the best place to get a quick answer. Follow the requirements exactly so that later on you don't discover you've forgotten to write down important details about the books you read or the information you found that you now need. Don't forget to note the date of access to any web-based material you may use.

The reason for giving references is so that anyone can go and find the same information that you did. You give the date of publication and the publisher as there may be different editions (hardback and paperback) between which the page numbering will differ. Without this information, it is difficult to find the words you are quoting if you don't have the right edition. The place of publication is important for the same reason – differences between editions. The author name comes first and that automatically stands out. The title is best underlined to stand out as that means you can use *italics* for articles in books and journals to distinguish them from the title of the book or journal (which is usually underlined). Your objective is clarity and accuracy and to find things quickly, which is why whether the section after the conclusion is called 'Bibliography' or 'References', the authors' family names should come first and be in alphabetical order. For example:

Bachmann, T. 2000. *Microgenetic approach to the conscious mind*, John Benjamins Publishing Company: Amsterdam and Philadelphia.

Baron-Cohen, S. 2001. Consciousness of the physical and the mental. In: *Finding Consciousness in the Brain*, P.G. Grossenbacher, ed., pp. 61–76. John Benjamins: Amsterdam.

Blake, R. and R. Fox, 1974. Adaptation to invisible gratings and the site of binocular rivalry suppression, *Nature*, 249: 488–490.

Bogen, J. E. 1997. Some neurophysiologic aspects of consciousness, SeminarNeurobiol., 17: 95–103.

Placing footnotes

As suggested in the previous section 'Using Citations and References', the practice in some subjects is to put the citation reference in numbered footnotes at the bottom of each page. This is one use of footnotes.

In other subjects, like English, Development or Environmental studies, footnotes can be used to add details that may detract from the main topic and also demonstrate wider knowledge of the subject, other sources or examples. For example, footnotes can:

✔ Add comments, which although you can bracket them, are more than one line long and so would disrupt the main text and make the message confused.

✔ Give examples of something mentioned in the main text or further, extra examples. This is a good way to demonstrate extra reading done while keeping the text focused on the main issue.

✔ Give definitions or alternative definitions to those in the main text to show your awareness that these exist.

✔ Add references to more detailed explanations than there's space for in the main text.

You may have seen footnotes that take up more than half a page, possibly in a literature commentary. If you're like me, your heart sinks at the sight. If the main text still makes sense without reading the footnotes, well and good. The two should be independent of each other in terms of understanding. The footnotes should add information but not be essential reading, but often, there's a kind of leak between the footnotes and the text and the reader has to skip back and forth between the main text and the footnotes. As always, put yourself in the position of the reader. Jumping about like this is tiring on the eyes, irritating and uses up more brain space, all of which takes up more time.

Check on the practice in your department regarding footnotes, whether you are or are not allowed to use them and for what purpose. If you do use footnotes, use them with care and think about the reader.

Using longer quotations

Quotations that take up more than three lines are usually treated differently to shorter ones. Instead of using quotation marks, increase the size of both margins in comparison to the main text and use single spacing. This clearly distinguishes the text you wrote from the text you're quoting.

Although long quotes can be useful to set the scene or provide in-depth definitions, make sure that you don't use too many and that you use them appropriately as the reader easily spots how much of your work you've made up with long quotes. Using long quotes appropriately means making sure that the whole quotation is relevant – that is, does it need to be that long? – and linking it into your text to explain why you're referring to it.

Watching Your Back – Making Claims and Hedging

Politicians often refer to their 'beliefs' or 'visions for the future'. Cynics point out how these tend to change and vary over time, depending on which party is in power. Politicians seek to persuade and influence the electorate with passionate speeches as much as reasoned argument. Academic writers, by contrast, must use evidence, cold logic, explanations and evaluations as tools to persuade their readers. The validity or reasonableness of their argument should be independent of any particular individual's personal influence or manipulation. However, readers quickly challenge any loose statements or inadequately supported claims, so for debates to proceed or for hypotheses to be discussed and ideas exchanged, writers need to watch their backs and develop defence mechanisms, normally by *hedging* or softening the language they use.

If a writer uses 'claim' as a verb to refer to another writer's work (*Smith claims*. . .) this often signals they intend to criticise that work. 'Claim' as a noun refers to an idea or concept that someone strongly supports or to an earlier idea or hypothesis that was later accepted or is now proved to be true. Copernicus, supported by Galileo, couldn't prove his claim that the sun was the centre of the universe, but his claim is now accepted as true. Using the verb 'claim' or 'is/was (not)' or 'must (not) be' puts you on very danger-ous ground to defend, so it's best to avoid these terms unless you're talking about things where there's no possible dispute – general truths or dates, for example.

Use 'suggest' as in 'recent research suggests' to discuss interesting ideas which have some evidence to support them because 'suggest' isn't a claim, merely a possibility. A claim would be to say 'homosexuality *is* due to biologi-cal causes' ('is' being a strong, 100 per cent claim), which isn't the case as homosexuality has many causes. It's very difficult, almost impossible, to pro-vide evidence or examples to show something is 100 per cent true or not true except for general truths like 'the sun rises in the east' or 'all men are male', so avoid making strong claims.

Verbs such as 'indicate' or 'suggest' allow you to discuss issues within the framework of the available knowledge. You can also use hedging phrases like 'seems' or 'appears' to be, or add adverbs such as 'probably' to 'is/was (not)' thus avoiding being challenged so you can get on with the job of hypothesis-ing and explaining.

Hedges are vocabulary items which help you to avoid commitment to a set idea. (The verb *hedge* means to equivocate or withhold full support.) The hedges in Table 16-1 may help you avoid confrontation with your reader and at the same time allow you to analyse, suggest and interpret with caution and safety.

Table 16-1	Useful Hedging Vocabulary
Useful verbs	*Example*
Suggest	Research *suggests* there *may* be a link between birth order and homosexuality
Indicate	The results *indicate* that flu jabs for under fives can benefit the whole population
Imply	The outcomes *imply* that there's a knock-on effect on the whole population
Seems, appears	There *seems/appears* to be a strong probability that the two effects are connected
Tend	Skirts *tend* to get longer during periods of economic decline
Modal verbs	
May (50/50 possibility)	Heroin addiction *may* be partly due to social conditions and partly to having an addictive personality
Might/could (less likely than 'may')	Early marriage *might/could* account for some girls dropping out of education, but there are several other factors involved
Adverbs	
probably, almost certainly	The sharp decline in smoking related deaths in Scotland in the last two years is *probably/almost certainly* in part due to the ban on smoking in public places
possibly, perhaps	*Perhaps/possibly* hundreds of species die out before they're ever discovered
Phrases	
It's likely/probable/almost certain	*It's likely/probable/almost certain* that more men are related to Genghis Khan than any other male ancestor
The evidence points to the likelihood	*The evidence points to the likelihood* of a small correlation between the size of nose and intelligence
A slim/slight possibility exists	*A slim/slight possibility exists* that birds evolved independently of dinosaurs
It is conceivable that	*It is conceivable that* people prefer branded pharmaceuticals to their generic counterparts (in spite of their higher costs) due to the power of advertising

Observing Other Language Features

Academic writing is different from everyday English in a number of ways. The use (or omission) of certain language forms in academic writing:

- ✔ Helps to make your work part of the academic writing community and so be taken seriously.
- ✔ Shows that you know the 'rules'.
- ✔ Avoids criticism or examination of language points, which can detract from the message you're trying to convey.

Academic readers (and that means your tutors) are highly tuned to certain turns of phrase, which they won't question, and highly sensitive to others, which they do question. The previous section gives examples of claims and hedging, perhaps the most important to be careful of, but there are a number of others.

Gender awareness

You may find some notes about gender bias in your course handbook, with some suggestions as to how to avoid this. In the past, even as recently as 15 years or so ago, all the actors – the people who did things or made things happen – in writing were almost always referred to as 'he'. This had been the norm for a very long time, so it wasn't until feminists took a long look at bias in academic writing and at male-related pronouns that awareness of this problem was raised in the academic community. This was not just a problem of detail. Women's contribution in general was overlooked or downplayed through lack of feminine pronouns!

Crick, Watson and Wilkins received the Nobel prize in 1962 for their discovery of the DNA double helix. In fact, their co-worker, Rosalind Franklin's photographs of the double helix provided the key evidence for their claim, but her name was never mentioned. She died in 1958 of ovarian cancer aged only 37 and, until recently, her part in the discovery of the double helix has been largely ignored.

So, the tendency to use male – he, his, him – pronouns may not be just a matter of bias but academically incorrect, as indeed happened in Rosalind's case.

Obviously, for named persons, where you know their gender, use the appropriate pronouns. For unnamed persons like teachers, doctors, students, aid workers and scientists who feature in your writing and whose gender is unknown, use feminine pronouns – she, her, hers. This is a deliberate choice and shows that you're gender aware and not assuming that all those involved in the action are male. You may note the use of 'she' to refer to unknown actors throughout this book.

You may feel that using feminine pronouns is going too far in the other direction, but it's preferable to using he/his. Other alternatives that can work in certain circumstances are:

- ✔ **S/he:** As in 'S/he works a 15-hour day for approximately US$1.50'

- ✔ **They as a neutral singular pronoun:** The nurse checked on the patient at four-hourly intervals, but from the notes, it wasn't clear whether **they** had administered the medicine at midnight or at 4.00 a.m.

It may not always be clear that 'they' refers to one person – as it clearly does in the example above – so you need to consider that when you choose a pronoun. The most important thing is clarity, and that means that you need to be clear whether you're referring to just one person or more than one.

Many students when referring to academic authors assume that they're male. Check the sex of those you refer to and make sure that you use the correct pronoun!

Your school notes may give you a list of other gender-biased forms to avoid. These often have 'man' as part of the word or male forms like 'master'; others are 'female' forms that people perceived as having low status and so you should avoid these too. The notes may suggest substituting gender neutral forms for gender biased forms, as indicated in Table 16-2.

Table 16-2	Avoiding Gender Bias
Gender bias	*Gender neutral*
Master copy	Top copy
Mankind	People
Chairman	Chair or chairperson
Foreman	Supervisor
Housewife	Homemaker
Actress	Actor

Gender zeal can go a bit too far. Some words containing 'man' like 'manuscript' or 'manufacture' derive from the Latin word *manus*, meaning 'hand' and so have nothing to do with gender and shouldn't be changed.

Use of pronouns

Apart from the use of pronouns to avoid gender bias and the use of 'I/my' in personal input I refer to earlier in this chapter, another important aspect of pronouns in academic writing is the avoidance of 'you/your' and 'we/our'.

Throughout this book I've used 'you/your' because it's a friendly manual giving advice about skills, not an academic text. The aim of academic writing is to be objective and unbiased and so 'you' is unsuitable as it is too specific and too personal. However, English can also use 'you' to mean anybody – as in this book – especially when giving advice or instructions. Academic writing, though, is not about giving advice or instructions, so 'you' is not appropriate on two counts. 'You' would definitely give the wrong impression of what academic writing was about. Table 16-3 gives a couple of examples.

Table 16-3	Avoiding 'You' Constructions
Friendly	*Academic*
You can find several meanings for 'development'	'Development' has several definitions
Your school notes may give you a list of	School notes may list

In many cases, the subject of the sentence tends to be impersonal – not a person – but an object or abstract idea (like development).

Another pronoun pair to avoid or at least take care when using is 'we/our'. The use of 'we' in academic writing implies either or some of the following:

- ✔ That the work is a cooperative effort with more than one author (for example, in reports).

- ✔ That as this is a 'didactic', that is, teaching form, you're teaching your tutor – maybe not how to suck eggs, but it challenges the relationship between you and your tutor and suggests you're superior, which isn't the best way to gain friends and influence people.

- ✔ That you're an economist and belong to a great community of economists who share certain values and world views. Check out the use of 'we' if you're an economist to see if your departments still accepts it.

- ✔ That you're making the assumption that everyone agrees with you – hardly academic.

- ✔ That you have two heads.

Avoiding passive forms

In general, you're best to avoid passive forms as they take up a lot more processing space in the reader's brain than active forms and that's always bad news. It means your tutor takes more time to read your work and time is precious.

Academic writing prefers more impersonal forms, but you can still use active forms by making the subjects impersonal. Think about what newsreaders say. They read from texts that are about the most formal things you're likely to hear on a daily basis and many sentences start with non-personal subjects.

✔ Gas prices are to rise throughout the rest of 2008.

✔ An accident on the M25 is causing mayhem.

✔ Pollution is the biggest threat to marine wildlife.

✔ Exam results are a fiasco.

✔ Trade Union membership is on the decrease.

Newsreaders start their sentences with the most important item – that is the news! However, the claims or predictions made through the use of is/are in the news are too strong for academic writing and the evidence presented in the news is less exacting than what is required for academic purposes, so in academic writing the judicious use of probably – pollution is *probably* the biggest threat to marine wildlife – or a similar hedge, would do nicely.

English in general puts emphasis on the first idea in a sentence, that is, you start with the most important thing. In academic writing, you can capitalise on these aspects of English – putting the most important idea or subject first and being objective about it.

If you can, avoid using the passive by making ideas or things the subject of active sentences. Everyone knows that gas prices don't rise by themselves, that it is the producers that raise gas prices, but making gas prices, for example, the subjects of active sentences makes for clear, shorter sentences – and saves both reading and processing time.

Sometimes, you just have to bite the bullet and use a passive form to keep the focus on ideas and results rather than people, and so be objective. Some passives can be expected, for example, when describing research events.

✔ Once the results *had been checked* against the predictions, the analysis of the differences began.

✔ Various forms of biological pesticide *were tried out* in the 1980s to control the cotton boll weevil, all with limited success.

Cutting out contractions

Everyday spoken and informal written language contains lots of contractions, which are a mark of informality and friendliness. However, in order to be taken seriously and to demonstrate the seriousness of the subject, you don't normally use contractions in formal or academic writing. The following is a list of common contractions and their complete forms to use in academic writing – to be on the safe side. Tutors may not insist that you use complete forms at first, but as you progress along the academic path, your work will get a better reception if you do, because these forms add a patina of academic credibility to your writing. Table 16-4 lists some common contractions, and their complete forms.

Table 16-4	Contractions
Contraction	*Complete form*
Isn't	Is not
Hasn't	Has not
Can't	Cannot
Won't	Will not
Would've /could've/should've	Would/Could/Should have
It'll	It will
It's	It is
I'm	I am
She's described her work	She has described her work
She's the first woman	She is the first woman
There've been several investigations	There have been several investigations
There's no need to repeat the exercise	There is no need to repeat the exercise

Addressing the dreaded apostrophe

If you ask tutors what the most annoying thing is that they have to cope with in academic writing, at least half of them say the misuse of the apostrophe – try checking this out as your own research project! The apostrophe can:

- ✔ Replace a letter, as in the contraction examples in Table 16-4.

- ✔ Show possession after a singular, for example 'The Union's finest hour was . . .'.

- ✔ Show possession after a plural, for example '*The researchers' objectives were . . .*

As contractions shouldn't be used in academic writing, the main use is to show possession. There's a meaning and communication difference between *The researcher's objectives* (one researcher) and *The researchers' objectives*, (two or more researchers) so it's important you make these distinctions clear.

However, if you look around you, you see rogue apostrophes everywhere. 'Potato's (potatoes) 15p per lb' is a common one – and not even metric – and small ads usually produce plenty of examples. It's not clear why people are so fond of apostrophes that they want to use them everywhere. Much misuse -- as in the potato example – is just wrong rather than creating a problem with meaning. However, tutors find this misuse exceedingly annoying and downgrade your work as a result.

In academic writing you only need to use apostrophes to show possession.

Other punctuation

Make sure that you don't overdo commas. In the title of Lynne Truss's 2004 book, *Eats, Shoots, and Leaves*, the extra comma has the power to turn nouns into verbs and hence presents a gun-toting panda that has a meal before shooting up the joint and is pretty nonchalant about the whole thing! The intention – no doubt – was to describe the eating habits of the panda, which *eats shoots and leaves,* just one verb (eats) and two plural nouns (shoots and leaves).

When you use a comma, you divide words into groups and this gives them a particular meaning, as in the example above, which may not be the one you intended.

Try saying your sentence out loud to see if it contains any pauses. If not, you don't need commas. If you're writing a sentence with *who* or *which* in it, see if you can replace *who* or *which* by *that*. The *who or which* in:

'The Chancellor of the Exchequer, *who* was Gordon Brown . . .' or ' Bridget Jones' diary, *which* I've read several times . . .' can't be replaced by *that,* so keep the commas.

However, *who* in 'The teacher *who* I was talking to comes from Austria' and *which* in 'I was sitting in the seat which is next to the air conditioner' can be replaced by *that,* so commas aren't needed.

You need to use brackets (. . .) in academic writing to put the author's name and date of publication in, for example, (Bell, 2004), so dashes can be useful instead of brackets in which to enclose aside comments, so that each piece of punctuation has a specific area of use and meaning, and thereby guides the reader. For example:

'Earthships – the latest is being built in Brittany – use rammed earth in old tyres to create their walls.'

Exclamation marks show emotion and are therefore biased and so aren't appropriate in academic writing.

Colons (:) are often useful in academic writing before lists. For example:

> 'Most mammals are placental, and include four main sub-groups: Rodentia – mice, rats and other small gnawing mammals; Chiroptera – bats; Carnivora – cats, dogs and other meat-eating mammals; Cetartiodactyla – sheep, goats and other herbivores, and whales.

Use semi-colons (;) to show big sub-groups and commas (,) to show smaller divisions within a group, as in the example above.

You can create categories and sub-categories by using colons and semi-colons, which help to make your work clear. For more on the detail of punctuation, check out *English Grammar For Dummies* by Lesley J Ward and Geraldine Woods (Wiley).

Acting on Acronyms

An acronym is an abbreviation formed from initial or significant letters of several words. For example, UNESCO, the full form of which is United Nations Educational Scientific and Cultural Organisation. The initial letter of each word forms the acronym, which is pronounced as a word. Benelux is another example of an acronym (Belgium, Netherlands and Luxemburg), although the abbreviation is made up of more than the initial letter. Other acronyms, like the BBC or USA are only pronounced as letters, not words.

Some acronyms can have more than one meaning. ESP, for example, can mean *Extra-Sensory Perception* or *Elite Security Products* or *English for Specific Purposes.*

In academic writing, to ensure that you make everything clear, use the full term the first time you refer to something that has an acronym and put the acronym immediately afterwards in brackets.

Light-emitting diode (LED) torches produce a brighter light than conventional torches.

You should also give a list of acronyms at the beginning of your work, after the 'contents' page, so that the reader can check the full meaning of the acronym without having to go back, perhaps through several pages, to find the first – and hence complete – reference.

Part V
Final Reckoning: Surviving (And Enjoying) Your Exams

'This is our concentration room – if you can study here, you can study anywhere.'

In this part . . .

Exams don't need to be a big hassle in your life. If you plan properly, do plenty of research and follow the advice in this part, you'll be able to tackle written exams, orals and interviews with confidence.

I kick off with some strategies for helping you to remember the details you'll need to produce in exams, then tackle the nitty-gritty of the different sorts of exams you'll be facing, and how to plan for each.

I also stress the importance of looking after yourself properly and finding a balance between revision and rest.

Chapter 17

Mastering Memory Strategies

In This Chapter

▶ Retaining important information

▶ Remembering key points and sequences

▶ Making memory and logical links

Most courses these days aren't assessed by exams alone: coursework forms a big component of the final grade. This means that you don't have all your eggs in one basket, but it also usually means you have to achieve a minimum mark for assessed coursework and a minimum mark for the exam as well in order to pass. For some exams, you may be given the questions in advance so that you can research the answers. However, it's less stressful and more useful if you have a continuous review plan throughout the academic year to revise your knowledge and refresh your memory.

Some subjects – pure science, for example – are more information dense than others. Even so, at least 30 per cent of any subject is about what to do with information, rather than information itself, and this is reflected in exam questions. Setting up more links to the information you already have empowers you by giving you more choices, and more potential outcomes for your knowledge in the exam. However, different kinds of information need different memory strategies, and this chapter takes a look at some which are worth trying out.

Key Information and Memory Strategies

The first strategy for remembering information is to consider two types of information: first, what you have to recall in exactly the same form, and second, what you can work out as long as you have a memory prompt. The kind of things you have to remember 'by heart' include the names of:

✔ Key academics and the theories they were associated with;

✔ Key people like prime ministers, presidents, monarchs, generals, assassins or other political actors;

✔ Writers, artists and musicians and the titles of their works;

✔ The heroes, heroines and villains of literature and real events;

✔ Important places and dates, for treaties, wars and other key events;

✔ Key terms, equations and formulae used in your subject area and what they mean;

✔ Key sequences of processes or procedures.

The other kinds of information which can be brought to mind by more general prompts include:

✔ More fleshed out information, such as theories, the plots of plays and examples of various kinds

✔ The relative importance of events or ideas

✔ The similarities and differences between people, events and ideas

✔ Arguments and rationales for and against certain views and theories

✔ Opinions and evaluations of ideas and events or theories, often from two or more perspectives

Generally, things you have to remember exactly – items in the first list – can be the prompts for what you have to know about in more general terms – the items in the second list. It takes quite a long time to learn a lot of information by heart unless you are a trained specialist, and even specialists have difficulty finding information if questions don't come in the order they learned the answers in.

The other main group of memory strategies involves drawing comparisons and deductions from the way the questions are written and applying what you already know to find answers. If you experience your mind going blank in an exam, or if you have a date in your mind but can't remember the event that goes with it, the second set of strategies can get you out of trouble. The good news is that using your learning diary, preparing for classes, reviewing your notes, and discussing topics should have set up lots of useful links to help you work out what at first seems bewildering.

Questions in exams are not always presented in the same way as the topic in class. You may have to compare two things not compared in class or take the opposite view to a theory discussed in class. This means you cannot rely on rote memory (learning by heart) alone. You have to consider things in a more rounded way.

Remembering Key Points and Sequences

These days you have a lot to remember, what with phone numbers, access codes and passwords, and if you have several of each and don't use one for a while, you will notice how difficult it is to recall it. At other times you feel the numbers are in the right order or the password is correct – then realise as your are denied access that you've used them for the wrong application. Remembering dates and details is easier and more useful if you can connect them to something else by use mnemonic memory aids.

Mastering Mnemonics

Mnemonics are memory aids that you can use to help you remember something. You make an association between them and what you want to remember. When you create a password, you are often asked to provide a password hint to help you remember the password if you forget it. This is making a link between something you know well – the hint – and something you want to remember. Most of us use mnemonics every day. If you learned music, your teacher probably taught you the mnemonic FACE to remember the five notes in the spaces on the scale and EGBDF – Every Good Boy Deserves Favour – to help you remember the notes on the five lines of the treble clef.

Make sure you choose the right memory aid, one that can have only one answer. For example, if you make a link through your boyfriend's or girlfriend's name, by the time you need to use the link to remember important information, they may be history, so the link may be lost or forgotten.

Assessing audio stimuli

For some people a rhyme or beat stimulus works well. At school, most people learned the rhyme 'divorced, beheaded, died, divorced, beheaded, survived' – the fates of the wives of Henry VIII – and similar rhymes can help you remember other pieces of information. You might find that a rap beat helps as well. There are several websites and some software that can create rhymes for you like this one for a name and date:

US President in 1947 was Harry S. Truman, who's now gone to heaven.

But the really meaningful rhymes are those you create yourself. Your brain is capable of millions of connections, so make sure the memory aid and what you want to remember have a one to one relationship. You can have several girlfriends, but only one mother!

You can always kill two birds with one stone and exercise while committing information to memory. You can successfully combine skipping with chanting what you want to remember so that it fits in with the beat. If you can find rhymes as well, the beat and rhymes will reinforce the learning and help you recall the information later. Skipping and chanting can be quite staccato and beat out formulae or equations, like 'base plus acid = salt plus water'. Of course, you can't skip in exams, but you can beat out the skipping rhythm quietly on your knee. Most mnemonics are useful for small or important pieces of information which are crucial to get right. However, 'raps' can be used for longer pieces of information and the repetition of the chorus is an extra support.

Dangers exist in simply rote-learning large amounts of information, especially if you don't use a mnemonic aid as well. Without other reference points, all information has equal importance, and so specific parts are difficult to retrieve. You might have to recite quite a lot out loud (or under your breath in an exam) to get to the bit you want. This takes time and can be quite nerve-racking in exam conditions. Actors tend to break what they need to remember into chunks by linking it to their position on stage for each cue or the prompt line from another actor, so helping them to recall what they need. Relying on your ability to recite alone is rarely enough. As a last minute technique, when you've just realised you've forgotten something and really have no time to set up a mnemonic or logical link, rote-learning may see you through if what you need to recall is not long, and you only need to remember it for a day or so. Physical stimuli, like the pain of pinching your arm to make you form an association with what you want to learn is very efficient for very important last minute things, but you can really only use the pinch once, or the memory wires get crossed and you'd be covered in bruises.

Learning with loci

'Loci' means 'places' in Latin, and is a useful tool when you have to remember a process or a sequence of events in a particular order. It could be an alternative way to rapping for remembering all of DH Lawrence's novels in their order of publication, or for remembering processes like how to wire a plug.

To do this (see the nearby sidebar 'Looking at loci' for the historical background) imagine you are entering your house through the front door and think of the order you will arrive at other rooms and whether they are on the right or left. You can use the stairs as well, and if you run out of rooms to put your information in, you can use the fridge, oven or washing machine to make more places. Any building you know well, even a garden will do, as long as you keep the same order of going to each room or place. In other words, the sequence of the rooms (places) and where they are must stay the same and any additions to extend the number of places must be logical. Then put each piece if information in the place and sequence you need to recall it in.

Drawing a floor plan – a bit like an architect's map – is not only useful in helping you visualise the loci and the sequence they come in, but can show you how many places you have so that you disrupt the sequence as little as possible to add in more places. As a rough guide, about 10–15 loci are ideal for this kind of memory aid. You can put more than one thing in a particular place, but you then have also to remember the number per place as well as the items, so this puts more strain on recalling your important information.

Some people find visualising pigeon-holes (similar to a table or grid system) and putting information into particular boxes helpful. You can also practise revising by actually drawing up a grid. If you've taken notes in a grid pattern, then you already have that aid and you can see how much you can recall and fit into a blank grid. The boxes in the grid can be located on a numerical/alphabetical grid, with, say, 1–7 on the horizontal axis and A, B, C, D, E, F, G. on the vertical axis, so information locations are 1C or 6D for example, as in the game 'battleships'. The boxes really form another version of loci. Instead of using numbers and letters, some people colour code their boxes or loci or use symbols like dolphins or E-type jaguars on the front of the boxes to help them remember what's inside. Whatever works for you is fine.

Loci work particularly well for remembering key facts for a short time for exams because the loci are always the same and the sequence is familiar, but you change what you put in each place according to what you want to remember. You can use the same system of loci for various exams, by changing the information as appropriate. Because you reconstruct the sequence of the loci to remember what's in each place, you are unlikely to be plagued by odd pieces of information or rhymes that pop into your head without being able to remember what they relate to. Equally, if you want to, you can often recall the information in the loci as long as you can remember the sequence of places or rooms.

Looking at Loci

Loci is a Latin word, but the practice of using loci as memory aids is older. In ancient Greece, when after-dinner speaking was even more popular than it is today, rivalry was great between different speakers. Those who were more entertaining and had more stories to tell would get more work. The work depended on what they could remember, so they carried round clay tablets with their 'notes', usually symbols to represent the order of the talk. They imagined walking through their house and placed a piece of information at the front door, in the vestibule and so on, in a specific sequence which mapped the progress of their talk. They used what they were familiar with to anchor new information. This ensured they got the sequence right and left nothing out.

Other ways to remember key facts

If you have to remember abstract things like formulae, sound and picture aids are useful. For example, you can attach sound and picture prompts to abstract entities to make things like a set of symbols easier to remember. Recalling a formula is often the first stage in answering an exam question, as you usually then have to apply it. Recalling the symbols then becomes the prompt or link to their meaning or use. For example, in the mathematics operator ' d/dx,' you can pronounce 'dx' to sound similar to 'ducks' and probably the best known duck is Donald so you can make an aural and visual memory of Donald with his two nephew ducks (d/dx). The same method – using the sounds and pictures suggested by symbols and linking them together to make a story – can help you remember longer strings of formulae or data. With luck, the formula you have to use in the exam will be given in the exam question, but you still have to recognise it even if you don't have to produce it.

Acronyms like OPEC (Organisation of Petroleum Exporting Countries) are said as words and are so well-known and used that you rarely have to produce them in full. You can create your own acronyms in order to remember other sets of information. For example, you can remember the Great Lakes of North America from the acronym HOMES (Huron, Ontario, Michigan, Erie and Superior). You can then chant them, colour then and put them in loci if you need more memory support.

Most of these techniques, although essentially a form of rote-learning, do engage more than one part of the brain – for example, the aural and visual senses, so give you back-up, and more than one way to get at what you want to remember.

Whatever technique you use, make sure the memory aid and what you want to remember have a one-to-one relationship.

If you want to remember something, you need to concentrate on it. If you try to word process while having a phone conversation, you will notice some of that conversation popping up in your typing. In the same way, distractions can leach into your memory exercise. If your sensory memory lacks input or the input is muddled, then either you won't remember much at all or won't be able to retrieve what you need because you won't know where it is without stimuli or prompts.

Another form of visualisation, used in systems like Neuro-linguistic Programming, can help calm your nerves in exams. Imagine yourself in a place you love, where you are comfortable and happy, and bring up this image in the exam whenever you feel the need for calm. For the full low-down on NLP, check out *Neuro-Linguistic Programming For Dummies*, by Romilla Ready and Kate Burton (Wiley).

Making Memory and Logical Links

Mnemonic memory aids are great for recalling short, key pieces of information to prompt you to recall more information. This helps you to develop your exam answers in greater depth. While you need to have key information at your disposal, it is only a starting point for more logical and extensive treatment. Mnemonics are not much more than rote-learning, but where they involve two or more of the senses, they engage more of the brain, and are likely to then be more thought-provoking (literally) and produce more links or reactivate links to what you know, but has perhaps been buried for a while.

If you can remember more than one link or pathway to the various pieces of information and knowledge that you learn and are examined on, then you can develop several ways to recall and reconstruct the information you need in the exam.

Developing a historical perspective

Generally speaking, courses start with the most general or the most basic information and then proceed to more specific details. The information presented over a series of classes in a term or a year may be *incremental*, with each class adding new information related to the previous one. For example, in Maths or Economics courses, each piece of new learning depends to a large extent on understanding what went before. The development of the course may be organised historically. Neo-Classical economic theory, for example, usually comes before Keynesian economic theory and Monetarist theory. In this sense, these topics are incremental, part of a hierarchy, as each presents a criticism of an earlier theory and a new development.

In another sense, these theories are parallel to each other because they all strive to explain the same set of circumstances – key areas of macroeconomic interest like unemployment and inflation. Sometimes, in the pressure to work in the moment, a student can easily lose the overview of a course and miss seeing how all the parts link together.

Considering how one theory develops as a reaction to an earlier one, gives you a historical perspective and most represents the order in which you were taught. You can also start with a problem or event and compare how different theories or viewpoints consider or explain it. In this way you create two pathways to remember key information. The second method is one you can best develop yourself when reviewing your work.

Making memory maps

When you are revising and even jotting notes in the exam, mind maps or spider pictures with key ideas at the centre can help you see how much you can recall and which key idea brings the most links. For example, thinking of Henry VIII and divorce is likely to set up various possible memory paths. He had two divorces (two thought paths). The first (from Catherine of Aragon) had profound political, religious, economic and foreign policy implications, all separate thought paths (though with some overlaps). The second (from Anne of Cleves) was lower key, by mutual agreement and had no profound repercussions. Key ideas at the hub of a wheel generate connections to other ideas, even in other subject areas. In the Henry VIII example, you will be aware of the relevance or otherwise of the Ann of Cleves divorce from your course, or perhaps be reminded of the importance of Sir Thomas More and the Act of Supremacy.

 You can use a circle to represent, for example, a common macro-economic debate – inflation and unemployment – as the body of a 'spider', while the 'legs' of the spider can each represent a particular theory, and then the key differences or extensions to the theory be added on to the legs as shown in Figure 17-1.

 When revising, it's always a good idea to use a different method from the original – even a different mind map – because to do this, you have to transfer information across from one system to another, creating another link in your mind. You're also more likely to spot gaps in knowledge and weaknesses in argument or logic if you do this.

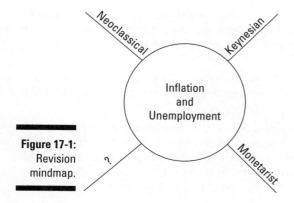

Figure 17-1:
Revision
mindmap.

Start with what you know – make your mind map (or grid) from the knowledge in your head without looking at your notes. When you see gaps, use your notes to remind you how to fill them.

Revising from Notes

If you've been using a learning diary (see Chapter 1 for more on keeping one), you'll have some preparatory questions that you thought about before going to each lecture, and perhaps notes of what you thought or discussed with friends after the lecture as well. You also have your lecture notes and maybe some notes from reading around the same topic, and probably some Internet or other references. Chapter 7 covers the skill of taking notes in lectures. You may also have written essays on some of the examined topics. Thus you already have several information sources that you've expressed in your own way or modified or added to – that you've captured as your own. This means you already have a memory trace to build upon when revising for exams.

Other advantages to starting off revision by using your notes include the following:

✔ **Notes represent different episodes in your learning over time.** The way your notes change illustrate how you've changed and progressed – what you now understand better.

✔ **Notes represent different sources.** Because they cover lectures, seminars, web and library sources, they can give you a rounder picture of a topic than you had before.

As with the spider diagram/mind map above, your notes taken together can potentially give you several different takes on the same topic and help you to create or reinforce several memory paths.

✔ **Notes allow you to go back over your initial questions.** If you consider some of your initial pre-lecture questions about a certain topic you may find now that you can answer these questions better or create more appropriate ones.

The process of recycling and reviewing ideas in your notes reinforces your knowledge and can also stimulate your thinking strategies to make new logical links.

✔ **Notes help to identify problem areas.** Working from your notes – or creating new ones using mind maps or tables to summarise the information you already have is likely to alert you to areas you're still unsure of and to which you need to find answers. You can then focus on these areas or ask for help from your tutor, and so make the best use of your time.

Taking notes in various ways as you learn, and using these notes to begin your revision, involves not just thinking skills, but provides listening, visual, diagrammatic, spatial and time memory aids, all of which can reinforce each other and help to make you an active learner. Conversely, if you don't take advantage of what you already know and have worked on and instead consult paper or web resources as the first step in your revision, you risk missing the information you really need as you're not so readily aware of what you already know and what you specifically need to find out. You may waste time that you could have spent doing some stress-busting activities, and gain nothing that you can use in the exam because you weren't properly focused.

Examination questions typically ask you to combine in some way – usually by comparison or contrast – information you received over a period of time, not just from one or two lectures within a week or so. In other words, you need to practise thinking about topics from different parts of the course which are similar, or at the same level, like two wars at different times, because although their relationship has not been covered in class, it might be in an exam question. Relationships like that between central and local Government, or between colonial boundaries in Africa and current economic problems there may not have been discussed as a topic in class but you should consider these relationships and links between elements of the course. Draw them up as a mind map as part of your revision, because it is very difficult to recall in this way under exam conditions if you have not already practised some alternative ways of thinking about the subject.

If you don't like mind maps, use a grid to put similar things together and causal or dependent (and superior) things together to maximise the potential of your information and knowledge in the exam. It's sad when students have good factual knowledge about one part of a question but not another and thus can't use their knowledge effectively. This restricts their response to mainly regurgitating information and their maximum mark to 50 per cent or less, because they're not able to make the links between the two topics under examination conditions. They may well know a lot more than they're able to demonstrate in the few hours of the exam. They just haven't thought about it or practised it before!

Making Memories

Memory is extremely important in general terms, because without memories you wouldn't know who you are. You'd have no identity or concept of yourself. In everyday life, you unconsciously build up links that can take you back to a former time. The smell of hay can link back to a farm holiday, or the taste of a particular ice cream to a fairground ride. You naturally have memories embedded in all five senses and any one sense can prompt a memory coming up to the surface of your conscious mind. If your A-level English syllabus included *Much Ado About Nothing*, your teacher probably watched the film version with you, and you may find you can visually recall scenes and hear the actors' voices in your head. The memory of the actors speaking certain lines have made committing them to your memory easier and more interesting. More input paths means easier access to memory. It's a bit like a pinball machine. The more lights the ball hits on its passage, the better.

TIP

Memory mechanics

From a psychological point of view, memory refers to the ability to store, retain and retrieve information. Initially, you have *sensory memory*, when something you perceive through the senses for just a few milliseconds can be recalled for a few seconds. Sensory memory has very limited storage capacity.

Some of this information then passes into *short-term memory*, which has a bit more storage capacity and allows something to be recalled from between a few seconds to about a minute. In 1956, George A. Miller introduced the idea of the Magic Number (7 plus or minus 2) as an estimate of how many items can be held in short-term memory, that is, approximately seven items – plus or minus two – though modern estimates are a few less. However, local phone numbers (without the area code) usually contain about six digits and most people can dial them without asking the numbers to be repeated or having to write them down. Mobile phone numbers on the other hand are much longer, but can be easily stored in the handset and so don't have to rely on human memory.

Long-term memory has infinite capacity, that of a life time, and this is your main memory in terms of establishing your identity You may also remember telephone numbers for many years if you've constantly used and repeated them. This is the key to saving things in long-term memory – rehearsal and repetition, use it or lose it.

Sometimes this transfer between short-term and long-term memory is referred to as *processing memory*. It is often compared to an old fashioned telephone system. As the connections from other phones to a particular phone number increase, so does the likelihood of it ringing. The connections can come through different initial inputs to sensory and then short-term memory and then through repetition, setting up different cognitive networks through noting, discussion and so on.

In an exam situation, you want to consciously bring to mind certain information. If you can use several pathways or links, you then have several possible ways of getting at that information. You have back-up! The problem may not be the information itself, but how to access it. At the end of exams, people often realise that they knew the answer to a question, but they didn't recognise the question in the form it was presented. They didn't make the links!

There's more than one way to skin a cat. If you need to remember information, try to create more than one sensory or cognitive link.

Collating and Recycling Information

Collating information, or pulling together everything you know, is the best way to assess your current state of knowledge and find out what you need to pay attention to. You may have already used mind maps (or spidergrams) to represent what you hoped to learn or had learned at certain points – after lectures, seminars and reading texts. Mind maps are also a great technique for exam preparation. If you draw a mind map of your understanding of a topic without looking at any notes first, this gives you the current state of play in your mind and illustrates the gaps in your understanding. You can then have a good idea of where to look in your notes to fill in the gaps, and add that information to your current mind map. In this way you collate information using what you know to find out what you need to know and add that on.

Because mind maps can extend indefinitely you can also add rhymes or pictures or other mnemonics to them, and so use various techniques simultaneously (and both sides of your brain). Basically, in battle terms, there's no need to call for the cavalry – they're already there!

When you try to find out what you don't know and use this to collate the missing bits of information, you're effectively testing yourself. Can you cheat? This is a possibility as you may have slipped into a comfort zone and stopped challenging yourself.

As with learning, you're better to revise with a friend – four sides of a brain are better than two. If you and your friend both draw a mind map or one of you interprets the mind map of the other or any other memory aid you've devised, then the act of talking about these serves as a memory aid itself as well as a diagnostic tool to help you decide what to check up on!

In a similar way, if you study more than one subject you may find it interesting to see one subject through the eyes of another. You may be able to recycle knowledge from one subject and apply it to another. For example, studying Boccaccio reveals how Shakespeare recycled his plotlines – and added to and improved them without taking anything away from the status of Boccaccio. If you happen to study Philosophy and another subject, you know that philosophers have a take on everything. Other subjects can, in turn, provide examples to agree (or disagree) with philosophical or theoretical concepts.

The more you recycle what you know and use it for other purposes, the better you understand the advantages and limits of the ideas you're studying. Doing this in conversation with others – because speaking and listening engage more areas of the brain than reading or writing – means you use more of your brain and create more links to core concepts to support your memory of them.

In certain circumstances, it may be easier to talk to yourself. Record yourself while you do the cooking. Ask yourself questions as a supporter of the Big Bang theory for example, and see if you can make a good defence. It's important to record these out-loud musings as they pinpoint for you where you got lost or any gaps you need to fill or checks to make. The recording enables you to concentrate and focus on the task of explaining and defending, at the same time picking up any gaps or misunderstandings, which you can check up on later.

It's always a good idea to play 'devil's advocate' in these speaking situations because:

- Doing so distances you from your own views and helps you to be more objective.

- You have to consider much more carefully the evidence from the other side of the argument.

- You have to see how to defend your real view through logic and argument and not passion.

- You think up good arguments and then discover what factual information you need to check out in order to support them.

- If you 'dry' in the exam for a bit (go to the 'happy place') you're more likely to catch the first threads to pull yourself to safety by remembering these spoken arguments.

- This exercise is good preparation for any formal academic situation – that is, that is marked – presentations, essays or other written work or exams.

Reflecting on Beliefs and Feelings

Reflecting is good to do throughout your course. If you use a learner diary, go through it at least once a week to reflect on where you are now and where you were a week ago. Recycling is reusing information you've gathered in new ways. Reflecting is more about considering your attitude and how you feel about certain subjects or aspects of the course and is much more about the emotions. The result of reflection may be that you need to talk to your tutor or student adviser because you feel uncomfortable about something that you can't specify as clearly as you can the need to find out a date or a definition. Reflection can allow doubts as well as satisfaction to come to the surface, and both emotions are good. If you know that you have doubts, you can do something about them. If you bury them, you deny them their role, which is to let you know when you need to get help – a bit like an early warning system. Simply the ability to express them out loud (another use for the recorder) can help you to recognise them and take steps to sort things out.

In the run up to exams it's particularly important that you reflect at the end of each day. Congratulate yourself on what you've achieved and promise yourself to sort out any niggling worries the next day.

All in all, if reflecting and recycling by using some of the strategies suggested become regular habits throughout your course, you'll find that examinations aren't so bad – just bit more of 'business as usual'.

Chapter 18

Preparing for Your Exams

. . . .

In This Chapter

▶ Checking up on exam requirements

▶ Perusing past papers and rubrics

▶ Trying out some self-testing

▶ Timetabling for the exam period

. . . .

Knowledge is power, and never more so than when you're preparing for exams. The kind of knowledge that's most important at this stage – and in life in general – is about how to make the best of the circumstances you find yourself in and where to find useful information to help you do so. One important point to remember is that it's in everybody's interests that you do well. No one wants to put barriers in your way. A course's reputation is based on success stories. In these days of league tables, university and university subject comparison tables, success rates are public information and open to public scrutiny. Success brings an institution greater access to government funding and makes it more attractive to private investment.

Add that to your own ambitions, and it's a pretty powerful team, with all parts pulling in the same direction. To this end, various support facilities or help and information contacts are available – including some online and perhaps email support – some of which are particularly useful to you as you approach exams. Make sure that you know what they are, where they are and that you make good use of them at the right time – not the last minute, if you can avoid it.

This chapter looks in detail at the exams process, covering the different types of exams you may face, the questions in them, and how to make sure you are properly prepared.

Examination Requirements and Conditions

You probably had a look at the exam requirements near the start of the course. In any case, it's time to refresh your memory. This information is probably in your student information pack, so that's a good place to start looking. Otherwise, the school or subject office or course website normally contain all the rules and regulations regarding your course. You need to find out the specific circumstances of each exam you take on your course, including the following:

- ✔ Is the exam a term test or does it count towards your degree or other qualification?

- ✔ If it does count towards your final qualification, what percentage of the final mark does it represent?

- ✔ What are the consequences of failing?

- ✔ What is the procedure if you're ill at around the exam time? Who should you inform and do you need a doctor's certificate?

- ✔ Under what circumstances can you re-sit the exam?

- ✔ Can you postpone the exam if you have a heavy burden of other exams to take? (This can happen where several different degree or certificate courses share a common exam. The timing of the exam may be better for some students than for others.)

Assessing the importance of your exams

You need to find out how important each exam is to your future. Generally speaking, you have to sit several exams over a couple of weeks or so. Ideally, you want to give of your best in all of them. However, if not all exams are equal, and you have to choose how best to spend your energy (for various reasons), it's important that you make the right choices and focus on the exams that count most, even if they're the topics you find most difficult.

Touching on timetabling

It's not unusual for there to be exam timetable clashes when different major subject students take a common exam (a *shared-course exam*, as it's sometimes called). When this happens, students can't sit two exams at the same time, so the exam-writers devise two versions of the exam to allow those with the clash to sit an equivalent exam at a later date, without finding out the questions from the first group to sit the exam.

If your exam is a shared course exam, it's worth checking whether the exam is timetabled for more than one slot, and if so, whether a different slot would suit you better – perhaps you have a heavy load of two three-hour exams on several days in one week and then very few exams the following week. Of course, this depends on the number of desks available in the exam room (rules govern the distance between desks to make cheating difficult), but there are often a few spare desks and sometimes students are allocated to take exams on the basis of being free at a particular time, rather than that being the best time for them. Devising exam timetables is no easy business, but there may be some flexibility, so it's worth asking.

Sorting out your individual needs

Your university or college is committed to making the playing field as level as possible for all students, so if you have a learning difficulty such as dyslexia or have to use special equipment to help you study, you've probably made that known already and been given support.

However, it is worth making sure that all those who set the exams (check with the subject or school office) are aware of your needs and have made arrangements to accommodate them in the exam. For example, if you're dyslexic, you may be given more time.

Allowing for illness and anxiety

If you're ill before the exam period, you must let your tutor know as being ill can cut down your revision time. You should get a doctor's certificate. It's also important to let your tutor know if you're taking medication during an exam, so the invigilator knows what you're doing – not just 'pill-popping'. If you have a temporary problem that affects your sight you may be able to get support with taking the exam, for example, someone to write answers for you, as in the case above if that is better for you than to sit the exam at a later date.

Although everyone is very sympathetic to real problems, last-minute exam freak out is not a good idea for you or anyone else. If you feel bad in any way – physically or emotionally – talk to someone sooner rather than later, ideally your tutor or a student counsellor. With advanced warning comes flexibility, and you can work things out. Nothing is more important than your health and wellbeing. You can find ways of sorting things out, even sitting an exam a few days late in your bedroom with an invigilator, or in your tutor's office.

This exam, and many others, is soon be nothing more than a vague memory. Focus on the day after the last exam and think about all the great things you're going to do then.

Perusing Past Papers

Past papers form a very important part of basic exam preparation because they make exams concrete. What you find out about is never as intimidating as what you don't know or what you imagine to be the case. You can normally obtain past papers from your school or subject office, and papers are also often available on line from your subject of study web page. Sometimes, previous years' students hand in their papers to the Student Union office. If you're sitting an external exam you can request copies of past papers from the appropriate examinations board, although there may be a small charge.

From past papers, you can find out:

✔ How long the exam is – three hours, one hour or whatever.

✔ How many questions are set.

✔ How many questions you have to answer – how wide your choice is. (For example, twelve questions may be set, but you may only have to answer three.)

✔ Whether the exam has sections and if you have to answer a certain number from each section or have open choice.

✔ How much time, on average, you can spend on each question.

✔ What type of questions are asked – essay or short answer type. (For example, if you're a Maths or Pure Science student you may have to answer a series of short questions each worth a few marks, or questions divided into three or four subsections with specific marks allocated to each.)

✔ Whether you can submit answers in note form if you run short of time.

✔ Whether you can get hold of 'takeaway papers' to answer on your own within a certain time limit.

✔ Whether you're given the exam questions in advance to give you time to research the answers before sitting the exam in the normal way.

✔ Some typical rubrics. See the next section for more on rubrics.

Reading Up on Rubrics

Rubrics are the instructions that you have to follow in order to answer the exam questions. The general rubrics appear at the top of the paper and tell you how many questions you have to answer, how much each question is worth, how long the exam lasts, or whether you can write on one or both sides of the paper.

Here's an example of the type of general rubric you may find in an undergraduate Maths exam.

> There are 10 questions in this exam: number 4 is worth six points and number 8 is worth fourteen points. All the others are worth ten points each. In questions with multiple parts, the questions are divided equally among the parts.
>
> Show all your working out, as credit may be given. Use of books, calculators, notes or mobile phones aren't permitted during this exam. Please make sure that mobile phones are switched off.

The actual mark sheet may be printed on top of the questions paper and the marks for each question are clearly stated. In some cases, you may actually write your answers on space provided on the question paper. However, you're always given rough paper on which to work out your answers and which you must hand in with the answers as credit may be given for rough work. If you're running out of time you may decide to leave questions like number 4 in the example to last, as it is worth the least number of marks. Maths, Science and Engineering subject rubrics are generally very direct and similar to the example.

When preparing for exams you must read carefully the general rubrics and as many different example question rubrics as you can find to ensure that you understand them, because you must do what they tell you. Brilliant answers that don't follow the instructions of the rubrics may earn no marks, even if they're factually accurate.

The question rubrics are also the guidelines for marking your paper – though not always stated as directly as in the example above – so you need to be clear about what they mean.

For example, this Ecology question says:

> Give four reasons why it is essential to protect what remains of the Amazon rainforest for future generations.

Most essay type or longer answers (where more than a few lines are expected) have a few bonus points on offer for doing a little more, so if you gave four very good reasons and a bit more, you might be in line for a bonus point or two. However, if you only give three reasons, no matter how well you express yourself you're only eligible for three-quarters of the total mark. In this way, the rubrics of the question control the mark scheme in Humanities as well as Science subjects – though not as clearly – so you need to read them carefully.

Arts and Humanities rubrics are open to some interpretation, to give you some freedom of response. In addition, it's not possible to spell out exactly what is required without giving the game away. The exam writer probably had in mind a range of possible answers to the rainforest question, probably several more than four, but any four may be acceptable. The exam writer has specified this in the mark scheme as marking is probably shared by several people. This contrasts with the rubrics of Pure Science and Maths that relate to answers that are correct or incorrect, though credit is given for workings out, so you can gain some marks for a wrong answer.

This is an example question from an undergraduate Maths exam.

> Question 1.(a) 2 points
>
> Find the distance from the point (2,-2,1) to the *x-z* plane

(Question 1 has three parts: Part a) is worth two points – part b), three points and part c), five points. The questions increase incrementally according to difficulty, and so the marks increase correspondingly. Abstract subject rubrics may give more precise instructions and marking information than Arts subjects, but the principles are the same.)

If you find rubrics difficult to make sense of, now is a good time to ask your tutor to explain them to you. There's a fair chance that the exam you sit has been written by the same group of people (most exams are written collectively by several people) or if not, it has to be – as far as possible – of the same standard as past papers, so it is similar. If you don't follow the rubrics, you won't answer the questions properly and thus lose marks, even if you have all the appropriate knowledge. Again, it's not what you know, but what you're able to do with what you know.

Discussing rubrics with classmates can be as productive as discussing the topics to be examined, and at best, the two should go together. Working out rubrics is a way of getting into the head of the examiner, and that, essentially, is how you achieve good marks in exams. It's worth asking your tutor who writes the questions for certain topic areas. If you've been taught by that person, you have an idea of how she thinks. If you aren't a member of her group find someone who is or go directly to the tutor concerned or if you can, express your problem in a quick email. However, a workshop would probably be better, so suggest your tutor runs one to go over some of that tutor's and other rubrics with you and your fellow students.

This sort of suggestion is normally welcomed because it shows awareness and concern – for all exam-takers. You can always encourage your friends to ask for help too – the savvy tutor realises that one workshop to a group of students is a better use of everyone's time than a stream of students trooping to her door asking the same questions.

A questionable question

'Describe the moor in *Othello* and the heath in *Wuthering Heights'* – apparently a real rubric in a school certificate exam from some 60 years ago – would no longer pass the exam test phase. The question writer probably thought it was a clever pun, but what did she imagine the answers would be? This is certainly not clear. Is a comparison expected between the moor (Othello) and the Yorkshire dales or is this 'witty' pun a reference to Heathcliff, the hero of 'Wuthering Heights'? As it doesn't pass the first post (clarity) it certainly doesn't comply with the other rules of communication.

Not all examiners write brilliant or clear rubrics. Rubrics should follow the rules for good communication: honesty, clarity, reality and relevance. The rubrics shouldn't be there to trick you but to tell you exactly what you have to do to answer the question. If the paper asks for four reasons, three are not eligible for full marks. However, examination writers today are generally better trained than in the past.

If what a question wants you to do really isn't clear, then it's beast to avoid that question. If you have to answer it, write: 'This is my understanding of what the question asks me to do . . .'. In general, it's always a good idea to say what you understand, what you're doing, why you're doing it and how, because then you're assessed on your merits and the marker doesn't have to guess what those are.

Essay-type questions

Some rubrics – in the Arts or Social Sciences, for example – require you to define certain terms – in a similar way that essay titles require you to define terms.

The anatomy of essay-type questions

Consider the following rubric from a History examination:

> **Either** 'Socialism is incompatible with freedom' Discuss.
>
> **Or** 'Fascism is a product of modernity.' Discuss.

The time allocated to answering the question was one hour. A standard procedure exists for dealing with questions like these.

- ✔ **Understand the structure of the question:** A choice exists within this question, indicated by the '**Either/Or**' in heavy type. If you answer both parts, you only get marks for one, normally the first. If you're very lucky, the marker may read both answers and give you the marks for the best answer of the two.

- ✔ **Define the terms:** You need definitions to show your understanding of the terms 'socialism' and 'freedom' for the first question or 'fascism' and 'modernity' for the second.

- ✔ **Make sure that you do what the question asks:** Both sub-questions make statements that you're asked to discuss. 'Discuss' is part of the rubric as well and means you have to give both sides of the argument with reasons for and against the statement in the question. You don't have to agree or disagree with the statement. You can say that both arguments (for and against) have their merits.

In most essay-type questions, you should plan your answer roughly because if you don't have time to finish the question, the plan can show where you were going. You get credit for that. In other words, the plan can be marked. Rough notes for 'Socialism is incompatible with Freedom' may be something like this:

- ✔ **Introduction:** The question presupposes there's no overlap between socialism and freedom – two separate, non-touching circles.

- ✔ **Define socialism:** The economic theories of Marx, Owen, Blanc and others.

- ✔ **Define freedom:** From social economic perspective; laissez faire government or personal freedom? Does capitalism give freedom? Is individual freedom possible? Is all freedom limited?

- ✔ **Freedom within socialism:** Possible and what sort? (Small circle within a larger circle?).

Freedom is a very wide concept and defining it within the context of being incompatible with socialism, implies discussing capitalism, or aspects of non-socialist governance.

Both before the exam as preparation and in the exam itself, it's always a good idea to rough out how you'd answer a question. Ideally, put down your rough ideas on paper as a sequence (as above) or a mind map; doing so reveals not only what the question rubrics ask directly but also what they *imply* – that is, indicate, but don't state directly. For example, the word 'capitalism' may not appear in the title of an essay, but you may still need to discuss it in detail. Once you're used to spotting these implications, they become much easier to handle.

The following question – in the form of a question this time, not a statement – is also part of a History exam from the same source.

> To what extent are 'gender' and 'race' cultural constructs?

Not all the examinees are History majors; some have a different major, so this is an interesting 'crossover' question because the terms ' gender' and 'race' can be studied within many disciplines. *To what extent* suggests the answer shouldn't be a straightforward 'yes or no' type , but should deal with degrees of opinion, implying a range of possible opinion.

The terms to define are *gender*, *race* and *cultural constructs*.

The implied terms, which are not stated (and may relate to the other subjects the students study) may be *social construct* or *political construct* and a possible argument is whether *social construct*, *cultural construct* and *political construct* are separate concepts.

In a question like this, be sure to discuss *gender* and *race* separately, not together, and make sure that you give them roughly equal weight in your answer. You can argue that one is a cultural construct, but not the other. The rubric guides you to give equal consideration to each topic (gender and race) and if you write a lot about one, but little about the other, it affects your mark. Plan out your points in terms of a paragraph for each, you then have an idea of the balance of your answer.

Essay-type exam instruction words

Essay-type exam questions can have several rubric instruction words similar to *discuss, compare and contrast, to what extent*. Table 18-1 gives some common instruction words found in exam questions and essay titles, together with what you have to do.

Table 18-1   Standard Instruction Words and Their Meanings

Instruction word	What you have to do
Analyse	Take apart an idea, concept or statement and examine and criticise its sub-parts in detail. You have to be methodical and logical.
Assess	Describe a topic's positive and negative aspects and say how useful or successful it is, or consider its contribution to knowledge, events, processes. (Usually about how important something is.)
Criticise	Point out a topic's mistakes or weaknesses as well as its favourable aspects. Give a balanced answer. (This will involve some *analysis* first.)

(continued)

Table 18-1 *(continued)*

Instruction word	What you have to do
Compare	Put items side by side to see their similarities and differences – a balanced (objective) answer is required
Contrast	Emphasise the differences between two things
Define	Give the meaning of an idea, either a dictionary definition or from an academic authority in your subject of study (technical definition)
Describe	Give details of processes, properties, events and so on
Discuss	Describe, explain, give examples, points for and against, then analyse and evaluate the results
Evaluate	Similar to 'discuss', but with more emphasis on a judgement in the conclusion
Examine	Take apart and describe a concept in great detail
Explain	Give detailed reasons for an idea, principle or result, situation, attitude and so on. You may need to give some analysis as well.
Illustrate	Give concrete examples – including figures or diagrams. 'Illustrate' is usually added on to another instruction
Interpret	Explain and comment on the subject and make a judgement (evaluation)
Justify	Give reasons to support a statement – it may be a negative statement, so be careful!
List	Provide an itemised series of parts, reasons or qualities, possibly in a table
Prove /disprove	Provide evidence for or against and demonstrate logical argument and reasoning – you often have to do this for abstract or scientific subjects
Relate	Emphasise the links, connections and associations, probably with some analysis
Review	Analyse and comment briefly, in organised sequences – sentences, paragraphs or lists – on the main aspects of a subject
State	Give the relevant points briefly – you don't need to make a lengthy discussion or give minor details

Instruction word	What you have to do
Suggest	Give possible reasons – analyse, interpret and evaluate. (This is also the verb most commonly used to quote another author.)
Summarise or outline	Just give the main points, not the details
Trace	Give a brief description of the logical or chronological stages of the development of a theory, process, a person's life and so on. Often used in historical questions

Some Biology exam papers – the example here is from animal social behaviour – share the same instruction words as Arts and Humanities papers and have a similar choice of questions, for example, three questions out of eight in three hours. (Candidates are also asked to use information from other Biology courses and diagrams when appropriate.)

Discuss how game theory has contributed to our understanding of animal social behaviour.

Multiple-choice questions

The questions you can take away to answer and those you're given in advance before you answer them under normal exam conditions tend to be essay-type questions, as discussed above. You may also be presented with multiple-choice questions. These are often used as a quick way to assess knowledge of basic or key points, for example in psychology, as in the example below:

Sensation, perception and memory are of particular interest to which group of psychologists?

a) Psychoanalysts

b) Behaviourists

c) Humanistic Psychologists

d) Cognitive Psychologists

You may be familiar with this type of question, usually with four possible answers (sometimes three or five) from your A- or AS-level examinations, or even quiz games like *Who Wants to be a Millionaire?* They may seem superficially easy, because you're given the answer, but you'll probably recall how difficult it can be to guess correctly. (The correct answer in the example is d), incidentally.) Multiple-choice exams are easy to mark. How good they are for checking basic understanding depends on the skill of the exam writer. If too few correct answers are a), or if you can get more correct answers by chance, simply by ticking a particular letter for each question, then they have limited value.

Bearing that in mind, multiple choice tests provide a useful means of revising basic concepts. You can access various subject websites by Googling 'multiple choice practice tests' to test yourself (for example, for American History www.historyteacher.net/USQuizMainPage.htm, and for Chemistry, chemistry.boisestate.edu/people/richardbanks/organic/mc/mcquestions317.htm.

Other types of questions

Undergraduate Engineering exams typically have questions subdivided into about three parts, each with a problem to solve or proof to demonstrate. Thirty minutes to complete each question means that each sub-part allows about ten minutes. The exam usually consists of a choice of two questions out of three to be completed in an hour.

All exams are about using knowledge, but Science and Technology subjects are more likely to require the direct use of abstract symbols or formulae that you need to remember or memorise, whereas Arts and Humanities subject exams generally require argument or logic, of which you need to find examples, or reasons for.

Finding the fun in facts

A less serious way to prepare for exams and check your memory skills for facts is to write some multiple choice questions to test fellow students, and they can do the same for you. They can be as silly as you like to help you remember the facts by association. For example:

Endorphins are produced:

a) in the Mediterranean and Adriatic seas.

b) in the pituitary gland and hypothalamus.

c) only during sex.

d) only by people under 40.

Strategies to identify common topics

One of the problems of exams that give you a wide choice of questions is to map common topics, and just as importantly, the form of the questions about them. Where fewer choices exist (generally in Maths and Engineering), it can be easier to see what the commonly examined topics are as they tend to turn up regularly, as these subjects are incremental in terms of knowledge.

In either event, it's important to look at recent exam papers in your subject area. If your course is fairly new, the exams may only go back a few years, so there may not be many examples.

Ask your tutor for help to get a better idea of the exam format. She may be also able to suggest other institutions that offer a similar course where you can find some examples of exams that are likely to be similar. Alternatively, Google your course title to look for similar courses and where you can find sample exams.

The best way to identify likely topics is to start with your list of lecture and seminar topics for the year. Using a colour code:

✔ Mark any of these topics that appear in the most recent exam.

✔ Do the same for the last three or four years.

✔ Using another colour mark any essay topics that appear in the most recent exam.

✔ Do the same for the last three or four years.

This should give you a fair idea of common (or *core*) exam topics and topics that appear both in coursework essay subjects and exam questions. Note, however, that the exam topic is likely to have a different focus than the essay topic, where both are the same. You should also note the range of choice – likely to be small for Maths, Science and Technology, but wider for Arts, Humanities and Biology.

In doing this exercise, note that many questions have usually two or three sub-topics, which can appear in different combinations with other topics. You may be able to identify core topics that appear more frequently, but don't forgot to note the secondary topics as well.

Once you've done this, you can identify:

- ✔ Topics that you know a lot about or are comfortable with.
- ✔ Common topics about which you know less.
- ✔ What you need to revise to give yourself an adequate choice of questions.

Most essay-type questions offer a very wide choice. This may be to cater for different groups of students taking the same exam. Decide the minimum core of information you need in order to cope with the topic combinations likely to occur from your frequency research, and add on a few more for safety's sake. If, for example, you have a choice of three questions out of eight, then covering the topics to answer four of the questions you think likely to come up may be a bit tight, so another one or two may be better for safety's sake. You probably don't need to prepare to potentially choose any of the eight questions, as much of that preparation would be redundant. It's best to concentrate your efforts where they're most likely to be fruitful.

Testing Yourself

Wherever possible, find some classmates to discuss how you'd tackle certain questions using the instruction words and possible implications and also discuss how much you can do in the time allocated for each question. You can get a rough idea of this by drawing a mind map. (For more on mind maps see Chapter 7.) With Science and Technology questions, consider how much information you think you need to get the marks allocated to each question.

Find an hour or half an hour to tackle a question – whatever the time allocated to a question is. Be quite strict about this as you need to know how quickly you can write and how much you can reasonably cover in the time given. If you can answer and write on a computer, so much the better, but many exams are still handwritten although most people rarely write by hand these days. Practise handwriting answers as you may have no idea how fast or slow your handwriting is.

Testing yourself against the clock is also where you get an idea as to whether you have the balance of a question with two topics right, or if you've given too much space to one – or only arguments in favour and none against. Always check what you're doing against the rubrics.

If you can do these tests with classmates and can exchange papers and put on a marker's hat, you quickly see what is clear and what is not. If you can't find someone to exchange with (it's a really quick way to learn a lot) then take a look at your own work after a time lapse – sleep on it at least – and you may see things that would make your answer better or remember things you've left out.

Your school or subject of study office may have examples of old exam answers, although for various reasons they're normally shredded. It's worth asking your tutor for a *sample answer* – an answer specifically written by an expert as a model of the way the question should be answered – these can be very helpful.

If your tutor or another tutor wrote the sample answer in essay form, neither is likely to have done it under exam conditions, so it may be somewhat unrealistically elegant as a goal. If however, they noted the core facts, the argument or the discussion they were looking for, this can be very helpful.

Timetabling the Pre-Exam Period

Coursework normally stops a week or so before exams start, so this is a period of consolidation. By now, with luck and some of the strategies described earlier in this chapter, you probably have a good idea of what you're comfortable with and what niggles you still have at the back of your mind. This is now the time for pacing yourself and sorting out any niggles.

As soon as you have your exam timetable and know the order of the exams and the gaps between them, you can start to make daily plans for spreading your workload and getting enough exercise and sleep. Because timing is important at this point, it's a good idea for you to check on topics, methods and theories you're still not confident about but which you've identified as likely to come up in the exam. Then decide on the best place to look for help. Ideally this should be in the week or so before the exams start, so you can plan your final revision period effectively.

Niggles are good. Listen to them. They point out where a gap exists. Sit back with your eyes shut and relax. After a moment of relaxation, meditation or whatever suits you, the niggles become clearer, which helps you to sort them out. Deal with the niggles like this:

- ✔ If you've forgotten which tutor gave the lecture or seminar related to a niggle, check your learning diary or timetable; or ask classmates.

- ✔ Find out when her office hour is and make an appointment. If you know that she's in her office regularly take a note to explain exactly what you want to ask about, or send an email, or do both.

- ✔ Copy the above to your personal tutor, who may also be able to help, or copy your query to any student mentors who may have been helping you.

- ✔ Copy the same to class members and any students in the year above that you know.

In other words, by scattering your request you bring in more answers. Some will make more sense than others, but the principle is that it's better to read several versions of the same thing than the same version over and over again. You can return to later after reading the others.

You also need time to absorb information and mull it over, so now is the time to be super-organised. Talking to a tutor or classmates about concepts you find difficult is best done before you start your full-on daily subject revision in the examination period. If you leave this too late, you'll have gaps in your understanding that affect other areas of your revision.

Your 'week before exams start' diary should have a balance between general revision – things you need to check up on, perhaps working with other people – and exercise, socialising and practical needs. Once the exams start, it's more difficult to programme working with friends as they may have different timetables, depending on what they study, and different free time. Some may prefer to work on their own. Socialising in free time is another matter, as long as it doesn't turn into escapism or exam avoidance. They're always easier to do than not do, as the repercussions are greater.

Your pre-exam (week before) timetable plan may look something like Table 18-2.

Table 18-2	A Typical Pre-Exam Timetable
Monday	Morning: Library (read journals)
	2.15 p.m.: Tutor meeting re. Econometrics
	5.00 p.m.: Swimming at . . .
	Evening: Watch DVD with flatmates
Tuesday	Morning: Revising with Fred
	Afternoon: Shopping
	Evening: Chores (washing clothes and so on)
Wednesday	11.00 a.m.: Viewing booked in library to watch Charles Handy DVD with George
	3.00 p.m.: Dentist
	Evening: My turn to cook supper then read through notes at home

Thursday	10.30 a.m.: Meeting with tutor group and tutor re exam techniques
	Afternoon: Lunch, then discussion with group till 3.30p.m.
	Evening: Cinema at 5.00 p.m. with Bev (cheap tickets before 6.00 p.m.)
Friday	Morning: Lie-in
	Afternoon: Timed-essay practice with Fred and swopping to mark, then pub for an hour with friends
Saturday	Morning: Library to check on details not sure of after timed essay (quiet on Sat. a.m.) and checking sample exam answers not available off-campus
Sunday	Long bath, relaxation, four-mile walk to village pub for lunch

Things tend to get a bit tighter when the actual exams start, but you still need to timetable-in some fun. A revision timetable for when the exams are actually underway may look more like Table 18-3.

Table 18-3	Revision Timetable During Exam Time			
	Morning	**Afternoon**	**Evening**	**Comment**
Monday	Revision – note, read through for exam 1. Salad for lunch	2.00–5.00 Exam 1	Wash hair; revision exam 4	Pub for an hour at 9.00 p.m.
Tuesday	Revision exam 2	Shopping, wash clothes	Revision exam 5	Early night
Wednesday	9.00 – 12.00 exam 2	swimming	Revision exams 5 and 3	Watch TV 9.00–10.00 p.m. bed
Thursday	Last-minute checks exam 3	Exam 3	Jogging for one hour, revision exam 4	
Friday	Exam 4	Exam 5	Gym, then cinema	

Have enough socks and underwear washed before the exam – or a good friend to borrow some from – as you don't want to have to make choices between cleanliness or revision!

By the week of the exam you probably don't want to do more than a quick overview revision as writing exams is tiring, so you need to conserve your energy. If you've been reviewing, recycling, researching, discussing and practising as you've progressed through your course, you may find the exam is itself quite enjoyable, as you can now offload all that stuff that's been in your head waiting for this moment!

Chapter 19

Coping with the Countdown to Your Exams

In This Chapter

▶ Getting to grips with the where, when and how of exams

▶ Preserving a healthy mind in a healthy body

▶ Believing you can succeed

▶ Reviewing your results

You need to put exams in context. They last over a period of two or three weeks in most cases. They can be the icing on the cake after a term or year of study, your chance to show how you have benefited from your course and what you can do in a few hours. Exams don't just assess you. They assess the quality of your course. Everyone wants you to do well. If you have attended class and done your assignments, had feedback and asked your tutor how you can do better, then exams can slot in as just another part of the course, nothing exceptional. They are certainly not the end of the world and not the only things you are assessed on. Your coursework – contributions to seminars, presentations, projects, essays and so forth – and being a generally kind and helpful human being is also part of the picture.

Exams can also teach you a lot as well. If you have an oral exam, you can think of it as practice for a job interview. Exams serve as practice for working under the time and pressure constraints of the real world of work in order to meet deadlines. Preparing for exams as well as the exams themselves gives you practice in planning, prioritising and creating goals in order of importance. You get to decide what you have to have and what you can do without, and discover how to manage tasks on a day-to-day basis, and longer term. Exams can be very good at focusing the mind. All in all, going with the stream in exams – rather than reluctantly resisting the current and then being swept along by it later – can be a very positive experience. You can challenge yourself to successfully manoeuvre within the time and space exams and exam preparation occupies so that these become a support rather than a constraint. You are then indeed in charge.

A Time and Place for Everything

Everybody needs certain things to sustain a healthy life. There are other things which are fun and a bit more self-indulgent, but while in term-time you have more flexibility to make up for three late nights or early mornings on the trot mid-week by sleeping in the day time, for example, in the exam period, you need to ration some things and rationalise others. What this boils down to is time.

Making time for revision – and life's necessities

During the exam period it is important to get your priorities right to maintain your health, your energy levels and not least, your sanity. This means you need to have enough sleep, food and exercise on a daily basis to stay healthy. This section covers balancing your requirements for sleep, food, work and play. The later section 'Keeping a healthy mind in a healthy body' has more detail on looking after yourself.

Whereas outside the exam period you might work on a weekly or longer basis to catch up on sleep, have a healthy diet and enough exercise. During the exams, you need to prioritise and divide your time between:

✔ **Sleeping:** Getting seven or eight hours sleep each night, ideally beginning at least one hour before midnight, sets you up well, mentally and physically, to cope consistently with the demands of the exam period. It's important to maintain a sleeping routine , as this make you feel calmer and more secure. Without proper sleep, you won't function at your best.

If you have difficulty in relaxing and getting to sleep, the old remedies of a mug of hot chocolate or cocoa, a drop of lavender oil on your pillow or a relaxing bath and a hot water bottle or your favourite cuddly toy at bedtime work well for most people.

✔ **Eating:** A balanced diet is more important than ever to maintain your energy levels and immune system. It is very important not to skip breakfast, especially when you have long morning exams. Boiled eggs for breakfast are quick and easy, or porridge (quick in the microwave) will also give more energy and nutritional value than ordinary cereal or toast. Don't forget your five portions of fruit and veg a day. Bananas are good to take into exams for a burst of energy along with some bottled water so you don't get dehydrated – the main cause of headaches and tension. If you don't feel much like cooking, then prepared salads and cold meat, along with beetroot, are good things to eat in the evening. Chunky soups can also be a good source of vegetables and very comforting.

Salads may only keep for about three days in the fridge, so make sure you can get some fresh food mid-week, either by making a buying rota with a friend or by turning the need to shop into a diversion and a change of activity.

✔ **Socialising.** You can combine socialising – meeting with friends – with other activities like sports, going to the gym, cycling or walking, sharing a meal, watching a film, especially on Friday nights or at the week-ends, when you have more time to relax. Ideally, you should take breaks when nobody mentions. Exercise – including skipping to a beat to help you remember facts – will help you sleep better. Watching a film or play will involve you in the moment. Even ten minutes chat on heavy exam days will remind you there is more to life than exams, so plan to have some encounters with other people every day. Chat to people at the bus-stop, have a haircut and chat to the hairdresser – whatever it is, make sure you have some social interaction every day.

If you have no exams and you want to revise all day and it's pouring with rain, then take a break and use your mobile. If you haven't seen a class-mate for a few days, ring them up and ask how they're doing. Best of all, plan to have a break with them for an hour or so when the rain stops. It's very important to get out of your room for a bit and have a change of scenery.

✔ **Revising:** The exam timetable may mean that the gaps between exams are not ideal. Planning last minute revision needs to take into account what gaps you have available after you've sorted out sleeping, eating and socialising. You may need to do your main last minute revision for a certain exam one week before you have to sit it, with just an hour or so free the day before or on the day of the exam itself. This is actu-ally good news. In the period after your main revision some points will arise because part of your brain will have been mulling them over in the intervening period, making your very last minute efforts before the exam highly focused and productive.

If you can arrange to do your final revision for each exam several days or a week before you have to sit it, you will find any last minute revision is much more focused.If you have been going over your notes and reviewing your course as you went along, especially for a course that ended before Easter and is examined in June, with the exam in mind, you will have already prepared the ground well. This also cuts you some slack in the exam period if you feel ill or need to have a day off to rest. In fact, your brain will still be working on the revision you've already done, so you will have lost nothing. Wherever possi-ble, build in some reflection time to help you pace yourself and allow your mind to mull over the issues. You will find some remarkable ideas will pop up to the surface of your conscious mind as a result. There's plenty of extra capacity in your brain, so use it. Most of us only use about ten per cent of our brains. Reflection allows the brain to add on and extend the topic of the reflec-tion by tapping into other related areas which your conscious mind may not have thought of.

Timetabling a good balance between sleeping, eating, socialising (including taking exercise, even if it's just a walk) and revising will put you in charge and give you both intellectual and emotional support during the exam period. It also works well on the economics of when to undertake certain activities and for how long to get the most out of them individually and within the overall planning for the exam period.

Keeping a healthy mind in a healthy body

Keeping your body healthy – as healthy as it can be given individual circumstances – should come first, or your mind will become distracted. As well as being careful to eat a balanced diet, including fruit and vegetables, it also important to:

- ✓ **Avoid excessive alcohol intake, especially during the week.** A glass of red wine for a treat, when you're not driving, is fine for most people. Don't overindulge on Saturday or Sunday as you won't have enough time to recover, given the other stresses and strains of exam time.

- ✓ **Avoid taking painkillers unless you have to.** Paracetamol seems to suit most people, but ibuprofen (present in many over-the-counter drugs, especially for period pain and such like) can cause depression in some people, while aspirin can be a stomach irritant. Instead, for headaches, massage the back of the neck and temples using a little lavender oil, lie down on you back for a while, or try a face massage. If possible, avoid taking any new medication during exam periods in case it has a side-effect.

- ✓ **Take precautions against minor ailments.** If colds and flu seem likely, then echinacea or bee propolis taken daily, help to build up your immune system. St John's Wort can be very helpful in times of tension. It is best to try these out before the exam period, although side–effects are rare.

- ✓ **Keep hydrated and carry a small bottle of water with you.** Most people can't tell the difference between tap water kept cool in the fridge over night and spa water.

- ✓ **Loosen up those muscles every day.** Jigging round the room to your favourite record for 15 minutes morning and night, or have a jigging break during revision, will keep you hanging loose.

If you practise meditation, this can be very helpful during exam periods. It helps you to keep things in proportion and see the bigger picture. If you're not used to sitting quietly and calmly, then this might be the time to try it out in a park or open space. If you live near a Quaker meeting house and have never been in, then the shared silence can be very uplifting. Everyone is welcome at a Quaker meeting – you don't have to be a Christian.

The most important thing is to anchor your thoughts to what is happening now and what you need to do now to take care of yourself. You are a unique and important human being every moment of every day. The future will take care of itself.

If you take care of yourself, you are in a better position to cheer others up. You can plan phone breaks during revision as a change of activity to check up on your friends' progress and remind them to set their alarm or arrange to go to the exam together. Cheerful chats with friends are good. If you feel very moany, it's better to phone someone like your mum, who 's left exam-taking far behind, and so will be less affected by your complaints than your classmates.

All the little practical tasks like setting your alarm and putting out your clothes at night ready for the next day, checking you and your mates have the right tools – pens, pencils, rubbers, rulers and so on – all serve to ground you in reality, and make you feel more secure. These are the things you can control and make sure you're in charge of, so it's important to do just that.

The economics of time, self-bribery and treats

It can be very difficult to get down to revising if your mind wanders or you're hungry or just plain bored. It's easy to get distracted by email or Youtube. If you're really tired, the best thing to do may be to take a nap – think of it as a siesta. An hour's sleep in the afternoon can set you up for several hours of work later on. Trying to carry on with your eyes propped open with matchsticks is usually a waste of time. You learn nothing and you don't get any rest either.

At a time like this, be aware of your body and what it wants to do. While it is generally best to get an hour's sleep before midnight, if you occasionally wake in the night and feel alert, it may be better to put in a spot of revision, perhaps some reading – to tire yourself out if nothing else – than to toss and turn and not sleep a wink.

It can help your concentration if you build in small bribes and treats to break up your revision, provide goals and give you something to look forward to. You know yourself and what can motivate you, but the following list offers a few suggestions that might help you complete a task or work consistently (with coffee/tea or loo breaks included) for a couple of hours. Promise yourself the reward and make sure you deliver.

- ✔ A relaxing bath with scented bath oil, alternatively, do the washing up with lots of lovely suds and hot water to blow bubbles with as well, if you're short of time.

- ✔ 45 minutes in the pub with friends, back in time to get to bed before 11.00 p.m.

- ✔ A really delicious oral indulgence – dark chocolate coated ginger, seaweed peanuts, chewy salami – taking time out to savour whatever you fancy.

- ✔ A quick spot of window-shopping nearby in the early evening, when it's quiet, to look at that great dress, jacket or pair of shoes.

- ✔ Television break to catch the news for half an hour or watch a favourite soap.

- ✔ 30 minutes to listen to some favourite music – really listen, not as a background to revision.

- ✔ 15 minutes to knead dough with your hands, or rub butter and sugar into flour to make breadcrumbs for crumble. (These can be put in the fridge to bake the next day.) It's very tactile and relaxing.

- ✔ Half an hour or so to read a chapter of a thriller or other non-revision reading.

- ✔ A foot or shoulder massage to your flatmate and get them to return the favour.

- ✔ Time to stroke the cat/dog that lives nearby, or any other furry, accessible creature.

- ✔ Ten minutes to stand in front of a window and practise deep breathing, especially on days when you won't go out till later in the day.

- ✔ Listen to 'A Book at Bedtime' (on BBC Radio Four) in bed. Being read to conjures up feelings of warmth and security in many people.

Make sure you get out every day, even for a short period of time, for a change of air and scenery.

Little bribes and treats should include some that appeal to several senses as these can help you relax as well. They will also work as markers or a framework on either side of the revision you are doing and help you remember it. You will also find that you can get more out of the time between treats than you could if you just carried on working, with no breaks or 'bribes'. This is where you hit the rule of diminishing returns. You need to spend more time to learn less if you don't build in breaks and little escapes after an hour or so of concentrated work.

Getting Down to It: Sitting Your Exams

Exams can't eat you. They can't drink you. In fact, they can't do anything to you at all if you don't let them. Think of people like Sir Richard Branson, Sir Alan Sugar, or successful racehorse trainer Jenny Pitman OBE, none of whom considered the need for taking exams after the age of 16. They have been successful through getting on with the practical side of things, having great self-confidence (pretending and being convincing is good enough) as well as drive. They also use their *emotional intelligence* (the ability to understand other people's emotional responses and work with them) and have a knack for spotting winners.

Indeed, you can have fun in preparing for exams and then finding out how good your preparation was, how well it served you in the real thing. That's all about developing the knack of spotting winners – much more useful in the long run. It is indeed all in the preparation. You've gone through that process by the time you get into the exam room, so you've already learned some of the most important life skills you need. The exam itself will help you to evaluate the skills you have used in the preparation period.

 Exams only test one kind of intelligence – intellectual intelligence – on a particular day for a certain amount of time. This kind of intelligence is neither a necessary nor sufficient condition for success, but no one has quite worked out how to test other forms of intelligence and give them marks on a scale.

Last minute exam behaviour checks

Make sure you know where each exam rooms is – there may be several – how to get there, where the nearest loos are. With luck, you'll have been there before, but if not, make sure you've been inside the room so that it is familiar to you by the day of the exam. The more you know, the less there is to surprise you or make you nervous. You may never need to use the loos, but knowing where they are can be very comforting.

Read through the course instructions and other instructions you've been given about the day of the exam carefully. These should tell you:

- ✔ **What time the exam starts and ends and what time you have to get to the room by:** If you are late, you may not be allowed to sit the exam.

- ✔ **What you have to take to the exam with you:** For example, your student ID card or other form of identification, and possibly a candidate number previously given to you.

✔ **What you are allowed to take into the room and what not:** Books and calculators may not be allowed, but chocolate bars, crisps and water may be.

✔ **Where you can store your stuff:** You may arrive with your coat, bag, books and other items you may need to take with you, but can't keep with you by your exam desk.

✔ **The arrangements for going to the loo or attracting attention during the exam:** You are not normally allowed to speak during the exam, or leave your place without permission, but there must be a system in place to attract the attention of the invigilator should there be a problem.

✔ **How the desks are arranged in the room:** You need to know which way they face, and how the desks are allocated to candidates – whether they're allocated in alphabetical order by surname, or by candidate number. You may find that you're sharing the exam room, if it's a big one, with candidates taking another subject, so you may not know your neighbours at the nearest desks.

✔ **What materials you need and what you are given:** You need to know whether you have to write on the question paper and hand it in or whether you will write on A4 paper or be given graph or other paper and be able to keep the question paper.

✔ **Whether you are allowed to leave the exam room early:** Sometimes you are not allowed to leave in the last ten minutes, as this can be disturbing to other candidates, but can leave thirty minutes before the end of the exam, for example.

It's always good to know what the practical arrangements for an exam are so that you don't have to waste time or energy wondering what they are if a problem arises during an exam. If they are not clear or you think the exam instructions have left something out, then ask – even in the exam room before the exam starts.

Carrying on regardless

A candidate in an exam had a nose bleed and fainted, something she and her classmates were used to as it happened fairly often. The invigilator was busy marking her own tests, so did not look up. The students had been told not to speak or leave their desks. The invigilator finally looked up after a sustained bout of coughing from every student in the room. The sight of the student on the floor in a pool of blood caused the invigilator herself to faint. The student with the nose bleed came round of her own accord after a few minutes, mopped herself up and continued with the exam – as did her classmates. The invigilator came round to a sight of perfect peace and calm. All the students were busily engrossed in the exam.

In particular, if you have any health problems or if you need to take medication with you into the exam room, make sure your course tutor knows about it and also mention this to the invigilator in the exam room.

Exam Day Preparation

You should have checked to see that you had your key, money, paper handkerchiefs, mints and other necessities in your bag the night before the exam. Your alarm will have gone off, and you'll have enjoyed your boiled eggs or your porridge.

Make sure you are wearing layers, so that you can take something off if it's too hot or add a layer if you feel chilled. A favourite scarf can help as can shoes you can slip on and off easily so that you can wiggle your toes and retain a sense of freedom. It's important to be comfortable.

If you can, walk to the exam. It will help balance out being in one place for several hours and you can take in some good lungfuls of air. Make sure that you leave in good time and don't have to rush. Try to keep a measured, controlled pace, and you will feel on top of everything. If you smoke, try chewing liquorice to help you get through long exams if you can't manage to give up.

Sizing up the exam room

In the exam room, look around you, note where the doors and windows are, where your desk is in relation to them and the invigilator. St down carefully, making sure that you are planted squarely on your seat, and can sit with your spine straight and in a comfortable position. Push the chair to see if it scrapes or makes a noise, so that you can be aware of that and try to avoid making a scraping noise during the exam. Arrange your pen and other implements in a convenient way so that you can get to them easily without knocking them onto the floor. Notice the space in front, behind and to the sides of you. Close your eyes and take a few deep breaths.

Being aware of the space around you and the space you occupy in the exam room can make it your space, under your control, your little haven for the duration.

Checking the exam paper

When everyone is in their place and the exam is ready to begin, the invigilator writes the start time and end time on the board. Every exam room should also have a clock that is clearly visible to all the candidates – the invigilator will probably check that it is. You should be given some rough paper, and if not, you can ask for some.

Once the exam papers have been handed out and the exam has started, you need to read carefully through the general instructions on the first page. You've probably already read several exams of a similar kind and so you know more or less what to expect of the general instructions and layout of the exam and the number of questions to answer, so there should be no big shocks waiting for you. The general instructions or rubrics on the first page tell you:

- How long the exam lasts
- How many questions you have to answer
- Perhaps the marks allocated to each question
- Other requirements like using diagrams and whether you have to hand in the question paper at the end of the exam.

You almost certainly can answer the questions in any order that you like and this is normally stated in the general rubric.

Don't rush your initial check as it's important you understand the general rules. If they are not clear, then ask the invigilator by raising your hand or do whatever is permitted under the exam conditions. As long as the question is about the meaning of the general rules, not individual questions or their content, it should be permitted. Sometimes there are typing errors or other printing mistakes in exam papers, so if you spot something like that, you will be doing everyone a favour, as the invigilator can point out the error to the other candidates.

Assessing the questions

Once you know the number of questions you have to answer and how much choice you have, read through them all to see what key words link to areas you know a fair bit about, and which instruction words seem clear and straightforward. When writing essays, you might be attracted to the more obscure and unusual, but in exams, it's usually safest to go for the most clear and direct questions. Select the easiest question first, rough out the structure of the question or any maths or other calculations you need to do, and start writing, noting the time and then roughly dividing the time left by the number of questions you have to answer.

Don't rush this initial reading of the questions. You must read them carefully to make sure you understand the underlying or indirectly stated requirements. A few extra minutes spent reading the questions carefully and not rushing at them is time well spent and can avoid a later realisation that the question actually referred to something quite different from what you understood. I once mistook a kidney for a tomato in a Biology exam through rushing things! In answering essay-type questions, it is always a good idea to state your understanding of the question and its possible implications at the outset, just as you would in an essay, to show the parameters of your thoughts and ideas.

If you're struggling with the meaning of a question, it's best to continue to the next clearest question that you feel you can answer. If you're running out of time towards the end of the exam, then don't worry about beautiful sentences. List the points you intend to make (important theories and experiments) in note form or use a flow chart, with arrows and common symbols as links. If possible, try to find time to add your own view (evaluation, analysis, critique, comment etc.) as well at the end.

The good thing about exams is that they don't last long. The time may zip by and the whole thing may be a bit of an anticlimax. If you do leave early, go quietly and don't speak till you are well away from the exam room so that you don't disturb others who are still working.

Once you've left the exam room, well, you've done it! You've sat an exam and conquered the experience!

Approaching Oral Exams

Not all exams are written. *Oral exams*, in which the candidate speaks directly to an examiner can be of various kinds:

- ✔ **Language exams:** All language students have to demonstrate their oral proficiency in exams, that is, that they can actually speak the language they are learning at a certain level.

- ✔ **Doctoral *vivas*:** Doctoral students have to make a defence (called a *viva voce*) of their thesis to an internal and an external examiner as part of their examination process.

- ✔ **Project orals:** Some students are orally examined on their dissertations, experiments or projects, sometimes individually and sometimes in a group. This oral examination can be in the form of a presentation, which is then assessed individually and/or collectively.

- ✔ **Grade boundary interview:** Some students' exam results may fall close to a class level boundary (2.1 or 2.2, for example) so they are invited to an oral interview with usually two or three examiners, to help the examiners decide which is the appropriate class of degree for them.

- ✔ **Assessment checking:** External examiners often interview a selection of students with different levels of competency in both term work and in the examination, to check that the assessment of the students is fair and accurate and that the exam results accurately reflect the ability of the students. For example, if a high achieving student does badly in an exam, she may be invited to interview to determine why this has happened and to see whether there was a problem with the exam or the marking system for the exam.

✔ **Suspicion of cheating:** In cases where collusion or cheating in exams is suspected, an oral exam and interview may be used to clarify the situation. It is quite difficult to cheat and get away with it in exams. People caught talking are more likely asking to borrow a rubber, but they can be given zero marks. On the other hand, if two exam papers are similar, it may be because two friends have revised together, rather than anything untoward happening in the exam room. A diagram of the layout and the seating plan for each exam is made to show where each individual sat. If there is suspected collusion, two candidates sitting next to each other will fall under greater suspicion than two sitting much further apart.

For whatever reason, if you have an oral exam or interview related to an exam, this is your chance to be heard, to put your case and take the initiative. As always, it is your right (as well as the most sensible thing to do) to find out what the questions' parameters are, how many people are going to take part in the oral examination and how long it is likely to take.

Human beings make up their minds about people in the first few seconds after they meet. Oral exams and interviews, especially with people you don't know, give you a great opportunity to get in there and make a good impression. They can also be great practice for job interviews later on. Regardless of the type of examination you will be undergoing, don't wait for them to take note of you, but take the initiative by:

✔ Smiling and looking the examiner in the eye;

✔ Moving or leaning towards them with your hand outstretched;

✔ Greeting them and giving your name (in whatever language is appropriate);

✔ Saying you are pleased to meet them and asking how they are;

✔ Being polite and looking at their faces.

These first few moments establish the relationship between you. If you are positive and upbeat, even in a difficult situation, this shows the examiner that you are making an effort to co-operate and things will go more smoothly. Basically, you will be removing some anxiety from the examiner and opening up the communication channels. No one likes to have meetings where there is some stress, but you can do a lot to remove it both from your own shoulders and those of the examiner or interviewer.

In whatever situation you find yourself, do your best to make it as smooth and pleasant as you can regardless of what has gone before.

Language orals

If you are a language student, ask your tutor if there are taped examples of oral exams you can watch in the Language Laboratory. Your tutor will give you the general format and examples of the type of exam questions you are likely to encounter, and the topics you discuss are often given ten minutes or so before the exam so that you can prepare them. The number of examiners is usually one unless the oral counts towards your degree grade, when there may be two.

In some examples, doctoral students have to make a public defence of their thesis. If you are a doctoral student and get the chance to attend a public defence, take it, even if the subject is far removed from your own, because you will be able to get a general idea of how the viva works. In general, the (usually two) examiners' role is to make you comfortable and the questions are more like a discussion about how and why you reached the conclusions you did, your own evaluation of your research and contribution to knowledge. They will also pick out details in your thesis script which need correction or explanation. Most examiners will tell you early on in the proceedings whether you have reached the required standard, or what kind of changes you have to make to reach it.

Project or dissertation orals

If you are orally examined on your dissertation, perhaps randomly selected as part of the procedure for evaluating the reliability of the assessment or marking system, then you will be invited to express your ideas or explain what you did. In this case, it is the assessment procedure that is being assessed, not you, so take the opportunity to make observations and comments as these may be very helpful.

Other kinds of oral exams

Whether your work is being assessed as part of the exam process or because it falls on the boundary between two grades, matters very little. You can still adopt the same attitude and explain your understanding of the exam questions, what you did and why you did it.

If you have an oral exam or interview because of suspected cheating or collusion, then you should be given formal written notice of the precise reason for the interview, who you will be interviewed by and when. Don't panic if this happens at it is just part of a formal procedure. You should contact your tutor and the Students Union for advice. Normally, you can nominate someone to attend the interview with you and take notes of the proceedings to make sure everything is open and fair. Where the matter is considered serious, you also usually have the right to nominate a tutor to speak in your defence.

For whatever reason this happened, the situation can be redeemed if you co-operate and work calmly and openly with the system to find out what happened and explain why there was a problem. If you should take some responsibility for what happened, do so, rather than blaming others. Your maturity in doing this will be rewarded in the long run. If you are entirely blameless, underline this by being polite and co-operative.

After the Exams

Once the exams are over, forget them. You are never going to have to face the same paper again. Some people, however, like to have extensive post mortems after exams. If it pleases you to estimate your results in private, that is fine. It is not a good idea to get dragged into someone else's insecurities about how they have done. They may want to compare what you and they did to feel more secure. Even if what you both did was inappropriate, they may feel better if they were not alone in making a mistake. They may want to feel that they gave a better answer by comparing theirs to yours. All of this activity is energy-consuming and makes no difference to what happened in the exam. That's in the past and there's nothing you can do about it. You can't do anything about how it will be marked either, so why waste energy on speculating about that?

Put the exams behind you and start having a bit more fun. You can now plan a bit more into the future – holidays, for example, usually follow exams.

Understanding the marking process

How important the results of exams are depends on whether they are term tests or count towards your degree or qualification, but you can get something from all results. Terms tests can help to show you where you are in terms of your understanding of a subject (or how to do exams) and what you need to improve or what you need to pay more attention to.Any exam that contributes towards a qualification should have more than one examiner unless:

- ✔ The questions were multiple-choice, in which case, no interpretation of the answers is necessary and indeed, some answer sheets are marked by computer programme or clerical staff.

- ✔ There is a simple right/wrong answer format, with no marks given for effort or working out.

The procedure for marking essay-type or more complex questions requiring calculations and so forth is approximately as shown in Table 19-1:

Table 19-1	Exam marking procedure
	Action
1.	Scripts are collected after the exam and sent to the chief examiner for that subject.
2.	Scripts are divided into piles for first markers (tutors) who normally mark some exams of students they did not teach to act as a check and balance system. If the marks do not count towards a qualification, the scripts may be returned to the students and gone over in class within a short period of time. Students can challenge the markers' arithmetic and ask for clarification of the marks. This is part of the learning process.
3.	If the exams count towards a qualification, the same answers are independently marked by a second marker. Neither marker writes on the exam scripts.
4.	First and second markers independently record their marks for each student.
5.	First and second markers meet to discuss marks. If there is a big difference in the score or they cannot agree on a particular mark, the exam script may be sent to the external examiner.
6.	The external examiner may agree with one marker, suggest quite a different mark, or send the script back to the original markers and ask them to explain their decisions. In some institutions, the external marker has the final say on the mark given. In other institutions, the external marker works in a purely advisory capacity, though she can ask for access to any documentary or other information she deems relevant.
7.	The external marker may ask for a selection of exam scripts which have been allocated high, medium and low marks to check the standard levels. She may also ask to interview some students who have been selected on a similar basis.
8.	When all the marks have been agreed by the markers, including the external marker (s) if appropriate, the exam board meets to discuss any problems. For instance, if it seems that the exam has been particularly difficult, they may lower the pass mark to make it consistent with previous years, or vice versa.
	If there are any students who are in danger of failing the course, they should be identified and their tutors informed so that the students can be given help and support.
	If there are any other anomalies that the exam board wishes to sort out before announcing the results – any interviews with students and so forth – these should be arranged now.
9.	If all the procedures have been followed and accepted, the marks are given to the students and made public.
10.	Students are normally given some feedback comments from the markers, sometime highly detailed, to help them with future work.
11.	Students can ask for clarification, especially if the mark given seems at odds with the comments made, or even for their work to be remarked by the external or another examiner.

The procedures for assessing students through either essays or exams are normally formally laid out on the home page of the subject of study. These procedures are designed to be as clear and open as possible, but within manageable time limits. Markers, for example, will be given a set amount of time within which to hand in marks to the chief examiner (usually the course convener, the tutor in charge of the course). However, every institution is open to external scrutiny through the three or four yearly assessment visits by external assessors to check the quality of the course – how it is taught and assessed (the star system) – as well as having the system of invited experts in the field from other institutions to act as external examiners.

The Course Convener may not call the first meeting of all the tutors teaching on a course to discuss the exam results (the exam board meeting) and general student progress until March. This means that students who need help and support may not be identified till then, which is very late in the academic year – near the Easter break – especially for students following a one year course. If your term and exam marks were low, don't wait until the exam board meeting, but informally ask your tutor for help and support as soon as you think you would benefit from them. This will do you no harm, but possibly a lot of good and you will get brownie points for taking the initiative. There may be a mentoring system, or your tutor may introduce you to a student in the year above who can offer help.

Querying an exam mark

Everyone is human, and everyone makes mistakes. These can be simple things like an examiner taking a break in the middle of marking your paper and leaving out a question or not adding up the marks properly. If you think that something like that has happened, you can politely ask if you can have a look at your paper. This is not always possible if it counts towards a qualification. In any case, go to you tutor and express your concern. If you have been told the marks for each section and are pretty sure you answered enough of the questions to get most of the marks, yet your overall marks are low, then this kind of informal low key approach is the best way to get things sorted out – probably with an apology. It does pay to be vigilant, though. Don't assume mistakes can't be made.

Before you decide to make a formal application to have your marks checked, tell your tutor your problem. Most likely, she will try to sort out the problem as described above. If you feel that a particular examiner marked you harshly, for example, when the addition of the scores was correct, so that was not the problem, your tutor may feel this is outside her remit. Do ask advice of the Students Union.

As with all challenges of this kind, you may be warned, especially if an external examiner is involved, that your marks may go down as well as up. This is worth considering if the margin of difference is small. If you feel strongly that you have suffered discrimination or don't have confidence that the mark you have been given is fair then you can:

- ✔ Ask for your work to be remarked by two or three completely different examiners. Your institution may suggest this, but you will then be bound by that mark.

- ✔ Ask to re-sit the exam that is, take one of the same standard. This might be the fairest solution for you and the examiners.

In all cases, you need to discuss the situation so that you can sort out your anger and disappointment on the one hand, and look at what action is practical and good for you in both the short and longer run.

Student counselling, the Students' Union, your personal tutor can all help. Don't keep the problem to yourself. All of these have more experience than you of the best way to deal with this sort of problem. It is remarkable what can be done unofficially. For example, it may be that a similar complaint was made in a previous year and your point has added to the evidence. The chief examiner or convener may undertake an investigation of her own, and, with her more extensive knowledge, be able to sort out the problem quietly. Not only that, but she will be grateful that you tactfully pointed something out so that she can avoid the problem in the future.

Sometimes it is enough for you to go to your tutor to for an explanation of the complaints procedure and how to have your work reassessed. No tutor wants her student to lack confidence in the system, so she may well privately take steps and report back with her assessment of the situation and a solution.

Things should not only be clear but be seen to be clear. Undoubtedly, the situation is not perfect yet. Students who do not behave appropriately are not always reprimanded, and examiners are not always trained to be as clear as they should be. This situation is continuously improving. All institutions now have far more fail-safe and checking and assessment procedures in order to improve the quality of education and standards across courses in similar institutions than they ever did in the past. Meetings are set up between subject experts and administrators in different institutions for the exchange of ideas and examples of good practice – including how to deal with assessment to make it clear and open to public scrutiny and understanding. Education is no longer in the hands of an elite few who 'knew what was best and how things should work'.

You are always entitled to a second opinion. Making your point politely, with confidence and making sure that you have the relevant information, evidence and understanding of the procedures involved will go a long way to helping you get what you want – and make friends and influence people as well.

Angry and head-on challenges leave little room for manoeuvre – for you as much as anyone else – and are best avoided.

However, if you are sure of yourself and have the backing of the Student Union's Counselling service and your tutor, proceed in a quiet and firm way and that in itself will be to your credit.

Part VI
The Part of Tens

In this part . . .

The Part of Tens: every *For Dummies* book has one, and this one is no different.

Here you can find pithy and useful hints and tips on how to save yourself valuable studying time, how to broaden your horizons as a student and get full value from your time at college, and finally some great advice on how to polish up your written work.

Chapter 20

Ten Time-saving Techniques

In This Chapter

▶ Planning to use your time effectively

▶ Prioritising your work

▶ Avoiding perfectionism and procrastination

Time can seem a very rare commodity when you're studying. Looking at reading lists, coursework and exam preparation – not to mention attending class – can give you a headache before you start. You might feel you have to rush immediately to do something and even the idea of taking a little time out to plan can seem like a waste of time. Don't panic.

As everyone pays tuition fees these days, imagine how cross you'd feel if you only had a few books to read and the occasional class to attend and no exams and no certificate. You'd feel short-changed, wouldn't you? Course writers also feel the need to justify their courses (and their jobs) in a much more detailed and explicit way than in the past, and this is all to the good. Just remember, in most courses (and also exams) there are options, and the course description has to cover all possible choices. You make your selection from these – you don't have to do everything.

The tips in this chapter will help you organise your study time effectively, efficiently, and – most importantly – enjoyably.

Asking Direct Questions

Take charge and save time by asking direct questions that get straight to the point, things like: 'My understanding of x is y. am I right?' or 'Does that mean . . . ?' Don't waste time speculating, wondering or trying to reconcile things that don't make sense to you – lists, timetables or instructions that seem crazy, odd or that you don't understand. Don't assume you've made a mistake or got it wrong and worry about it. Go and ask someone – your course tutor, the departmental office – someone who should know the answer or who can find it out for you, and do it sooner rather than later. If you've made a mistake, there's no harm done and you'll have helped by showing that some instructions weren't very clear, or something was missing or maybe a date or time was wrong, so that the problem can be cleared up. When you get the answer, tell everyone else.

Planning to Do Things at the Best Time

You can get carried away by planning. Some people turn it into an art form, and a substitute for action. However, practical planning, doing things at the best and most useful time, saves you not only time but a lot of worry.

Certain things are planned on your behalf, and you can't change – class time-tables, when coursework is due and when exams take place – but these can be very useful as a framework. Start from what is fixed so you can then see what time gaps there are between activities and so make the best use of that time. Start with daily, routine activities like class preparation, as in Table 20-1 below, and then move on to find time gaps for weekly, monthly or once a term activities.

In the timetable below, there is a class first thing on Monday and then nothing till 4 p. m. Preparation for the 4 p. m. class could fit into some of the space between the two Monday classes. Preparation for Tuesday's class could fit into the morning of Tuesday, and later on Tuesday could be used for Wednesday's class, leaving some time on Wednesday morning for Thursday's classes, as the afternoon is for sports. There is some time on Thursday morning for preparation for Friday, as well as Friday morning, which also leaves time to prepare for Mondays' class, leaving the weekend free for other things.

	9–11.00	11–1.00	2–4.00	4–6.00	Evening
Mon	class			class	
Tues			class		
Wed		class	sports	sports	
Thur		class	class		
Fri			class	class	
Sat					
Sun					

Activities tend to expand into the time available, so using fixed time gaps helps you use time well and save time for other things.

You get an idea fairly quickly of how long you need to prepare for different classes (the amount of reading you have to do, for example) and how far that can help you with other tasks. There is likely to be a fair amount of overlap, so class preparation is likely to save you time later as well as help you get the most out of classes.

Prioritising Your Workload

Once you know your timetable you know how much time you have left in which to carry out other assessed tasks. Weekly tasks have weekly deadlines, so slots for sorting them out should be straightforward. You can then plan fortnightly, monthly, or ask for end of term hand-in dates to make sure you allow time to complete tasks. Check when the relevant topics are covered in class, so that while you have your plans, questions and outlines in place early, the final version can use information from the discussion in class. In other words, an optimum time exists for doing tasks which makes the best use of the available amount of time and the points in time at which information resources become available.

Unless you are studying a subject with a mathematical base where it is possible to get 100 per cent as a mark, it is important to remember that the highest mark in practice for many subjects is considerably less than that. This means that no matter how long you spend on a piece of work, you may not increase your mark by much, if at all. There is a glass ceiling. Penalties also exist if you exceed the word limit by more than 10 per cent and you risk introducing irrelevant information or making mistakes as your work gets longer. Of course, sticking to your plan and research questions will help you avoid this.

The law of diminishing returns is also worth bearing in mind when planning to use your time to its best effect. For example, you may have to learn and remember 10 sentences of similar length. On average, you can learn 7 in 30 minutes, but it will take you another 30 minutes to learn the last 3. If 7 is enough to pass or get a suitable grade and 10 impossible (as in many arts and humanities subjects) then it might be better to spend that second half hour on a different task. This means you can get the equivalent of 7/10 for two tasks in an hour, compared to only possibly more than 7 for one task in an hour.

It is a better use of your time to cover two (or however many) tasks well, to the 7/10 level. If you then have spare time and are sure the extra work will polish up a particular task, then go for it. Don't put all your eggs in one basket. Most courses require you to get a certain grade average, and this is easier to maintain if you treat all tasks at a certain level as equal in terms of the time and effort you spend on them. Sadly, if you perform one task very well, but at the expense of another which gets a low mark, your grade average can be much lower than if you did a little less well on the task with the higher grade and had spent a bit more time on the other.

Nobody's Perfect – Thank Goodness!

Perfection, like beauty, is in the eye of the beholder. It's all relative, so trying to be perfect is a waste of time as it means different things to different people. The creator of a piece of work may feel it has faults, but a tutor may be blind to them and think it's very good, certainly in terms of work at that level. The tutor may also make her judgement in comparison with other people's efforts, and her experience of standards. If you think about it carefully, perfection means there is no room for improvement. It's a stagnant static state, so why would anyone want to go there? After all, if you get A++ for your first piece of work, what happens next in the perfection stakes?

First of all, if that happens, congratulations. You will know if you spent ages on that piece of work, or whether you are a genius or just well organised. At different times, there will be different pressures on your time, so rather than being a perfectionist, it's more sensible to do your best at any particular time and recognise that different judges or markers have different ways of assessing work. You might not be able to please some people even if you had a 100 years to try, so do your best and please yourself.

Claiming to be a perfectionist can sometimes lead to reasoning that because it is impossible to do a certain thing perfectly, it is therefore better not to do it at all. That might be true for 'Strictly Come Dancing', but most things worth doing are worth doing to the best of your ability, because they have intrinsic value, not because you are looking for accolades.

Avoiding Procrastination

Get difficult things done sooner rather than later. The longer you spend worrying and dreading doing them, the more difficult they get, not easier. Do difficult things first – once you've asked any necessary questions. You can spend ages dreading and worrying about something and it won't get any better. If you make a start, you'll get a more specific idea of the problems you need to solve. You can then break down them down into smaller tasks, which are easier to solve.

It is also difficult to gauge how much of your time difficult tasks are going to use up, so they make overall time planning a nightmare if you don't tackle them sooner rather than later. In other words, there's a knock-on domino effect on your other work. Put yourself back in charge, take a long cool look – don't rush – and make a mind-map or whatever is your favourite strategy and start breaking the task down so you can decide what questions you need to ask and answer to get moving.

Put strict time limits on how long you are going to spend on difficult tasks – remember the perfectionist rule – to stop yourself wavering and thinking about the difficulty of the task rather than the task itself.

Learning to Say 'No'

If you are prone to distraction, you are likely to jump at the chance of escaping from whatever you are doing if someone asks for your help or suggests another activity. People who can't get on with their work often feel better if they can persuade someone else to take time out as well. Sometimes it seems easier to agree than to argue the case for saying 'No'. You might even be conditioned to always say 'Yes'.

Saying 'No' when you're a toddler helps you separate from your mother and develop into an independent being. Saying 'No' as an adult is just as important. It means taking responsibility for your own actions, being self-reliant and making your own judgements. Be strong and give yourself permission to say 'No' if that seems right. For example, to protect yourself from being interrupted or allow you to finish something that is near completion or do something which has higher priority.

Everybody needs a change of activity, so a more positive way of tackling the interruption problem is to anticipate breaks and use them to frame periods of study. For example, you can make a pact with your friend that you will both study independently and finish at a certain time. You can then plan an activity together. Use the break as an incentive to work up to that point. Bribe yourself with a party at the weekend, so that you consolidate work in the week. You sometimes have to say 'No' to yourself, just like you do in your diet plan when you're about to swallow the third chocolate biscuit! 'No, I will not sit in the bath for an hour and a half as I usually do. I will sit in the bath for 20, minutes, read over my class notes and make notes in my diary for half an hour, and then do a preparatory reading for half an hour.'

What is amazing is that if you actually time how long tasks take, they often take a lot less time than the things that distract you, especially if you can break them down into chunks. Think how much better you will feel if you've had a bath and completed a couple of tasks in less time than you normally take to have a bath – and your skin won't be all wrinkly either!

Having a Quiet Place and Time

To help you set boundaries, find a time and a place when you are not to be disturbed and let everybody know about it. For example, you could go to the library for an hour or two each day at a specific time, and that could be your time off the radar, when you are not contactable. You could have a yoga class or meditate or use private time to call your mum or check your bank statements, or whatever else you need to do. Everyone needs private time and as it is only for a couple of hours, there is no reason for anyone else to break into it. You also need to be strong and make sure you respect your own boundaries and don't allow anyone to break them.

Private time, when you can be sure of no disturbances, allows you to concentrate more completely, reflect and generally recharge your batteries. It will help you use other time to better effect.

You also need a suitable place to have your private time. The library is ideal for working, the practice room for yoga and maybe you bedroom for other activities. It is a good idea to make a 'Do Not Disturb Between 5p.m. and 7p.m.' type sign as this is more likely to be respected than a general 'Do Not Disturb' sign. Of course, you can have as many 'private' times and places as you like. Some people prefer to state when they are available to be contacted, for example, between 12.00 and 2.00pm. However, that can be very off-putting, and suggests people need to make an appointment! You are still a social being, but you need your private space to be respected, so make boundaries, but not the Great Wall of China!

Building In Some Flexibility

Of course, emergencies do happen and some things are just too good to miss – like last minute tickets for your favourite group – so build in some flexibility so that you can take advantage of gift horses and make up time elsewhere. You will soon find out where you can cut corners – maybe survive an extra day without going food shopping or hoovering. to find time for an unforeseen event. (Don't put off cleaning the bath, though). You will probably get better at some things and need less time to get them done or not need to do them as often as you think (and still keep the bath clean). You might combine activities by walking or jogging to post letters, for example, so that you can get exercise at the same time as completing a task.

Building in some flexibility also means leaving gaps, so that not every bit of the day is accounted for. Some parts – like a quiet time and space – are pretty much sacrosanct, but it is very good for the morale and hence efficiency to find you have gaps to do other things that you don't need to do very often, like cleaning football boots or having a haircut and actually quite enjoying them as a bonus.

Using Big Blocks of Time for Big Tasks

The law of diminishing returns suggests that after something like three hours of study, not only does nothing much go into your brain, but what you learned in the previous three hours can become seriously unstuck. However, with screen breaks at least every hour, coffee breaks and loo trips and time to eat, you can break things up into smaller bite-sized chunks and so avoid the kind of unremitting intensity that reduces your learning.

Big blocks of time – a whole afternoon, for example – are best used for big tasks rather than a series of minor tasks, albeit with suitable breaks. For example, you might get part of an essay done or the preparation for giving a presentation. Big tasks have a continuity of theme, purpose or method, so that when divided into chunks, there is a clear relationship between the sub-parts that has to be kept in mind while each individual task is carried out; hence, they are better done in big blocks of time. Too many interruptions can jeopardise the continuity of purpose of big tasks and cause thoughts and ideas to fragment, which leads to a lot of repetition and revision of the same tasks. In the long run, the task can take up more time and can be very frustrating.

The trick is to identify and use well small blocks of time for small tasks. For example, never spend hours on your email. Resist the sudden urge to break into a big block of time and check your email – it's probably a *displacement activity*, a way of putting off something you know you have to do. It's fine to take a break and check your email, but if you're working online, taking a screen break would be better.

Big Projects Need Big Plans

Big projects, like research or experiments that you are going to write up as a dissertation or thesis, need long term planning built in and a good deal of flexibility. For example, you might need to consider, among other things:

✔ How many people you need to approach, and who they are. How difficult are they likely to be to get hold of and how long it is likely to take.

✔ What the best way to contact them is: mail, phone, email or by meeting them in person and depending on which you choose, how long it is going to take.

✔ Whether you can easily get hold of information you need or if you have to wait for an inter-library loan.

✔ How long it is likely to take to write, test, or have subjects complete a questionnaire or test sheet, and how many you need to be completed to make your results valid.

✔ Whether there is a better way of getting the information that you need so that your whole enterprise is less risky.

✔ Which information or methods are crucial to the success of your project so that you give them priority, and which you can drop if you have to.

✔ How long it will take you to get the results of an experiment and research and how far you can design the format to fit the analysis and so save time.

✔ How you can pace your work so that you don't end up having to do a lot of work at the last minute.

✔ How to identify the weak spots in your project and prepare plan B.

In certain types of project you can prepare and write up the general background to your work and the theoretical part while you are waiting for the results, but you must keep a really tight hold on any information you need people to provide you with.

The crucial aspect of long-term planning is managing the sequence in which you expect things to happen. Plan this carefully, so that you are not left twiddling your thumbs. Some writing up can happen before the results are in, so think of the research and write-up as a single process, not two separate ones. Then you can identify which information has to be in before another part can be produced, like the results precede the analysis, and which parts are mainly dependent on a literature search, and can be written earlier.

Time itself is not the enemy; there is always enough time to do what needs to be done. It's a questioning of identifying and getting rid of what doesn't need to be done and finding the best times for what does.

Revisiting Reading Lists

Reading lists have core texts or books you should read and that others that are optional choices, usually to provide more detail if you choose to study a particular topic in depth. If your teachers refer to their own books in a reading list, they often feel obliged to add a few more so they don't look too pushy. If you can, fold over the list so that you can just see the ones you have to read, and that looks better already. Essential reading may be no more than a quarter of a reading list and can be a lot less.

Chapter 21

Ten Ways to Have Fun While Studying

In This Chapter

▶ Being creative

▶ Making links

▶ Helping out

Allll work and no play makes Jack a dull boy – and Jill a dull girl, for that matter. Without a change of activity, you will only be stimulating certain centres in your brain. The rest will be quite dormant. If you work alone in your ivory tower for too long without interacting with other people, you will tend to become over-concerned with some things and neglect others. The image of the nutty professor – hair on end, tie covered in egg-yolk, shirt hanging out, dirty cups with cigarette butts strewn all over the floor and piles of paper everywhere – is not entirely without truth.

We are social animals – even if some prefer socialising with a computer. Studying can be hard work and you need to break it up with more light-hearted moments. In particular, you need to meet up with other people, talk about mundane things, sort out minor issues of everyday life, forget about essays and other things. Remember the law of diminishing returns. You actually get more work done if you have time out than if you continue working and don't take proper breaks for eating, sleeping and other necessities. All play and no work is equally difficult, as eventually, you will need to double or treble the amount of work you could normally do in the same amount of time, or give up the attempt. A good balance is always best, and mundane things help to ground you in reality.

Being the Best Host

One way to have fun and make sure you socialise at least once a day, especially during exam times, is to take turns at cooking an evening meal with a group of friends. If five or six of you share accommodation and everyone cooks a meal, then each person will cook once a week or so. It's not much more difficult in the long run to cook for 6 than for 1, and think of the time you will save and how green you will be by saving energy! You could also cook in pairs, and organise a clearing-up rota.

To make your meal more interesting and entertaining, you can ask each friend to suggest two or three well-known people, dead or alive, that they would like to invite to dinner. If each person is allowed one guest, then who should be invited can be debated during the meal. You can decide whether there should be an equal number of male and female guests, whether footballers will mix with politicians, and who should sit next to whom.

Once you have made the decision as a group, each person can prepare to take on the character of their 'guest' as a role-play and dress for the part as well, at another meal – this usually works well on Friday nights. Mixing pleasure with business, if you have a particular study hero or heroine, you can immerse yourself in their character and try to imagine what their views might be on various current issues.

Throwing Perfect Parties

Having parties is usually an important part of student life and a great way to meet new people who are studying different subjects or who you would not get the chance to talk to on a routine basis. However, getting people to mix and leave the kitchen or wherever they are stationed clutching a bottle is not always easy, so they might not enjoy themselves as much as they could do.

Party puzzles can be useful to arouse even a jaded curiosity. Arm yourself with some adhesive labels upon which you have written the names of well-known characters. When guests arrive, stick a label onto their forehead, making sure they have not seen it and cover any mirrors. They are allowed to ask only questions which have the answer 'Yes' or 'No', for instance, 'Am I dead?' or 'Am I male?' or 'Do I live in the USA?' You can limit the number of questions, say to 20, or make other rules, like no drink till you've guessed who you are (harsh) or limit the range of characters, for instance to exclude fictitious characters.

A variation is to find your other half. This is easier, so better with larger groups. It may also be better to put the sticky labels on people's backs, as this requires more movement to talk to people. The same rules apply – only the use of 'Yes/No' questions and possibly only 10. For instance, if you find Romeo, then the question to ask is 'Am I Juliet?' You might have to make a rule that guests should not cheat by pointing out people's other halves. More obscure pairs might be Anna and the King of Siam, Bubble and Squeak or Emu and Rod Hull.

Joining Up

There are always many different clubs and activities organised by or through the Student Union, or at least advertised there. If you go to Freshers' Week, you will no doubt be handed a lot of information about these and you may well be spoiled for choice. Remember, team sports like football or hockey are likely to be free and activities that come under the heading of 'Sports' if not free, are likely to be subsidised. This is your chance to try out something new, like scuba diving, archery or even taster flying lessons. If you prefer your feet on the ground, dance classes like salsa or tap are likely to be a lot cheaper through the student union than private classes. These are often organised at lunch time or in the late afternoon, so make a welcome change of activity between classes.

Most universities have a gym or access to one, and you can usually book a time, having been shown how to use the equipment, to fit in with your time-table. The same goes for badminton and squash courts. There are likely to be walkers or ramblers clubs as well.

If you prefer self-expression, then there will be a drama club, where costume designers and make-up artists are needed as well as actors, and photography and painting clubs. There will also be plenty of clubs to meet people, like the debating club and the international club (home students are usually welcome). Many clubs will arrange visits to places of interest at very reasonable prices, so here's your chance to do things you would not normally manage on your own and to make the best use of week-ends for farther away trips.

Getting Out in the Local Community

If the separation between town and gown is not to your liking or you feel the need to get away and do off-campus things, various ways exist to get involved in the local community and meet local people. If the local pub runs pub quizzes, then these are usually good fun and a way of meeting local people. You might ask to join a team or take some of your pals along to form a team of your own. The competitive spirit will be fun and you will be surprised at some of the answers – and who knows them – to the more obscure questions. Sometimes, if you win, you can write the next quiz, which is also fun. (A variation can be used for revision purposes, whereby small group teams write revision questions for each other.)

You can volunteer to work for some hours in a charity shop. Apart from meeting local people, you will get a discount on any purchases you make, a good source for costumes for 'guests'. Volunteer work is always good for your curriculum vitae, and if there is a volunteer bureau, you can do things from walking dogs to house-painting to help other people.

Supporting Sweet Charity

As well as working in a charity shop, there will be other charity work which the Student Union supports. For instance, there are usually many sponsored activities, from swims and walks to snail-eating, to support immediate needs, like disaster funds, as well as regular events like Children in Need. Dreaming up novel ways to get the public to part with their money and being allowed to do slightly outrageous things can be fun and useful at the same time. Most colleges have a rag or charity week, with floats and people in costume to represent various parts of the college and collect money for charity. Offering your services to the rag committee to help dream up themes and design floats or costumes or help with the general organisation can be great fun. You also get to see the product and know what the profits from your time and efforts are fairly quickly.

Student Unions also often organise sending educational books which are still usable but surplus to requirements to universities or colleges with no book-buying budget and whose libraries are outdated. Because many subjects are published primarily in English and students are taught through English in many parts of the world, these books can still play an important role.

Other work can involve collecting relief good to fill a Student Union van to send to an area in need, for instance, nappies, toiletries and spectacles. Drivers and people to do the paperwork will also be needed. You can make a difference and enjoy the experience.

If you see a need that you don't think is being met and you'd like to help, talk to the Students Union for help and advice about setting up some support. For instance, one university is now involved in protecting badgers and foxes on campus by ensuring rubbish is properly secure so they can't harm themselves and another helps the Royal Society for the Protection of Birds by ringing and counting migrant birds on campus.

Working as a Student Helper

It's sometimes fun to be with people outside your age-group, especially if you have younger brothers or sisters that you miss. If you like playing with children and organising activities for them, you may find there is an after-school and holiday club organised by the Student Union Welfare committee for the children of students. As well as Blue Peter- type projects, going swimming and playing games are also usually part of the programme. If you have a life-saving badge or sports interest, that may increase your chances of getting paid work in this area. You will also need to have a CRB (Criminal Records Bureau) check to work with children, though your employer (probably the Students Union) will pay for this to be done and it doesn't take long. (It can be done online for a small fee, about £7.00.)

Maths or English coaching is often requested for children through the Students Union, which also runs a student employment unit, including for baby-sitting. The Students Union will decide the rates, usually quite generous, and spending time in someone else's house with access to their music and books can be interesting and bathing the baby fun!

Another rewarding activity is helping fellow students with mobility problems navigate around campus in their wheelchairs or picking them up from class and helping them get back to (usually) their campus accommodation and perhaps doing the odd errand for them. There is usually some paid work as well, and it is very popular, but you would need to live near the student who wanted support.

Reporting for Duty

Your college or university probably has a student newspaper, so if you've ever fancied working in journalism, here's your chance. You can offer your services in a number of ways – layout, graphics, photography, cartoons, agony aunt, letters to the editor, book, film and theatre etc. reviews, even horoscopes. If any of these columns don't currently exist, you can also offer to start them. In addition, there will be the more serious reporting of campus news and politics, the goings-on in the Senate and whatever protest is current, which the student body need to be aware of as it can affect them.

The Student Union is usually given complementary tickets to films, concerts, theatre productions, exhibitions and the like, which are often handed on to the student newspaper critics or journalists, possibly with a photographer, in exchange for writing a review. Sometimes the tickets and reviews are shared round between the newspaper team, so that everyone has a chance of a free ticket. If this is not currently happening, you might ring the local cinema or theatre, explaining you are the student newspaper critic (with the editor's agreement) and ask for complementary tickets. If sales are low, you'll probably get them, as any publicity may be helpful. With luck, you might set a precedent and get tickets for the really hot stuff.

Similarly, publishers are often willing to give away complementary books to get a review, though these will probably be fiction. However, this can be a pleasant change from course book reading and writing a critique which is not going to be marked can be liberating and fun, but don't be cruel. The role of book reviewer can be shared in rotation and so can the books.

All of this can be fun and good for the CV.

Discovering DJing

Student radio is becoming more popular, especially where student residences exist on campus, so if you have ever fancied being a DJ or presenter, now might be your chance. Sometimes Tannoy or public address systems are used as well as radio frequencies, and broadcasts are normally restricted to campus and to the evenings and week-ends, though sometimes there are early morning calls during exam times. Radio slots are usually shared by a number of students, perhaps an hour each, and include birthday greetings, requests for items, offers of items, information about events and general campus news as well as music.

Some DJs seem to have Robin Williams in *Good Morning Vietnam* as their role model as well as various Radio 2 DJs, so there is the opportunity to tell jokes, try out funny voices and have the occasional interview as well as select the music you love to play – or introduce new or unusual music, world music perhaps, or play requests.

There is always the need for technical broadcast skills as well, so if that's your forte or interest, you will probably be welcomed, especially if you have a knowledge of equipment, or fancy being a programme producer.

Some institutions have a television studio with cameras, and if your interest lies there, enquire at the Students Union as there might be a club you can join to make short films. The cost of using the studios is quite high, so not something you could do alone, indeed, any form of broadcast will involve team work.

Diving into Student Politics

If you have become involved in any of the activities of the Student Union, you may take a bigger step in your second or third year and stand for office. There are various posts, from President of the union to Student Welfare Officer, Head of Sports or Entertainment. You will have fun planning your campaign, probably with the help of a campaign manager, and create posters, badges, mission statements and generally make sure everyone knows who you are, either through stunts and outrageous costumes or making sure you are interviewed by a student newspaper reporter or on student radio.

You can be as serious or as light-hearted as you like, but if you want to get elected, you will have to work to get the support you need and have some experience of working at a lower level in the area of the position you are standing for. Many institutes have a male and female head for each post. If you are more of a facilitator, then helping out your more extroverted friend as campaign manager or general fixer can be even more fun and get you access to people and places you would not normally come across.

Two students (one male and one female) are also elected by the student body to sit in the University Senate, along with the elected representatives from the various faculties, schools and institutions, the library and the administrative staff and other areas of the university as an institution. The Senate is where the general matters that affect all those involved in the university are discussed and minuted, though not all the representatives have a vote. Student representatives are usually observers, and their role is to report back to the student body and keep them updated on what's going on. They can lobby another sympathetic representative to ask a question on their behalf. While Senate meetings are not for the faint-hearted or sleepy, it can be very interesting watching how the representatives work as a group – or not – and see familiar faces in a different role. A bit like parliament.

Being a Mentor or Coach

After your first year of study, especially if you have had a student mentor and benefited from the experience, you might enjoy doing the same for others. Student mentors normally receive general training from the University Counselling Service and often share general training (maybe a day or half a day at a week-end) with members of the University teaching staff, so you are treated like a professional. Shorter training sessions may also take place, which you are invited to.

You will normally be employed by a particular area of study and for a particular purpose, for example, to attend a statistics seminar with student from a lower year and go over the questions or points discussed, and perhaps helping them with any questions set for an hour. You will need to write a report of each session and any problems encountered. For example, if there are too many students for you to talk to in an hour, you could ask for another mentor to help you. You are normally supported by the Counselling service as well, though paid by the school of study or faculty whose students you help.

If you are very organised and bomb-proof, you might enjoy being a residence mentor. In this case, you will be there to help students who are in the same hall or residence as you, and will be on call at certain times. This post is usually shared by two or more students so that they can go out on some evenings, as that is when most requests for help are made. These can include not knowing how to replace a light bulb, flooding the bath, getting locked out, having lost something, not having enough bedding and being cold or needing a pain-killer. Most requests are usually simple and sometimes students just pop by to tell the mentor they are in or going out – touching base. The residence mentor is supported by caretakers in the day time, who can help with practical requests for bedding and light bulbs or taps that don't work, and by security staff at night, via an emergency on campus number.

This is a paid post. Some students really enjoy taking on the role of parent or older sibling and many form strong friendships.

While you'll probably wait till your third year before standing for election as Head of Sports, you can gain valuable experience by helping out with coaching, perhaps for racquet sports as well as team games, or you might find it is more fun to be a referee! If, for example, you use the gym, there will be some professional coaches employed to show you how to use the equipment and specific exercises for particular purposes. You can then use this knowledge to help coach the college football team, for instance.

Of course, as coach, you can travel with the team on the bus for away matches and celebrate or drown your sorrows in different waterholes, get to visit other parts of the country and learn some songs your mother would never have taught you.

Chapter 22

Ten Essay Writing Tips

In This Chapter

▶ Getting organised and making frameworks

▶ Sorting out details

▶ Working with others and in other ways

▶ Reflecting on your work

*O*n courses with a large amount of written work, writing essays sometimes seems to take up an awful lot of your time. If you don't have to write essays, you probably have to write reports or exercises or log the procedures and results of experiments. Some form of written work is the most popular method of assessment and some essays or other pieces of writing will count towards you final mark or degree award. For this reason, you may have weekly, monthly and term essays, records or reports in addition to dissertations or other written work that count for a larger percentage of your overall assessment.

While regular, weekly written work can seem a bore, the practice and feedback you get are all part of the preparation for longer and more serious work, which would be almost impossible to do without building up to through smaller, regular pieces of written work. That would be a bit like climbing Everest – or certainly the Matterhorn – for your first mountaineering project! This chapter helps you through the foothills of essay writing.

Getting Feedback You Can Use

Your tutor should give you feedback comments on your work so that you know what to improve and how to do it. You tutor should also have a record of their comments so that they can monitor your progress from one piece of written work to the next. A copy of this information can help you to follow your progress as well and help sort out any problems or misunderstandings.

Sometimes feedback comes in the form of a general impression comment on a piece of work. This is usually fine if your work is of an acceptable standard, but is probably of little help if you need to improve, because it is likely to be too vague. If your subject area uses a feedback form like the one in Table 23-1, this gives a better idea of what you need to tackle and also makes it easier for both you and your tutor to compare different pieces of written work over time.

Table 23-1:		A typical feedback form		
Name	**Good**	**Satisfactory**	**Needs Improvement**	**Suggestions**
Answers question?				
Refers to appropriate sources?				
Use of sources				
Balance between sources and own ideas				
Argument				
Analysis				
Reasoned conclusion				
Use of charts, diagrams etc.				
General layout, contents, page numbers etc.				
Punctuation, paragraphing				

The categories on the left refer to areas in which you need to achieve a level of competence. Overlaps exist within the categories, and the same problem may be identified under more than one heading, but the right hand 'suggestions' column helps with this. Both student and tutor can see where more effort should be concentrated and where improvements have been made. If your subject area does not use this kind of form, you could ask your tutor to use this one (or something similar) to help you both pinpoint any problems. the form makes record-keeping easier, and is also useful to refer to when you are writing a new piece of work, so that you can learn lessons from previous written work.

Defining Your Terms

Most essay titles your tutor sets will contain key words that you need to define in order to understand how to tackle the question. If you create your own title, you will also need to give a definition of the key words you have used. A general dictionary (there are several online ones) will provide you with definitions. For instance, 'revolution' in the political sense can mean the overthrow of one government and its replacement with another (www.thefreedictionary.com/revolution) or the overthrow of a government by those who are governed (www.wordreference.com/definition/revolution). The first definition describes an event whose effects are not so far-reaching as the second, so be sure that you get your definition right.

You may feel quite sure you know the meaning of the key words in your chosen essay title, but you must use dictionary definitions or references from the literature on your subject, that is, independent authorities, to define the meanings you want to use. This makes your terms of reference quite clear and explicit to your reader. She may have a different concept or understanding of a key word, so it is important to set the definition you have decided to use as the basis for the discussion. It's your essay and your call! Definitions provide you with a framework for your work and help the reader understand and evaluate the points you make within the meaning framework you have chosen. If you don't define your terms, the reader will guess, perhaps wrongly, and you may be misjudged.

You can also compare different definitions in the body of your work and suggest which particular event fits which definition. For example, the velvet revolution in Czechoslovakia in 1989 was a popular uprising, so is more like the second definition I mentioned at the start of this section. Definitions thus help you analyse your work as well.

Finding Your Voice

Your work will encourage you to have a 'voice': your own ideas and independent thoughts, expressed in your own style. At the same time, you have to refer to other people's work and use objective terminology and definitions. This is not an easy balance. The best way to approach it is to start from your own reactions to an essay title. Check any key word definitions and references to what you remember from your lecture programme or any reading you have already done. Use this to guide your research. This means creating your own questions or hypotheses before you do anything else, so that your voice is at the centre of your work. You will do this best by reflecting when having a bath, cooking or jogging, for example, not with your nose in a book full of someone else's ideas.

As you reflect, you may well challenge some of the ideas you have been taught or realise that you require more information to understand them properly. This is your voice asking the questions, this is putting your voice at the centre of your research and your essay. If you Google your questions, you may find some factual information around which you can build your challenge to a method or make your own ideas central to a discussion. Limiting yourself to repeating ideas that you have been taught means you have no clear voice at all.

Avoiding Style Giveaways

Some of the books you read are textbooks, rather than academic books or articles about theories or research. An important difference exists. Textbooks are general study manuals and designed to teach using phrases like 'We shall now turn to the question of' or 'As we shall see, this proved to be more of a problem than previously thought'. These and other similar phrases are the giveaway teaching (or didactic) phrases that textbooks use.

Your written academic work, on the other hand, is more like a report of work or research undertaken, the results, analysis, evaluation and discussion of a specific project. You are presenting information to the reader for their consideration, not to teach them, so avoid the standard phrases. For instance 'As we shall see' points to a future and suggests an overview of a problem, and is suitable in a textbook. However, academic work is reported in logical or time sequence, so this future reference is inappropriate. The use of 'we' is also unusual in academic writing unless the piece is written by several authors. However, in a text book, 'we' suggests a group or a class of the type of student or level that the book aims at.

If you use these or similar phrases, it will suggest that either you have taken them and what follows afterwards from a textbook, which will look like plagiarism, or that you are using an inappropriate style for an essay or piece of academic writing. It may sound as though you are teaching your reader rather than demonstrating your understanding, knowledge and skills to them for their consideration.

In either case, a problem exists, so avoid phrases with 'we' and inappropriate verb forms.

Sorting Out Your Verb Grammar

Academic style often has relatively simple tense grammar. For example, you can use simple present tense to describe how the parts of the essay work: 'In this section, I outline the main constituents of . . . ' or future ('I will outline'). 'I outline' means this is a fact. It usually occurs in the introduction and shows that it was written – or at least reviewed – last, after everything else had been written, indicating the true state of affairs and what really is in the rest of the essay. 'I will outline' is actually a promise of what is to come, rather than a fact about what is there. Both are possible, but in general you want to keep things simple.

When you use direct quotations from books or other documents, you can refer to them in the present tense: ' As the Bible *says'*, 'As Marx *points* out'- because documents are regarded as being eternal. It is their writers who die. However, if you are talking about an historical argument or where someone changed their mind and disagreed with something they had written earlier, then you can use past tense to indicate the change. For instance, 'Ptolemy *said*, then Copernicus *said*, then Newton *claimed*, then Einstein *claimed*, then Post-Einstein Gravitational Effects theory *claims'*. All the past tenses show a change in the main idea, or *paradigm shift*, the point at which the most popular theory or idea gives way to a new one. The last item – 'Post-Einstein Gravitational Effects theory *claims'* – has the verb in the present tense, because Post-Einstein Gravitational Effects theory is one of a number of current ideas.

Conclusions review the rest of the essay and often use forms like 'This essay *has considered/examined/discussed*' and 'lessons *have been learned'*. When facts or events are reported, the tense changes: 'I *analysed* the results.' These switches, which we may not think of consciously, are important meaning signals and help make the voice of the writer clear to the reader.

Using Gerunds

Some tutors find the use of -ing words used as verbal nouns (gerunds) very sophisticated, especially at the beginning of sentences in academic writing. Such sentences also avoid complicated verb structures and are usually objective and factual. Here are some examples.

- ✔ **Estimating** the impact of global warming on the migration patterns of birds is essential to a better understanding of local ecosystems.

- ✔ **Considering** the evidence presented so far, this topic deserves in-depth research.

- ✔ **Exploiting** the difficulties the poor have in obtaining credit has been the mainstay of money-lenders since time immemorial.

- ✔ **Analysing** the results, the most surprising was that cost was not the first consideration when choosing to fly with a particular airline.

- ✔ **Observing** the behaviour of immature male elephant seals, it seems clear that they adopt female attitudes in the presence of dominant males to avoid attack or injury.

Exchanging Essays

Get a friend to exchange draft essays with you (not on the same topic, so that there can be no argument about pinching ideas). If possible, use the feedback form suggested here or one similar, some days before the hand-in date. The form will help you and your reader be more focused and analytical in your reaction to each other's work and will give you both something more concrete to discuss.

It is not easy to critique someone else's essay without a framework. You can say 'It's OK', which doesn't help much, either because you don't want to upset your friend or because you don't want to spend time and energy on it or because it's quite difficult to pinpoint what you feel unclear about. With a framework, you can say, for example, the right sources were used, but there wasn't much comment or criticism of them, or you're not sure what the point was in referring to certain sources.

These comments can help make your writing more reader friendly before you hand it in, and in explaining your intentions to your friend, you are likely to think of other points to add or clarifications to make. If you keep your feedback form and the points you considered before you handed in your work and compare this with your tutor's feedback, you will have a more rounded view of your work. Such feedback is also useful as a record of your thinking and your essay development, if you need to discuss some issues or problems later with your tutor.

Allowing Reflection Time and Self-criticism

Always leave some reflection time after each section you are writing. Sleep on it and reread what you have written the next day. In that way, you can be your own critic. Some parts will seem brilliant and other parts will clearly need more explanation and examples than you have given. You will even wonder yourself what on earth you were on about – and get some idea of how your reader might react. Everybody can make mistakes, especially when tired, so reflection can help you to weed out silly errors. After several hours or longer, you have to reconstruct what you have written from cold, and you will notice more easily if something is wrong and can either leave it out or find something else to add in.

Give yourself time as well to absorb and reflect on feedback from your classmates and from your tutor, if you can get some before the hand-in date. This is to help you fully appreciate the points they have made. If you've managed to use a framework form, then you will know which parts or sections you don't have to worry about and which you can improve. Again, sleep on it to help absorb what they've said. You don't have to agree with it, but seeing things from their perspective can help you argue your case better.

Assessing Your Satisfaction Levels

Note in your learning diary before you start work on your essay, which part of the research and writing process you think will give you the most satisfaction, which part you think you will find difficult or troublesome and which you thought would be easy. Note how your views change during the process of writing your essay.

If you found things rather different from what you expected, then think why this was so. Did you enjoy the research part more than you thought? Was it more like playing detective? Did you find exchanging essays and reading them quite fun? If you found discussing your essay with classmates stimulating, then you can build on that and consider whether to work with a classmate earlier in the process – to brainstorm ideas, for example – as well as later on to swap drafts.

Working through a process with a set of different procedures always tells you something about yourself and how you prefer to work, what things you'd rather not bother with and then what impact not bothering with them has on your marks and feedback. If, for instance, you don't bother with page numbers as a time-wasting unnecessary bit of protocol, you tutor may not agree if your work is badly attached and pages come loose. It is very annoying and time-consuming trying to reconstruct the sequence and the longer the essay, the more annoying this can be. Certain aspects of the presentation of your work are an act of courtesy (or otherwise) to your reader, including explaining the purpose and layout of each part in the introduction, as well as numbering pages. These affect the impression your work makes so are certainly worth bothering with. Not doing so can spoil the effect of an otherwise good piece of work and lower your marks.

Overcoming Blocks

Sometimes you can really get stuck in a rut or feel you're at a dead end if you can't get hold of the material you want. To get moving again, you can either abandon what you've done and start again (but risk the same thing happening again) or you can modify what you've already started. It's probably a good time for a chat with your tutor. However, to get going again you can:

- Take another look at the key words – can you change the emphasis with a different definition or reference to theory in the literature? Can you narrow the angle (better than widening it)?

- Can you demonstrate the same ideas with different examples, case studies and so on?

- If you have the case study or experiment information, but think you need to change the theoretical aspect, can you find another case study or experiment to compare it with? If so, this will probably help you sort out the theoretical parts more easily.

- Have you gone through all the possible differences between 2 sets – age, height, weight, gender, etc.? This might help if you've made an assumption or followed someone else's assumption without really being conscious of doing so before. If you find some assumptions in received wisdom, this can be your essay – a critique.

- When in doubt, break down things into the smallest possible bits. Doing this can also write you essay for you, especially if you deconstruct some received wisdom at sentence level and find a sentence in paragraph one is inconsistent with another in paragraph five. Take a look at definitions. These often take on a different meaning after a few pages.

Any of these strategies can lead to a modification (plan A1) so that you don't throw the baby out with the bathwater. However, if you get a surge of enthusiasm for plan B, go for it!

Index

• *Numerics* •

7up project (longitudinal study), 133, 134, 138

• *A* •

abbreviations for note-taking, 104–105
abstract (academic text), 157
abusive personality type, 78
academic argument, 44–46, 47
academic books, 156–159, 344
academic opinion, 50–51
academic reasoning, 44–45
academic titles, 15
academic voice, 51–52
academic writing
  academic voice in, 51–52
  characteristics of, 221, 263
  feedback on, 253–254
  models for, 224–226
  organising your information, 238–241, 247–253
  organising your writing, 237–238
  orientation, 232
  outline plans, 232–235
  paragraph structure in, 158–159
  presentation formats, 241–247
  principles of communication for, 52, 222, 293
  quotations or references in, 169
  reason for, 167
  reflection time, 286, 347
  section organisation, 156–158
  set essay titles, 226–230
  structural elements, 221–226
  style of writing used in, 121, 255, 344
  text organisation, 156–159
  tips for, 341–348
  working titles, 230–231
accommodations, 29, 30–31
accuracy, checking data for, 119
acronyms, 117, 178, 269

action research, 143–144, 242–243
active learning
  framework for new information, creating, 100
  lectures and, 68–71
  overview, 67
  during seminars, 72–79
  tutorials and, 79–82
addressing administrative staff, 15
administrative staff, 15, 16–17
adult education, 62
adverbs, linking, 252–253
ageism bias, 181
aggressive personality type, 77
alcohol, 308
analysing
  argument/logic, 44
  claims and evidence, 47–52
  reading materials/text, 178–181, 223–224
  research findings, 250
  your writing, 240
analysis and evaluation (text), 155, 158
analytical framework, 129
analytical thinking. *See* critical thinking
anti-virus and anti-spy software, 56, 59, 62
anxiety, dealing with, 289
apostrophe, 267–268
appendices (academic text), 158
Apple Mac computers, 54, 55
Archive of European integration website, 195
archived material, 136
archives, television, 191–192
argument/logic
  academic argument, 44–46, 47
  in academic writing, 248
  evaluating, 44, 155
  evidence supporting, 44, 119
  feedback on, 114, 119–122
  identifying the stages in, 43
  space guideline for, 238
  syllogism, 45–46
Aristotle, 84
aspirin, 308

audience
  attention span of, 70
  engaging, 91–92, 93
  feedback, 96–98
  seminar, 76
audio stimuli for memory recall, 275
audio-visual resources, 159–160
Australia, writing culture of, 197
automatic correction feature, software,
    62–63

• B •

Background Reading (bibliography), 168
background section (academic
    writing), 157
backing up computer files, 61
balance and bias, checking for, 184–185
banks, 32
bar charts, 210–211, 245
BBC website, 160, 191–192
behaviour and etiquette
  addressing administrative staff, 15
  misconduct, avoiding, 38
  preventing plagiarism, 38–40
  sorting out problems, 16–18
  student/tutor interactions, 14–15
behaviour patterns, 76–79
beliefs and feelings, reflecting on, 286
bell curves, 142, 212–213
bias, checking for, 180–181, 184–185, 196
bibliography. *See also* references
  adding books to, 110, 168
  Background Reading subsection, 168
  building, 109–111
  models for, 224
  online, 189–190
  using, 158
big projects, planning and studying,
    331–332
biography websites, 194
blocks, overcoming, 348
BNC (British National Corpus), 38, 195
body language, demonstrating, 92
books
  academic, 156–159, 344
  listing in bibliography, 110, 168
  text books, 188, 344

boundaries, setting, 330
brackets, commas, and dashes, 268–269
brain size, 130
breaks. *See* downtime; fun activities
British English
  American English spelling versus,
      62–63, 122
  largest collection of, 38
  studying, 195
British National Corpus (BNC), 38, 195
British society, study of, 133
browsers, Internet, 57
building names or numbers, 11
Burton, Kate (*Neuro-Linguistic Programming
    For Dummies*), 279
business websites, 194

• C •

cafes, locating, 11, 14
calculator, online, 190
campus
  computers, 13–14, 54–55, 135
  financial services, 27
  finding your way around, 11–12
  health emergencies, 31
  living on, 30–31
campus map, obtaining, 11
cancelled lectures, 34, 60
card indexes, 109
case studies, 50, 138–139
chair for seminar, 75, 83, 95
character reference, from tutor, 34
charity work, 336
charts
  bar charts, 210–211, 245
  flow charts, 213–214
  pie charts, 209–210
chat breaks, 25
chat rooms, online, 188
cheating, 316, 317
childcare and nursery places, 29
children, critical thinking of, 47
chores, weekly, 25
citations and references, 182, 257–258
claims and evidence
  academic opinion and, 50–51
  academic voice, developing, 51–52

evaluating the evidence, 43, 44, 49–50
making a hypothesis, 47–48
necessary and sufficient conditions, 48–49
claims, making, 256, 261
clarity
principle of, 169, 222
writing with, 52, 238
class handouts, 106, 107
class notes, downloading, 106
classes
code numbers for, 10
preparing for, 326
prioritising, 17
"classical" theories, 130
clothing, for exam day, 313
clubs and activities, 335
clusters of computers, 54, 61
coaching, 339–340
code numbers for classes, 10
collating and recycling data, 284–285
colons, 269
commas, brackets and dashes, 268–269
communication principles, 222–223
comparison and contrast, 177–178
computer. *See also* Internet; laptop computer; software
buying, 53–54
on campus, 13–14, 54–55, 135
courses, 61, 62
field research using, 135
hardware, 53–55
housekeeping, 61
laboratories, 54, 57
problems with, 62–63
taking breaks from, 24, 184
troubleshooters for, 61
upgrading, 135
concentration, developing, 25, 309–310
concepts, 120
conclusion
assessing, 123
described, 51, 157, 240
essays, 51, 52, 123
identifying, 43
jumping to, avoiding, 171
need for, 237
space guideline for, 238
title matched with, 123
writing, 52, 250–251
conditions, necessary and sufficient, 48–49
constructive criticism, 79
contents page (academic text), 238, 252
contraception and abortion advice, 29
contractions, 266–267
counselling services, 29–30
coursework. *See also* feedback
computer education, 61, 62
distance-learning courses, 196
extension or break from, 35
feedback on, 114, 116–117
marks for, 273
online material for, 59–60
penalties for, 18, 327
prioritising, 18, 327
requirements and assignments, 17–18
software classes, 61
student information pack, 10, 288
substituting, 17
switching courses or institutions, 34
timetable clashes, 17
credit cards, 32
credit system, 17
crisis centres, 29
critical thinking
in academic arguments, 44–46
analysing claims and evidence, 47–52
overview, 41–42
skills of, 42–44
using in the real world, 45
criticism, constructive, 79, 234
cross-checking data, 171, 183, 185, 196
culture websites, 195

• ***D*** **•**

daily breaks, 24–25
daily routine, 326
The Daily Telegraph (newspaper), 192
dashes, commas and brackets, 268–269
data. *See also* evidence
collating and recycling, 284–285
comparing, 42, 171–175, 176–178
cross-checking, 171
evaluating, 44
fact versus opinion, 43

data *(continued)*
  incomplete, 240–241
  missing, 43
  organising, 238–241
  questioning, 156
  researching, 155
  sources and access, 134–135
  summarising, 175–176
  triangulating, 50, 132, 146
dean (head of faculty), 14
debating society, 90
decimals, fractions and formulae, 202–204
definitions, researching, 155
dehydration, 308
dentist, on campus, 32
departmental culture, 16
Der Spiegel (newspaper), 162, 192
descriptive text (academic text), 238, 247
desktop publishing (DTP) programs, 57
devil's advocate, playing, 232, 233, 285
diagrams
  bar charts, 210–211, 245
  bell curves, 142, 212–213
  described, 208–209, 218
  flow charts, 213–214
  graphs, 215–216
  histograms, 211–212
  pie charts, 209–210
  tables, 121, 216–218, 242–243
  technical, 214–215
  using, 245–247
  Venn diagrams, 209
Dialogues (Plato), 84
diary, learning
  creating, 21–23
  feedback requests recorded in, 243
  lecture preparation notes in, 68
  passwords recorded in, 60
  pinpointing changes needed, 118
  reading-sources noted in, 170
  reflecting on beliefs and feelings, 286
  satisfaction levels assessed in, 347–348
  tutorials recorded in, 81
  for workshop participants, 89
dictionary, 343
diet, 24, 306–307
difficult tasks, dealing with, 328–329
diminishing returns, law of, 310, 327, 331, 333

dissertations, 136, 235, 317
distance-learning courses, 196
distractions, dealing with, 329
"Do Not Disturb" sign, 330
doctoral vivas, 315, 317
downtime. *See also* fun activities
  daily breaks, 24–25
  importance of, 24
  lectures using, 70, 71
  screen brakes from the computer, 184
  weekly breaks, 25–26
Dragon Naturally Speaking Voice
    Recognition software, 55
DTP (desktop publishing) programs, 57
dyslexia, 36, 289

• *E* •

economics students, 117
economics websites, 136, 194
The Economist (website), 136
e-learning (electronic learning), 195–197
email. *See also* Internet
  accounts, 57
  interviews, 144
  regarding workshops, 89
  time spent on, 331
  using effectively, 61
emergency
  crisis centre, 29
  health emergency, 31
  phones, locating, 30
emotional intelligence, 311
emotional versus factual comments, 120
empirical research, 127, 136
employment
  as computer troubleshooter, 61
  doing surveys, 140
  locating, 29
  making time for, 26
encyclopaedia (Wikipedia), 192–193
English, British versus American, 62–63, 122
English Grammar For Dummies (Ward and Woods), 269
essays. *See also* academic writing
  buying or plagiarising, 225–226
  conclusion, 51, 52, 123
  critiquing with friends, 346

evidence of the writer in, 223
introduction, 52
length, assessing, 123
models/examples, 123, 224–226
online, 184, 186, 225–226
outline plan, 233–234
past papers, reading, 164–165
requirements for, 17
set essay titles, 226–230
style of writing for, 344
title for, 123, 343
tutors' review of, 123–124
working titles, 230–231
writing tips, 341–348
etiquette and behaviour
addressing administrative staff, 15
misconduct, avoiding, 38
preventing plagiarism, 38–40
sorting out problems, 16–18
student/tutor interactions, 14–15
evaluation section (academic text), 250
evidence
evaluating, 43, 44, 49–50
lack of, 119
sources of, 223
weak or circumstantial, 50
evidence-based medicine, 240
exam preparation. *See also* exams
behaviour checks/practical
arrangements, 311–313
benefits of, 287
for exam day, 313–315
exam paper, checking, 313–314
exam requirements and conditions,
288–290
exam topics, identifying, 299–300
health and energy levels, maintaining,
306–308
mental health, maintaining, 308–309
past exams, obtaining copies of, 20, 290
questions, assessing, 314–315
revisions, making time for, 307
rubrics, reading up on, 290–298
sample answers, asking for, 301
self-bribery and treats, 309–310
self-testing, 300–301
timetabling the pre-exam period, 301–304
workshops for, 292
exam rooms, 311, 312, 313

exams. *See also* exam preparation
benefits of, 305
calming your nerves during, 279
cheating on, 316, 317
copies of, 20, 290
importance of, assessing, 288
marking process, 273, 292, 318–322
oral exams, 315–318
postponing, 288
pre-testing for, 141
questions used in, 274, 281
requirements and conditions, 17, 288–290
re-sitting, 113, 321
sitting for, 311–318
timetable clashes, 288–289
Excel, 62
exclamation marks, 269
exercise, 25, 308
experimental research, 136, 141–143
extension to complete classwork, applying
for, 35

• F •

facilitators, 76, 77, 78, 94
factual versus emotional comments, 120
feedback
audience, 96–98
coursework, 114, 116–117
defined, 113
examples of, 116–122
form and guidelines (example), 342
guidelines, asking for, 115
on layout/structure, 114, 121–122
on logic and argument, 114, 119–122
marking system and, 115–116
from peers, 124, 254, 346
reflecting on, 347
tutors giving, 116–122, 253, 341–342
feminine pronouns, using, 263–264
field research, 135
files, naming and saving, 61
final grade, assessing, 273
financial services, 27, 29, 32–33
Financial Times (newspaper), 192
finding your way around campus, 11–12
fire emergencies, 31
First Aiders, 14
flexibility, building in, 330

flow charts, 213–214
footnotes, 259–260
formal writing style, 255–256
fractions, formulae and decimals, 202–204
framework
  analytical, 129
  for new information, 100
  theoretical, 129–130, 239, 248
Freshers' week, 13
friends/colleagues. *See also* students
  critiquing essays with, 346
  discussing material with, 187
  drawing mind-maps with, 284
  essay outline plan discussed with,
    233–234
  making, 28
fun activities. *See also* downtime
  charity work, 336
  clubs and activities, 335
  cooking for housemates, 334
  importance of, 333
  mentoring or coaching, 339–340
  off-campus, 335–336
  parties, 334–335
  student newspaper, 337–338
  student politics, 339
  student radio DJs, 338
  treats/rewards, 25, 309–310
  volunteer work, 336
  working as a student helper, 337

• *G* •

Gauntlet, David (professor), 195
gender bias, 180–181, 263–264
general information package, 10, 288
genetic engineering, 128
gerunds (verbal nouns), 345–346
global warming, 47–48
Google search
  avoiding plagiarism and, 185–187
  on course title, 299
  features of, 190
  for keywords, 153
  for multiple choice practice tests, 298
  online news from, 162
grades. *See also* marking system
  final, assessing, 273
  grade average, 327

grade boundary interview, 315
  low, bouncing back from, 116, 320
  querying, 320–322
  understanding, 115
graphics software, 56
graphs, 215–216
Greenpeace (environmentalist
    organisation), 179–180
group work
  benefits of, 84–85
  giving presentations, 90–98
  reading groups, 163–165
  study groups, 20–21
  workshops, 85–90
The Guardian (newspaper), 161, 162, 192

• *H* •

handouts, 101–102, 106, 107
hardware, computer, 53–55
headings and sub-headings (academic
    text), 252
Health Centre, 14, 32
health issues. *See also* illness
  dehydration, 308
  dentist, on campus, 32
  getting help with, 32
  health and energy levels, maintaining,
    306–308
  health emergencies, 31
  medication, painkillers, 308
  mental health, maintaining, 308–309
  minor ailments, preventing, 308
  painkillers, 308
Health Service student counsellor, 30
hedging or softening the language, 261–262
helper for seminar, 75
histograms, 211–212
history websites, 194
honesty principle of communication, 110,
    222, 258
honesty, writing with, 52, 238, 249
horseshoe seating arrangement, 93
hours of study, recommendations, 331
hypotheses
  in academic writing, 248
  defined, 47, 127
  described, 239
  developing, 47–48, 127–128

fact versus, 43
relating theoretical framework to, 130

• *I* •

IBV's ViaVoice Software, 55
icons used in this book, 5
ICT (Information and Communication
  Technology). *See also* computer;
  Internet; software
  online material, 59–60
  problems with, 62–63
  systems learning and support, 60–62
illness. *See also* health issues
  preventing, 308
  taking a break from studies for, 35
  taking exams and, 289
incomplete data, 240–241
The Independent (newspaper), 161, 192
inferences, making, 44
information pack for students, 10, 288
information-based seminars, 91
initiative, taking, 316
instruction words for essay-type
    exams, 297
intelligence, types of, 311
interactive learning, 83
inter-library loans, 13, 60, 187
International and European law
    websites, 195
Internet. *See also* email
  access limitations, 59–60, 135
  books sourced through, 187–188
  connecting to, 57–60
  cross-checking data from, 183, 185, 196
  as data resource, 134–135
  e-learning (electronic learning), 195–197
  inappropriate web pages, 184
  online chat rooms, 188
  plagiarism, avoiding, 185–187
  as research tool, 136, 188–195
  search engines, 185–186, 190
  security system, 56, 59
  for up-to-date information, 176
  wireless connection, 58–59
Internet Public Library (IPL) website, 194
interviews
  described, 144
  grade boundary, 315

pitfalls to avoid, 147
related to exams, 316
introduction section
  described, 157, 221, 239
  essays, 52
  model for, 224
  writing, 247, 250–251
Intute website, 136, 193–194
IPL (Internet Public Library) website, 194

• *J* •

job interview questions, 68
journals, in bibliography, 110
judgements, making, 44
jumping to conclusions, avoiding, 171

• *K* •

keywords, 153–154, 343

• *L* •

laboratories
  computer, 54, 57
  Language Learning Laboratory, 55, 57
  Online Writing Laboratories (OWLs), 197
landlord's responsibilities, 29
language. *See also* punctuation
  acronyms, 117, 269, 278
  apostrophe, 267–268
  body language, demonstrating, 92
  contractions, 266–267
  feedback on, 114
  gender bias in, 180–181, 263–264
  hedging or softening, 261–262
  indecent or abusive, 38
  oral exams, 317
  passive forms, 265–266
  pronouns, 52, 180, 263–265
  too strong for evidence, 122
  using "claim" versus "suggest," 261
language exams, 315
Language Learning Laboratory, 55, 57
laptop computer. *See also* computer
  note-taking with, 102, 104–105, 109, 111
  sockets for, 58
law of diminishing returns,
    310, 327, 331, 333

law websites, international, 195
laws, attitude toward, 179
layout for class rooms/seminars, 92–94, 312
layout/structure, 114, 121–122
Le Figaro (newspaper), 162, 192
LEA (local education authority), 55
learning. *See also* active learning
  by asking questions, 175
  co-operative, 20
  distance-learning courses, 196
  e-learning (electronic learning), 195–197
  hours spent in, 24
  interactive, 83
  rote ("by heart"), 273–274, 276
  Socratic method of, 84
learning diary
  creating, 21–23
  feedback requests recorded in, 243
  lecture preparation notes in, 68
  for organising your study, 21–23
  passwords recorded in, 60
  pinpointing changes needed, 118
  reading-sources noted in, 170
  reflecting on beliefs and feelings, 286
  satisfaction levels assessed in, 347–348
  tutorials recorded in, 81
  for workshop participants, 89
learning difficulties/disabilities, 37, 55, 289
lecture theatres, 11, 58
lecturers
  contacting, 15
  described, 14
  presentation style, 69–70
  presenting his own views, 105
lectures. *See also* note-taking during lectures
  asking questions at, 71, 99, 105
  cancelled, 34, 60
  choosing a place to sit, 101
  class handouts, 106, 107
  follow-up seminars for, 72
  introductory, 101
  methodological, 101
  missing, 17, 28, 69
  online material for, 59–60
  preparing for, 68–69, 87–88, 99
  sequential, 101
  size and structure of, 69–71

timetable clashes, 17, 72
timetable for, 19
tutorials and seminars precedence over, 72
leisure. *See* downtime; fun activities
length of essay, 124
library
  catalogue, 60, 187
  inter-library loans, 13, 60, 187
  Internet Public Library (IPL) website, 194
  local, 61
  locating, 13
  research dissertations/theses from, 135
Library of Congress website, 136
linear note-taking, 106–107
listening, attention span for, 70
literacy programmes, 37
literature review (academic text), 157, 247
living on campus, 30–31
loans, student, 32
local education authority (LEA), 55
loci, memory tool, 276–278
logical reasoning, 44–45, 47
logic/argument
  academic argument, 44–46, 47
  in academic writing, 248
  evaluating, 44, 155
  evidence supporting, 44, 119
  feedback on, 114, 119–122
  identifying the stages in, 43
  space guideline for, 238
  syllogism, 45–46
longitudinal studies, 133–134
long-term memory, 283
long-term planning, 332
loos, locating, 11, 311, 312
lost and found office, 31
low grades, bouncing back from, 116, 320

• *M* •

Manikiw, Greg (Harvard professor), 194
map of the campus, obtaining, 11
marking system. *See also* grades
  coursework, 273
  for exams, 292, 318–322
  final grade, assessing, 273
  glass ceiling for, 327
  minimum requirements, 115

overview, 113
querying an exam mark, 320–322
symbols used for, 115
understanding, 115–116, 318–320
mean, median and mode, 204–206
measurement conversions, online, 190
media resources
audio-visual resources, 159–160
online newspapers, 162–163, 192
print media, 161–162
radio, 160–161
sharing, 163–165
television, 160, 191–192
websites, 195
medication, painkillers, 308
meditation, 37, 308
memory stick, 54
memory strategies
audio stimuli, 275
collating and recycling data, 284–285
drawing comparisons and
deductions, 274
historical perspectives, 279–281
for key points and sequences, 275–278
loci, 276–278
mechanics of, 283
memory prompts, 273, 274
mind maps/spidergrams as, 280–281
mnemonics, 275
overview, 283–284
revising from notes, 281–283
rote ("by heart") memory, 273–274, 276
mental health, maintaining, 308–309
mentors, 31, 163, 339–340
methodological lecture, 101
methodology. *See also* research tools
described, 135–136
feedback on, 121
Internet research on, 188
methodology section (academic text), 158,
248–249
Microsoft Office Word 2007, 56
Microsoft Word, 54, 55
Microsoft Works, 56
mind maps/spidergrams, 107–108, 228–229,
280–281, 284
minor ailments, preventing, 308
misconduct, avoiding, 38
missing data, 43

missing lectures, 17, 28, 69
missions, differences in, 180
mnemonics, 275
models of academic writing, using, 224–226
MP3 player, 161
multiple-choice exam questions, 297–298

• *N* •

naps/sleep, 25, 306, 309
Nature website, 194
necessary and sufficient conditions, 48–49
nerves, calming, 279
Neuro-Linguistic Programming For Dummies
(Ready and Burton), 279
New York Times (newspaper), 192
New Zealand, writing culture of, 197
newspapers
campus, 14
online, 162–163, 192
researching, 161–162
student, 337–338
night school classes, 62
"no," saying, 329
note cards, 182
note-taking during lectures. *See also*
lectures
abbreviations, 104–105
adapting and reflecting on, 109–111
choosing a place to sit, 101
discussing with classmates, 111
handling handouts, 101–102
laptop computer for, 102, 104–105
linear note-taking, 106–107
non-linear note-taking, 107–109
organising your thoughts, 105–109
on paper, 102, 103
preparing for, 100
recording equipment used for, 99
revisions, 281–283
symbols for, 103
note-taking from academic books
analysing reading materials, 178–181,
223–224
citation/quotation and note cards, 182
comparing and contrasting data, 176–178
cross-checking information, 171
devising research questions, 170–171
jumping to conclusions, avoiding, 171

note-taking from academic books *(continued)*
  purpose of, 167–168
  reading up-to-date material, 171, 176
  summarising information, 175–176
  using several sources for, 171–175
notice-boards, 29, 60
null hypothesis, 47
numbers
  building names or numbers, 11
  code numbers for classes, 10
  describing, 175
  fractions, formulae and decimals, 202–204
  mean, median and mode, 204–206
  page numbering, 121, 122
  percentages, 201–202
  questioning, 175
  standard deviation, 206–208
  statistics and statistical significance,
    200–201
nursery places, 29

• O •

observation, 140–141
off-campus activities, 335–336
once-a-week treat, 25
online chat rooms, 188
online essays, buying, 186
online newspapers, 162–163, 192
online study support, 37, 38
Online Writing Laboratories (OWLs), 197
open access computer, locating, 13–14
"Open Office," free word-processing
    software, 56
opinions
  academic, 50–51
  checking the accuracy of, 98
  facts versus, 43
  open, 51
oral exams, 315–318
organising workshops, 88–90
organising your information (academic
    writing), 238–241, 247–253
organising your study. *See also* time-saving
    techniques
  group study, 20–21
  learning diary for, 21–23
  timetable for, 18–20

organising your thoughts, 105–109
organising your writing, 237–238
orientation for academic writing, 232
outline plan for writing, 232–235
overgeneralisations, 181
OWLs (Online Writing Laboratories), 197

• P •

page numbering, 121, 122
painkillers, 308
paragraphs
  in academic text, 158–159
  average length of, 121
  first sentence in, 252
  using correctly, 121, 122
participant observation, 141
participation, benefits of, 98
participatory action research, 143–144, 242
parties, 334–335
passive forms, avoiding, 265–266
passwords, recording, 60
penalties, coursework, 18, 327
percentages, 201–202
perfectionism, avoiding, 328
personal tutorials, 80
personal tutors, 12, 33–34
personal voice, showing, 256–257
personality types, 76–79
philosophy websites, 195
photographs, 246–247
pie charts, 209–210
plagiarism
  Internet, 185–187, 226
  preventing, 38–40
  tutors checking for, 39
planning
  for big projects, 331–332
  doing things at the best time, 326
  essay outline plan, 233–234
  importance of, 9
  long-term, 332
  outline plan for academic writing,
    232–235
Plato (*Dialogues*), 84
play. *See* fun activities
politics, student, 339
porters, 31
postponing exams, 288

power bases, 179
PowerPoint, 56, 60, 62
pregnancy, 51
premise of an argument, 45, 46
preparation. *See also* exam preparation
  for lectures, 68–69
  for seminars, 74–75
prescriptions, obtaining, 32
presentation software, 56
presentations. *See also* diagrams; seminars
  audience feedback and, 96–98
  engaging your audience, 91–92, 93
  formats for, 241–242
  graphs, 215–216
  handling questions, 95–96
  photographs, 245–247
  room layout, 92–94
presenter for seminar, 75
principles of good communications, 52,
  222, 293
print media, 161–162
printer, 54
private time, need for, 330
procrastination, avoiding, 328–329
project or dissertation orals, 317
pronouns
  in academic writing, 264–265
  feminine, 263–264
  gender bias and, 52, 180
psychological stroking, 76, 94
punctuation
  apostrophe, 267–268
  exclamation marks, 269
  other, 268–269
  tips for, 122

• *Q* •

qualitative research, 131–132
quantitative research, 131, 132
questionnaires
  overview, 139–140
  pitfalls to avoid, 147
  planning for, 233
  return rate, 233
  turnaround time for, 146
  unfinished, 249
  using, 135

questions. *See also* research questions
  direct, 325–326
  job interview, 68
  learning by asking, 175
  during lectures, 71, 99, 105
  multiple-choice exam questions, 297–298
  querying an exam mark, 320–322
  during seminars, 72, 95–96, 98
  "who, what, when, where, why," 230
Quick MBA website, 194
quiet place and time, 330
quotations
  long quotes, 260
  recording method for, 182
  researching, 155, 190
  using, 169
  verb grammar for, 345

• *R* •

Radical Statistics Group website, 194
radio
  resources, 160–161
  student, 338
RAM (Random Access Memory), 54
rambling personality type, 78
raw scores table, 243–244
readers, 14, 15
reading as research. *See also* research
  about, 149
  area of interest and, 170
  getting credit for, 168–170
  preparing for lectures, 87–88
  purpose of, 152, 169–170
  questioning the data, 156
  research questions, 136–138, 152–153,
    169, 170–171, 239
  skim reading, 124, 154
  text organisation and, 156–159
  time-saving techniques, 153–155
reading groups, 163–165
reading lists, 150–152, 332
Ready, Romila (*Neuro-Linguistic
  Programming For Dummies*), 279
reality principle of communication,
  52, 222, 238
reasoning, academic, 44–45
recording equipment for note-taking, 99

recording yourself, 285
reference cards, 182
references. *See also* bibliography
   importance of, 40, 259
   recording, 182, 259
   used in essays, 122, 124
   using correctly, 169, 259
reflection time
   in academic writing, 286, 347
   building in, 307
   for information given, 42
   learning diary for, 286
relevance principle of communication,
      169, 222
relevance, writing with, 52, 238, 239
report seminars, 90, 96
research. *See also* reading as research;
      research tools
   data sources and access, 134–135
   dissertations and theses, obtaining
      copies of, 135
   empirical, 127, 136
   evaluating, 146
   field research, 135
   hypotheses, developing, 47–48, 127–128
   longitudinal studies, 133–134
   methods for, 131–135, 239, 248–249
   pitfalls to avoid, 146–147
   pre-testing, 249
   qualitative, 131–132
   quantitative, 131, 132
   reassessing data, 133
   theoretical framework for, 129–130
   unpublished, 135
research questions
   creating, 136–138, 152–153
   described, 239
   devising from notes, 170–171
   redesigning, 169
research tools. *See also* Internet
   action research, 143–144, 242–243
   archived material, 136
   case studies, 138–139
   experimental research, 141–143
   interviews, 144, 147
   media resources, 159–165, 195
   observation, 140–141
   online, 188–195
   overview, 135–136

questionnaires, 135, 139–140, 147
   storytelling research, 145
   websites, 136
residence mentor, 340
re-sitting exams, 113, 321
resources, media
   audio-visual resources, 159–163
   online newspapers, 162–163, 192
   print media, 161–162
   radio, 160–161
   sharing, 163–165
   television, 160, 191–192
   websites, 195
results section (academic text), 158, 249
rewards/treats, 25, 309–310
rhymes, 275–276
room allocations timetable, 10
room layout, 92–94, 312
room numbers, 11
rote ("by heart") learning, 273–274, 276
rubrics. *See also* exams
   defined, 290
   for essay-type questions, 293–297
   for multiple-choice questions, 297–298
   overview, 291–293
   understanding, 314
Russian Federation, 184–185

• *S* •

satisfaction levels, assessing, 347–348
scholars, researching, 190
school (faculty)/department office, 11
Science Daily website, 194
Science Direct website, 194
search engines, 185–186. *See also* Google
      search
secretary for seminar, 75
section headings, 122
section organisation (academic writing),
      156–158
security, 30–31, 56, 59
semi-colons, 269
seminar groups, studying with, 20–21
seminars. *See also* presentations
   active participation in, 98
   cancelled, 60
   follow-up, 72
   giving presentations, 90–98

information-based, 91
interactive, 90
online material for, 59–60
participants in, 75–76
personality types in, 76–79
precedence over lectures, 72
preparing for, 74–75, 87–88
report seminars, 90, 96
room layout for, 92–94
room name or code, 11
size of, 72
small-group teaching seminars, 73
structure of, 96–97
timetable clashes, 17
timetable for, 19
tutorials precedence over, 72
work-in-progress seminars, 73, 90, 96–98
workshop seminars, 73–74
senior tutors, 14, 15
sensory memory cue, 92, 283
sentence structure, 120, 121
sequential lectures, 101
set essay titles, 226–230
7up project (longitudinal study),
    133, 134, 138
shared-course exam (common exam),
    288–289
short-term memory, 283
silent personality types, 76–77
skim reading, 124, 154
skipping and chanting, 276
sleep/naps, 25, 306, 309
small case study research, 50
small-group teaching seminars, 73
smoking, 31, 32
sniper personality type, 78–79
socialising, 34, 307
Socrates, 84, 171
software. *See also* computer
    anti-virus and anti-spy, 56, 59, 62
    automatic correction feature, 62–63
    courses for, 61
    desktop publishing (DTP), 57
    files, naming and saving, 61
    graphics, 56
    learning to use, 60, 61
    presentation, 56
    spell checker, 62–63
    spreadsheet programs, 56

tutorials, 60
voice-recognition, 55
word-processing, 56, 62–63
Spam folder, 57
specific objectives section (academic
    writing), 157
spell checkers, 62–63, 122
spelling
    avoiding errors, 122
    British versus American English,
        62–63, 122
spidergrams/mind maps, 107–108, 228–229,
    280–281, 284
sports
    coaching, 340
    making time for, 335
    time set aside for, 22
spreadsheet programs, 56
staff, teaching, 12–13. *See also* tutors
standard deviation, 206–208
statistical significance, 200–201
statistics
    help in supplying evidence, 50
    statistics and statistical significance,
        200–201
    websites, 194
storytelling research, 145
Student Financial Adviser, 33
Student Helpline, 29
student information pack, 10, 288
student life. *See also* students
    adapting to, 28
    behaviour and etiquette, 14–18
    checking out teaching staff, 12–13
    downtime, 24–26
    finding help or counselling, 29–30
    finding way around campus, 11–14
    living on campus, 30–31
    organising study-time, 18–23
    student information pack, 10, 288
    university services, 28
student loans, 32
student residence mentor, 31
Student Union
    activities organised by, 335, 336–337
    computer course information, 61
    Student Financial Adviser, 32
    Student Helpline, 29
    study support, 37

Student Union bar, 14
Student Welfare services, 36, 37
students. *See also* friends/colleagues;
    student life
  character reference from tutors, 34
  evaluating others' work, 123
  feedback from other students, 114, 115
  getting early feedback from, 117
  giving feedback to tutors, 124
  information pack for, 10, 288
  pre-and post-lecture chats with, 68, 71
  publishing essays on the Internet, 189
  as seminar chair, 75
study support
  obtaining, 29
  study groups, 20–21
  types of, 36–38
study time
  for big projects, 331–332
  law of diminishing returns,
      310, 327, 331, 333
  number of hours for, 331
  online study tips, 197
  organising, 18–23
  prioritising, 17
  for small tasks, 331
subject or project tutorials, 34, 80–82
subject treatment, feedback on, 114,
    118–122
subject tutors, 34–36, 69, 114
summarising information, 175–176
summary (academic writing), 157, 238
support for students. *See also* study
    support
  from administrative staff, 16–17
  finding, 29–30
  welfare services, 28
suspending studies for a year, 35
switching courses or institutions, 34
syllogism, 45–46
symbols
  for marking, 115
  for note-taking, 103
synonyms, researching, 190

• T •

tables, 121, 216–218, 242–243
talking to yourself, tape-recording, 285
teaching rooms, locating, 11
teaching staff, 12–13. *See also* tutors
technical diagrams, 214–215
technical symbols, for note-taking, 103
technical terms, "common" knowledge, 39
technician, computer, 13–14
technology. *See* ICT (Information and
    Communication Technology)
teen pregnancies, 51
telephone, emergency, 30
telephone interviews, 144
television, 160
television archives, online, 191–192
tenant/landlord responsibilities, 29
text. *See also* note-taking from academic
    books
  analysing, 178–181, 223–224
  buying, 19, 187
  finding on the Internet, 186–188
  organisation for, 156–159
  researching online, 190
  sharing for exams, 21
text books, 188, 344
theatre or concert ticket, discounts, 32
theoretical framework, 129–130, 239, 248
thinking, critical
  in academic arguments, 44–46
  analysing claims and evidence, 47–52
  overview, 41–42
  skills of, 42–44
  using in the real world, 45
thoughts, organising, 105–109
three-point rule, 96
Tim Johns' University of Birmingham
    Kibbitzer pages, 38
time. *See also* study time
  planning to do things at the best time, 326
  spent on email, 331
  spent on research, 146
time frame considerations, 179
The Times (newspaper), 192

time-saving techniques. *See also* organising your study
  asking direct questions, 325–326
  avoiding perfectionism, 328
  avoiding procrastination, 328–329
  big projects need big plans, 331–332
  building in flexibility, 330
  having a quiet place and time, 330
  learning to say "no," 329
  planning to do things at the best time, 326
  prioritising your workload, 327
  reading and research techniques, 153–155
  reading lists as, 332
timetable
  clashes, 17, 72, 288–289
  creating, 18–20, 326
  exam time, 301–304
  example, 19, 326
  obtaining, 10, 11
  weekly, 10, 16, 19, 21–22
title
  academic, 15
  checking against text, 124
  conclusion matched with, 123
  for essays, 343
  Google search on, 299
  keywords in, defining, 343
  set titles, 226–230
  working titles, 230–231
toilets, locating, 11, 311, 312
treats/rewards, 25, 309–310
triangulation, 50, 132, 146
troubleshooters, computer, 61
tutorials
  overview, 79
  personal tutorials, 80
  precedence over seminars, 72
  software, 60
  subject or project tutorials, 34, 80–82
  timetable clashes, 17
tutors
  addressing, 15
  checking for plagiarism, 39
  contacting, 12, 15, 16
  emailing, 61
  essay outline plan discussed with, 234–235
  feedback form and guidelines (example), 342
  feedback from, 116–122, 341—342
  help with low grades, 116
  helping student prepare for lectures, 69
  model essays by, 225
  office hours, 12
  personal tutors, 12, 33–34
  reviewing essays, procedure for, 123–124
  as seminar chair, 75
  sending weekly updates to, 81
  student giving feedback to, 124
  subject tutors, 34–36, 69, 114
  volunteer tutors, 37
  work-in-progress reviewed by, 114, 247, 248, 253

• U •

Union café, 14
unit converter, online, 190
universal education, 232
university court, 38
University of Aberystwyth website, 195
U.S. government, 179–180
U.S. writing culture, 197

• V •

Venn diagrams, 209
verb grammar, 345
verbal nouns (gerunds), 345–346
Vice Chancellor, 15
visual representations, 245–247
vocabulary, 195, 262
voice
  academic, 51–52
  developing your, 343–344
  formal and personal, 255–256
voice-recognition software, 55
volunteer tutors, 37
volunteer work, 37, 336

• W •

Ward, Lesley (*English Grammar For Dummies*), 269
weekends, study-free, 26
weekly breaks, 25–26
weekly timetable, 10, 16, 19, 21–22
"who, what, when, where, why" questions, 230
Who's who list, example, 13
"Why?," asking, 44, 171
WiFi, 58–59
Wikipedia (online encyclopaedia), 192–193
wireless network adaptors, 58, 59
Woods, Geraldine (*English Grammar For Dummies*), 269
Word 2007, 55, 109, 111
word choices, 122
word limit, penalty for exceeding, 327
word-processing skills, 54
word-processing software, 56, 62–63
working titles, 230–231

work-in-progress
  feedback on, 253–254
  seminar for, 73, 90, 96–98
  tutor reviewing, 114, 247, 248
workshop chair, 87
workshop seminars, 73–74
workshops
  benefits of, 85, 89–90
  for exam preparation, 292
  format for, 86
  housekeeping, 89
  for lectures/seminar preparation, 87–88
  organising, 88–90
  participating in, 98
  for self-study, 87
writing by hand, 54
writing order for academic text, 247–254
writing styles. *See also* academic writing
  described, 255
  formal and personal voice in, 255–256
  textbooks versus academic books, 344

FOR DUMMIES®

Do Anything. Just Add Dummies

UK editions

BUSINESS

978-0-470-51806-9

978-0-470-99245-6

978-0-470-75626-3

FINANCE

978-0-470-99280-7

Tax For Dummies

978-0-470-99811-3

978-0-470-69515-9

PROPERTY

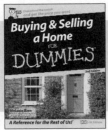

978-0-470-99448-1

Understanding and Paying Less Property Tax For Dummies

978-0-470-75872-4

978-0-7645-7054-4

Backgammon For Dummies
978-0-470-77085-6

Body Language For Dummies
978-0-470-51291-3

British Sign Language
For Dummies
978-0-470-69477-0

Business NLP For Dummies
978-0-470-69757-3

Children's Health For Dummies
978-0-470-02735-6

Cognitive Behavioural Coaching
For Dummies
978-0-470-71379-2

Counselling Skills For Dummies
978-0-470-51190-9

Digital Marketing For Dummies
978-0-470-05793-3

eBay.co.uk For Dummies,
2nd Edition
978-0-470-51807-6

English Grammar For Dummies
978-0-470-05752-0

Fertility & Infertility For Dummies
978-0-470-05750-6

Genealogy Online For Dummies
978-0-7645-7061-2

Golf For Dummies
978-0-470-01811-8

Green Living For Dummies
978-0-470-06038-4

Hypnotherapy For Dummies
978-0-470-01930-6

Available wherever books are sold. For more information or to order direct go to www.wiley.com or call +44 (0) 1243 843291

13902_p1

FOR DUMMIES®

A world of resources to help you grow

UK editions

SELF-HELP

Cognitive Behavioural Therapy For Dummies
978-0-470-01838-5

Neuro-linguistic Programming For Dummies
978-0-7645-7028-5

Emotional Freedom Technique For Dummies
978-0-470-75876-2

HEALTH

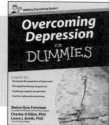

Overcoming Depression For Dummies
978-0-470-69430-5

IBS For Dummies
978-0-470-51737-6

Low-Cholesterol Cookbook For Dummies
978-0-470-71401-0

HISTORY

British History For Dummies
978-0-470-99468-9

Twentieth Century History For Dummies
978-0-470-51015-5

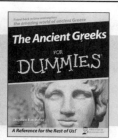

The Ancient Greeks For Dummies
978-0-470-98787-2

Inventing For Dummies
978-0-470-51996-7

Job Hunting and Career Change All-In-One For Dummies
978-0-470-51611-9

Motivation For Dummies
978-0-470-76035-2

Origami Kit For Dummies
978-0-470-75857-1

Personal Development All-In-One For Dummies
978-0-470-51501-3

PRINCE2 For Dummies
978-0-470-51919-6

Psychometric Tests For Dummies
978-0-470-75366-8

Raising Happy Children For Dummies
978-0-470-05978-4

Starting and Running a Business All-in-One For Dummies
978-0-470-51648-5

Sudoku For Dummies
978-0-470-01892-7

The British Citizenship Test For Dummies, 2nd Edition
978-0-470-72339-5

Time Management For Dummies
978-0-470-77765-7

Wills, Probate, & Inheritance Tax For Dummies, 2nd Edition
978-0-470-75629-4

Winning on Betfair For Dummies, 2nd Edition
978-0-470-72336-4

13902_p2

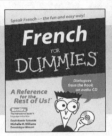

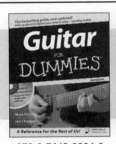

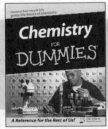

FOR DUMMIES®

Helping you expand your horizons and achieve your potential

COMPUTER BASICS

978-0-470-27759-1

978-0-470-13728-4

978-0-471-75421-3

DIGITAL LIFESTYLE

978-0-470-25074-7

978-0-470-39062-7

978-0-470-17469-2

WEB & DESIGN

978-0-470-19238-2

978-0-470-32725-8

978-0-470-34502-3

Access 2007 For Dummies
978-0-470-04612-8

Adobe Creative Suite 3 Design Premium
All-in-One Desk Reference For Dummies
978-0-470-11724-8

AutoCAD 2009 For Dummies
978-0-470-22977-4

C++ For Dummies, 5th Edition
978-0-7645-6852-7

Computers For Seniors For Dummies
978-0-470-24055-7

Excel 2007 All-In-One Desk Reference
For Dummies
978-0-470-03738-6

Flash CS3 For Dummies
978-0-470-12100-9

Mac OS X Leopard For Dummies
978-0-470-05433-8

Macs For Dummies, 10th Edition
978-0-470-27817-8

Networking All-in-One Desk Reference
For Dummies, 3rd Edition
978-0-470-17915-4

Office 2007 All-in-One Desk Reference
For Dummies
978-0-471-78279-7

Search Engine Optimization For
Dummies, 2nd Edition
978-0-471-97998-2

Second Life For Dummies
978-0-470-18025-9

The Internet For Dummies, 11th Edition
978-0-470-12174-0

Visual Studio 2008 All-In-One Desk
Reference For Dummies
978-0-470-19108-8

Web Analytics For Dummies
978-0-470-09824-0

Windows XP For Dummies, 2nd Edition
978-0-7645-7326-2

Available wherever books are sold. For more information or to order direct go to www.wiley.com or call +44 (0) 1243 843291

13902_p4